MODERN MEXICAN CULTURE

EDITED BY
STUART A. DAY

MODERN MEXICAN CULTURE

Critical Foundations

THE UNIVERSITY OF
ARIZONA PRESS
TUCSON

The University of Arizona Press
www.uapress.arizona.edu

Printed in the United States of America
22 21 20 19 18 17 6 5 4 3 2 1

ISBN-13: 978-0-8165-3426-5 (paper)

Cover design by Leigh McDonald
Cover photo: *Las icónicas torres de Satelite* by iivangm/ Flickr

Publication of this book is made possible in part by the proceeds of a permanent endowment created with the assistance of a Challenge Grant from the National Endowment for the Humanities, a federal agency.

Library of Congress Cataloging-in-Publication Data
Names: Day, Stuart A. (Stuart Alexander), editor.
Title: Modern Mexican culture : critical foundations / edited by Stuart A. Day.
Description: Tucson : The University of Arizona Press, 2017. | Includes bibliographical references and index.
Identifiers: LCCN 2017012664 | ISBN 9780816534265 (pbk. : alk. paper)
Subjects: LCSH: Mexico—Civilization. | Mexico—History.
Classification: LCC F1236.7 .M63 2017 | DDC 972—dc23 LC record available at https://lccn.loc.gov/2017012664

♾ This paper meets the requirements of ANSI/NISO Z39.48-1992 (Permanence of Paper).

CONTENTS

MODERN MEXICAN CULTURE

INTRODUCTION

The Art of History

STUART A. DAY

THIS BOOK OFFERS READERS a profound understanding of key ideas and events in Mexico and beyond by explicitly combining art and history in order to encourage a multidimensional understanding of Mexican touchstones and watersheds. Each chapter provides a historical grounding of its topic in the initial pages, followed by a multifaceted analysis through various artistic representations that provide a more complex (if still incomplete) view of Mexico. Through this approach the authors of the following pages—all experts in the field—demonstrate the power of art and artists to question, explain, and influence the world around us. The initial reference page of each chapter lists readily available murals, political cartoons, plays, pamphlets, posters, films, poems, novels, and other cultural products, like documents and documentaries, that teachers can use to build syllabi or independent learners can use to enrich their knowledge of Mexico; the chapter endnotes list suggestions for further reading.

One example of an artistic representation that brings to life the history and culture of modern Mexico is Diego Rivera's mural *Sueño de una tarde dominical en la Alameda Central* (Dream of a Sunday Afternoon in Alameda Central). The mural is fascinating for its critique of high-society wealthy elites, one of its common and compelling interpretations; yet it also contains within it keys to a multitude of other stories that intersect with it as part of a web of historical memory. Of the many events and concepts that can be explained by studying

Rivera's mural, two in particular—the Mexico City earthquake of 1985 and the role of Catholicism in Mexico from the Conquest to the present—can be used to highlight the main purpose of this book: to investigate what art adds to our understanding of key events and ideas. Painted in the mid-1940s, the mural is a complex rendition of Mexican history, which, because Rivera himself was a key figure in postrevolutionary Mexico, includes many colorful characters from his own life. The work of art—brilliant in its depiction of Frida Kahlo, José Guadalupe Posada, Sor Juana Inés de la Cruz, and over a hundred more figures—is housed close to the park for which it was named, though its location in a custom-made museum is a bit tricky to find. (As I will explain below, it is relatively new and therefore not as prominent as the other museums in the area.) The massive mural, the history it depicts, and even its physical journey from the Hotel del Prado to the small, built-to-suit Museo Mural Diego Rivera after the 1985 earthquake hold answers to many of the questions readers might ask about Mexico. As mentioned above, two brief examples—the earthquake and its devastating aftershocks, as well as the role of Catholicism in Mexico—demonstrate the value of a cultural studies approach to our academic endeavors; namely, the use of multiple cultural artifacts to explain the world around us and to expose intersections and entanglements of specific power dynamics. Such analyses, emerging out of the Birmingham School of Cultural Studies beginning in the 1950s, are now common practice for teacher-scholars in the United States.

A central term epitomizes the period following the earthquake: *displacement*. The historical accounts that narrate the disaster and the government's feeble, delayed, even arrogant response, which showed incompetence at the same time that it bolstered civic participation (out of necessity), underscore the political and social impact of the earthquake. Studied from only one angle, the impact of the earthquake can be *understood*; studied from a variety of views, it can be *felt*. Historical writing can make use of and be combined with, for instance, Elena Poniatowska's book *Nada, nadie: Voces del temblor* (Nothing, Nobody: The Voices of the Mexico City Earthquake, 1988), which relays personal stories of the devastation (much as her book on the 1968 Tlatelolco massacre of students and others at the hands of the government does). Through these mediated testimonies it is evident that, as with the 1968 tragedy, people saw corruption exposed, as another account of citizen engagement, this time from a member of the group called the Coordinadora Única de Damnificados (Victims' Coordinating Council), relates: "Reconstruction was made possible by the popular organizations that already existed and by those that were created, and also by a great, well-channeled solidarity. I believe this was the first defeat the PRI [Partido Revolucionario Institucional] suffered. I first realized this one day . . . when Cosío Vidaurri, Secretary General of the Government of [the] Federal District, arrived with his famous water barrels, the ones that were brought by an international society to provide us with drinking water. We got the word that those barrels had been held up for four or five days because they had to put the PRI's logo on them" (Joseph and Henderson 579). The same sentiment that showed yet another fault line in the PRI's rhetoric led to renewed faith in people working together to solve their most immediate problems. Indeed, true or not, many lament the absence today of what they explain as much stronger civil society in the mid-1980s. In 2015, for instance, noted historian, editor, and essayist Enrique Krauze wrote the following on his Twitter account: "La sociedad civil reaccionó con cientos de iniciativas prácticas ante el terremoto de 1985. Ahora está paralizada" (Civil society responded to the 1985 earthquake with hundreds of practical initiatives. Now it's paralyzed) (@EnriqueKrauze). In a sense, people in 1985 had a common goal, recovery, and an increasingly common enemy—the PRI.

What might Rivera's mural add to our understanding of the events of 1985, and specifically the tension between civic activists and the government? Amid the ruins of the earthquake the government preserved the mural as a testament to the past, which, despite controversies surrounding the work of art itself, at the same time preserved key myths that in many ways sustained the PRI. After the earthquake severely damaged the Hotel del Prado, writes William Stockton, a new venue for the mural was found: "Another hotel across the street from both the Hotel del Prado and the Alameda [collapsed] during the earthquake. In its place, the government built another park. The adjacent site where the hotel parking lot stood was vacant, and this was chosen for the mural. . . . In the weeks prior to the move, while workers labored amid the ruins of the second-floor lobby of the del Prado to prepare the mural, other workers hurried to lay the concrete foundation of a new building. The plan is to build the walls and roof of the salon around the mural, solving the problem of maneuvering the unwieldy object through a door or window of some other structure."

The elaborate strategy came to fruition, and a video of the move on YouTube shows an impressive, eminently well-staffed and engineered choreography that stands in stark contrast to Mexico's weak humanitarian response to the earthquake: mariachis play as every detail is taken care of and observed by local and foreign press. A reporter for the Spanish newspaper *El País* writes about the dangerous move, noting that a crane "capable of lifting 250 tons" moved the mural, which was covered in a special coating to protect it from changes in temperature. An engineer "estimated that the cost to move the mural was upwards of 120,000,000 pesos but that 'it must be done, even in times of economic crisis, because it's about preserving Mexico's heritage.'" The heritage—or patrimony—in this case is complicated. Shortly after the 1985 earthquake the mural could be understood to both celebrate and condemn the ruling party, the PRI, whose neoliberal technocrats were at the time already working to privatize the ejido system, which under the revolutionary Constitution had finally returned land to campesinos (to give just one example of the changes the 1980s and '90s brought). Thus, the revolutionary right-hand section of the mural, which among others celebrates an insurgent Emiliano Zapata on horseback, is alive only in Rivera's fresco—the mural is a mythical underpinning for the regime.

As happened in New York, when he was commissioned by the Rockefellers to create one of his stunning murals in 1932, Rivera expressed his political ideas through art. Following the direction of his sponsor to show society at the crossroads, he juxtaposed communism and capitalism—with communism coming out the clear winner in a mural that, as one can imagine, didn't please the Rockefellers. In Mexico, Rivera's politics also played out through art. His work was tightly tied to the Revolution, as was another important touchstone of the time: Catholicism. The Cristero War represented a reaction to the 1917 Mexican Constitution that sought to eradicate the influence of the Catholic Church by legislating away its grip on Mexican politics (through a host of prohibitions, including one on religious education). In 1926, when a new president, Plutarco Elías Calles, took office, these prohibitions became critical—the two previous presidents left them in writing. Calles brought the words on the page to life, for example, as the historical document—the Constitution—related to education: "Freedom of religious beliefs being guaranteed by Article 24, the standard which shall guide such education shall be maintained entirely apart from any religious doctrine and, based on the results of scientific progress, shall strive against ignorance and its effects, servitudes, fanaticism, and prejudices." Reading the Constitution itself in conjunction with historical texts related to Rivera begins to provide a more complete picture of Rivera and his epoch. Historian John Chasteen writes, "Like many other Mexican intellectuals of the 1920s and 1930s, Diego Rivera and Frida Kahlo thought Mexico needed a social revolution. They joined the Communist Party and offered their home to exiled

Russian revolutionary Leon Trotsky, who lived with them for several months. Their nationalism was widely shared in Mexico during the 1920s and 1930s. Everything *national* had become fashionable" (221). In *Sueño de una tarde dominical en la Alameda Central* one can see this nationalism displayed, for instance, in the depiction of the Revolution in the panel to the right.

The story of this midcentury mural also offers information about (anticlerical) nationalism; as seen in the 1932 mural he painted for the Rockefellers, Rivera was revolutionary as an artist and as a proponent of the Revolution. He painted one of his subjects in *Sueño de una tarde dominical* stating, "Dios no existe" (God doesn't exist) and, as one can imagine, caused a vehement religious response. The mural was damaged by pro-Catholic attackers after local church officials refused to bless it. Interestingly, this revolutionary move was mitigated by Rivera himself in the next decade. William Stockton writes, "In 1956, little more than a year before his death, Mr. Rivera made peace with the Roman Catholic Church and changed the wording on the scroll to merely reflect the 19th-century meeting at which a Mexican politician had spoken the words. After making the change, he descended from the scaffold and told waiting reporters, 'I am a Catholic.'"

If one mural helps articulate so many stories, how can *multiple* artistic viewpoints add to our understanding of Mexico? Before offering an additional example of my own, let me preview one of the following chapters to offer a more concrete idea of the modus operandi of the authors represented in this book. Jacqueline E. Bixler's chapter on the 1968 massacre, after a historical introduction, analyzes the following cultural expressions to add nuance to our understanding of the tragedy: graphic art created during the time of the 1968 Olympics and again on the fortieth anniversary of the massacre; Elena Poniatowska's testimonial narrative *La noche de Tlatelolco* (1971); the film *Rojo amanecer* (1990); Flavio González Mello's play *Olimpia 68* (2008); and the Plaza de Tlatelolco itself, a *lieu de mémoire*, or site of memory, which, as Bixler shows, "includes a memorial to the victims as well as a permanent museum exhibit titled *Memorial del 68*." Bixler contends that "Mexico's writers and artists, in particular, have ensured that 'el dos de octubre no se olvida' (October 2 will not be forgotten) by counteracting the politics of amnesia with a steady stream of collective memories, ranging from chronicles and commemorative books to works for the stage and the silver screen. These cultural products serve as 'counter-memories,' which underscore 'the disparities between history as it is discursively transmitted and memory as it is publicly enacted by the bodies that bear its consequences.'" Bixler provides various views of the topic not solely for the sake of offering more comprehensive and multifaceted information, a worthy task in and of itself, but also in order to counter official histories, to interrogate the role of memory and amnesia in sociopolitics, and to become, herself, part of a chain of authors that keep the memory of October 2 alive—as will the readers of this volume. Bixler's essay can be combined with others in the volume to form thematic clusters that, in turn, inform additional, broader concepts.

An exploration of one further example—the concept of "impunity"—will suffice to illustrate the principle of this volume: how art helps us to enrich our understanding of society. It is clear that impunity—defined by the Oxford English Dictionary as "exemption from punishment or penalty"—is a pertinent notion in the United States, even though the term is not widely used. After all, there is no dearth of examples—in the daily press, virtual and otherwise—of people who escape justice, illegally, or, as is often the case, because laws and the justice system favor the wealthy and powerful. In Mexico, the term is regrettably part of daily vocabulary. From petty theft and small- and large-scale bribery (as when Walmart bribed officials in order to erect a massive store within sight of one of Mexico's archaeological wonders, the pyramids at Teotihuacán) to murder and massacres (as of this writing, forty-three disappeared students from the Ayotzinapa rural teaching college are still unaccounted for under President Enrique Peña Nieto, who already had one massacre to his name from when he was a state governor), the percentage of prosecuted crimes is dismal. The Universidad de las Américas Puebla puts out the well-known Global Impunity Index (IGI), which (among many other bleak statistics) offers the conclusion that "less than 1% of crimes in Mexico are punished" (Le Clercq Ortega and Rodríguez Sánchez Lara). The one blind spot of the summary report is that "punishment" does not always mean justice. That is, when most people convicted of crimes in Mexico never see a judge, and when those with ties to business, government, and narco-traffickers have an even higher level of impunity, the 1 percent of crimes that result in incarceration includes the convictions of innocent people.

The abovementioned impunity index speaks to the need beyond government entities (though they hold primary responsibility) to combat impunity: "Se necesita la atención y participación urgente de otros actores no gubernamentales como la sociedad civil, sector privado, academia, medios de comunicación y organizaciones internacionales" (Urgent assistance and participation from NGOs is needed, like the civil society, the private sector, academia, the mass media, and international organizations). Of these groups, historians and artists, especially when their work is considered together, as in the pages that follow, play an important role in exposing, ridiculing, and at times combating impunity.

What might help people who live outside of the country to understand impunity in Mexico? One way to get at the concept in a U.S. classroom is to define it and then look, not to Mexico, at least initially, but closer to home. For my students this means an exploration of definitions in a variety of English- and Spanish-language dictionaries (this alone is a useful activity) and web-based research on groups like the Innocence Project, which helps to free innocent people from prison. The latter has a recent connection to my university: A group of University of Kansas (KU) students and professors worked to free a man who had served well over a decade in prison for a murder he didn't commit. During this time served, it was discovered, in part by KU law students and professors, that the real murderer was able to run free (it was the convicted man's brother, who had originally confessed to the crime and who did so again in a suicide note). The Project for Innocence and Post-Conviction Remedies at KU is linked with the Midwest Innocence Project and the national Innocence Network. Students and professors have worked to exonerate many, including Floyd Bledsoe, the man forced to serve time for his brother and whose case, according to project director Jean Phillips, had "several hallmarks of a classic wrongful conviction, including prosecutorial misconduct, ineffective assistance of trial counsel and an inadequate investigation. . . . Studying Floyd's case helps students understand what issues to investigate while working on their own cases in the Project and later as practicing attorneys" ("KU Law's Project").

False incarceration is the other side of the coin of impunity, which does not imply solely a system where criminals are not punished. It also relies on the incarceration of innocent people and the almost uniform impunity for prosecutors—even in cases where the activities of prosecutors and the police are clearly criminal. The study of unjust convictions in the United States, seen most prominently in hundreds of DNA exonerations, prepares viewers for a Mexican documentary called *Presunto culpable* (Presumed Guilty) in a way that creates a sense of solidarity instead of (the usual) feelings of exceptionalism. The heroes of this unit become not systems of justice in the United States or Mexico but rather students and professors—and their respective institutions of higher learning—who see empowered peers taking on the system(s). The 2008 documentary, directed by Roberto Hernández and Geoffrey Smith, follows two Mexican lawyers, Hernández himself and Layda Negrete, who were simultaneously also graduate students at the University of California, Berkeley, as well as the protagonist, a young man named Antonio Zúñiga, who was unjustly arrested and convicted of murder. The documentary explores a patently corrupt police force and an absurd judicial process. The following description of a key scene in the film offers insight into the affective side of the documentary and, more broadly, into the affective potential of documentaries: The defendant

> Zúñiga is . . . forced to cross-examine the original suspect and lone eyewitness accuser, Victor Daniel Reyes, a member of a gang allegedly involved in the shooting and the victim's cousin. As the two stand almost nose-to-nose [with the defendant behind bars], Reyes sticks to his story. Then Zúñiga asks Reyes whether he knows that Zúñiga tested negative for gunpowder, as did Reyes. Matching Zúñiga's slow and deliberate pacing (for the benefit of the court typist), Reyes drops a bombshell: "I did not know that they did the same test that you now mention. And it is true I did not see who fired the gun." (POV Communications)

Reviewers and commenters on social media mention the fact that Mexicans were surprised, and often infuriated, to see their justice system laid bare, as one of the producers explained on the film's website: "So many Mexicans believe that we have an American courtroom—that we will have the prosecutor, the defense, the judge and the trial. They believe that! Because they have never been in contact with a trial" (*Presumed Guilty*). That is, people seemed to react not to the shocking injustice seen in *Presunto culpable* (this would not have come as a surprise) but rather to the fact that the system itself—not just the *funcionarios* who staff it—was fundamentally flawed.

The contrast to the U.S. system—presumed innocent versus presumed guilty—would be stark to viewers who had not recently studied the various innocence projects in the United States. What becomes evident in this context are not differences but rather a key link: despite dissimilarities, the United States and Mexico have a shared imaginary of judicial systems that follows a mainstream Hollywood narrative, fictional stories in which justice prevails. As Mexico struggles to implement new laws that require oral trials as opposed to paper processes, confessions that are to count only if spoken before a judge, and a presumption of innocence—changes that were to occur largely over the last decade—the technical differences between the two systems diminish further. In a classroom, the viewing and discussion of *Presunto culpable* can be followed up by an activity in which students explore the social impact of this and other documentary films, discover recent changes in Mexico's legal system, and then craft two laws—one for Mexico and one for the United States—that would ameliorate respective judicial injustices. It is particularly interesting to observe group work on this activity: almost all my college students, no matter their individual political views, indicate that people should serve time only for crimes they committed (as opposed to the idea in some conservative circles that people behind bars have committed *some* crime at *some* point and therefore justice has been served).[1]

Other artistic expressions from Mexico that treat impunity embrace a Hollywood-esque scenario in which good deeds defeat profound corruption—and concomitant impunity. The 2000 film *Todo el poder* (All the Power), while not a masterpiece of Mexican cinema, is an enjoyable example of an intellectual who seeks and finds justice (albeit limited) in a system where corruption is endemic. In the blog *Íncipit 50*, Erika Issela points to the topic in *Todo el poder* that most frustrates people, and which underscores that problems of corruption and impunity are structural: "Al final nos muestra como el sistema es como un círculo vicioso que tal vez nunca llega a poner punto final al problema puesto que cuando descubren a un policía corrupto ya tiene un suplente de la misma calaña que el anterior" (In the end it shows us how the system is like a vicious circle that might never lead to a solution, since when they discover a corrupt police officer they have a replacement of the same ilk at the ready). The film demonstrates that a local hero can have an impact on society but that without stronger civil society and a sound, well-funded justice system, the systemic impunity will outlast individual heroics. Similar in theme is the film *La ley de Herodes* (Herod's Law, 1999), which begins and ends with the exact same scene (but with different actors/characters): A couple drives up to a small village. He's the new municipal president, or mayor, ready to take on a new role as he (surely) moves up in the party toward a governorship. A wary mestizo greets them in front of a dilapidated municipal building. The wife of the new mayor says it all in a line that will be repeated by every arriving (and soon to be corrupted) official: "Here?" as in, "This is where they've stationed us?" Set in the 1950s, the movie eviscerates corrupt politicians and Catholic clergy and is particularly focused on the PRI. In one scene, a governor and presidential hopeful offers a PRI pin to an underling, explaining its origins—the president himself. The next shot is of his desk drawer, which contains dozens of the same pin. This duplication—and duplicity—suggests that if impunity is the root of Mexico's problems, callous corruption is its major indicator.

Cinema offers outstanding examples of day-to-day life in a society where impunity is a common key word—as does theater, a closely related art form in Mexico because of the ways the genres interact and because the same players (actors, writers, and others) are often involved in both. For example, Vicente Leñero, one of the screenwriters of *La ley de Herodes* and dozens of other films, penned a play called *Nadie sabe nada* (Nobody Knows Anything, first produced in 1988) that in its form and theme complement his cinematic work. The play represents an art form he calls *teatro de simultaneidad*, which allows multiple scenes to occur onstage at once, much like a split screen in a movie. The audience is drawn deeper and deeper into the underworld of newspapers in Mexico as multiple scenes portray the struggle to remain honest in a corrupt system. Leñero comes from this world—in addition to fiction he was a well-known figure in Mexican journalism—and his play offers a street-level view of the power of impunity that engulfs the common person. The green Volkswagen taxis (formerly ubiquitous in Mexico and accessible to many in the middle class) crossing the stage are just one indicator that the author presents not the world of the wealthy or of impoverished Mexicans but that of everyday people struggling to get by in the metropolis. Leñero's play, with its journalists and their constant talk of bribes—who gives them, whether or not to take them—resonates today, though amazingly it seems a bit quaint.

Mexican journalists are now under even more pressure than in the 1980s to bend to both cartels and the government, and the murder rate continues to grow. Reporters Without Borders puts it succinctly: "Land of the drug cartels, Mexico continues to be the western hemisphere's deadliest country for the media. Murders of journalists are typically carried out in cold blood, like executions, and almost always go unpunished. This impunity accounts for the widespread corruption. Some elected officials are directly linked to organized crime. Ownership of the broadcast media is extremely concentrated, with two media groups owning almost all the TV stations." The organization ranks Mexico one hundred and forty-ninth on the World Press Freedom Index, right between Russia and Tajikistan; and the Committee to Protect Journalists rates Mexico seventh on its list of countries with the highest rates of impunity for murdering journalists, between Afghanistan and Colombia. *Nadie sabe nada* looks like the good old days, when threats seemed more common than murders for reporters and when censorship might mean that the government would make sure you couldn't buy the paper on which to print your newspaper (as happened to Leñero when he was cofounding the news magazine *Proceso*). So too does Mexico's most famous play, *El gesticulador* (The Impostor, 1938) by Rodolfo Usigli, who is generally considered the father of Mexican theater. Usigli's play, usually studied for its relationship to Octavio Paz's essay "Mexican Masks," is at its core about an unsolved murder: only one person knows who murdered the revolutionary César Rubio, so when a professor decides to impersonate Rubio, the murderer must remain quiet. The play is a reminder that impunity was not born with the drug cartels, though the level of violence Mexicans might now experience on a daily basis seems unsurpassable.

The topic of impunity can be seen in myriad genres that dismantle façades of the rich and powerful, in many cases communicating the anger people feel in a way historiography cannot. Such is the case of the Molotov song "Que se caiga el teatro" (Let the Theater Fall), which enacts visceral connections with listeners in a way that hard rock and punk often do. Like Rage Against the Machine with songs like "Killing in the Name" (about police brutality, corruption, and impunity in the United States), Molotov expresses the rage many people feel toward the government. In "Que se caiga el teatro," the lead singer hammers away at the powers that be:

Hay algo más fuerte que el poder de la mente
El poder de poder eliminar a la gente
Tener la vara alta y además ser prepotente
México, el país donde es libre el delincuente.

There's something stronger than the power of the mind
It's the power to eliminate people
With influence and arrogance
Mexico, the country where the criminal is free.

Molotov's iconoclastic lyrics also call to task seemingly naïve bands, like Maná, that sing songs of light social protest, offering hope to listeners but at the same time leaving the status quo unchallenged. One of Molotov's CDs, *¿Dónde jugarán las niñas?* (Where Will the Girls Play?), is a parody of Maná's environmentally conscious *¿Dónde jugarán los niños?* (Where Will the Children Play?). Molotov is blatantly sexist (as seen in this album-cover parody and many of their lyrics) and homophobic, a problem not uncommon in social protest of many sorts in Mexico and elsewhere. The violence of some forms of music in Mexico can boomerang back on musicians, especially if they are commissioned by or otherwise tied to cartels. Yet some groups have even been able to criticize narco-traffickers and lived to tell about it. The legendary band Los Tigres del Norte's song "La Granja" (The Farm), loosely inspired by George Orwell's *Animal Farm*, for example, takes swipes at the government of Vicente Fox, the wealthy, politicians, and the drug dealers who all, in one way or another, make the lives of campesinos untenable. The Orwellian link in the song and its accompanying music video provide intertextual but also intercultural context (*Animal Farm* brings up multiple referents, from Joseph Stalin and the Spanish Civil War to present-day North America).

Though far from lighthearted, the cartoon music video for "La Granja" is easily relatable to the daily political cartoons that challenge impunity, as well as other types of humor that often provide just enough protection from persecution. Two well-known Mexican intellectuals, Denise Dresser and Jorge Volpi, compiled a parodic Mexican "history book" titled *México: Lo que todo ciudadano quisiera (no) saber de su patria* (Mexico, What Any Citizen Would [Not] Like to Know About Their Country). Though in part fiction, it is, sadly, only slightly exaggerated, as in the following play-by-play timeline of activities (bribes, et cetera) required to recover a stolen sedan:

> Totales
> Gastos totales por denunciar el robo de mi auto: $240 325.00
> Costo del carro en el mercado: $75 000.00
> Tiempo invertido: más de 80 000 horas
> Noches sin dormir: más de 3 000
> Años de cárcel (para el ladrón): 0
> Años de cárcel (para mí): 3
> Costo de tener un sistema de justicia mexicano: no tiene precio.
> Para todo lo demás está: Mastercard. (165)
>
> Totals
> Total expenses for reporting my car's theft: $240,325.00
> Cost of the car in the marketplace: $75,000.00
> Invested time: more than 80,000 hours
> Nights with no sleep: more than 3,000
> Years in prison (for the thief): 0
> Years in prison (for me): 3
> Cost of having a Mexican justice system: priceless.
> For everything else there's: Mastercard.

Fiction can tell the truest tales, as seen in this ad takeoff, but laws—and the process of making laws—do too. One section of Dresser and Volpi's book details the advent of the executive branch of government. In a chapter that begins with a Claymation image of a politician and the words "La ley de Herodes: La única ley que obedecen los diputados" (Herod's Law: The only one followed by congressmen), the authors write that the 1917 Constitution required three branches of government (executive, legislative, judicial) but that the PRI "consideró que esta división era sólo una sugerencia" (considered this division to be only a suggestion). The authors explain that after 1997, "en el México del Cambio™, las cosas sí cambiaron" (in the Mexico of change™, things did change) (133). In describing a new, ineffective Congress, they conduct a faux survey of people in Congress to determine its purpose. One humorous "response" parodies Congressman Manlio Fabio Beltrones of the PRI, a fixture on Mexico's political scene: "Lo de legislativo pos la verdad no nos importa mucho, pero lo de poder, pos eso sí que sí. Poder pa' hacer negocios, poder pa' actuar impunemente" (To be honest, we don't care a lot about the legal part, but the power does matter. Power to do business, power to get off scot-free) (134). Parodies, counterhistories, subversive scenes or lyrics, and other forms of exposing or enduring impunity and its concomitant feeling of helplessness are often parallel to civic engagement efforts—for example, a move to require more transparency for government officials. Kirk Semple writes of a civic group that spearheaded transparency laws in Mexico:

> At the center is an ambitious initiative to impose public disclosure rules for all public servants, at all levels of government. Called "3 de 3"—or "3 out of 3"—the initiative would require government officials to reveal their assets and potential conflicts of interest, as well as prove that they are paying taxes. If passed, the initiative, which would also compel close relatives of public officials to reveal their assets, would be among the farthest-reaching public disclosure measures in the world, its authors say. "Mexico has to aim for the best," said Eduardo Bohórquez, one of the principal authors and the executive director of Transparencia Mexicana, a watchdog group.

Semple notes that in addition to citizens being fed up with impunity, especially after recent high-level examples of corruption, business leaders might also be increasingly interested in change: the transparency initiatives "also received the support of influential business associations, leaving some analysts to speculate that spiraling bribes may have cut too deeply into profits." While many in Mexico see new transparency as an absurd continuation of the façade of democracy, the involvement of citizens (Semple indicates that more than 600,000 signatures were collected to force the most recent transparency measure) is a key indicator of a democracy's strength.

As scholars—university or armchair—consider different ways to understand Mexico, outlining similar topics and the historical and artistic examples that explain them leads to engaging intellectual explorations. In one of my courses, for instance, students explore pachuco culture as they prepare to explain and analyze a topic of their choosing, following the same model as this book: historical contextualization and artistic representation. The section in the course on pachucos explains Mexican American youth culture around the time of World War II, focusing on the Zoot Suit Riots in Los Angeles. In addition, the historical overview offers students significant details about migration from Mexico, wartime Los Angeles, the internment of Japanese Americans, post-Depression migration within the United States, the uncomfortable role of wartime ally that Mexico played, and newspaper articles from the time that show blatant racism (not to mention the power of the press). Artistic representations include Luis Valdez's film and play *Zoot Suit*, which was successfully staged in the United States and has now been staged in Mexico City (I share interviews with the play's actors and producers); music from the era, with a focus on videos of dance and a guest lecture by a dance professor that includes a jitterbug demonstration; political cartoons from Mexico and the United States depicting pachuco culture; interviews with zoot-suiters on the PBS documentary program *American Experience*; Octavio Paz's famous essay "The Pachuco and Other Extremes"; and murals that depict the evolution of the term *pachuco*. There are many other key words, events, and ideas that students can explore on their own or collaboratively using a similar model: for example, the Zapatista movement, coloniality, Afro-Caribbean cultures, street vendors, gay rights, transportation, the *maquila* industry—the possibilities are endless.

The chapters described below point to many of these topics and can be read independently; they are designed to guide readers in a way similar to a university course. In the initial chapter, "Youth and Migration: American DREAMers and Mexico," Marta Caminero-Santangelo emphasizes the many ways people in Mexico and the United States (and specifically students!) are connected socially, culturally, and politically and gives our U.S. audience a sense of their own participation in history. Through DREAMers' testimonies, films, performance, novels, and other cultural products, Caminero-Santangelo argues that DREAMers, approximately 70 percent of whom are from Mexico, create testimonies that, because of their public political goals, emphasize an "American" identity and the "American Dream." She finds something very different in other art forms: the portrayal of undocumented youth is "more ambivalent and transnational," offering a nuanced view of migration that allows for association with Mexico (as opposed to the disassociation that testimonies seem to require) and, in general, more room for agency on the part of DREAMers, as they are able to "keep one foot in Mexico." Caminero-Santangelo offers varied representations of undocumented activists that depict the truncated dreams of graduates, representations that refuse to buy into a narrative allowing only for unadulterated allegiance to the United States.

The subsequent chapters further enhance the reader's knowledge of Mexico, as topics progress in chronological order from pre-Columbian times to the present, always looping to both the past and the future to illustrate the porousness of historical timelines in order to facilitate deeper understanding. In "Milpa: Mesoamerican Resistance to Agricultural Imperialism," Analisa Taylor continues the cross-border connection seen in Caminero-Santangelo's chapter, but with a perspective that crosses centuries. Several widely distributed U.S.-based documentary films, such as *Super Size Me* (2004) and *Food, Inc.* (2008), as well as books such as Michael Pollan's *The Omnivore's Dilemma*, have drawn our attention to the health consequences for consumers and the environmental devastation wrought by the genetic modification and the fossil-fueled cultivation of food. Taylor draws on the documentary films *Migrar o morir/Paying the Price* (2008) and *Food Chains* (2014) to recenter the discussion on the first-person accounts of people who experience the perils of the U.S.-based agro-industrial complex as migrant laborers. Whereas Caminero-Santangelo offers a more complex view of the DREAMer experience, including a section on DREAMers who return to Mexico (*los otros* DREAMers), Taylor addresses the topic of growing food, an issue that—in some cases because of mammoth companies like Monsanto—links people in Mexico and the United States in unique ways. In both countries, government rhetoric favors the small farmer, but corporations ultimately control the market.

In "Charros: A Critical Introduction," Christopher Conway describes the charro as "a theatrical and stylized Mexican cowboy." Unlike the vaquero (cowhand), the charro is "a dandy on horseback, with embroidered clothes studded with silver buttons, rings and chains, and that fancy sombrero." Conway argues that by the turn of the century, the figure connoted violent masculinity and could be found in all social classes: "bandits, rurales, and aristocratic landowners all put on his costume." He traces the evolution and construction of the charro in novels, films, and song. In doing so he provides a framework useful for anyone who seeks to understand the way that figures and events function at the service of national ideologies. Conway shows that narrative, tradition, space, and iconography are employed to accomplish nationalist identification on the individual and collective levels.

Ryan Long's chapter, "The People's Print Shop: Art, Politics, and the Taller de Gráfica Popular," is unique in that the artistic representations he studies—prints and illustrations—are the product of the group he studies, the Workshop for Popular Graphic Art (TGP). The artists of the TGP, like those who manipulated the image of the charro, aimed to engage and influence the political topics of the day, which included the aftermath of the Revolution and the Cristero War through the 1950s. In the historical section of his chapter, Long traces the roots of the TGP and its commitment to justice and equality—a commitment that extended far beyond Mexico to engage, for example, Nazism and the Holocaust. He argues that a clear but less direct precursor to this engaged political art can be found in José Joaquín Fernández de Lizardi's novel *El periquillo sarniento* (The Mangy Parrot, 1816) and, at the turn of the century, Ricardo Flores Magón's writing and work as editor of the journal *Regeneración*; both writers, in different times, shared the idea that art could be a critical tool. Long traces an even more direct influence on the TGP: the world-famous printmaker José Guadalupe Posada, "whose satirical work inspired the TPG in terms of both medium and message."

The idea that art is instructive can also be seen most prominently in the role of the Mexican educational system after the Revolution. David Dalton, in "Educating Cohesion: The Teacher as an Agent of the Postrevolutionary State," traces the role of the teacher after Mexico's Secretary of Education José Vasconcelos began to sponsor art to educate the masses. Dalton shows that rural teachers were "the most celebrated actors of the cultural missions" promulgated by Vanconcelos in order to "civilize" Mexico. Of the different artistic representations of teachers Dalton studies, two murals by Diego Rivera, *La maestra rural* (The Rural Teacher) and *Alfabetización: Aprendiendo a leer* (Literacy: Learning to Read) send particularly potent messages: "Armed peasants may have overthrown Porfirio Díaz and Victoriano Huerta, but schoolteachers will ultimately rebuild the nation by educating the people into a cohesive national identity and assimilating even the nation's military heroes." The strength of the state can be understood through myriad vehicles (for example, the abovementioned teachers) but—as with Porfirio Díaz, who was famous for his *pan o palo* (carrot or stick) leadership—the PRI (and later the PAN, or Partido Acción Nacional) resorted, and resorts, to violence to maintain power.

In "*M* for *Murder*: Mexico and Its *Democratic* State," Fernando Fabio Sánchez traces state violence and the way it is represented and imagined through art. Sánchez refers to the Tlatelolco maccascre of 1968 as the beginning of a series of massacres for which the Mexican people hold the PRI and PAN responsible. Of the many examples he employs, perhaps the graffiti art on a wall during the remodeling of the Alameda Park (the same park seen in Rivera's Sunday afternoon mural) is the most striking. Sánchez describes death as President Peña Nieto "among all the graffiti and collective statements" on *The Wall of Truth*.

If La Santa Muerte is a constant in Mexico, so is solitude. Robert McKee Irwin, in his chapter on the topic, contrasts this against the solitude described by Nobel laureate Octavio Paz: "Solitude, it would seem, is indeed a concept that runs deep in Mexican culture. However, the sentiments and meanings it evokes differ significantly from those described by Paz. If Mexico is a labyrinth of solitude, it is a solitude that is much more emotive, more histrionic, more communal, more cathartic, more colorful, and more fun than the dreary labyrinth proposed by Paz." Irwin also argues that while solitude is tightly tied to Mexican history and national identity, some of the meanings the word took on in postrevolutionary Mexico are anathema to nationalist constructs. From the homoerotic art of writer Xavier Villaurrutia to the solitude in songs that emigrants listen to (and find solace in), like those of Los Tigres del Norte, Irwin takes a concept that has been theorized by intellectuals and shows how it relates to multiple facets of Mexican popular culture. His analysis of solitude exemplifies the ways art can help to explain the human experience at a level perhaps deeper than what historical texts can offer.

The chapter "Democracy: The Idea of Democratic Transition" by Ignacio M. Sánchez Prado is crucial to helping us understand both the process of democratization in Mexico and the fragility of Mexico's current democracy. Sánchez Prado traces new electoral practices that began in the 1980s and the electoral defeat of the PRI in 2000 (and its return in 2012) as well as the concomitant move toward neoliberal economic policies (for example, austerity programs and the selling off of state enterprises). After outlining the historical process, he looks at the way literature, cinema, and popular culture represent the transition. From chronicle essays and political manifestos by prominent Mexican intellectuals (including the Zapatistas) to the films of Luis Estrada, which focus on electoral democracy, economic inequality, the drug war, and the return of the PRI and rock music, Sánchez Prado shows a level of skepticism so pervasive that it leaves in doubt the very concept that underlies the chapter: democratic transition.

Sánchez Prado's chapter on Mexico's transition to democracy precedes Emily Hind's "Classism: *Gente Decente* and Civil Rights; From Suffrage to Divorce and Privileges in Between." Reading in this order, though it may seem counterintuitive, offers the reader appropriate information about democracy in Mexico in order to better comprehend the relevance of the suffrage movement and other key themes in Hind's chapter. Hind critiques "citizen privilege" as defined by the mainstream Mexican notion of *gente decente* and looks to a variety of artistic works (from Rosario Castellanos's farce *El eterno femenino* to Alfonso Cuarón's *Y tu mamá también*) to argue that "the select groups that trample the civil rights of others correspond to the sectors that imagine themselves to be socially superior, the *gente decente* (decent people)." Two videos available on YouTube, *Gentleman de Las Lomas* and *Las Ladies de Polanco*, show how colonialism—or coloniality, the vestiges of colonialism in the present—operates today, as young, light-skinned Mexicans are seen disparaging darker-skinned Mexicans of a lower social station, thinking themselves to be *gente bien* (nice people).

Jacqueline E. Bixler's "1968: Archiving Amnesia; Tlatelolco and the Artfulness of Memory" presents perhaps the most well-known touchstone for understanding present-day Mexico, as I have already mentioned. It ties in with a variety of themes in postrevolutionary Mexico and, in its theorization of amnesia, speaks to *lieux de mémoire*, "sites of memory," including the site of the next two chapters, both of which focus in part on the real and mythical northern border.

Rafael Acosta Morales, in "Medusa's Head: The Drug War Commandeers the People," traces the myth of the drug lord to the years surrounding Mexico's independence in 1810 and to prohibition, during colonial times, of alcohol and tobacco. The more recent link to prohibition in the United States, as well as the concept of Robin Hood, allows readers from beyond Mexico to understand the common portrayal of narco-traffickers as heroes, as one finds in other parts of Latin America (think of Pablo Escobar in Colombia). Acosta Morales also questions the legitimacy of Mexico's current war on drugs, which was started—seemingly out of the blue—by President Felipe Calderón, of the

PAN. He refers to Mexican intellectual Jorge Castañeda, who speculates that "what Calderón tried to do was to legitimize himself. Facing the accusations of electoral fraud that surrounded his election, he decided he needed a foundational act of his administration."

In their chapter on femicide, "Expanding Outrage: Representations of Gendered Violence and Feminicide in Mexico," Dana A. Meredith and Luis Alberto Rodríguez Cortés provide a detailed background of the murders of women in Ciudad Juárez, ultimately pointing to the reality that the border city is no longer an outlier: the violence depicted in the plays, films, art installations, and mixed-media publications point to the proliferation of violence throughout Mexico. The authors base their chapter on the work of Melissa Wright and the "myth of the third world disposable woman," first tracing some of the earliest widely known cultural products related to the femicides, like Lourdes Portillo's documentary film *Señorita extraviada* (Missing Young Woman, 2001) and the investigative journalism of Sergio González Rodríguez in his book *Huesos en el desierto* (Bones in the Desert, 2002). This book, as Meredith and Rodríguez Cortés point out, is an excellent example of the influence fiction has on nonfiction and vice versa: González Rodríguez's book "became a foundational source for Roberto Bolaño's novel *2666*, published posthumously in 2004." This blending is seen in what the authors call "parodic inversion" (following the work of Linda Hutcheon)—that is, to use Hutcheon's words, "repetition with critical distance" that allows for audiences to engage meaningfully with works of art. Through many art forms, including plays like *Antigone* and Mexican author Edeberto "Pilo" Galindo's 2002 *Lomas de Poleo*, Meredith and Rodríguez Cortés show the value of reworking the past as well as the challenge of depicting violence.

Oswaldo Zavala's essay on El Norte, "The North in Contemporary Mexican Narrative, Poetry, and Film: Relocating National Imaginaries Beyond the Mythology of Violence," offers a profound analysis of northern Mexico through a variety of art forms produced by artists "who may not come from the North, might not reside there, or, in some cases, are not even natives of Mexico" but who, despite intellectual colonialism, present the North in ways that "have contributed significantly to the country's most important cultural trends." He argues that the North is "the ultimate frontier of Mexican modernity [and that] certain works of art allow for a productive understanding of the North as a privileged space of geopolitical signification in Mexico." Zavala works with thinkers like Slavoj Žižek, Jacques Rancière, Étienne Balibar, and Giorgio

Agamben to conceptualize the North as something other than merely a site of violence in the Mexican imaginary.

In "Media from Above/Media from Below: An Alternative Topography of the Mexican Mediascape," Magalí Rabasa looks at a common topic from an uncommon angle, offering the reader a nuanced view of the media with a historical perspective that explains the present-day context of violence—which seems to increase daily—toward reporters and others in the Mexican media. Rabasa combines Arjun Appadurai's concept of the mediascape with Clemencia Rodríguez's idea of "fissures in the mediascape" to present elite-controlled mass media (media from above) and media that question and contradict it (media from below). In Rabasa's chapter, as she puts it, "objects being analyzed (the works of art) are also examples of the subject they represent (media)." The different angles from which she examines media in Mexico highlight the fact that controlling the media is a high-stakes endeavor and demonstrate the massive power of the media with a capital *M* as well as the profound influence small-scale operations can have.

Debra A. Castillo's chapter "Net.art" closes out the book with a look at where the arts and humanities are headed in the age of the Internet, specifically in a Web 2.0 environment. In order to answer this question she studies the ways net.art, Arte Útil, and post-Internet art enable people to carve out spaces of creativity and resistance. Castillo's case studies focus on the work of Mejor Vida Corp. (Better Life Corp., or MVC, created by Mexican artist Minerva Cuevas) and the Transborder Immigrant Tool (TBT, a collective project of Ricardo Domínguez, Micha Cárdenas, Amy Sara Carroll, and other collaborators in b.a.n.g. lab's Electronic Disturbance Theater). The TBT is an excellent example of the conjunction of history (in this case, the history of the Mexican-U.S. border) and art (in this case, art in and as technology), since the TBT is designed to guide migrants to safety while providing—on the screen of a flip phone—poetry to inspire, educate, and orient. This combination—history and art—is the underpinning of this book, which can be read, just like history and fiction, in or out of order.

NOTE

1. *Presunto culpable* was released two decades after the U.S.-produced *The Thin Blue Line* (1988), Errol Morris's documentary about Randall Dale Adams, who

was wrongfully sent to death row and exonerated after the release of the film. In both documentaries, imagined systems of justice are juxtaposed with what for many is a clear, obvious reality based on social inequity; and in both the protagonist himself is the most solid evidence of the power of documentaries.

WORKS CITED

Chasteen, John Charles. *Born in Blood and Fire: A Concise History of Latin America.* W. W. Norton, 2001.

Dresser, Denise, and Jorge Volpi. *México: Lo que todo ciudadano quisiera (no) saber de su patria.* Aguilar, 2006.

@EnriqueKrauze. "La sociedad civil reaccionó con cientos de iniciativas prácticas ante el terremoto de 1985. Ahora está paralizada." *Twitter,* 13 Sep. 2015, 12:34 p.m., twitter.com/EnriqueKrauze/status/643115494870941696.

Issela, Erika. "Reseña de la película *Todo el poder.*" *Íncipit* 50, 16 May 2015, decada50s .blogspot.com/2015/05/resena-de-la-pelicula-todo-el-poder.html.

Joseph, G. M., and Timothy J. Henderson. *The Mexico Reader: History, Culture, Politics.* Duke University Press, 2002.

"KU Law's Project for Innocence Frees Man Wrongfully Convicted of Murder." *KU School of Law,* 21 Dec. 2015, law.ku.edu/news/ku-laws-project-innocence-frees -man-wrongfully-convicted-murder.

La ley de Herodes. Directed by Luis Estrada. Artecinema, 1999.

Le Clercq Ortega, Juan Antonio, and Gerardo Rodríguez Sánchez Lara, editors. *IGI-MEX: Global Impunity Index Mexico (2016).* Fundación Universidad de las Américas Puebla, 2016, www.udlap.mx/igimex/assets/files/igimex2016_ENG.pdf.

Leñero, Vicente. *¡Pelearán diez rounds!; Los hijos de Sánchez; Nadie sabe nada.* Grupo Editorial Gaceta: DDF, Secretaría General de Desarrollo Social, 1994.

"Mexico." *Reporters Without Borders,* rsf.org/en/mexico. Accessed 13 Apr. 2017.

Molotov. "Nostradamus mucho (Que se caiga el teatro)." *Dance and Dense Denso,* Universal Music Latino, 2003.

POV Communications. "Trials of Antonio Zúñiga Expose the Nightmare of Mexico's Justice System in POV's *Presumed Guilty.*" 2010, pov-tc.pbs.org/pov /downloads/2010/pov-presumedguilty-press-release.pdf.

Presumed Guilty: The Movie. www.presumedguiltythemovie.com/.

Presunto culpable. Directed by Roberto Hernández and Geoffrey Smith. Cinépolis, 2008.

Semple, Kirk. "Grass-Roots Anticorruption Drive Puts Heat on Mexican Lawmakers." *New York Times*, 28 May 2016.

Stockton, William. "Rivera Mural in Mexico Awaits Its New Shelter." *New York Times*, 4 Jan. 1987.

The Thin Blue Line. Directed by Errol Morris. Miramax, 1988.

1

DREAMers

Youth and Migration: American DREAMers and Mexico

MARTA CAMINERO-SANTANGELO

PRIMARY MATERIALS:

- *Dream Act Now* by Lalo Alcaraz (cartoon, n.d.)
- *Dream Girl* by Lalo Alcaraz (cartoon, 2014)
- *GOP Santa Gives It to DREAM Act Students and to Latinos* by Lalo Alcaraz (cartoon, 2016)
- *The Guardians* by Ana Castillo (novel, 2007)
- *Under the Same Moon*, directed by Patricia Riggen (film, 2007)
- *Underground Undergrads: UCLA Undocumented Immigrant Students Speak Out*, edited by Gabriela Madera et al. (testimonies, 2008)
- *Into the Beautiful North* by Luis Alberto Urrea (novel, 2009)
- *Return to Sender* by Julia Alvarez (novel, 2009)
- *Which Way Home*, directed by Rebecca Cammisa (documentary, 2009)
- *Papers: Stories by Undocumented Youth*, edited by José Manuel et al. (testimonies, 2012)
- *Los Otros Dreamers*, edited by Jill Anderson and Nin Solis (multimedia project, 2014)

IN THE PAST DECADE AND A HALF, undocumented immigrants who arrived in the United States as children have been among the most vocal and visible activists for the passage of legislation for immigration reform. They have been called DREAMers, referring specifically to their eligibility for the proposed DREAM (Development, Relief, and Education for Alien Minors) Act, which would provide a path to legalization for undocumented youth meeting certain conditions. The general rhetorical argument constructed in support of the DREAM Act goes something like this: DREAMers were brought to the United States by their parents, not of their own volition; the United States is in many cases the only country they remember; they are often high-achieving, meritorious students; they could make substantial contributions to U.S. society but are currently unable to do so because of their legal status.

By far the majority of DREAMers (roughly 70 percent) are originally from Mexico. And according to the Migration Policy Institute, undocumented immigrants from Mexico who are currently eligible for DACA (Deferred Action for Childhood Arrivals) are approximately 14 percent of the total undocumented population from Mexico. DACA is the policy instituted by President Barack Obama in the wake of the repeated failure of the DREAM Act or more comprehensive immigration reform to pass Congress, to allow work permits and a temporary deferral of deportation for qualifying undocumented youth. In this essay I address the question, How does Mexico operate in the DREAMer cultural imaginary? I examine a range of art both by and about undocumented youth in the United States, including (1) first-person narratives by DREAMers themselves in collections such as *Papers: Stories by Undocumented Youth*, *Underground Undergrads: UCLA Undocumented Immigrant Students Speak Out*, and *Los Otros Dreamers*, as well as on the Internet; (2) visual art and music by and about DREAMers; (3) novels by U.S. Latinx authors, such as *The Guardians* by Chicana Ana Castillo, *Into the Beautiful North* by Chicano Luis Alberto Urrea, and the young adult novel *Return to Sender* by Dominican American Julia Alvarez, with narrators who are undocumented youth from Mexico; and (4) films such as the documentary *Which Way Home* (about Central American unaccompanied minors) and the drama *Under the Same Moon* (La misma luna), about an undocumented minor who travels to the United States from Mexico in search of his mother.

Because publicly disseminated DREAMer testimonies (drawing on the Latin American genre of *testimonio*, or life narrative told as part of a "political imperative" [Sommer 134]) are crafted to further a particular political agenda (legal incorporation into the United States through the passage of the DREAM Act), representations of ties to and identity with Mexico in such testimonies are often muted, while representation of their U.S. American identities is drawn in bold strokes, emphasizing their allegiance to the host country and their embrace of the ideal of the American Dream. Other forms of artistic representation, by contrast, substantially complicate this rather singular narrative of U.S. American belonging. The identity of undocumented youth portrayed in novels by U.S. Latinx writers, for instance, is, ironically, more ambivalent and transnational; filmic representation of the growing phenomenon of unaccompanied undocumented minors complicates further the justificatory narrative that DREAMers were brought by their parents and therefore not willful agents in their own (unlawful) migration.

DREAMer TESTIMONY AND ADVOCACY

As I have already suggested, part of the rhetorical case that DREAM activist youth make for passage of the DREAM Act is that for many, the United States is the only home they remember; in building communities of solidarity they have identified more closely with DREAMers of other national origins than with Mexico as their country of origin, and they have understood and represented themselves culturally as undocumented U.S. Americans rather than as Mexican. Representations of Mexico as point of origin and as a cultural identity thus are largely invisible, or at least obscured, in the visual art and activist narratives of DREAMers. Indeed, Mexican DREAMers share with other DREAMers—from Central and South America, Africa, and elsewhere—plot lines that seem to shed the markings of the nation and culture of origin in order to insistently demonstrate commonality among DREAMer stories and even to create a sense of a collective identity for (all) undocumented youth. As one DREAMer, José Manuel, a co-editor of the volume *Papers: Stories by Undocumented Youth*, writes, "There are undocumented people from all over the world, and when reading their stories, I saw that they have suffered in many of the same ways, either in the countries they were born in, during the journey they undertook to get here or in their lives once they arrived. These are immigrants who can see a future here in the United States, not in the countries of their birth" (Manuel et al. vii). On the website of the National Immigrant Youth Alliance (NIYA), the pitch soliciting support for the DREAM Act is accompanied by strong language of a collective and shared experience that utterly obscures countries and cultures of origin while insisting on a shared, collective identity and common struggle in the United States: "Together we are coming out of the shadows. . . . The experience is empowering and liberating for each of us, as well as for all of us as a community." Activists quoted on the NIYA site are listed by organizational affiliation, not country of origin.

The public rhetoric of DREAMer activists in their testimonies emphasizes a strong personal sense of identification as American and adheres to a narrative pattern of the potential for immigrant contributions to American society. This strategy corresponds with Bonnie Honig's observation, in *Democracy and the Foreigner*, that "movements need myths. Activists can make up new myths, or they can take those already in existence and recycle them. The latter strategy is preferable because it takes advantage of existing cultural resources" (103). As the acronym DREAM attests, the myth "recycled" by activists for the passage of a DREAM Act is, in part, the myth of the American Dream of meritocracy rewarded: "We have worked long and hard, we have risen to meet every challenge and we have made this country a better place for all. . . . We are empowering ourselves to seek a better future, a future in which we are respected, in which our families live with dignity, in which our American Dream is possible" ("Are You Undocumented"). Jessica Esparza, originally from Durango, Mexico, recounts on a YouTube video testimony her honors and achievements as a student: even in Mexico, "I was always student number 1; [I] went to competitions for first and sixth grade—state competitions—and always got first place." When Jessica was brought to the United States at age eleven, "I managed to get all A's and one B in seventh grade without speaking English fluently." In eighth grade she won a scholarship to the NASA Space Academy for the summer ("I'm a Dreamer"). Veronica Valdez, who came over the border from Mexico with her mother when she was four and who graduated from the University of California, Los Angeles, recalls that she "worked very hard in school and earned good grades" and "had always had aspirations of becoming a professor" (Madera et al. 43). Her education represented, for her, "one component of the American dream" (41).

Honig has posited that the American national narrative contains within it contradictory notions of immigrants: there is the "good immigrant" constituted by "exceptionalist accounts of . . . the myth of an immigrant America"; in such accounts, "the immigrant functions to reassure workers of the possibility of upward mobility" and supposedly confirms "that the economy fairly rewards dedication and hard work" (74). On the other hand, national discourse equally depends on the construct of the "bad immigrant" (commonly understood to be undocumented) who, rather than giving to the nation through hard work, only takes: "[She or he] takes things from us and has nothing to offer in return. [She or he] takes up residence without permission; [she or he] takes services without payment" (96). The testimony of DREAMers stridently counters the "bad immigrant" construct with insistence on the posture of the "good immigrant" who wants only to contribute, to give back. Jessica Esparza talks about her ambition to be a nurse in terms of being "able to provide health care to other community members, maybe able to make a difference, I might . . . save a life" ("I'm a Dreamer"). Carlos Roa, a Venezuelan-born DREAMer, explains, "It's frustrating, the fact that I want to give back, I'm willing to serve this country in military service, and I don't even have the option to do so" ("Carlos").

DREAMer testimony challenges the bad immigrant narrative in other ways as well. The rhetorical justification of the DREAM Act has typically included the reasoning that DREAMers did not make the choice to "[take] up residence without permission," since they were brought here by their parents; thus their unauthorized status punishes them for something that was not their fault. As José Manuel, one of the cofounders of El Grupo Juvenil—the group responsible for the documentary film *Papers: Stories of Undocumented Youth*—writes in his foreword to the follow-up book *Papers*, "Youth face these obstacles because of the decision of their families to immigrate, a decision that they had no say in" (Manuel et al. v). (The very problematic nature of this rhetoric, which implicitly *does* blame the parents, has been pointed out by immigration reform activists.) Jessica Esparza echoes this sentiment: "I had no knowledge or no saying on any of my parents' decisions" ("I'm a Dreamer"). In another YouTube testimony, Piash argues, "We came here with our parents when we were ten, five, twelve, at a very young age when we had no control over our future. We went wherever our parents told us to go. So how could I have broken a rule that I had no clue existed?" ("Undocumented and Unafraid"). A poem titled "The Undocumented," included in *Papers*, reproduces the general gist of this line of reasoning:

> And if?
> If they are innocent in being here
> if they had no choice in getting on
> that bus, boat, plane, train
> If they had no idea
> of the consequences
> of following their parent

> If they were too young
> to make a legal or sound decision
> Do they still
> Deserve to be called and classified as
> the undocumented? (Manuel et al. 34)

This poem echoes the argument in which migrant youth are "innocent" of "legal" violations, and therefore exonerated from the act of illegal immigration through their own lack of "choice" in the matter of going where their parents went. What such a representation obscures, emphasizing as it does that young migrants don't "deserve" the consequences of their adult parents' decision, is the implication that the parents *do* deserve those consequences—that is, that migrant parents are the "bad immigrants" (a rather risky strategy in advocating immigration reform). In Honig's analysis, the dominant U.S. construct of the "illegal immigrant" imagines a person who defies the basic principle of consent of the governed to their government: he or she "never consents to American laws, and 'we' never consent to his presence on 'our' territory" (96).

DREAMer testimonies, however, are often uneasy with suggesting that parents made "bad" decisions. Thus, in several DREAMer narratives, what emerges is a fraught relationship to that parental decision—a relationship that manifests itself as one of debt and obligation to the parent(s), who took grave risks in seeking a *better life for their children* than was available in the home country. The unspoken subtext is a deficit model for the country of origin—dreams can be achieved in the United States but not in Mexico (or other home countries). José Manuel says, "Their families just wanted safety, food, shelter or a better future for their children" (Manuel et al. v). In *Underground Undergrads* Antonio Alvarez, who came to the United States from Mexico at age four, explains that his mother "'did not see a future for us in Mexico and viewed the United States as the answer to our problems" (52). In an unpublished *testimonio*, "Rogelio" explains his parents' decision to come to the United States from Mexico:

> My parents brought me when I was six months old . . . to save my life, pretty much. . . . When I was born, for some reason I would not eat at all. I just kept on crying and crying, and the doctors didn't know what was wrong with me. . . . I got tested for broken bones, damaged organs, mental retardation, any diseases, HIV AIDS. . . . The doctors gave up on me, and they told my parents, "I'm sorry, there's nothing else we can do for you." . . . My parents didn't want to accept

> that . . . they had heard that the United States had better medical treatment, way advanced, back in Mexico. And so they had to decide. The biggest decision of their lives was either stay back in Mexico and hope for a miracle to happen or take the risk of coming here. . . . So they came to the United States, and within two weeks they figured out what was wrong with me—the doctors figured out that I was lactose intolerant. ("Rogelio")

This narrative strain also facilitates a pronounced *dis*identification of DREAMers with Mexico; DREAMer narratives frequently emphasize their lack of knowledge of the home country. In Anne Galisky's introduction to *Papers*, she tells the story of Hector Lopez, a college student in Oregon who was deported to Mexico—a country he had no memory of and which he had not lived in since he was an infant of six weeks. Hector did not even know about his undocumented status. In response to what happened to him, Hector protested, "I don't even speak Spanish! I got a 'C' in Spanish! . . . We didn't even eat Mexican food at home. We had meatloaf. I don't even know where the accent marks are supposed to go on my name!" (Manuel et al. xii–xiii). When Hector was deported, he was—perhaps predictably—read as American, not Mexican, in Mexico, and harassed accordingly by gang members: "They assumed I had money. They hung up an American flag across from where we lived. . . . It's almost like you don't exist anymore, like you've gone into a black hole and are floating outside of the universe. You're there, but you're not real" (xiii). For Hector, having been stripped of the only national identity he knew and being sent to what was, for him, a foreign country, it is in some sense Mexico itself that is the "black hole," a space signifying the erasure of all sense of personhood and identity. Briana, a Mexican-born DREAMer whose story is also included in the collection *Papers*, succinctly declares: "I was raised in the USA. This is my home. Here I have a home and a school and dreams to accomplish" (28). Veronica Valdez insists, "I consider myself American. My friends, boyfriend, family, hopes, and dreams are in this country. Thus, I work in every way I can, in every moment I can, to be recognized by the nation I have lived in for so long" (Madera et al. 44).

PICTURING DREAMers

Visual art representing DREAMers furthers the political and activist goals of the DREAMer collective identity, through a strongly U.S.-facing posture and a lack of identification with their country of origin. The stylized illustrations of the volume *Papers*, drawn by artist Julio Salgado (who grew up gay and undocumented in the United States) in bold, contrasting colors with stark backgrounds mostly lacking in detail, bear witness to the commonalities of experience and to the DREAMers' identity as "Americans" above their shades of difference. Almost completely lacking in the illustrations is symbolism or overt reference to *any* country of origin (Manuel et al. vii). The foreword to the volume is illustrated by a drawing depicting two arms and hands—one white skinned and one brown skinned—upholding the words "United States," all in capitals and colored in red, white, and blue (vii). The drawing thus explicitly anchors the collection in a U.S. context while advancing a vision of multiethnic American identity. In another illustration, a single figure stands in the foreground, while a Statue of Liberty—blacked out in shadow—stands in the background (43). A repeated visual theme in the illustrations is the importance of documents themselves—those documents that are next to impossible to obtain, that mark the difference between national belonging and a shadow existence, that signify unmet aspirations and (collective) failed dreams, or that designate the threat of deportation and literal removal from the United States. One illustration of two figures, for instance, contains graphic, larger-than-life depictions of a work permit and driver's license as the only background (37). Another shows a letter from Immigration and Customs Enforcement (ICE) in the background, again larger than life and represented in roughly the same dimensions as the human figure of a young woman in the foreground—a life determined by the force of documents (35).

Visual art representing DREAMers frequently emphasizes the theme of stunted potential through youth depicted in graduation regalia. In one illustration accompanying *Papers*, for instance, a graduate stands next to a wall that stretches higher than her head, and reaches (but not quite) for the top of the wall with her hand (20). Nationally syndicated political cartoonist Lalo Alcaraz, creator of the comic strip *La Cucaracha*, depicts a DREAMer with her graduation cap hovering in midair above her head, suggestive of the just-out-of-reach aspirations facing undocumented youth in the United States (*Dream Girl*). In another, a DREAMer in graduation regalia is posed as the Statue of Liberty, holding a torch high in the right hand and a diploma in the left (*Dream Act Now*). In a third, an elephant dressed as Santa Claus—but with "GOP" printed on his coat—hands a graduating DREAMer a piece of coal, with the word "NO" written on it (*GOP Santa*). The political protests staged by DREAM activists in recent years, likewise, call overt attention to the ways in which current immigration law stunts the dream of graduation as commencement, or beginning. The annual mock graduations in Washington, D.C., organized by United We Dream for many years drew hundreds of DREAMers from across the country every summer, dressed in caps and gowns and marching to the tune of "Pomp and Circumstance," to perform the plight of high school graduates unable to secure financial aid for college because of their status. These depicted a singularly U.S.-focused experience and were devoid of the markers of transnational ties, such as Mexican flags, that have marked other rallies and marches related to immigration issues or Latinx heritage. In July 2013, DREAMers staged their first-ever mock citizenship ceremony in Washington, D.C., in a forceful performance of their allegiance to the United States at the expense of other national attachments.

The song "ICE el Hielo," performed by the band La Santa Cecilia and made by director Alex Rivera into a music video featuring undocumented actors, portrays what Peter Orner calls a "culture of anxiety" (10) in which ICE agents roam the streets and "nunca se sabe cuando nos va tocar" (we never know when they are going to strike). One of the song's verses replays the theme of the stunted ambitions of DREAMers; it describes an undocumented youth, Marta, who can't pursue her education because of her status, while those "born here" will garner the academic awards and scholarships:

> Marta llegó de niña y sueña con estudiar
> Pero se le hace difícil sin los papeles
> Se quedan con los laureles los que nacieron acá
> Pero ella nunca deja de luchar.
>
> Marta arrived as a girl and dreams of studying
> But it's hard without papers
> The laurels go to those who were born here
> But she never gives up struggling.

Additional cases of potential deportation depicted in the song lyrics focus on adult workers (a gardener, a maid) and on the children who will be traumatized by the deportation of their parents, who simply made the mistake of having a job ("Eso pasa por salir a trabajar" [That's what happens when you go out to work]). However, other children, like Marta, have different fears: the fears that they will never achieve their dreams. The music video, notably, focuses specifically on Marta's deportation. (I will return shortly to the subject of deported DREAMers.)

Some DREAMer visual art demonstrates a concern with the sense of invisibility of undocumented youth in the United States, who feel unrecognized in their own country despite their achievements. In a 2011 cartoon not included in *Papers*, but very much in the same style, Julio Salgado represents another DREAMer in graduation regalia; on her gown are depicted the words "I am . . . Your Brother, Your Sister, Your Neighbor, Your Cousin, Your Partner, Your Lover, Your Teacher, Your Student, Your Friend, Your Dreamer . . ." The litany emphasizes that undocumented youth are all around us, that they are in our schools and communities, that they have families (and in many cases U.S.-citizen family members), and yet they are often invisible in mainstream American society. As a direct challenge to that invisibility, the cartoon bears the heading (in large black block letters) "Undocumented, unafraid and unapologetic," the slogan of DREAM activists. The graduate's tassel consists of the word "HOPE." Another Salgado drawing emphasizes DREAMers' existential dilemma: a graduating DREAMer with the words "I exist" is detained by what appear to be two Border Patrol agents (Carrasquillo).

The cartoonist Alberto Ledesma, who grew up undocumented and is a PhD and Chicano studies scholar working in higher education at the University of California, Berkeley, also explores the theme of DREAMer invisibility and lack of recognition, through visual references to Ralph Ellison's *Invisible Man*. One drawing depicts a teenaged boy reading the novel; the illustration is headed "Diary of a Dreamer" and contains the text (in handwriting): "You should know that I never wanted to lie, that if I ever misled you it was because I had no choice"—repeating the refrain of innocence in the decisions that brought DREAMers to the United States. In another cartoon, a boy again reads *Invisible Man*, while wearing a Batman costume. This time the text running along the side of the picture explains DREAMers' sense of responsibility to their families, their compulsion to fly "under the radar," their awareness that coming out of "the shadows," even as an act of political activism and agency, puts their loved ones as well as themselves at risk: "It was because of my love for family, because I did not want to put them in jeopardy, that I remained in the shadows all those years when I was undocumented. . . . I knew that any misstep would affect more than my own dream." In another drawing, the superhero as undocumented immigrant is now Superman, being detained by a Border Patrol agent; Ledesma and others have repeatedly played on the fact that Superman too was an "illegal alien" (Carrasquillo).

Taken as a whole, these artists are doing explicitly political work; the content of their drawings continues and extends the activist DREAM narrative of lack of choice, the thwarted potential for significant contribution, the deserving nature of the DREAMers, and their sense of (unrecognized) belonging in the United States. The cultural content (Batman, Superman, American flags, the Statue of Liberty, state drivers' licenses) is American; Mexico is, for all practical purposes, invisible.

THE OTHER DREAMERS

A significantly more complex picture of young immigrants' continuing relationship to Mexico is, unsurprisingly, derived by looking at the testimonies of undocumented youth who have returned to live in Mexico, either by choice or through deportation and removal, gathered in the volume *Los Otros Dreamers*. These youth vastly complicate the definition of "DREAMer" because the American Dream is no longer the mythological structure of their dreaming—and, in many cases, because they never fit the exact criteria for the DREAM Act to begin with. Several of these *testimonios* attest to their having had their dreams blocked and thwarted in the United States because of their undocumented status and suggest that it is in fact in Mexico that they have experienced human dignity and the ability to pursue their ambitions. Rather than insisting that the United States is their home and that they are "Americans, just without papers," they have laid roots and laid claim to a home in Mexico that gives them a sense of belonging many never felt in the United States. Maru ascribes to Mexico the values typically associated with the United States; she describes wanting to get "out of the U.S., out of the place that was incarcerating me" and leaving for Mexico "to see what this pursuit of happiness and being free were like" (Anderson and Solis 63). Other testimonies suggest the desire to reconnect to their cultural heritage, to rediscover the language and traditions of their home countries, and to sustain a fully bicultural and transnational sensibility—an idea that most DREAM narratives in the United States shy away from, no doubt for fear of feeding into the dominant culture's ascription of them as foreign and outsiders. Indeed, sometimes for repatriated DREAMers, this bicultural sensibility is suggested in the language itself.

Samantha Maribel, for instance, writes in Spanish about how she feels that Mexico is her home: "No quiero regresar porque me siento feliz, satisfecha viviendo en mi país. Me siento parte de algo" (I don't want to go back because I feel happy, satisfied living in my country. I feel a part of something) (75). But she switches to sentences in English precisely when she is declaring her fullest sense of belonging in Mexico, as though to simultaneously assert her continuing cultural ties to the US: "Returning to Mexico just felt right. . . . I felt it was my responsibility and commitment to come back" (79). Maru notes that she has found her life's purpose and fulfillment (at least for the time being) in working with the L@s Otr@s Dreamers Collective in a project that inherently recognizes the dual cultural pulls and contradictory struggles of living in the United States as undocumented or in Mexico as a former U.S. American: "My passion is borderless now" (66).

Interestingly, just as, for these "Other Dreamers," the poles of the geography of dreams fulfilled versus dreams deferred are reversed, so too is the geographic locus of undocumented identity considerably complicated. For several students who returned to Mexico after finding that they could not pursue their educational aspirations in the United States because of their undocumented status, it is a shock to realize that, as far as education goes, they are equally undocumented in Mexico, because their U.S. education cannot count without transcripts (their documents), which some schools in the United States will not release without their being personally present to sign for them—a presence that is, of course, impossible. As Rufino explains, "I couldn't fix my papers. . . . It is frustrating. I can't study here, and I couldn't study over there" (56). Thus Mexico emerges more contradictorily in the imaginary of the "Other Dreamers" as a place of potential and belonging and simultaneously as dismayingly mirroring the United States in the obstruction of potential through a Catch-22 of dependency on *U.S.* documentation.

TRANSNATIONAL DREAMers

Fictional representations of undocumented youth in the United States elaborate and expand upon repatriated DREAMers' more transnational sensibility, in which the Mexican national identity need not be sacrificed in an embrace of the U.S. American one. A repeating figure in novels by Castillo, Alvarez, and Urrea, as well as in novelist Reyna Grande's memoir *The Distance Between Us*, is the absent or missing parent. The DREAMers' continuing and in some cases dominating ties to Mexico are largely a product of that stretched relationship, in which imaginary ties to missing parents reach across the border.

Dominican American writer Julia Alvarez's young adult novel *Return to Sender*, which writes across lines of national origin, depicts a family of Mexican migrant workers who come to a Vermont farm community, where the undocumented eldest daughter, Mari, makes friends with the white son of the owners of the farm where her father works. Mari's mother is lost while crossing the border "on her way back from a trip to Mexico" (118–19) to visit her own ailing mother. The literary figure for migration in *Return to Sender* is the swallow, who flies north but then *returns home*, or attempts it: "When a Mexican dies far away from home, a song known as '*La Golondrina*' ('The Swallow') is sung at the funeral. The song tells of a swallow that makes the yearly migration from Mexico to *El Norte* . . . sometimes that swallow gets lost in the cold winds and never finds its way back. This is the fear of those who leave home as well as those who stay behind awaiting their return" (322). In this imaginary, those who leave home are expected to return—quite a different construct than that of DREAMer activist *testimonios* that insist on the United States as (the only) home. On the eve of the Mexican Independence Day, Mari declares allegiance to Mexico in a letter that she writes to the U.S. president—but she also leans heavily on American-identified values and rhetoric ("liberty and justice for all" [72]) in making her argument.

Ana Castillo's novel *The Guardians* tells the story of a family of immigrants, some of whom have been lost or killed at the border, leaving an undocumented teenaged son, Gabo, whose identity is far more fluid than that which DREAMer activist *testimonios* present. Among other things, the fact that his father, Rafa, is a missing border crosser complicates the narration of a strictly U.S.-American identity. As Rafa's sister Regina, who is a naturalized U.S. citizen by marriage, notes, "Sometimes I like to think [Rafa] is back in Chihuahua with a pregnant wife and that we just never heard from him because he became too selfish and didn't care about Gabo no more or his past life with Ximena" (12). Despite the potential devastation of this fantasy, the fact is that Regina *imagines her brother in Mexico*, and his disappearance only prolongs indefinitely the identification of Mexico with family. Imaginatively, then, the DREAMers' identities in these novels are not focused exclusively on families and communities on the U.S. side of the border but keep one foot in Mexico, while communities and families themselves are seen as spanning the border and defying national boundaries. Gabo is surrounded by family and community members who signal the persistent presence of transnational ties and collective history. Miguel, the Chicano schoolteacher who helps Regina in her search for her missing brother, posits the voice of the Chicano/a community, which "felt our hermanos and hermanas on the other side had every right to be here" (124), thus extending a familial identity to the other side of the border even before any crossing has taken place. And El Abuelo Milton, Miguel's grandfather, who articulates the long history of Mexicans along the border, notes that it was the institution of the Border Patrol in 1924 that marked the point "when Mexicans got to be fugitives on our own land. Whether you lived on this side or that side, all Mexicans got harassed" (72). Thus, even while Gabo grows up and goes to school in the United States (where he seems increasingly unhinged), all of those who surround him narrate a collective history that spans two countries. That is to say, while DREAMer testimonies and political art focus squarely on U.S. identity, novelists like Castillo, privileged no doubt by their U.S. citizenship to push *back* against rigid constructions of national belonging, write of more encompassing DREAMer identities inserted into larger transnational communities that move back and forth across the border.

DESERTED DREAMers

It is notable that in both *The Guardians* and *Return to Sender*, part of the transnational imaginary involves the loss of a DREAMer's parent; the pervasiveness of ties to Mexico is brought home by the fact that the parent might well still be in Mexico and that thus the DREAMer's familial and social network extends beyond the current U.S. context. In both novels, circular migration accounts for the possibility of parental loss for DREAMers who have laid roots in the United States. The opposite movement, however, is also true and is also represented in Latinx writing. Also missing from the more frequently heard DREAMer activist narrative is this alternative story of the children who are left behind in Mexico and Central America when their parents migrate to the United States in search of increased economic opportunities so that they can support their families back home; the stories told by and about these young people are quite different in tenor than the public stories told by DREAMer activists. Instead of advocating the right to stay in the United States, these stories might just as easily be seen as testimony to what David Bacon has called, in *The Right to Stay Home*, "the right to not migrate" (xii), that is, as narratives of forced migration that separates families because of economic necessity, with enormous psychological and familial consequences. Further, children who come north in search of parents are often conscious and deliberate agents in the decision to migrate, in a counter to the dominant activist narrative of lack of choice and agency. And while DREAM activists invoke as part of their rhetoric the ideal of the "American Dream," for these other DREAMers—those for whom their parents' migration north has resulted in at least a perception of abandonment—the United States is the place where the person representing love and security vanishes: a nightmare, not a dream. Further, familial reunification does not heal the traumatic ruptures of separation in these texts, which are repeatedly represented as running too deep for tidy resolution. The youthful protagonists' arrival in the United States is not a happy ending but rather its own infinitely deferred dream.

The novel *Into the Beautiful North* by Luis Alberto Urrea represents a village that has been such a source of out-migration by men that there are virtually none left; the main character, Nayeli, decides to embark on a quest to the United States to literally bring back some men to Mexico. She also hopes to find and reunite with her father in the United States and then *to bring him back home* to help save her village. Nayeli is bitterly disappointed when she travels to Kankakee, Illinois, and realizes that her father has, in fact, abandoned his life in Mexico and established an entirely new life and family in the United States. Nayeli doesn't perfectly fit the definition of a DREAMer—she is already nineteen when she migrates to the United States (too old to be a DREAMer, strictly speaking), and she does not stay long enough to become a long-term resident. Nonetheless, her story of migration in search of a missing parent is a common theme reflected in other narratives.

The dream of reunification with the absent parent, which drives much of Reyna Grande's memoir *The Distance Between Us*, fails once again to be matched by the less-than-idyllic reality of reunification. The memoir details the young Reyna's sense of abandonment when her mother leaves Mexico to follow her father north and does not keep her promises to return within a year. In the child's emotional reality, Mexico represents the unwanted; but it is the United States that bears the onus of rupturing families. Grande likens the United States to the legendary ghost La Llorona. In the first section of the memoir, rather defensively titled "Mi Mamá me Ama" (My Mother Loves Me), Grande recounts how

> my father's mother, Abuela Evila, liked to scare us with stories of La Llorona, the weeping woman who roams the canal and steals children away. She would

> say that if we didn't behave, La Llorona would take us far away where we would never see our parents again. . . . Neither of my grandmothers told us that there is something more powerful than La Llorona—a power that takes away parents, not children.
>
> It is called The United States. (3)

The United States becomes the geographic locus of anxieties that the parents will never return to the "motherland," Mexico. Grande reflects that she was "too young [then] to know about the men who leave for El Otro Lado [the Other Side] and never return. Some of them find new wives, start a new family. Others disappear completely" (8). As the memoir progresses, it is precisely this fear that is in danger of being realized. Mami calls to tell Reyna and her siblings that she is pregnant again; Grande's sister Mago responds, "They're replacing us. . . . They'll leave us here and forget all about us" (33). And Reyna too sees the new baby as more desirable to her parents than its Mexican-born counterparts: "Now, with this new baby on the way, Mami's plans had changed. Why would she come back to Mexico to have her baby, when she could stay on that side of the border and give birth to an American citizen? . . . Why would they want us now, when they're going to have American children?" (33, 37). The dynamic of migration and familial separation produces a strange sort of transnational sibling rivalry, with the Mexican-born children longing to be part of a family made in the United States that would not be subject to the risks of migration and separation that plague the family structure in Mexico.

The fantasy of reunification in Grande's memoir, however, eventually turns out to be as hollow as the American Dream itself. The parents separate when the father acquires a new woman, and the mother returns to Mexico; but she leaves them again repeatedly for various men, so that physical reunion never heals the rift for Grande: "if truth be told, I never really got my mother back" (6). Eventually, the father returns to Mexico for a visit and is persuaded to bring his children back with him to the United States; but this reunification, too, proves to be an imaginary happy ending rather than a real one, since it is subsequently the father's defense when he beats them—"I came back for you, didn't I?" As Grande explains, "Even the time he punched me in the nose so hard it broke . . . I told myself that maybe he was right. We shouldn't expect anything better from him. He didn't forget us, after all. We were here because of him. *I* was in this country because of him. I *begged* him to bring me. I got what I wanted, after all. How could I complain now, simply because things weren't all that we had hoped for?" (256). Grande's childhood dream is to have her family restored; but the dream of reunification, even when physically accomplished, proves hollow, infinitely deferred.

Grande eventually adopts a more standard DREAMer's dream—graduating from the University of California, Santa Cruz, becomes the new dream. Yet even in the memoir's epilogue, when Grande is looking retrospectively back on her dreams fulfilled, her narrative only partially corresponds to the more familiar DREAMer narrative of U.S. belonging: "The United States is my home; it is the place that allowed me to dream, and later, to make those dreams into realities. But my umbilical cord was buried in Iguala, and I have never forgotten where I came from. I consider myself Mexican American because I am from both places. Both countries are within me" (320). While this narrative of hybridity and transnational belonging is certainly a familiar one in U.S. Latinx letters, it is, as we have seen, almost entirely absent from DREAM activist testimonies.

IN SEARCH OF PARENTS: UNACCOMPANIED MINORS

As I have already discussed, the rhetorical justification for the DREAM Act has typically included the reasoning that the children brought to the United States with their parents had no choice in the matter. Some artistic representation, however, depicts a different sort of DREAMer—the child who sets out on his or her own authority to find an absent parent. While the Central American minors of the documentary *Which Way Home* are traveling through Mexico and toward the United States for many different reasons, some have parents in the States whom they hope to rejoin. Ten-year-old José, from El Salvador, who is being held as an unauthorized migrant in a Mexican detention center, cries as he recounts that he has not seen his mother or father in three years—they live in New York. Juan Carlos's father left for the United States when he was five, to make money to send home. Nine years later, Juan Carlos, a thirteen-year-old from Guatemala, is heading to New York as well. For all of these youth, Mexico is a dangerous passage on their journey to their final destination. In several cases, the youth are quite explicit that the decision to travel north was theirs alone. Juan Carlos left his mother a letter explaining his decision to go to the United States. Like Juan Carlos, Kevin, aged fourteen, from Honduras, goes north to work so that he can help his mother financially. Fito, Kevin's thirteen-year-old traveling companion, admits that he did not even tell his mother he was leaving.

Under the Same Moon (La misma luna) dramatizes a similar plight—and sense of youth agency—through the story of a young Mexican boy, Carlitos, who sets out to find his mother in Los Angeles, where she has been working for several years. When the nine-year-old boy's grandmother dies, he decides to rejoin his mother, Rosario, and makes a series of deliberate decisions calculated to get him across the border and to his mother. Carlitos wrongly interprets his mother's four-year absence through the lens of his father's prior abandonment of both of them and asks, "Why don't my parents love me?" But his road trip buddy, an undocumented worker, corrects him: "Tell me how you've liked these past few days. You *liked* hiding from La Migra?" Of course, the worker's point is that this is what Carlitos's mother has been going through for his sake, in order to send money home. But a never-stated implication of this lesson is that if Carlitos does find his mother and stays in the United States, the underground life of an undocumented immigrant will also be his.

The last scene is, on its surface, a happy ending: Carlitos and Rosario are ostensibly reunited as they find each other at a busy L.A. intersection and wait to cross safely. But the scene, which freezes them while they are still separated by a busy street, only anticipates the actual reunification. (The crosswalk sign changes from the red "stop" hand to the white crosser, with the film ending on that shot.) In other words, the happy ending illusion depends on the film concluding before it can represent what the reality would entail: Carlitos growing up as an undocumented youth, perhaps a DREAMer, possibly unable to get a job or a driver's license or a college fellowship or to study abroad; unable to find a way to legalize himself. He might be a DREAMer, but one with a much more fraught and complicated story than even activist narratives of American Dreams deferred would allow for.

CONCLUDING REMARKS

In recent years, DACA has more or less dampened the production of DREAMer narratives, as those who would be eligible for the DREAM Act have, for the moment, been able to work legally in the United States without immediate fear of deportation. Thus an ameliorative measure arguably slowed efforts toward more comprehensive legislation and immigration reform. But this Band-Aid measure entailed many risks. The 2016 election of Donald Trump, who vowed during his campaign to repeal DACA and to deport all undocumented immigrants, presented renewed fears of deportation for all those young people who took advantage of the policy. Although the White House has recently announced that DACA will remain for now, the unstable grounds continue to feed an immigrant "culture of anxiety." We have yet to hear the testimonies of DREAMers that may emerge in this newly shifted world.[1]

NOTE

1. Suggestions for further reading, in addition to the testimonies and narratives discussed in this chapter, include *Underground America: Narratives of Undocumented Lives* (2008), edited by Peter Orner; *The Dreamers: How the Undocumented Youth Movement Transformed the Immigrant Rights Debate* (2013) by Walter J. Nicholls; *Dreamers: An Immigrant Generation's Fight for Their American Dream* (2015) by Eileen Truax; *The Border Patrol Ate My Dust* (2004) by Alicia Alarcón; and *We ARE Americans: Undocumented Students Pursuing the American Dream* (2009) by William Pérez.

WORKS CITED

Alarcón, Alicia. *The Border Patrol Ate My Dust*. Houston: Arte Público Press, 2004.

Alcaraz, Lalo. *Dream Act Now*. n.d. *Lalo Alcaraz*, laloalcaraz.com/portfolio. Accessed 14 June 2016.

———. *Dream Girl*. 2014. *Lalo Alcaraz*, laloalcaraz.com/lalo-alcaraz-signed-prints-for-sale/dreamgirl. Accessed 26 Apr. 2017.

———. *GOP Santa Gives It to DREAM Act Students and to Latinos*. 2016. *TwitPic*, twitpic.com/3iiqb6. Accessed 14 June 2016.

Alvarez, Julia. *Return to Sender*. Alfred A. Knopf, 2009.

Anderson, Jill, and Nin Solis, editors. *Los Otros Dreamers*. Offset Santiago, 2014.

"Are You Undocumented and Unafraid?" Dream Activist, action.dreamactivist.org/callout/. Accessed 26 Apr. 2017.

Bacon, David. *The Right to Stay Home: How U.S. Policy Drives Mexican Migration*. Beacon Press, 2013.

"Carlos: The Story of an Undocumented Student." *YouTube*, 21 July 2010, www.youtube.com/watch?v=kTnr-Cd-iSE. Accessed 14 June 2016.

Carrasquillo, Adrian. "22 Powerful Images by Dreamers: A Window into Life as an Undocumented Immigrant in America." *BuzzFeed News*, 3 Jan. 2014, www.buzzfeed.com/adriancarrasquillo/22-powerful-images-by-dreamers-a-window-into-life-as-an-undo?utm_term=.dpPwrwVd12#.faJDKDw3vz. Accessed 16 May 2015.

Castillo, Ana. *The Guardians*. Random House, 2007.

Grande, Reyna. *The Distance Between Us*. Washington Square Press, 2012.

Honig, Bonnie. *Democracy and the Foreigner*. Princeton University Press, 2001.

"I'm a Dreamer." *YouTube*, 29 Aug. 2013, www.youtube.com/watch?v=1PWJFowo1u4. Accessed 13 June 2016.

La Santa Cecilia. "ICE el Hielo." *YouTube*, 8 Apr. 2013, www.youtube.com/watch?v=o1NJviuYUEQ. Accessed 15 Jan. 2017.

Madera, Gabriela, Angelo A. Mathay, Armin M. Najafi, Hector H. Saldívar, Stephanie Solis, Alyssa Jane M. Titong, Gaspar Rivera-Salgado, Janna Shadduck-Hernández, Kent Wong, Rebecca Frazier, and Julie Monroe, editors. *Underground Undergrads: UCLA Undocumented Immigrant Students Speak Out*. UCLA Center for Labor Research and Education, 2008.

Manuel, José, Cesar Pineda, Anne Galisky, and Rebecca Shine, editors. *Papers: Stories by Undocumented Youth*. Graham Street Productions, 2012.

Migration Policy Institute. "National and State Estimates of Mexican Populations Eligible for DAPA and DACA Programs, 2009–2013." 2014. *DACA at the Two-Year Mark: A National and State Profile of Youth Eligible and Applying for Deferred Action*, www.migrationpolicy.org/research/daca-two-year-mark-national-and-state-profile-youth-eligible-and-applying-deferred-action. Accessed 6 May 2016.

Nicholls, Walter J. *The DREAMers: How the Undocumented Youth Movement Transformed the Immigrant Rights Debate*. Stanford University Press, 2013.

Orner, Peter. "Introduction: Permanent Anxiety." *Underground America: Narratives of Undocumented Lives*, edited by Peter Orner, McSweeney's Books, 2008, pp. 5–13.

Pérez, William. *We ARE Americans: Undocumented Students Pursuing the American Dream*. Stylus, 2009.

"Rogelio." Personal Interview. 15 Aug. 2011.

Sommer, Doris. "No Secrets." *The Real Thing: Testimonial Discourse and Latin America*, edited by Georg M. Gugelberger, Duke University Press, 1996, pp. 130–57.

Truax, Eileen. *Dreamers: An Immigrant Generation's Fight for Their American Dream*. Beacon Press, 2015.

Under the Same Moon. Directed by Patricia Riggen, performances by Adrián Alonso and Kate Del Castillo. Weinstein Company, 2007.

"Undocumented and Unafraid." *YouTube*, 28 Feb. 2011, www.youtube.com/watch?v=xdOrxLLHooU. Accessed 11 June 2016.

Urrea, Luis Alberto. *Into the Beautiful North*. Little, Brown, 2009.

Which Way Home. Directed by Rebecca Cammissa. HBO Films, 2009.

2

MILPA

Mesoamerican Resistance to Agricultural Imperialism

ANALISA TAYLOR

When the corn kernel sprouts, I feel that we prolong our days upon the earth.
It is our heart that germinates and grows,
it is the pozol, the tortilla, the world, life itself.

JUAN GREGORIO REGINO

PRIMARY MATERIALS

- *Food Chains*, directed by Sanjay Rawal (film, 2014)
- *Mesoamérica Resiste* (Mesoamerica Resists) by the Beehive Design Collective (poster, 2014)
- *México Profundo: Reclaiming a Civilization* by Guillermo Bonfil Batalla (book, 2007)
- *Migrar o morir/Paying the Price: Migrant Workers in the Toxic Fields of Sinaloa*, directed by Alexandra Halkin (film, 2008)
- *Our Sacred Maíz Is Our Mother: Indigeneity and Belonging in the Americas* by Roberto Cintli Rodríguez (book, 2014)
- "Fin de fiesta: El espectro del hambre recorre el mundo" (End of the Party: The Specter of Hunger Roams the Earth) by Armando Bartra (article, 2008)
- *Sin maíz no hay país: Las semillas de la dignidad* (Without Corn There Is No Country: The Seeds of Dignity), directed by Jonathan Cadiot and Arthur Rifflet (film, 2008)
- *Sin maíz no hay país* (Without Corn There Is No Country), edited by Gustavo Esteva and Catherine Marielle (print, 2007)

TO MAKE MILPA is to engage in an ancient yet dynamic agricultural practice central to the development of the diverse indigenous cultures of Mexico and of the greater Mesoamerican diaspora. The milpa is a cornfield, intercropped with beans, squash, and a wide variety of other useful plants. Most of corn's biological diversity is still located in the heart of Mesoamerica, in the *milpa*. Yet today roughly one-third of the corn consumed in Mexico is imported from the United States; this imported corn is a relatively new creature in agricultural history, uniformly ultrahybridized, uniformly yellow, and much of it genetically modified (GM).

The 1994 North American Free Trade Agreement (NAFTA) and the introduction of GM corn since the early 2000s have allowed a few agribusiness giants to hoard crops in order to manipulate prices and monopolize the Mexican corn market. As of 2009, Archer Daniels Midland–Grupo Maseca (Gruma) had gained control of roughly 73 percent of Mexico's corn flour market, while Minsa and Cargill gained control of virtually all the rest (Hussain 45).[1] Smallholder maize producers have been forced to compete with these highly subsidized U.S.-based industrial-scale producers. Compounding the vulnerabilities that small-scale farmers (campesinos) have faced in this newly transnational corn market is the fact that they have historically been relegated to the least productive lands and often coerced into selling their crops to intermediaries under extremely disadvantageous terms.

Millions of small and even midscale farmers have abandoned or partially abandoned milpa farming in search of wage labor outside their communities. As the documentary films *Migrar o morir/Paying the Price: Migrant Workers in the Toxic Fields of Sinaloa* (2008) and *Food Chains* (2014) illustrate, people who migrate to northern Mexico and points north of the U.S.-Mexico border to work in large agribusiness operations confront systematic human rights abuses, including enslavement, child labor, and dangerous exposure to toxic chemicals. This mass rural out-migration often entails other losses as well, such as that of indigenous linguistic and agricultural knowledge, kinship networks, land stewardship, and structures of self-governance. A central feature of NAFTA was the 1992 annulment of Article 27 of the Mexican Constitution, which dissolved the collective ejido land-use system and opened the door to the large-scale privatization of lands that had previously been held in usufruct. The deregulation of national food markets beginning in 1994 resulted in further losses of food and labor sovereignty at national and local levels (Bartra 2002; Fitting; Otero; Richard 2008).

Elizabeth Fitting has shown that since the mid-twentieth century, the cultural narratives of the Partido Revolucionario Institucional (PRI), or Institutional Revolutionary Party, have emphasized corn and campesinos as symbols of popular national identity, but its agricultural policies have consistently penalized and blamed them for the failures of the state on the grounds that they practice backward and inefficient farming methods (14). The Mexican government's response to destitute farmers who decry these losses has been to urge them to become more productive, to scale up and embrace genetically modified organisms (GMOs), to cultivate other crops—specifically export-oriented cash crops—or to find some other line of work.

"Sin maíz no hay país" ("Without Corn There Is No Country") surfaced in 2007 as a slogan chanted by destitute farmers protesting the conditions of falling corn prices, unregulated commercialization of GM corn seeds, and the cynical dismissal of campesinos, particularly indigenous *milperos*, as stewards of Mexico's agricultural heritage. The protests exposed the fact that, despite its pro-campesino rhetoric, the PRI was shaping Mexico's agricultural policies to fit the demands of transnational biotechnology and agribusiness rather than those of campesinos.[2] The movement has grown into a broad civil society organization characterized by horizontal leadership. Among its ranks are public intellectuals, activists, musicians, artists, workers, and farmers, whose unifying message is that the biological diversity of corn and the opportune stewardship of the milpa have value to the nation that cannot be tied to the global market.

In this chapter, we consider various types of cultural production that have been generated within and alongside the *Sin maíz no hay país—y sin frijol tampoco* (Without Corn—and Without Beans—There Is No Country) movement. Although we will be looking at only a few here, these include a wide range of posters, performances, street art, documentary films, music, a website, several books, and many other forms of cultural expression. Some of these works center on vindicating the agrarian roots of the Mexican Revolution, beseeching the government to stem the tide of neoliberal globalization. However, a more complex emblematic thread runs through many of these works as well, one in which Mesoamerica is conjured as the cradle of milpa agriculture and the epicenter of a global struggle against what Gabriela Pechlaner and Gerardo Otero call the "neoliberal food regime." For example, in the photograph below, a group of protestors parades the large figure of a Maya god(dess) of corn, who points an irate finger at the World Trade Organization (WTO). At the feet of this

FIGURE 2.1. Protestor with a sign reading, "LOS DIOSES MAYAS CONTRA LA OMC" (Maya gods against the WTO) at the World Trade Organization ministerial conference in Cancún, Mexico, 2003.

towering effigy, one of the protesters holds up a poster that reads: "Los dioses mayas contra la OMC" (Maya gods against the World Trade Organization). Off to one side, a nearby group of protestors holds up another poster that proclaims "500 years of indigenous resistance" (figure 2.1).

This image starts us on a path toward identifying ways in which Mesoamerica is depicted as ground zero in the global struggle against agricultural imperialism in an array of visual, literary, and performative expressions, from the ephemeral (slogans, chants, protest signs, graffiti, performances, happenings) to the more tangible (books, documentary films, graphic arts, and others). One example we will look at here is the dizzyingly detailed and expansive interactive double-sided poster *Mesoamérica Resiste* by the Maine-based Beehive Design Collective. This collaborative work shares in the task of creating what Roberto Cintli Rodríguez has termed "new sacred maíz narratives": stories, signs, and images that affirm the existence of a people whose identity is derived not from nation-state citizenship but from a relationship or dialogue with maíz.

CORN INVENTED AND REINVENTED

Approximately seven to ten thousand years ago, inhabitants of southern Mexico began to manipulate the reproductive process of the now-extinct wild teosinte grass, eventually creating an entirely new plant species: the robust, carbon-rich *Zea mays* (Esteva and Marielle; Pollan). Each juicy grain of heirloom corn is also a seed that spirals back to this modest agricultural revolution, bearing the genetic traces of its earliest ancestors. Unlike any other crop, corn was not simply domesticated but was created whole cloth out of another very different plant. As corn cannot reproduce on its own, each grain/seed owes its existence to the hundreds of generations of human ancestors who have optimized its genetic material from one growing cycle to the next, from one generation to the next, and from one region to another. As Gustavo Esteva and Catherine Marielle describe it, "Corn is our invention, and in turn, corn has invented us" (11). Guillermo Bonfil Batalla identifies this corn-human bond at the heart of Mesoamerican culture in similarly reverent terms: "Corn is a human plant; it is culture in the most profound sense of the word, because it would not exist without the intelligent and opportune intervention from the human hand; it is not capable of reproducing itself. Corn taught us how to mark the passage of time and to organize space in relation to its rhythms and needs . . . and became the essential referent through which to understand [our] forms of social organization [and] modes of thought" (qtd. in Esteva and Marielle 5; my translation).

Over thousands of years, the indigenous peoples of Mesoamerica have produced countless varieties of corn adapted to diverse regions, conditions, and tastes following the milpa agricultural system. In *1491: New Revelations of the Americas Before Columbus*, Charles C. Mann notes that milpa crops are nutritionally and environmentally complementary:

> Maize lacks the amino acids lysine and tryptophan, which the body needs to make proteins and niacin; diets with too much maize can lead to protein deficiency and pellagra, a disease caused by lack of niacin. Beans have both lysine and tryptophan, but not the amino acids cysteine and methionine, which are provided by maize.

> As a result, beans and maize make a nutritionally complete meal. Squashes, for their part, provide an array of vitamins; avocados, fats. The milpa, in the estimation of H. Garrison Wilkes, a maize researcher at the University of Massachusetts in Boston, "is one of the most successful human inventions ever created." (225–26)

Corn is delicious when harvested and eaten fresh, but when ancient Mesoamericans began to store and nixtamalize it,[3] soaking it with lime before grinding it into a dough, and complementing it with beans, squash, and other foods, they created the readily available food surpluses necessary for the development of highly sophisticated cities such as Paquimé, Tula, Teotihuacán, Tenochtitlán, Mitla, Monte Albán, Palenque, and Tikal, which often influenced one another through far-reaching networks of communication and trade. In *Decolonize Your Diet*, Luz Calvo and Catriona Rueda Esquibel explain that *nixtamal* comes from the Nahuatl word *nixtamalli*, which means "unformed corn dough." They describe nixtamalization as the "process of soaking corn in an alkaline solution, such as 'cal' or wood ash. This soaking process makes the corn more digestible and the nutrients in the corn more accessible to the body" (57).

When harvesting, farmers save the ears of corn they deem most favorable for future plantings, often trading or giving some away as precious gifts. Through this cyclical recombination of seeds, *milperos* commune with their ancestors and provide the basis of life for future generations. This sacred relationship is reflected in Mesoamerican origin stories; although they take many forms, all feature corn and humanity woven together in an intimate co-creative web. The *K'iche'* Mayan *Popol Vuh* (Book of Council) provides the best-known written account of this symbiosis: the gods formed the first humans out of corn, and in turn, humans gained the favor of the gods through their stewardship of corn—and would be forsaken by them if they were to become careless with it (Christenson 193–95; Álvarez Quiñones 18–19).

In *The Omnivore's Dilemma*, Michael Pollan describes corn's metamorphosis from revered companion of Mesoamerican agriculturalists to the internal combustion engine of our transnational capitalist food system. He suggests that we have indeed become careless with corn, turning its genetic malleability into a double-edged sword in the modern world. Traditional Mesoamerican farming methods have stimulated corn's biodiversity and optimized its qualities through thousands of years of experimentation and observation. In the hands of small-scale farmers who possess a deep knowledge of its behavior, corn is not a commodity but a living being that can be coaxed into adapting to radically diverse climates and conditions. As Pollan shows, however, botanists and biotechnologists have transformed it into a cheaply produced, disposable commodity as likely to be consumed as food as to be used as animal fodder, sweetener, or fuel. According to Pollan, this shift first came about after World War II under the guise of the Green Revolution, when scientists working for large agribusiness corporations transformed the biological substance of corn by creating "terminator" strains unable to reproduce themselves freely at the hands of farmers. Instead, these ultrahybridized seeds transformed the farmer from free agent to consumer. Uniform varieties of corn now blanket the American midwestern and much of the world's agricultural landscape. As Pollan notes, since corn is able to reproduce solely through human manipulation, it is also singularly responsive to human experimentation with its breeding:

> Early in the twentieth century American corn breeders . . . discovered that when they crossed two corn plants that had come from inbred lines—from ancestors that had themselves been exclusively self-pollinated for several generations—the hybrid offspring . . . produced genetically identical plants—a trait that, among other things, facilitates mechanization. Second, those plants exhibited . . . better yields than either of their parents [and] the seeds produced by these seeds did not "come true"—the plants in the second . . . generation bore little resemblance to the plants in the first. Specifically, their yields plummeted by as much as a third, making their seeds virtually useless. Hybrid corn now offered its breeders the biological equivalent of a patent. Farmers now had to buy new seeds every spring. (30–31)

Like their competitors in Iowa, Mexican farmers face pressure to produce a uniform product with the highest yields possible. However, as the documentary film *Migrar o morir/The Toxic Fields of Sinaloa* shows, many farmers who engage in this agribusiness model come to depend for their survival on the technologies, petrochemical inputs, and seeds sold by the agribusiness companies, depleting their soils and contaminating their communities. Instead of depending on their plants to reproduce themselves, they now depend on a corporation. As Guillermo Bonfil Batalla warned in 1982, twelve years before NAFTA went into effect, "Outside the popular paradigm, openly hostile to it in fact, stands another way of relating to corn, [one that] removes corn from its historical and cultural context in order to use it exclusively as a commodity, in ways that align with interests that are not those of the people. This paradigm renders corn an object of exchange, replaceable and even disposal" (qtd. in Esteva and Marielle; my translation).

MESOAMÉRICA AND AZTLÁN: THE PAST MADE PRESENT

In *México Profundo: Reclaiming a Civilization*, Bonfil argues that European colonization and the enduring postcolonial marginalization of indigenous peoples have fed into the idea of Mesoamerican civilization as a constellation of long-dead ruins and mysterious artifacts. He contends that while political elites have selectively appropriated elements of Mesoamerican antiquity as symbols of the Mexican nation, these same elites dismiss the integrity of Mesoamerican cultural practices and forms of knowledge among present-day urban and rural indigenous and mestizo communities.[4] Among these practices and forms of knowledge, Bonfil considers the cultivation and ritual use of corn to be central to this disavowed "dynamic continuity" between the diverse societies of Mesoamerican antiquity and their modern heirs (3–18).

If this indigenous Mesoamerican heritage has largely been trivialized by political and cultural elites in Mexico, it has been all but ignored in the United States. Growing up in the Chicano civil rights era, Davíd Carrasco became keenly aware that Chicanos and Mexicans in the United States were not considered heirs to a great civilization, but pairs of arms out of place when not tending to fields, factories, and the household needs of white America. In *Moctezuma's Mexico* he describes the gestalt he experienced in his first encounter with Mesoamerican artifacts at the National Museum of Anthropology in Mexico City when he was fifteen years old. Carrasco considers this his first "Aztec moment," a glimmer of all that he had not been taught in U.S. schools and in U.S. society in general regarding the civilizational accomplishments of his ancestors. Within the Chicano civil rights movement of the 1960s and beyond, challenging Anglo-American constructions of Mexicans and Mexican Americans as a people without a history, or as another in a long line of immigrant groups, meant embracing those accomplishments and emphasizing their continuity in the present.[5]

In *Our Sacred Maíz Is Our Mother*, Roberto Cintli Rodríguez identifies Carrasco's "Aztec moment" as one of many "new sacred maíz narratives" that affirm a connection between peoples of the modern Mesoamerican diaspora and their indigenous ancestry. Rodríguez refers to these narratives as the stories, images, symbols, and forms of ceremonial discourse that manifest the affective, often unconscious relationships that "Indigenous and de-Indigenized peoples" of Mesoamerica continue to have with corn (161). Whether found in poetry or in the graphic image on a tortilla wrapper in an Arizona grocery store, these narratives evoke Mesoamerica as a disavowed yet not defunct civilization engaged in a five-hundred-plus-year process of decolonization. They form a bridge between Mesoamerican civilizations and Chicano, Mexican, and Central American cultures of today. While "sacred maíz narratives" can be found in pre- and post-Conquest codices, murals, artifacts, and oral traditions, I distinguish these "new sacred maíz narratives" from their forebears is their romantic attachment or ironic commentary on the past as it lives in the present. Both old and new maíz narratives share a conceptualization of corn as a gift from the gods and as the central creative agent of human consciousness.

In new maíz narratives, however, indigenous peoples of the Mesoamerican diaspora assert that they are still here, in mourning for what has been taken from them and in celebration of what they have maintained through traditions, stories, and other strategies of resistance. One example of an "ancient maíz narrative," according to Rodríguez, is the thousand-year-old mural in Cacaxtla, Mexico, that depicts anthropomorphic ears of corn reaching out from their stalks. He finds examples of "new maíz narratives" in sources such as the contemporary rendition of this mural in a painting by Tanya Álvarez; in the many manifestations of elder epistemology he records and transcribes; and in his own rendition of an old creation myth, "Quetzalcoatl, the Ants, and the Gift of Maíz," a cosmic drama based on the Legend of the Suns recorded in the 1558 Codex Chimalpopoca (163). Each of these "new maíz narratives" is laced with intertextual references to ancient maíz narratives, and each bears witness to the resilience of maíz cultures in the face of colonization.

AGRICULTURAL IMPERIALISM EXISTS AND MESOAMÉRICA RESISTS

Many new maíz narratives point to the ways in which peoples throughout greater Mesoamerica have resisted the imperialist confines of the nation-states into which the continent has been divided. The four-and-a-half-by-nine-foot *Mesoamérica Resiste* poster provides us with a visual index of the ways in which new maíz narratives may animate social and environmental justice struggles. The BDC's website introduces viewers to a "full-screen flyover with narrative tour" that underscores the poster's explicit function as a consciousness-raising and organizing tool among activist groups and communities in resistance. Folded closed, the double-sided poster presents us with "the view from above," which evokes an Old World map of Mesoamerica. Layered over this colonial cartography, we find evocations of twentieth-century U.S. maps delineating sites of natural resource extraction, plantations, railroads, and ports.[6]

This cartographic collage draws parallels between the more than five hundred years of European colonization and the new forms of imperialist violence that threaten the region's people and ecology today. The focal point is a crudely rendered landmass stretching from the U.S. Southwest and Southeast in the north to Panama and Colombia in the south. This sinewy landmass is loosely rendered as a bound human body in fetal position, surrounded by oceans crowded with Spanish galleons, slave ships filled end to end with human cargo, and pirate ships replete with loot. Tightly binding this land is a tangle of superhighways, with rivers hemmed in by dams, refineries, factories, and megaports opening out to the Caribbean, Atlantic, and Pacific Oceans. Closer inspection reveals that the sails of these boats bear the ubiquitous images and icons of present-day transnational capitalism: Burger King, Citibank, Union Carbide, Monsanto, Walmart, and more. Crowding the waters further, gunboats, cargo ships, and oil tankers head south to dump cheap commercial goods (SpongeBob, Kool-Aid, Mickey Mouse) and extract raw materials. Riches are pumped out with monstrous Steampunk machines that might have been invented by Dr. Seuss. Overall, Mesoamerica is depicted as a mutilated body on which late capitalist industry feeds. This map explicitly refers to Mesoamerica as a space targeted for transnational megadevelopment under the "Plan Mesoamérica," also referred to as the "Mesoamerica Integration and Development Project." Across the top of the poster, we find an ornate scroll, unfurled to reveal the title: "Plan Mesoamérica: Every time history repeats itself, the price goes up." The map teaches us who benefits and who loses in this transnational trade deal, and it equates the WTO, the World Bank, and the IMF with stuffed shirts, an old form of conquest in a new guise or a new form of conquest in an old guise. This axiom, which evokes Marx's notion that history is lived first as tragedy and is then repeated as farce, is mirrored in the superimposition of new onto old cartographic imagery. The map's compass is rendered as a roulette wheel manned by Carmen Miranda of Chiquita Banana fame and the now-ubiquitous Starbucks mermaid.

Allusions to gun trafficking from north to south underscore the shady money-laundering relationship between big bankers and traffickers in human beings, drugs, and guns. As stated in the introductory sidebar in the narrative tour, "Outsiders who have no connection with the land have drawn this map, with motives of extraction and profit."

A detail from the poster, "A New Form of Violence Against People and the Land," focuses on agricultural imperialism in Mesoamerica (figure 2.2). According to the accompanying text:

> The tank-tractor merges the war machine with industrial agriculture, a new form of violence against people and the land. After World War II, factories that made tanks and explosives for war were put to new use and started pumping out tractors and fertilizers instead, leading to the world-wide Green Revolution and corporate control of agriculture. A mother stalk of corn is being assaulted and violated by the tank-tractor, sprayed with GMO seed and a toxic medley of

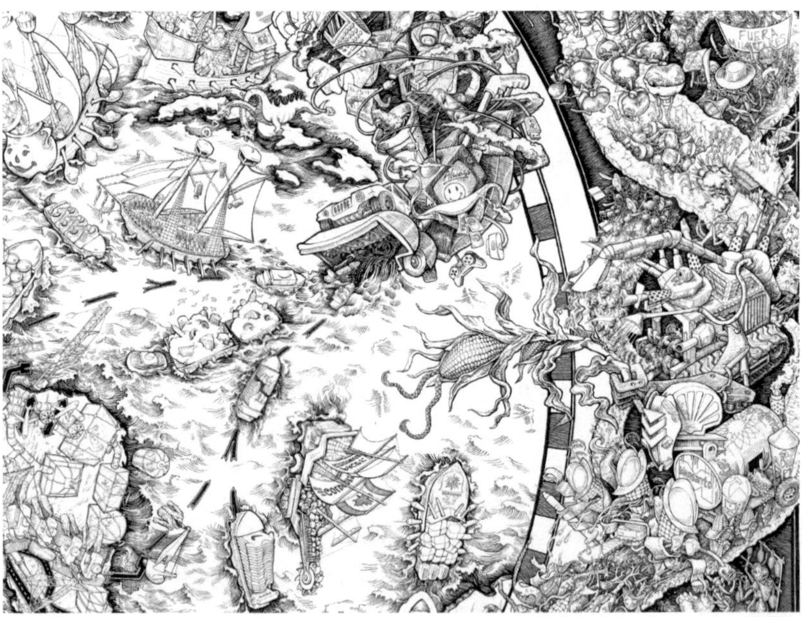

FIGURE 2.2. Beehive Design Collective, "A New Form of Violence Against People and the Land," detail from front of *Mesoamérica Resiste*, 2013. Double-sided folding poster.

FIGURE 2.3. Beehive Design Collective, "A New Form of Violence Against People and the Land," detail from reverse of *Mesoamérica Resiste*, 2013. Double-sided folding poster.

> chemicals. Like the Spanish conquistadors who used biological warfare, spreading disease to indigenous people of the Americas, these "*corn*quistadors" are destroying indigenous corn and food sovereignty with genetic contamination. One also wields a gas pump weapon as a reference to ethanol, an agrofuel from corn that is a false alternative to fossil fuels.

The poster's flip side, the "ant's-eye view," folds out to occupy a surface twice as large. In the words of the artists: "Our goal was to draw the good news twice as big." Whereas the view from above plays with the imagery of colonial and neocolonial cartography, this view presents us with an alternate cartography, one evocative of Mesoamerican codices and oral traditions and exhibiting an entirely different conception of space and time. A puffy, pointillist blue mist of DNA carrying the spirits of endangered and extinct animals spirals from the roots to the upper canopy of the sacred ceiba tree; the machines of industrial food production, depicted in heavy black and white around the edges of the poster, encroach to vacuum it up (figure 2.3). As the sidebar states: "Shopping carts pushed by genetically modified palm, corn, and soy creatures are rushing in on newly paved highways, attempting to invade a traditional local market with an arsenal of junk food and copyrighted genetic bombs. The market resists the invasion with the strength of its cultural and ecological diversity, forming a blockade of DNA strands to keep out these mono-cropped monsters of industrial agriculture."

Rendered in soft sepia, anthropomorphic animals of every type occupy the center of the poster, united in the creation of what Jaime Morales Hernández refers to as "the reconstruction of ecosystems and of the public spaces in which people who have been marginalized can generate viable economic, social, and environmental alternatives" (293–94; my translation). As the narrative in the poster's sidebar states, "A bee is blowing pollen on corn, beans, and squash, out of which rise the double helices of DNA, and saving seeds and beans for future planting. In this solidarity economy, the highest value is placed on seeds and eggs. The community assembly at the base of the *ceiba* tree exemplifies the ideals of horizontal communication."

BACK TO THE MILPA: CULTIVATING MESOAMERICAN LABOR AND FOOD SOVEREIGNTY[7]

Over thousands of generations, indigenous peoples of the Americas have stewarded much of the agricultural biodiversity on which people around the world depend for sustenance today. Corn and other native foods such as vanilla, cacao, and avocado have enriched much of humanity's culinary habits. Originating in southern Mexico seven to ten thousand years ago, corn's unique evolution made possible the development of complex societies and powerful empires in regions now part of Central America, Mexico, and even the southwestern United States. These societies flourished for thousands of years prior to European conquest and have survived more than five hundred years of colonial and neocolonial plunder and genocide. The cultivation of milpa has provided not just sustenance but also resilience to the indigenous and mestizo heirs of ancient Mesoamerican civilizations struggling against colonization.

Yet from the late twentieth century and into the twenty-first, Mexico has steadily increased its imports of corn and its exports of riches of every kind, including the labor and the very lives of its people. The dumping of cheap U.S. corn in the wake of NAFTA and of genetically modified corn since the early 2000s has provoked the collapse of the national agricultural economy, particularly in the majority-indigenous regions of southern and southeastern Mexico.

With the decline in traditional small-scale agriculture, millions of people have been forced to migrate, often at great peril, in search of new means of subsistence. As the documentary film *Sin maíz no hay país: Las semillas de la dignidad* (Without Corn There Is No Country: The Seeds of Dignity) shows, many of those who have continued to cultivate milpa have found themselves embroiled in a David-and-Goliath battle with a handful of powerful transnational corporations and the state over the biological integrity, economic value, and cultural meaning of corn.

In "Fin de fiesta: El espectro del hambre recorre el mundo" (The Party's Over and the Specter of Hunger Roams the Earth), Armando Bartra describes many of the same grave human, animal, and environmental costs wrought by industrial-scale or extractive agriculture that we have seen illustrated in this film and in the *Mesoamérica Resiste* poster: loss of biodiversity, depletion and erosion of soils, contamination and scarcity of water, precariousness of human rights, alienation of labor, and chronic refugee crises. According to Bartra, the modern industrial agricultural model has reached a point of diminishing returns; just as we have reached peak oil, Bartra argues, we have also reached peak cheap food. The broken link between food production and consumption, and the cruel inequalities that this fissure creates, point to the fact that we are in the midst of a global humanitarian catastrophe in which increasing prices of food and elevated rates of hunger will only escalate with our continued reliance on cheap fossil fuels (16–17).

Bartra reckons that cultivating milpa in the age of neoliberal food-market speculation is a profoundly anticapitalist and revolutionary act. Its strength lies not in its yields but in its encouragement of the biological diversity and intergenerational agricultural knowledge. In "El maíz y los pueblos indios," Trique writer Marcos Sandoval reminds us what is at stake in how we relate to corn, whether as companion or as commodity, as well as what is at stake in how we relate to the peoples whose ancestors have created it:

> They tell us that modified corn produced in their labs is better than our maíz. We don't know what that corn has gone and done over there, but we do know that it doesn't know our land, that it doesn't know how things are around here. But that is how it is with everything. If we build a house with our own materials, adapted to our climate, an architect comes and tells us that to live in dignity we must use industrial materials. If we invoke our ancient gods, religious people come and tell us that our spirituality is superstition and that they have come to bring us truth.

FIGURE 2.4. Favianna Rodríguez, *¡El Maíz es Nuestro!*, 2012. Digital print.

> That's why we want to say to the civilization of destruction that our way is a way of conviviality, and that we are still waiting for you to learn how to look upon us. (63; my translation)

Through more than five centuries of colonization, corn has provided not just sustenance but also resilience to the heirs of ancient Mesoamerican agriculturalists who crafted maíz from teosinte. Sandoval asserts that corn's significance to humanity transcends its shifting value as a commodity. The people whose ancestors created corn are likewise not reducible to an expendable labor force. The imagery and written expressions we have considered in this chapter cast Mesoamerica as a crucible in a global popular struggle against mega-corporations and the states that serve as their handmaidens. Rather than seeing Mesoamerica as a smattering of mysterious ruins from long-dead empires, these works evoke Mesoamerica as a diasporic and counternational *ethnos* constituted through a sacred relationship with the milpa as well as a shared history of resistance to agricultrual imperialism.

RESOURCES FOR FURTHER STUDY

Ashwell, Anamaría. "Campesinos, la milpa, y el maíz." *Artes de México*, Elementos, vol. 71, 2008, pp. 19–23.

Bowe, John. "Nobodies: Does Slavery Exist in America?" *The New Yorker*, 21 Apr. 2003, pp. 106–16.

Bowens, Natasha. *The Color of Food: Stories of Race, Resilience, and Farming*. New Society Publishers, 2015.

Cook, Scott. "Commodity Cultures, Mesoamerica, and Mexico's Changing Indigenous Economy." *Critique of Anthropology*, vol. 26, no. 2, 2006, pp. 181–208.

Cottom, Bolfy. *Los derechos culturales en el marco de los derechos humanos en México*. Porrúa, 2010.

Desmarais, Annette Aurélie. *La Vía Campesina: La globalización y el poder del campesinado*. Editorial Popular, 2007.

Domínguez Aké, Santiago. "La siembra del maíz." *Words of the True Peoples/Palabras de los seres verdaderos: Anthology of Contemporary Mexican Indigenous Language Writers*, edited by Carlos Montemayor and Donald Frischmann, vol. 1, University of Texas Press, 2004, pp. 86–87.

Guzmán Meza, Emilio. *Ixim, Maíz, Corn*. CIESAS, 2004.

Herod, Andrew. *Geographies of Globalization*. Wiley Blackwell, 2009.
Holmes, Seth. *Fresh Fruit, Broken Bodies*. University of California Press, 2013.
Levy Tacher, Samuel. *Raíces mayas para la restauración de selvas*. ECOSUR, 2011.
Lind, David, and Elizabeth Barham. *The Social Life of the Tortilla: Food, Cultural Politics, and Contested Commodification*. Springer, 2004.
Long-Solís, Janet, and Luis Alberto Vargas. *Food Culture in Mexico*. Greenwood Press, 2005.
Pilcher, Jeffrey M. *¡Que vivan los tamales! Food and the Making of Mexican Identity*. University of New Mexico Press, 1998.
Roberts, Paul. *The End of Food*. Mariner Books, 2009.
Sandstrom, Alan R. *Corn Is Our Blood: Culture and Ethnic Identity in a Contemporary Aztec Indian Village*. Yale University Press, 2010.

NOTES

The epigraph by Juan Gregorio Regino is quoted in Esteva and Marielle; the English translation is mine.

1. According to Groenewald and Niehof, "Since NAFTA came into effect, US maize exports to Mexico have almost doubled to some six million metric tons in 2002. . . . Between 1990 and 1998 domestic maize prices fell by 48 percent. . . . Market liberalization was accelerated by NAFTA, but did not begin there. Foremost among those changes was the 1992 cancellation of Article 27 of the Constitution, which opened the door to individual property ownership of previously collectively managed *ejido* lands. During the Salinas administration (1988–1994), the government restructure[d] the agricultural sector by implementing policies of privatization, deregulation, and trade liberalization, abandoning incentives to produce food locally and allowing market forces . . . to determine production according to the country's comparative advantages. . . . The most important reforms affecting the Mexican maize sector were the privatization of the land and capital market as well as the agricultural input markets for fertilizers, seeds, and pesticides" (202–3). See also *Subsidizing Inequality: Mexican Corn Policy Since NAFTA*, edited by Jonathan Fox and Libby Haight, Woodrow Wilson International Center for Scholars, 2010.
2. For a detailed account of the *Sin maíz no hay país* movement, see Richard, "*Sin maíz*."

3. "There is no precise date when the technology was developed, but the earliest evidence of nixtamalization is found in Guatemala's southern coast, with equipment dating from 1200–1500 BC" (Staller and Carrasco 317).
4. According to the Foundation for the Advancement of Mesoamerican Studies, the term *Mesoamerica* is not a native concept; it was coined by Paul Kirchoff in 1943 to designate "a geographical area occupied by a variety of ancient cultures that shared religious beliefs, art, architecture, and technology that made them unique in the Americas for three thousand years—from about 1500 B.C. to A.D. 1519. . . . Many aspects of the ancient cultures of Belize, El Salvador, Guatemala, Honduras, and Mexico continue to the present and several of these cultural inventions and traits have spread throughout the world." Some of its distinguishing features include "a common calendar based on the permutation of a 260-day sacred round cycle . . . a 365-day solar year count . . . hieroglyphic writing systems, bark-paper or deerskin screen-fold manuscripts . . . extensive astronomical knowledge based on horizon observation, a sacred ritual game played with a rubber ball . . . and a complex pantheon of gods and goddesses personifying natural forces" (Kowalski 3–4).
5. See Fields et al., *The Road to Aztlán*.
6. These images echo DeeDee Halleck's collage of film footage of U.S. government maps and Hollywood representations of Latin America as a land to be culturally, economically, and politically vanquished in her 1995 film *The Gringo in Mañanaland*.
7. See Bartra, "Dos prioridades mesoaméricanas."

WORKS CITED

Álvarez Quiñones, Francisco. *El Sistema alimentario de los Mayas*. Sna Jtz'ibahom, Cultura de los Indios Mayas, 2010, pp. 18–19.

Bartra, Armando. "Dos prioridades mesoaméricanas: Soberanía alimentaria y soberanía laboral." *América Latina en Movimiento*, 2002, www.alainet.org/es/active/1607.

———. "Fin de fiesta: El espectro del hambre recorre el mundo." *Argumentos*, vol. 21, no. 57, 2008, pp. 15–31.

Beehive Design Collective. *Mesoamérica Resiste*. Poster on paper, 2014.

Bonfil Batalla, Guillermo. *El maíz: Fundamento de la cultura popular mexicana*. CONACULTA, Museo de Culturas Populares, 1982.

———. *México Profundo: Reclaiming a Civilization*. University of Texas Press, 2007, pp. 3–18.

Cadiot, Jonathan, and Arthur Rifflet, directors. *Sin maíz no hay país: Las semillas de la dignidad*. Mille Plateaux Productions, 2008.

Calvo, Luz, and Catriona Rueda Esquibel. *Decolonize Your Diet: Plant-Based Mexican American Recipes for Health and Healing*. Arsenal Pulp Press, 2015, p. 57.

Carrasco, David, and Eduardo Matos Moctezuma. *Moctezuma's Mexico: Visions of the Aztec World*. University Press of Colorado, 2003, pp. 175–98.

Christenson, Allan J. *Popol Vuh, the Sacred Book of the Maya: The Great Classic of Central American Spirituality*. University of Oklahoma Press, 2007, pp. 193–95.

Esteva, Gustavo, and Catherine Marielle, editors. *Sin maíz no hay país*. CONACULTA, Dirección General de Culturas Populares e Indígenas, 2003.

Fields, Virginia. M., et al. *The Road to Aztlán: Art from a Mythic Homeland*. Los Angeles County Museum of Art, 2001.

Fitting, Elizabeth. *The Struggle for Maize: Campesinos, Workers, and Transgenic Corn in the Mexican Countryside*. Duke University Press, 2008.

Fox, Jonathan, and Libby Haight, editors. *Subsidizing Inequality: Mexican Corn Policy Since NAFTA*. Woodrow Wilson International Center for Scholars, 2010.

Groenewald, Sytske F., and Anke Niehof. "Social Limitations of Maize Farmers' Adaptation to Neoliberal Policy Reform in Mexico." *Latin American Research Review*, vol. 50, no. 4, 2015, pp. 197–218.

Halkin, Alexandra, director. *Migrar o Morir/Paying the Price: Migrant Workers in the Toxic Fields of Sinaloa*. Chiapas Media Project, 2008.

Halleck, Dee Dee, director. *The Gringo in Mañanaland*. 1995.

Hussain, Imtiaz. *North America at the Crossroads: NAFTA After 15 Years*. Universidad Iberoamericana, 2009.

Kowalski, Jeff K., editor. *Mesoamerican Architecture as a Cultural Symbol*. Oxford University Press, 1999, pp. 3–4.

Mann, Charles C. *1491: New Revelations of the Americas Before Columbus*. Vintage, 2005, pp. 225–26.

Morales Hernández, Jaime. *La agroecología en la construcción de alternativas hacia la sustentabilidad rural*. Siglo XXI, 2011, pp. 293–94.

Otero, Gerardo. "Neoliberal Globalization, NAFTA, and Migration: Mexico's Loss of Food and Labor Sovereignty." *Journal of Poverty*, vol. 15, no. 4, 2011, pp. 384–402.

Pechlaner, Gabriela, and Gerardo Otero. "The Neoliberal Food Regime: Neoregulation and the Division of Labor in North America." *Rural Sociology*, vol. 75, no. 2, 2010, pp. 179–208.

Pollan, Michael. *The Omnivore's Dilemma: A Natural History of Four Meals*. Penguin, 2006, pp. 30–31.

Rawal, Sanjay, director. *Food Chains*. Screen Media, 2014.

Richard, Analiese. "*Sin maíz no hay país*: Citizenship and Environment in Mexico's Food Sovereignty Movement." *Environment and Citizenship in Latin America*, edited by Alex Latta and Hannah Wittman, Berghahn Books, 2012, pp. 101–59.

———. "Withered Milpas: Governmental Disaster and the Mexican Countryside." *Journal of Latin American and Caribbean Anthropology*, vol. 13, no. 2, 2008, pp. 387–413.

Rodríguez, Roberto Cintli. *Our Sacred Maíz Is Our Mother: Indigeneity and Belonging in the Americas*. University of Arizona Press, 2014.

Rosin, Christopher, et al. *Food Systems Failure: The Global Food Crisis and the Future of Agriculture*. Earthscan Press, 2012.

Sandoval, Marcos. "El maíz y los pueblos indios." *Sin maíz no hay país*. Consejo Nacional para la Cultura y las Artes, 2003, p. 63.

Staller, John, and Michael Carrasco. *Pre-Columbian Foodways: Interdisciplinary Approaches to Food, Culture, and Markets in Ancient Mesoamerica*. Springer-Verlag, 2009.

3

CHARROS

A Critical Introduction

CHRISTOPHER CONWAY

PRIMARY MATERIALS

- *El Zarco* by Ignacio Manuel Altamirano (novel, 1901)
- *Allá en el Rancho Grande* (Out on the Big Ranch), directed by Fernando de Fuentes (film, 1936)
- "El ranchero y el charro" (The Ranchero and the Charro), performed by Diego Herrera and Leandro Ríos (song, 2015)
- "El Corrido del caballo blanco" (The *Corrido* of the White Horse, 1961) and "Las botas de charro" (The Boots of the Charro, 1972) by José Alfredo Jiménez (songs)
- "El charro mexicano" (The Mexican Charro, 1946) and "Yo soy mexicano" (I Am Mexican, 1941), performed by Jorge Negrete (songs)
- "Corrido del cuaco Lobo Gatiado" (*Corrido* of the Horse Named Lobo Gatiado) (song, n.d.)
- "Corrido del caballo Alazán Lucero" (*Corrido* of the Horse Alazán Lucero) (song, n.d.)

THIS CHAPTER EXPLORES TWO INTERRELATED TOPICS: the evolution of a national symbol over time and the specific ways that it is constructed in novels, films, and song. Our subject is the Mexican charro, a deeply influential symbol of Mexican identity that is universally recognized inside and outside of Mexico. To introduce his story we begin with general observations about nationalism and cultural invention, then examine the centuries-old history of the charro and the cultural uses to which he has been put. The charro is so ubiquitous in the modern Mexican and Mexican American imagination that he seems to be natural and eternal, but that isn't the case. In *Nations and Nationalism*, Ernest Gellner writes that one of the powers of modern nationalism is to give its inventions an aura of timelessness that transcends governments, ideologies, and individuals (47). To critically examine the charro, then, is to draw attention to the historical conditions of his emergence and to underline his ideological uses.

The most immediate questions at the outset are, "What is a nation?" and "What is nationalism?" Gellner writes that two people are of the same nation "if they share the same culture, where culture in turn means a system of ideas and signs and associations and ways of behaving and communicating" (7). We can understand how nationalism creates this shared system through the categories of narrative, tradition, space, and iconography. Each triggers a sense of communal identity because it manufactures, transmits, and perpetuates a symbolically meaningful feeling of belonging in a collective public.[1] After all, the whole point of nationalism is that it isn't *outside* of the people whom it designates as members of its family, but rather that it seeks to live *inside* them as a feeling. The first register, narrative, refers to storytelling, such as history textbooks that are widely read or used in schools, and to novels, stories, or films, all of which reinforce a community's symbolic claim to nationality. Another register is the "invented tradition," or a ritualistic activity designed to encourage civic pride in national collectivities, as in the case of the commemoration of Mexican independence in Mexico City on the night before September 16, when the president addresses a vast gathering of people with a litany of vehement "¡Vivas!"[2] Nationalism also makes use of space, situating its invented traditions and inspiring stories in specific places that in turn acquire a sacred aura. Through this process, ancient ruins, national monuments, and imposing buildings become meaningful locations in a country's culture. Finally, nationalism is iconic. What this means is that it manufactures or appropriates a thing, a person, a group, or an emblem and imbues it with meaning by continuously citing it as a symbol of nationality. In the case of Mexico, the repertoire of national icons includes the emblem of the eagle and the serpent, which appears on the country's flag, the Virgin of Guadalupe, pre-Columbian heroes, and well-known photographs of the revolutionary leader Emiliano Zapata. These registers—narrative, tradition, space, and iconography—are not separate from one another but deeply interdependent. Their overlap is so pronounced that it challenges our ability to explain them as separate categories or concepts. Here we present them separately just to emphasize the varied workings of nationalist culture.

Thanks to a profusion of charro imagery in tourist advertisements and in film, as well as to the fact that mariachis adopted his costume, the charro is arguably the most universally recognized emblem of Mexican identity around the world. His global presence as the embodiment of a nation may be compared to other universally recognized emblems, such as the Spanish bullfighter, the U.S. cowboy, the Argentinian gaucho, and the Ukrainian and Russian cossack, all preindustrial or agrarian masculine archetypes who were institutionalized as national symbols when modernization and city life began to overtake and alter the old, traditional ways of living. Like these mythological fellows, the charro is a rough, noble, and exotic male who pridefully commands the animals and men around him. In his extravagantly embroidered jacket and trousers, and wearing that formidably wide-brimmed hat, the charro is undeniably colorful. More importantly, he became the idealized prototype of the modern Mexican macho. He emerged through a powerful combination of rural traditions, post-revolutionary Mexican politics, and twentieth-century mass media, especially film and music. He is so intrinsic to the construction of the modern Mexican and Mexican American self, and is such a durable example of it, that he takes center stage at the Charro Days Fiestas of Brownsville, Texas, and the *charreadas* (rodeos) held to this day in Mexican and Mexican American communities throughout the U.S. Southwest.

The simplest definition of the charro is that he is a theatrical and stylized Mexican cowboy. Although he is a talented horseman trained to handle horses and cattle, he distinguishes himself from the working cowhand (the vaquero) by being a regal figure whose style and self-presentation is descended from the ranching aristocracy of the colonial era (Slatta 77–78). Indeed, the very word *charro*, which was originally used in Spain to describe a rustic or primitive country person, became an honorific meaning "country gentleman" in colonial Mexico (Sands 38; Palomar Verea 21). The charro's representative characteristic was his elegant style of dress; he was a dandy on horseback, with embroidered clothes studded with silver buttons, rings and chains, and that fancy sombrero. Despite this extravagance, to be a charro was to be a man's man, to know how to command horses, cattle, women, and other men. In the nineteenth century, these connotations intensified when the charro style was adopted by both bandits and the rurales (rural mounted police). One of the most notorious bands of nineteenth-century outlaws were the *plateados*, or "silver ones," who terrorized the countryside of Morelos, Veracruz, Puebla, and Guerrero in charro costumes richly studded in silver (Vanderwood 54–55). Many of these men had been schooled in chaos by Mexico's numerous civil wars, and when peacetime arrived they were not interested in putting down their guns to quietly go back to scraping by as farmers or artisans. In 1861, President Benito Juárez founded a special mounted police force, the rurales, to combat such bandits, and this force could not help but adopt the charro costume because to do otherwise would have been to admit weakness or a lack of virility. As Paul Vanderwood explains, the charro outfit symbolized a man's superior ability to ride, rope, shoot, drink, and womanize (55). Only a charro could be man enough to take on another charro. Thus, by the end of the nineteenth century, to be a charro was so symbolically connected to violence and manliness that it's not possible to pin him down to any specific class of person; bandits, rurales, and aristocratic landowners all put on his costume.

The charro was reinvigorated as a cultural icon and began his ascent as a true national symbol after the Mexican Revolution (1910–20). It is difficult to briefly convey how destructive and disruptive the Revolution was to Mexico. The conflict displaced thousands, and the combination of violence, famine, and disease killed anywhere between one and two million people out of a population of about fifteen million.[3] All families in Mexico, rich or poor, were touched in some way by the Revolution, either through direct experience or through the social, political, and cultural changes that it generated, such as the breaking up of large landed estates, the growth of cities, the dramatic rise in literacy rates, the emergence of new nationalist mythologies, and the creation of a state that was democratic in name only and that largely co-opted potential antagonists through political clientelism.[4] In comparison to the old days under Porfirio Díaz (1876–1910), Mexico had visibly and viscerally changed. One response people had to these shifts was to look backward in time and idealize the past, and the recovery and reinvention of the charro was an important part of this process of nostalgic recovery.

Eager to reinforce nationalist feeling through folklore and pageantry, the Mexican state and municipal governments co-opted charro imagery and established relationships with organizations dedicated to the promotion and regulation of charro identity and to the staging of *charreadas*. These associations could provide horsemen and entertainments for public display during nationalist and patriotic festivities, reinforcing the association of patriotism with charro culture. The alliance between the two players was paradoxical, because charro groups were nostalgic for the vanished ranching and landowning traditions of prerevolutionary Mexico. Although the Revolution had been fought to disrupt the old haciendas and liberate their peons, the postrevolutionary state now began to draw from nostalgic charro culture to build nationalist feeling. One friend of the National Association of Charros of Mexico City wrote an article that telegraphed the cultural agenda of charro organizations: "If our characteristic, symbolic type is the charro . . . the characteristic, symbolic house or palace of Mexico is the hacienda, that Mexican farm that nourishes the country, and which represents the loyal leveler and disseminator of its potential" (Carreño King 24). The idea that the charro was a treasured vestige from a vanished perfect society was not limited to newspaper articles or books. One of the founders of the National Association of Charros was the old aristocrat Carlos Rincón Gallardo, who used the following string of titles to identify himself: "Duke of Regla, Marquis of Guadalupe, and Marquis of Villahermosa." Rincón Gallardo tirelessly promoted charros and *charreadas*, published an influential handbook on charro life, and became involved in the nascent film industry. In 1929, he starred in a film called *La boda de Rosario* (Rosario's Wedding), in which he plays a charro landowner who rescues his beloved Rosario after she is kidnapped by a low-class person. The message was clear: haciendas are good, and their charro owners embody the valor and nobility of the Mexican character. One reviewer praised the film's intelligence and execution, but criticized it for being painfully trite in its idealization of folkloric types and for aligning itself with the most banal and embarrassing stereotypes of old Mexico.[5]

The conservative agenda of men like Rincón Gallardo aside, the charro was also a populist icon that could embody subversive meanings. The songs of the people, for example, known in Mexico as *corridos*, had as one of their most prominent subjects the lives of beloved bandit and revolutionary horsemen who were paragons of virility. Because different classes of people with different outlooks recognized and admired the charro, the Mexican government did well in adopting him as a patriotic symbol at official events and celebrations. In doing so it was tapping into a powerful symbol that had begun to be a dominant force in advertising, print media, and film. For example, one of the most popular comic books of the late 1930s was *El Charro Negro* (The Black Charro), and beginning in 1940, a young rodeo charro named Raúl de Anda began producing and starring in a series of westerns about a masked avenger titled *El Charro Negro* (which he claimed was not based on the famous comic but on local legend). The most famous and influential charro film of the twentieth century, *Allá en el Rancho Grande* (Out on the Big Ranch, 1936), spawned a new genre of Mexican film called the *comedia ranchera*. Throughout the 1940s and well into the 1950s, these musical melodramas captured the hearts of Mexicans, especially because their heroic charros were often played by the country's most beloved movie stars: Pedro Infante and Jorge Negrete. The early *comedias rancheras* were set in old haciendas, like *La boda de Rosario*, but later ones simply transposed the charro hero into modern times, as if he were an archetype of Mexican identity untethered from any one historical period, freely moving across time and space. In this case, what mattered about the charro was not that he was a kind of cowboy or that he represented an old way of living in the past but that he was *puro mexicano*. He was princely, passionate, honorable, prone to melancholy, and predisposed to sacrifice valiantly for love. Nowadays, these films play a key role in perpetuating the charro myth because most Mexicans have experienced the charro archetype through them, and through performers like Negrete and Infante, who died before their time and became beloved icons in their own right. Marcia Farr, the author of a study of how Mexican and Mexican American culture endures in Chicago in the twenty-first century, relates the story of how the inhabitants of so-called Chicagoacán treat the *comedia ranchera* as a vital cornerstone of their identity, keeping copies to watch on their televisions or dropping everything to watch them when they are screened on Spanish-language television stations. "Perhaps these films have appeal now," she writes, "in another era of confusion and upheaval, this time caused by massive migration to and labor in the United States" (41).

After the *comedia ranchera* faded, charro imagery continued to march through twentieth-century Mexico and the United States, as it still does today. Charro heroes continued to be foregrounded in grittier, harsher films, starring other male actors who were famous as recording stars, most notably Antonio Aguilar and Vicente Fernández. The fact that they dressed like charros when they played concerts solidified the association between charro dress and *ranchera* music. Parallel to these developments, another kind of charro maintained continual presence in the North American continent: the anonymous charro who performed astonishing feats of horsemanship and animal taming at the *charreadas*. To forget this dimension of the charro is to forget the true, living tradition that lies behind the different mass media versions of his myth. Kathleen

Mullen Sands calls the *charreada* spectacle a "complex folk tradition" that "draws the community together in a public, shared symbolic experience which ritualizes their collective history and reasserts their cultural identity" (4). In a *charreada*, which takes place outdoors in a circular arena with a narrow corridor attached to it, charros perform a series of stylized and challenging feats, such as horse tricks (*cala de caballo*), the roping of cattle (*piales en lienzo*), roping (*manganas*), bull riding (*jineteo de novillos*), and bronco busting (*jineteo de yegua*). In short, the charro is also a kind of athlete or performer linked to a sport that communicates his manliness and skill in dominating animals. The female counterpart of the charro, the china poblana in her long skirts and embroidered white blouses, also participates in *charreadas*, in choreographed riding drills called *escaramuzas* (skirmishes).

Now that we have briefly sketched some broad definitions and explored the general cultural history of the charro, we can turn to individual representations of this character and take a closer look at how he was variously constructed and for what purposes. We begin with the nineteenth-century association of the charro with criminality and banditry, as exemplified by one of Mexico's most famous nationalist novels, *El Zarco* (1901) by Ignacio Manuel Altamirano (1834–1893). Altamirano was an Indian born in the village of Tixtla in the state of Guerrero, into the humble yet respected family of the village's *alcalde de indios*, or Indian mayor. As a fourteen-year-old, Altamirano received a scholarship to study at the prestigious Scientific and Literary Institute in the town of Toluca, where he was deeply inspired by one of his professors, the influential liberal journalist Ignacio Ramírez. The rest of Altamirano's life was spent as a militant and uncompromising liberal activist; he fought in the country's civil wars and against the French occupation, and he tirelessly promoted liberal causes and cultural nationalism in a distinguished career as a writer. Altamirano's fame in cultural circles was so great that all the up-and-coming writers who sought his mentoring appreciatively referred to him as "Maestro" (Teacher), an honorific by which he is still remembered.

El Zarco was loosely based on a legend about a famous *plateado* bandit named Salomé Plascencia, who was said to have kidnapped a young woman from the village of Yautepec. In Altamirano's version of the tale, a *plateado* bandit named Zarco (Blue Eyes) comes to the same village and seduces an arrogant, light-skinned woman named Manuela, who has been rejecting the advances of an upright, noble Indian blacksmith named Nicolás. Indeed, she calls him an "ugly Indian," a nineteenth-century racial slur. In turn, Nicolás has been blind to the love of the virtuous mestiza Pilar, Manuela's godsister. After eloping with the bandit, Manuela lives to regret her choice because she discovers that real life among the bloodthirsty bandits does not conform to her idyllic, romantic idealization of them. Nicolás joins a posse that eventually captures Zarco and executes him by firing squad. Manuela, realizing that she has lost her place in the world and embracing her status as the bandit's mistress, is driven mad by the execution and dies on the spot.

There are various ways of reading the novel and its themes. One of the most common approaches is to see it as an illustration of the kinds of novels that Altamirano promoted in the name of Mexican nationalism. In other words, it is a morality play about how education, family values, and patriotism are linked together. Another key approach is the treatment of gender, since Pilar conforms to very traditional norms of femininity, whereas Manuela is undoubtedly a rebel and a more independent character. The character of Nicolás and a few references to Indians in the novel also invite readers to reflect upon the theme of acculturation and the idea that what matters is not the color of the skin but the quality of a person's character, most notably his or her commitment to family and to social and nationalist values. The novel's most important and influential interpretation is that of Doris Sommer, who saw it as an example of how nineteenth-century Spanish American "national romances" used love and marriage plots to establish symbolic reconciliations between different groups or interests in a country. In the case of *El Zarco*, the courtship of Nicolás and Pilar represents the future of Mexico and the love affair of Manuela and the bandit, its moral downfall (227–28).

The fact that Zarco is a charro is important because it roots the novel in the context of nineteenth-century Mexican banditry. *El Zarco* was, in part, a response to the romantic novel *Astucia, el jefe de los Hermanos de la Hoja; o, Los charros contrabandistas de la Rama* (Astucia, the Chief of the Brotherhood of the Leaf; or, The Charro Smugglers of La Rama, 1865–66) by Luis G. Inclán, an early promoter of charro identity. In Inclán's novel, which was inspired by the spirit of adventure and noble heroes of the beloved French novel *The Three Musketeers* by Alexandre Dumas, the charros are not bloodthirsty, terroristic *plateados* but rather "social bandits" and Mexican musketeers who live by a code, repair social evils, and embody a pure, unpolluted form of Mexican identity.[6] In contrast, Altamirano was eager to correct the literary record and unmask the charro's true character by focusing on the figure of the *plateado*. One of the ways he shows this is by exploring how self-presentation is a symptom of the quality of a person's character and propensity toward social good or evil. If the nation depends on productivity, peace, and patriotic feeling, the expression of personal egotism and greed through fashion signals a challenge to progress and a threat to the social order.[7] For example, let's consider Altamirano's dramatic and memorable description of Zarco's charro outfit:

> The rider was dressed like the bandits of that day and like our charros, like the most charro of today's charros. He wore a dark woolen jacket embroidered with silver and *calzoneras*, decorated down each side with a double row of silver *chapetones*, linked by little chains, and lacings of the same metal. The broad, flat brim of his dark wool sombrero was trimmed, as much on the underside as on the upper, with a thick, wide band of silver braid embroidered with gold stars; encircling the low, rounded crown was a double silver hatband from which dangled, at either side, two thin disks, also in silver, in the shape of medals, topped by golden rings. In addition to the woolen scarf covering his face, he was wearing a woolen shirt under his jacket, and on his belt a pair of pistols with ivory hilts, in their silver-worked, patent leather holsters. . . . It was an insolent ostentation, cynical and tasteless. The moonlight caused the silvery ensemble to gleam, giving the horseman the appearance of a strange ghost in a sort of silver armor, something like a picador in the bullring or a mottled centurion during a Holy Week procession. (74–75)

This charro is a dazzling and disturbing nocturnal and supernatural figure who inspires both awe and fear. Altamirano explains that Zarco was forged out of laziness, class envy, and greed, and Manuela is a feminine embodiment of these character flaws. She too is blinded by greed and materialism. In contrast, Nicolás, as well as President Benito Juárez (who has a cameo in the novel) and the leader of the posse who captures the bandit, are all men who dress in a sober and dignified way and whose motives are patriotic and selfless. For Altamirano, the charro is not a heroic national symbol but rather a symptom of personal vanity run wild that threatens to disrupt a national order deeply rooted in the concepts of family, law and order, and progress.

Our second cultural case study in the history of the charro is, by necessity, the enormously popular film *Allá en el Rancho Grande* (1936), which was remade in 1948. As already indicated, the film inaugurated a genre of musical melodrama that reigned in Mexico for two decades and that became deeply associated with the glamorous and iconic superstars Jorge Negrete and Pedro

Infante. Carlos Monsiváis, one of Mexico's most respected critics and cultural historians, called the genre a celebration of rural innocence that idealized all of its character types (charro, landowner, peasant, china, et cetera) and that pined for the purity of rural life (118). *Allá en el Rancho Grande*'s director was Fernando de Fuentes, who a few years earlier had directed a trilogy of hard-hitting movies about the meaning of the Mexican Revolution: *El prisionero trece* (Prisoner 13, 1933), *El compadre Mendoza* (Godfather Mendoza, 1933), and *Vámonos con Pancho Villa* (Let's Go with Pancho Villa, 1935). In these films, de Fuentes represents personal sacrifice, self-interest, political betrayal, and violence as the strands that define the Mexican Revolution as a collective event. *Allá en el Rancho Grande* took its criticism of the Revolution even further by celebrating prerevolutionary social and economic structures. In a period in which the Mexican middle class was wary of socialism and everyone was shaken up by the pace of postrevolutionary social change, *Allá en el Rancho Grande* touched a nostalgic and reactionary nerve (Mora 47). But at a more basic level, it caught on because it was full of recognizable types, contained familiar plot devices, and featured a catchy song that was an anthem to the comforts of country life: "The ranchero's pleasure / is to have a good horse / saddle him in the afternoon / go for a ride around the fence / . . . Over there in El Rancho Grande / where I used to live!"

The film tells the story of a charro landowner named Felipe, his charro foreman, José Francisco, and José Francisco's love, the virginal, long-suffering, Cinderella-like Cruz. At the beginning of the film, Felipe's father, a rich and benevolent hacienda owner, adopts little José Francisco after his single mother's death and raises him alongside his own son. After the patriarch's death, Felipe takes command of the hacienda and makes José Francisco his right-hand man. The motor of the melodramatic plot is that José Francisco loves Cruz, a servant who works for Angela, a scheming washerwoman who is cohabitating with the good-hearted village drunk and hacienda clown Florentino. José Francisco and the frail, virginal Cruz plan to marry but have to wait until he makes some money racing one of his horses at a meet. Meanwhile, Felipe, who is unaware that his best friend and Cruz are planning to marry, pays Angela to bring the young woman to him so that he can sleep with her. (The centuries-old Mexican and Spanish American practice of landowners taking advantage of the girls and women who render tribute to them or work their lands is called the *derecho de pernada*.) Cruz resists, and as she tussles against the landowner's advances she has a seizure, at which point Felipe renders aid, discovers the truth about her relationship with his best friend, and is filled with shame. He tenderly returns her to her home under the cover of night, but two peons see the pair and spread the word that Cruz is another of Felipe's "conquests." When José Francisco finds out about the rumors after winning his race and singing the song "Allá en el Rancho Grande" at a cantina, he is filled with rage; he rejects Cruz and challenges Felipe to a duel. However, Felipe is able to convince his friend that he did not know about his relationship with Cruz and that nothing untoward happened between them. The film ends with the joyous weddings of Felipe to his girlfriend Margarita, José Francisco to Cruz, and the scheming Angela to the newly sobered up Florentino. The latter wedding is significant because the film suggests that Angela's evil actions flow from Florentino's inability to dominate his woman. As the end titles roll, viewers are primed to believe that order has been restored to this paradisiacal place named Rancho Grande.

On one level, *Allá en el Rancho Grande* seems thematically straightforward: hacienda life is happy, the values of masculine honor are absolute, marriage tames sexual danger, and rural life, with its colorful charros and chinas, is a site of nationalist pride and unity. The problem is that the disturbing attempted rape at the center of the film reveals an unresolved undercurrent of tension, one that calls into question the idyllic nature of the hacienda as a benevolent hierarchy. Specifically, the film underlines that the *derecho de pernada* is something that Felipe has exercised before with other hacienda women, which begs the question of whether his father also practiced it. Was José Francisco taken into the "Big House" after his mother's death because Felipe's father, the hacienda owner, was also his father? Were the olden days better than the present or just as corrupt? In this light, the Rancho Grande becomes an ambiguous symbol rather than an uncomplicated, static, and happy utopia. The threat and reality of rape that loom over this tale and other Mexican cultural narratives echo the story of Malintzin, a young Maya woman who was taken by the conquistador Hernán Cortés during the Conquest of Mexico to help him translate during his march toward Tenochtitlán in 1519. As Octavio Paz argued in his book *The Labyrinth of Solitude* (1959), Malintzin (more commonly known as La Malinche) is the symbolic mother of modern Mexico and the embodiment of every Mexican macho's insecurities about his origin and his fear of being dominated (symbolically raped) by male rivals. Paz's arguments were not scientific, or even accurately sociological and psychological, but he identified an important narrative that recurs in Mexican culture, usually voiced through issues of paternity, rape, and illegitimacy. Be that as it may, the three marriages that finish *Allá en el Rancho Grande* suggest that taking formal ownership of a wife through marriage protects social systems against potentially dangerous disruptions, like the conflict between brothers. In particular, Angela the washerwoman, who is an amoral loose cannon, is finally tamed and dominated by Florentino in the final scenes of the film, which show her cowering under his threatening stares and gestures. Cruz, in turn, will no longer be available to tempt other men who might overpower her despite her resistance. And finally, Felipe, now married to an upper-class woman, might not wander as he did before, although that seems doubtful considering his history.

Our third and final case study relates to popular Mexican music. Thanks to *comedias rancheras* like *Allá en el Rancho Grande*, the charro became bound up with song. Song traditions about rural life that predated the *comedia ranchera* were co-opted into a musical culture that was associated with charro costumes and charro performers like Vicente Fernández and Antonio Aguilar, both of whom played charros on film. (Aguilar is lovingly known as "The Charro of Mexico.") Such iconic singers connected the virtues of folklore and rural life to the image of the charro and his costume. In this way, folk songs about horses landed in the symbolic world of the charro; this made sense, since the charro was Mexico's most regal and recognized horseman. Who better to sing the virtues of horses than he? Also, since in Mexico and the rest of the Western world horses are long-standing symbols of virility and strength, songs about horses are inevitability about masculinity, another key characteristic of charro identity. Some of the most canonical and enduring Mexican *corridos* are about horses, such as "Corrido del cuaco Lobo Gatiado" (*Corrido* of the Horse Named Lobo Gatiado, n.d.) and "Corrido del caballo Alazán Lucero" (*Corrido* of the Horse Alazán Lucero, n.d.) In the first, a man takes a mustang off the hands of a landowner in exchange for his mare and then turns around and bests the richer man with an expensive bet by taming the wild horse and then beating the mare in a race. In the second, Alazán Lucero is a horse that nobly allows a mare to win a race, a betrayal for which his owner shoots and kills him. Horses are either analogs or extensions of masculine power; the ability of men to command and control horses attests to their potential power over male rivals and their ability to command women. The power and vitality of horses also function as a reflection of male strength and self-sacrifice. One of the best and most beloved Mexican songs about a horse is by the legendary composer José Alfredo Jiménez, and it is called "El corrido del caballo blanco" (The *Corrido* of the White Horse, 1961). In the *corrido*, a white horse is set loose in Guadalajara, in central Mexico, and then travels heroically to the north, through the towns of Escuinapa, Culiacán, and Hermosillo, and then into Tijuana and down into Baja California, to El Rosario and Ensenada. The epic journey of the white horse, against adversity and suffering, is a rousing call to strength and endurance. In one of José Alfredo Jiménez's recordings of the song, the singer exclaims "¡No te rajes!" to the valiant horse, meaning, "Don't give in!" or "Don't surrender!," a phrase that is deeply associated with the construction of a boastful, aggressive, and ultimately defensive machismo that Octavio Paz explored in *The Labyrinth of Solitude* when explaining the cultural impact of La Malinche on the male Mexican psyche (51).

In addition to such tales about horses, there are also songs that explicitly explore the meaning of being a charro. The most canonical of these belong in the repertory of songs featured in the *comedias rancheras* of the 1940s and 1950s, and especially those sung by Jorge Negrete. The songs "Yo soy mexicano" (I Am Mexican) from the film *Ay, Jalisco, no te rajes* (Oh, Jalisco, Don't Surrender, 1941), and "El charro mexicano" (The Mexican Charro) from the film *Fiesta mexicana* (Mexican Fiesta, 1946) are cases in point. Both are nationalist anthems that argue the charro is the living embodiment of Mexican-ness and of a noble brand of machismo. "I Am Mexican" points to the distinctive charro costume, his command of horses and cockfighting, and his uncompromising courage and endurance, which likens him to the martyred Aztec warrior Cuauhtémoc. "The Mexican Charro" hits on the same themes and links the character to the holy triumvirate of La Virgen de Guadalupe, the homeland (*la patria*), and God. A noble dreamer and a loyal lover, he is also tough and proud because he likes to drink his tequila out of a rough pottery mug so that he can taste the earth in it. In short, these are the iconic, traditional, and official versions of the charro, tinted in glamorous nostalgia for simpler times and infused with boastful masculinity.

Some songs challenge the primacy of the charro and destabilize his monumental power. "Las botas del charro" (The Boots of the Charro, 1972), also by José Alfredo Jiménez, is a lament that represents charro identity in terms of class power; the mournful singer complains that his lover has left him because she prefers a man with expensive charro boots. "El ranchero y el charro" (The Ranchero and the Charro, 2015), by Salvador Aponte, is also critical. The song, a duet between Diego Herrera and Leandro Ríos, two twenty-first century superstars of norteño music, nudges the charro aside, making his symbolic power relative rather than absolute. Herrera sings the part of a charro from Mazatlán who brags about his superior skills as a horseman and a lover of women, while Ríos does the same, playing the role of a ranchero, or northern cowboy, from Los Ramones in Nuevo León. The resolution of the point and counterpoint is simple: neither is better than the other, because both love horsemanship, women, and loyal male friendship. The charro, which in Negrete's era had been an all-encompassing symbol of Mexican masculinity, is transformed here into one type or one equal among others (in this case, the icon of the ranchero from northern Mexico). In the music video for the song, the duet is represented through a *charrería* competition between the men, who take turns displaying their rodeo skills. Such imagery was pro forma in the *comedias rancheras* of the middle of the twentieth century, accenting the rivalry between charros eager to prove who was more skilled, daring, and courageous. Male rivals in these films ultimately discovered that they were allies and loyal friends because of their nobility of character, love of women, and commitment to a code of honor.[8] In the competition between Herrera and Ríos, we see how some of these old formulas are reinscribed and rewritten. For example, the charro is not dominant, but the *charrería* remains as the test of manliness. Also, although the rivalry between the men is not between two charros, the ultimate commitment to male friendship, honor, women, and horsemanship resolves the contest between the men, as it had before in the old movies.

In closing, it bears repeating that the charro is one of modern Mexico's most influential symbolic creations, one that harnessed the tremendous power of mass media through film and musical recordings. He is the stylized, aristocratic embodiment of machismo and male Mexican-ness. Everything about him—his dress, his song, his command of horses and cattle, his valor and loyalty, and his love of women—are merged into one persona that the Mexican and Mexican American public has accepted as something familiar, true, and personally meaningful. Although not a religious icon like the Virgin of Guadalupe, the charro is one of the truest articles of faith in modern Mexican culture and also one of the most complex.[9]

NOTES

1. My understanding of nationalism in relation to symbolism and culture is indebted to the work of Anthony Smith, author of *National Identity* (1991), who explores ethnic identity in relation to nationalist symbols and narratives (77). Also, I draw from the general themes of Benedict Anderson's enormously influential *Imagined Communities: Reflections on the Origin and Spread of Nationalism* (1983).

2. Eric Hobsbawm coined the phrase "invented traditions" in his introduction to the book *The Invention of Tradition* (1983), which he co-edited with Terence Ranger. "'Invented tradition' is taken to mean a set of practices, normally governed by overtly or tacitly accepted rules and of a ritual or symbolic nature, which seek to inculcate certain values and norms of behavior by repetition, which automatically implies continuity with the past" (1).
3. In 2001, Robert McCaa, of the University of Minnesota Population Center, published a paper online titled "Missing Millions: The Human Cost of the Mexican Revolution," which carefully reviews the secondary literature in English and Spanish on death statistics related to this event. See www.hist.umn.edu/~rmccaa/missmill/mxrev.htm.
4. For more on land reform after the Revolution, see *The Mexican Revolution: Federal Expenditure and Social Change Since 1910* (1970) by James Wallace Wilkie (76–77). Wayne Cornelius and Ann Craig's short *The Mexican Political System in Transition* (1991) provides an accessible sketch of how the Mexican state, as run by the PRI, used clientelism and the mass media to hold on to power.
5. My paraphrase is from an excerpt published by Tania Carreño King in *El charro: La construcción de un estereotipo nacional, 1920–1940*: "la tendencia a presentar un ilusorio México de charros y chinas poblanas . . . acabaría por consolidar definitivamente el 'México de pandereta' que ya circula en el extranjero" (the tendency to present an illusory Mexico of charros and chinas poblanas . . . would definitively consolidate that image of "Mexico, land of fiestas" that already circulates abroad) (54).
6. The debt to Dumas is obvious because of the use of the phrase "All for one and one for all" in Inclán's novel. The idea of social bandits refers to Eric Hobsbawm's famous conceptualization of bandits in certain kinds of societies as protorevolutionary and populist agents (*Bandits* 17).
7. In an important essay on the subject, Carlos Monsiváis explains that the issue of appearances, especially deceitful and seductive ones, are at the center of Altamirano's ethos as a novelist (253). Although society is sometimes incapable of reading the truth of a person on the basis of their appearance, Altamirano's narrators are always keyed in to the true significance of beauty and truth; external beauty is often an index of untruth, and truth is often dressed plainly or colored mestizo or Indian.
8. *Los tres García* (1947), starring Pedro Infante, is a good illustration of the *charrería* competition as a measure of manliness. The film *Los tres vivales* (1958),

which is a satire of *comedia ranchera* movies, lampoons the exaggerated *charrería* competition.

9. Students of the myth of the charro would do well to examine Kathleen Mullen Sands's *Charrería Mexicana: An Equestrian Folk Tradition* (1993), which is the best full-length study and synthesis about charros and *charrería* in English. Richard W. Slatta's *The Cowboy Encyclopedia* (1996) as well as his *Comparing Cowboys and Frontiers: New Perspectives on the History of the Americas* (1997) provide helpful and well-researched guidance on understanding charros. One of Mexico's most influential and important cultural magazines, *Artes de México*, did a special issue (no. 50, 2000) that contains invaluable and beautifully illustrated essays in Spanish on charros, nationalism, and *charrería*, as well as an appendix with English translations. The best modern history of the charro is Tania Carreño King's slim volume *El charro: La construcción de un estereotipo nacional, 1920–1940* (2000). Ignacio Manuel Altamirano's novel *El Zarco* is available in an English translation by Ronald Christ (2007). A standard reference work on the history of Mexican film is Carl Mora's *Mexican Cinema: Reflections of a Society, 1896–2004* (2005). Helpful studies of Mexican music in relation to charros include *Musical Ritual in Mexico City: From the Aztec to NAFTA* (2004) by Mark Pedalty, and Alejandro L. Madrid's *Transnational Musical Encounters: Music and Performance at the U.S.-Mexico Border* (2011). The finest book in English on *corridos* (Mexican and Mexican American folk songs) is the classic work of ethnography, "*With His Pistol in His Hand*": *A Border Ballad and Its Hero* (1958) by Américo Paredes. The volume *Masculinity and Sexuality in Modern Mexico* (2012), edited by Victor M. Macías González and Anne Rubenstein, is highly recommended for exploring charros within the topic of Mexican masculinities, especially the chapter titled "Mariachis Machos and Charros Gay: Masculinities in Guadalajara" by Mary Lee Mulholland (234–61).

WORKS CITED

Altamirano, Ignacio Manuel. *Zarco, the Blue-Eyed Bandit.* Translated by Ronald Christ, Lumen Books, 2007.

Anderson, Benedict. *Imagined Communities: Reflections on the Origin and Spread of Nationalism.* Verso, 1983.

Artes de México, no. 50, 2000.

Carreño King, Tania. *El charro: La construcción de un estereotipo nacional, 1920–1940*. Instituto Nacional de Estudios Históricos de la Revolución Mexicana, Federación Mexicana de Charrería, 2000.

Cornelius, Wayne A., and Ann L. Craig. *The Mexican Political System in Transition*. Center for U.S.-Mexican Studies, University of California, San Diego, 1991.

Farr, Marcia. *Rancheros and Chicagoacán: Language and Identity in a Transnational Community*. University of Texas Press, 2006.

Gellner, Ernest. *Nations and Nationalism*. Blackwell, 1983.

Hobsbawm, Eric. *Bandits*. Penguin, 1972.

Hobsbawm, Eric, and Terence Ranger, editors. *The Invention of Tradition*. Cambridge University Press, 1983.

Inclán, Luis G. *Astucia, el jefe de los Hermanos de la Hoja; o, Los charros contrabandistas de la Rama: Novela histórica de costumbres mexicanas con episodios originales*, edición de Manuel Sol. Universidad Veracruzana, Fondo de Cultura Económica, 2005.

Macías González, Victor, and Anne Rubenstein, editors. *Masculinity and Sexuality in Modern Mexico*. University of New Mexico Press, 2012.

Madrid, Alejandro L., editor. *Transnational Musical Encounters: Music and Performance at the U.S.-Mexico Border*. Oxford University Press, 2011.

Monsiváis, Carlos. *Las herencias ocultas de la reforma liberal del siglo XIX*. Debate, 2006.

Mora, Carl J. *Mexican Cinema: Reflections of a Society, 1896–2004*. McFarland, 2005.

Palomar Verea, Cristina. *En cada charro un hermano: La charrería en el estado de Jalisco*. Secretaría de Cultura Gobierno de Jalisco, 2004.

Paredes, Américo. *"With His Pistol in His Hand": A Border Ballad and Its Hero*. University of Texas Press, 1958.

Paz, Octavio. *The Labyrinth of Solitude: And the Other Mexico*; *Return to the Labyrinth of Solitude*; *Mexico and the United States; The Philanthropic Ogre*. Grove Press, 1991.

Pedalty, Mark. *Musical Ritual in Mexico City: From the Aztec to NAFTA*. University of Texas Press, 2004.

Sands, Kathleen M. *Charrería Mexicana: An Equestrian Folk Tradition*. University of Arizona Press, 1993.

Slatta, Richard W. *Comparing Cowboys and Frontiers: New Perspectives on the History of the America*. University of Oklahoma Press, 1997.

———. *The Cowboy Encyclopedia*. W. W. Norton, 1996.

Smith, Anthony D. *National Identity*. Penguin, 1991.

Sommer, Doris. *Foundational Fictions: The National Romances of Latin America*. University of California Press, 1991.

Vanderwood, Paul. *Disorder and Progress: Bandits, Police, and Mexican Development*. Scholarly Resource Books, 1992.

Wilkie, James Wallace. *The Mexican Revolution: Federal Expenditure and Social Change Since 1910*. University of California Press, 1970.

4

PRINT

The People's Print Shop: Art, Politics, and the Taller de Gráfica Popular

RYAN LONG

PRIMARY MATERIALS

- *El fascismo japonés* (Japanese Fascism) by Isidoro Ocampo (lithograph, 1939)
- *Profesor Ildefonso Vargas* by Leopoldo Méndez (lithograph, 1939)
- *Deportación a la muerte* (Deportation to Death) by Leopoldo Méndez (linocut print, 1942)
- *El libro negro del terror nazi en Europa* (The Black Book of Nazi Terror in Europe), edited by Antonio Castro Leal et al. (illustrated book, 1943)
- *El río Palizada* (Palizada River) by Alfredo Zalce (lithograph, 1945)
- *¡Victoria!* (Victory!) by Ángel Bracho (linocut print, 1945)
- *La negra Sojourner Truth* (The Black Woman Sojourner Truth) by Elizabeth Catlett (linocut print, 1947)
- *Pequeña Maestra, qué grande es tu voluntad* (Little Schoolteacher, How Great Is Your Force of Will) by Leopoldo Méndez (linocut print, 1947)
- *TGP México: El Taller de Gráfica Popular, doce años de obra artística colectiva* (TGP Mexico: The Workshop for Popular Graphic Art, a Record of Twelve Years of Collective Work), edited by Hannes Meyer (illustrated book, 1949)

A SOLDIER WITH A STEEL HELMET on his head and a rifle on his back shines a lantern into a boxcar filled with people. Inside the car a child clings to his mother's legs. Another soldier points at someone on the

FIGURE 4.1. Leopoldo Méndez, *Deportación a la muerte*, 1942. Linocut. Reprinted in Hannes Meyer (ed.), *TGP México: El Taller de Gráfica Popular, doce años de obra artística colectiva*, p. 8. Photograph by Ryan Long.

train. A man lying on the floor of the car is too weak to sit upright. The train extends to the horizon, where a plume of black smoke rises from either its engine or a crematorium. The lantern that exposes the huddling crowd also reveals to the world the nature of the Nazis' crimes against humanity in the linoleum-cut print titled *Deportación a la muerte* (Deportation to Death [Death Train], 1942) (figure 4.1), which Deborah Caplow (2007) describes as "one of the earliest-known images of the Holocaust by an artist outside the camps" (166).

It may come as a surprise to some readers that the image Caplow describes was created by a Mexican artist, the renowned printmaker Leopoldo Méndez. The volume in which the print originally appeared, *El libro negro del terror nazi en Europa* (The Black Book of Nazi Terror in Europe, 1943), was published in Mexico by a press associated with Alemania Libre (Free Germany), a German exile organization (Caplow, *Leopoldo Méndez* 161–62). Hannes Meyer, the Swiss-born architect and former director of the Bauhaus, lived in Mexico City from 1939 to 1949, and he was in charge of selecting the images that appeared in

El libro negro, thirty-two of which were made by ten different artists, including Méndez, who were associated with the Taller de Gráfica Popular (Workshop for Popular Graphic Art), or TGP (Meyer, *TGP México* xiv). The visual elements of *Deportación* are characteristic of much of the TGP's work. Formally, it uses contrast effectively, tying a dynamic relation between light and dark portions of the image into the development of its content. And even though the train in the image is stopped, the print suggests movement toward a place outside of its frame. Thematically, it is political and denunciatory. It highlights repression, injustice, suffering, and the need to call attention to these and other problems.

Throughout its most vibrant period, extending from its foundation in 1937 until the late 1950s, the TGP produced politically engaged art whose topics were relevant both within and beyond Mexico's borders. The TGP's early years transpired during a period of national and global transformation and upheaval. Mexico was recovering from the destruction and instability wrought by two wars, the Revolution, which lasted from 1910 until about 1920, and the Cristero War, which was fought from 1926 to 1929 but whose violent repercussions persisted for years. The relative stability of the 1930s and the reforms that took place during the 1934–1940 presidency of Lázaro Cárdenas, including significant land redistribution and the expropriation of Mexico's oil from foreign corporations, fostered and coincided with the efforts of many visual artists, filmmakers, writers, and other intellectuals to imagine and help make a better Mexico. Calls for justice, equality, and the defense of the oppressed were at the heart of the TGP's work. This is made clear in its contributions to projects like *El libro negro* and many others, including its earlier work condemning Franco's victory in the Spanish Civil War, the related rise of fascism in Europe and Japan, and the murders of rural schoolteachers in Mexico at the hands of reactionary forces. In the years before, during, and after World War II, the TGP made prints that addressed several centrally important themes, including poverty, illiteracy, racism, corruption, Nazism, the Holocaust, imperialism, capitalism, nuclear weapons, and equal rights for women.

The TGP's origins can be traced immediately to a previous group, the Liga de Escritores y Artistas Revolucionarios (League of Revolutionary Writers and Artists), or LEAR, and more indirectly to an established tradition of a critical press in Mexico, which dates back at least to the period of the war for independence from Spain. José Joaquín Fernández de Lizardi's serial novel *El periquillo sarniento* (The Mangy Parrot, 1816) is an emblematic example of a critical text that aimed to improve Mexican society by appealing to a wide audience, through humor in particular, and whose author suffered censorship for what he published. State persecution was an experience familiar to later writers as well, such as Ricardo Flores Magón, the anarchist editor of the critical journal *Regeneración*, who was forced into exile in 1903 during the climate of violent intolerance that characterized the period of Porfirio Díaz's rule (Adès 14), which extended almost uninterrupted from 1876 until 1910.

A clear predecessor to the TGP is José Guadalupe Posada, probably the best known of Mexican printmakers, whose satirical work inspired the TGP in terms of both medium and message. In a 1953 linocut titled *Homenaje a Posada* (Homage to Posada), for example, Méndez portrays Posada in his studio while Ricardo Flores Magón and his brother, Enrique, look over Posada's shoulder at the print he is working on. Posada is in the process of recording for history an event taking place at that moment just outside his window: soldiers on horseback wielding swords against an unarmed crowd of people protesting Díaz's reelection. This event was in fact portrayed by Posada in a print that appeared in the newspaper *La Gaceta Callejera* in May 1892 (Adès 13–14). Further evidence of the TGP's honoring of Posada is related to Hannes Meyer, whose work with the TGP was not limited to selecting prints for *El libro negro*. While in Mexico, Meyer was the financial director of the TGP. He also helped found La Estampa Mexicana, the TGP's publishing house, and directed it from 1942 to 1943 and again from 1947 to 1949 (Caplow, *Leopoldo Méndez* 176–77). Two of the Estampa's first publications were a series of prints by Méndez and another series of Posada's work. James Wechsler explains that these projects were intended to connect "the workshop's identity to these two master engravers" ("*Propaganda Gráfica*" 73).

The political climate that helped shape the TGP was generally more hospitable than that of either the period of the war for independence or the Porfiriato, as Díaz's reign is called. Nevertheless, political issues and conflicts were hardly limited to the content of the TGP's work. As a politically engaged, socially critical organization dedicated to collective work, the TGP often found itself negotiating conflicts both internal and external. Internal political issues that troubled the TGP included the organization's governance, economic independence, individual artists' self-promotion, and the pricing, marketing, and sale of the TGP's prints.[1] A dramatic early episode that placed the TGP at the heart of national and international conflict was the use of its workshop space for preparations by two of its members, Luis Arenal and Antonio Pujol, and the muralist and guest member David Alfaro Siqueiros for the May 24, 1940, assassination attempt against Leon Trotsky, who was in exile in Mexico City. Méndez did not support this act of violence, but he was implicated and briefly jailed, having lent Pujol the key to the workshop the day before the attempt on Trotsky's life. The TGP's relationship with Siqueiros was generally contentious,[2] and the Trotsky episode profoundly alienated him, Arenal, and Pujol from Méndez and other members of the TGP (Caplow, *Leopoldo Méndez* 154–56).

The TGP's emergence from its predecessor organization, the LEAR, illustrates how external political factors helped shape the former, especially party politics and connections with the Mexican state. According to Alison McClean, factors that contributed to the LEAR's disintegration in 1938, just four years after its founding, included pressure from the Communist Party and arguments among its members about how closely to work with the government of President Cárdenas (29).[3] Helga Prignitz-Poda writes, "Dadas las experiencias vividas en la LEAR, [los miembros del TGP] quisieron mantener a como diera lugar la independencia respecto a las comisiones y encargos estatales" (Given what they experienced in the LEAR, [the TGP's members] wanted to maintain as a priority their independence as it related to state-sponsored commissions and assignments) ("Taller" 260).[4] Deborah Caplow identifies Méndez, Raúl Anguiano, Luis Arenal, Ángel Bracho, and Pablo O'Higgins as founding members of the TGP in 1937 (*Leopoldo Méndez* 123). All of them had also been members of LEAR (McClean 29; Prignitz 280, 281, 293–94, 297–98). Caplow further explains that other early members of the TGP joined in 1938 (*Leopoldo Méndez* 123)—Fernando Castro Pacheco, José Chávez Morado, Xavier Guerrero, and Alfredo Zalce (who was also in LEAR [McClean 29]). Other members of the TGP who were in LEAR as well include Ignacio Aguirre, Roberto Berdecio, Francisco Dosamantes, Jesús Escobedo, and Elena Huerta (Prignitz 279, 282, 286, 287, 291). Born in part from a desire for independence from a previous group that had given its members an opportunity to develop or continue developing their talents and showcase their work, the TGP enjoyed relatively long-term success, maintaining a general degree of aesthetic quality and political relevance for roughly two decades, until the late 1950s and early 1960s, a period that, scholars tend to agree, defines the end of the TGP's most productive years in both aesthetic and political terms.[5]

Its relation to the LEAR is important to know in order to understand the fact that the TGP emerged during a time when politically committed art and artists, some of whom were directly associated with political parties, formed part of a broader dialogue about how to define the nation. In his retrospective volume about the TGP and his years working with it—which he published in two different venues, first in a book titled *TGP México* (1949) and second in a 1950 article for the Swiss magazine *Graphis*—Meyer highlights the activism and political nature of the artists in the TGP. For instance, he describes how some of the TGP's members engaged in the Ministry of Public Education's Misiones Culturales (Cultural Missions), "sea para pintar un mural en la escuela de una aldea, sea para investigar el folklore regional" (for such varied projects as painting a mural in the school or studying the folklore of the region) (*TGP México* xvi, xvii).[6] In Meyer's words, their portrayals of the problems that faced Mexico represented the efforts of the TGP's members to "use brush and pen as weapons in clearing the way to economic and cultural freedom" ("El Taller" 156).

An emphasis on collective efforts and politics defined the TGP from its beginnings. As Susan Valerie Richards notes, TGP founding members Méndez, O'Higgins, and Arenal were also members of the Communist Party (213), even if they didn't always agree with its politics, which at times clashed with their art (McClean 29). Concomitant with their party affiliation, TGP founders believed that a collectively oriented project must stem from collective production. As Richards puts it, "If art was *for* the people, it was created by more than one person" (16). Collective work and political commitment were clearly stated priorities of the TGP, as made evident by the group's March 1938 founding statutes, whose opening section, "Fines del Taller" (Goals of the Workshop), begins by explaining, "Este Taller se funda con el fin de estimular la producción gráfica en beneficio de los intereses del pueblo de México, y para ese objeto se propone reunir al mayor número de artistas alrededor de un trabajo de superación constante, principalmente a través del método de producción colectiva" (This Workshop is founded with the aim of stimulating graphic arts production in the interests of the Mexican people, and to this end seeks to bring together the greatest number of artists in a task of constant self-improvement, principally through collective production) (Taller de Gráfica Popular 22, 24).

Meyer's 1949 book about the TGP opened with a condensed statement of collective purpose that had by then replaced the 1938 statutes, titled "Declaración de principios del T.G.P." (Declaration of the Standards of the T.G.P.) and dated March 1945. The first two paragraphs of the "Declaración" emphasize the TGP's collective efforts and its overarching political goals:

> El Taller de Gráfica Popular es un centro de trabajo colectivo para la producción funcional y el estudio de las diferentes ramas del grabado y la pintura.
>
> El Taller de Gráfica Popular realiza un esfuerzo constante para que su producción beneficie los intereses progresistas y democráticos del pueblo mexicano, principalmente en su lucha contra la reacción fascista. (I)

> The Workshop for Popular Graphic Art is a center of collective work for a functional production and study of the different branches of engraving and painting.
>
> The Workshop for Popular Graphic Art undergoes a constant effort in order to benefit by its works the progressive and democratic interests of the Mexican people, especially in the fight against fascist reaction.

Antifascism in fact defines what Deborah Caplow calls the TGP's "first major collaborative effort" (*Leopoldo Méndez* 138), a series of posters that advertised sixteen lectures sponsored by the German exile group Liga Pro-Cultura Alemana en México (League for the Promotion of German Culture in Mexico), which took place from the fall of 1938 to the summer of 1939. The list of TGP artists who made the posters comprises the group's founding and earliest members, including Arenal, Bracho, Chávez Morado, Dosamantes, Escobedo, Méndez, Isidoro Ocampo, O'Higgins, Pujol, and Zalce (Meyer, *TGP México* 2–4). During the sixteen-week period of the Liga's lectures, the TGP put up 32,000 posters in Mexico City (Meyer, *TGP México* viii). Meyer emphasizes that the artists themselves worked day and night on the press that produced the copies of the posters (*TGP México* viii).

Unlike artists dedicated to muralism, probably the best-known manifestation of politically oriented visual art in Mexico, the members of the TGP used portable formats for getting their group's message across, such as the posters whose tens of thousands of copies Meyer describes, as well as fliers and pamphlets. Inexpensive paper and production methods, especially linoleum-block, or linocut, printing, enabled the TGP to keep costs low and production levels high (*TGP México* xii). Nevertheless, financial difficulties often plagued the TGP. An important means of balancing the group's books was the production and sale of fine art prints, often in thematically organized portfolios, such as the 1947 collection of eighty-five linocuts made by sixteen different artists titled *Estampas de la Revolución Mexicana* (Engravings of the Mexican Revolution). Meyer notes that of the 550 copies produced of this series, more than half were sold in one year, and 10 percent were donated to "organizaciones de cultura popular en el mundo entero" (progressive cultural organizations all over the world) (xiv, xv).

In addition to the help Meyer provided with the TGP's publications, financial management, and worldwide exposure—for example, in the case of the *Libro negro*—the TGP's international presence was developed by its members' connections to artists and institutions in the United States, Latin America, Europe, and China and the international backgrounds of many of its members and guest members. Already in 1949, when La Estampa Mexicana published the retrospective book edited by Meyer, there had been about twenty-five members and twenty-five guest members. In her book, which traces the TGP's history until 1980, Prignitz lists about one hundred members and guest members.[7] Clearly, the TGP attracted a significant number of artists who found a space to work on individual and collective projects. According to Meyer, at any given time in the twelve-year period he discusses, twelve to fifteen artists were actively involved with the TGP (*TGP México* xviii).

Within Mexico, the capital city was the most likely place of origin for the TGP's earliest members, including Arenal, Bracho, Dosamantes, and Méndez. Other early members were from Jalisco (Aguirre and Anguiano), Michoacán (Escobedo and Zalce), and Veracruz (Ocampo). The only founding member not from Mexico was O'Higgins, who was from Salt Lake City, Utah. Among foreign countries, the United States ranked first in terms of members' places of origin. In addition to O'Higgins, there were Elizabeth Catlett, from Washington, D.C.; James Heller, from New York; Margaret Taylor-Burroughs, from Louisiana; and Charles White and Mariana Yampolsky, both from Chicago. Catlett, Burroughs, and White were African American. James Wechsler observes that African American artists "found an atmosphere of acceptance in Mexico that they had not experienced in the United States" ("Taller" 208).[8] Like several other members of the TGP, White was also in the Communist Party (208). Other countries represented in the ranks of the TGP include Bolivia (Roberto Berdecio), France (Jean Charlot), Guatemala (Juan Antonio Franco), Ecuador (Galo Galecio), Cuba (Luis García Robledo), Israel (Moshe Gat), Belarus (Max Kahn), Spain (María Luisa Martín), Switzerland (Hannes Meyer), Poland (Fanny Rabel), and Czechoslovakia (Koloman Sokol).

The TGP's international relevance is certainly not fully explained by identifying its members' national origins, although this does give a quick sense of the group's diversity and prominence. Formal connections between the TGP and nations outside of Mexico were numerous and varied. For instance, Luis Arenal was employed briefly in the United States by the Works Progress Administration's Mural Division. The TGP, according to Wechsler, also "contributed prints to aid a Chicago newspaper guild strike against William Randolph Hearst's right-wing tabloids" ("*Propaganda Gráfica*" 67). Méndez won a Guggenheim Fellowship to travel to the United States in 1939, where, as Caplow observes, he was struck by the degree of poverty afflicting Mexico's northern neighbor (*Leopoldo Méndez* 152–53). In line with the TGP's emphasis on social critique, Méndez relayed a vivid account of a chain gang made up of African American prisoners (*Leopoldo Méndez* 153). Regarding its exposure abroad, by 1949 the TGP's work was owned by museums in Moscow, New York, and Chicago; and it had been exhibited in several other cities in the United States, as well as in Argentina, Panama, Poland, and Czechoslovakia (Meyer, *TGP México* xxiv). After World War II and as the Cold War intensified in the 1950s, the TGP's relationship with the United States became more difficult to sustain. According to Caplow, by the mid-1950s the frequency of visits by artists from the United States began to decrease (*Leopoldo Méndez* 218), a phenomenon associated with the intolerance of the period, when, for example, in 1951 the U.S. Department of State declared the TGP a "Communist front organization and prohibited members of the Taller from traveling to the U.S." (*Leopoldo Méndez* 218). As a consequence of the Cold War, the TGP's connections with other places grew stronger, especially Latin America, China, the Soviet Union, and Europe. In 1956, Ignacio Aguirre traveled to China to help with an exhibit about the TGP, inspiring a Chinese-published book titled *El arte mexicano* (Mexican Art) (1957), which included eighty-seven of the TGP's prints (*Leopoldo Méndez* 220). Additional travels and exhibits of the postwar period included Méndez's trip to Western and Eastern Europe in 1947, TGP exhibits in Sweden and Poland in 1950, and, organized with the help of guest member Roberto Berdecio, an exhibit in Bolivia in 1952 that coincided with the nationalization of that country's mining industry (*Leopoldo Méndez* 220).

The foreign exhibit of TGP work that coincided with an important domestic political event—the Bolivian mining industry's nationalization recalls the Mexican oil industry's nationalization in 1938—neatly summarizes the combination of international and national concerns that characterized the TGP's efforts. In 1942, for example, the same year that Méndez made the print condemning the Holocaust, the TGP's *Calaveras* (Skulls) series targeted truck drivers, shop owners, the press, pharmacists, and the distribution of tainted milk, developing relentless critiques of corruption, abuses of power, and exploitation of the poor (Meyer, *TGP México* 10–11). The *Calaveras* were a regularly published series of satirical prints inspired by Posada's famous caricatures of public figures as skeletons. They were often accompanied by mordantly critical, humorous texts in the form of *corridos*, or folk songs.[9] A particularly interesting print by Méndez combines the *Calavera* aesthetic with an international theme by portraying the Soviet general Semyon Timoshenko as a vengeful skeleton on a skeleton horse trampling the skulls of Nazis, an image that accompanies the text of the "Corrido de Stalingrado" (*TGP México* 11).

I will now turn to brief readings of six prints that reflect the varied topics, styles, and methods of the TGP's projects, both collective and individual. In chronological order, they are a two-color lithograph by Isidoro Ocampo that appears on a poster from the 1938–1939 lecture series for the Liga Pro-Cultura Alemana en México; a lithograph from Méndez's seven-print portfolio *En nombre de Cristo* (In the Name of Christ, 1939); a two-color linocut print that appears on a 1945 poster celebrating the Allied victory in World War II by Ángel Bracho; a lithograph from Alfredo Zalce's eight-print portfolio *Estampas de Yucatán* (Prints from the Yucatan, 1945); a 1947 linocut image of Sojourner Truth by Elizabeth Catlett; and a linocut that Méndez made in 1947 as a background for the credit sequence of Emilio Fernández's film *Río Escondido* (Hidden River, 1947). This small sampling of prints is not meant to be comprehensive, but I believe it will provide the reader with a general sense of the TGP's most important thematic and formal elements. I also hope it will serve as a point of departure for readers who want to explore further the work produced by these and other artists who belonged to the TGP.

Idisoro Ocampo was one of the earliest members of the TGP, and he participated in the collective project of publicizing the lecture series sponsored by the Liga Pro-Cultura Alemana. Particularly striking is the poster he made for the June 9, 1939, lecture by economist, essayist, and educator Daniel Cosío Villegas, which, like the other lectures in the series, took place in the highly prestigious venue of Mexico City's Palacio de Bellas Artes (Palace of the Fine Arts) (figure 4.2).

The lithograph featured in the poster presents a racist caricature of Japan's Emperor Hirohito as a giant insect whose swollen body and menacing legs completely overwhelm the Republic of China. In the section of his book titled "Cuadro comparativo de la técnica en litografía" (Comparative Plate of Five Lithographic Techniques), Hannes Meyer features Ocampo's use of very fine and densely arranged lines in reference to a different print (*TGP México* 35). In the 1939 poster, Ocampo uses this technique to great effect, portraying Hirohito

FIGURE 4.2. Isidoro Ocampo, *El fascismo japonés*, 1939. Lithograph. Poster in the collection of the Ibero-Amerikanisches Institut, Berlin. Photograph by Ryan Long.

as not only menacing but also utterly grotesque. Beginning from the top of the image, the lines that form the insect's body spiral downward in a clockwise direction, and they are picked up outside of the figure in the space symbolizing China, right under that nation's name. The insect's legs mirror the lines' spiraling motion, adding to an overall sense of vertiginous movement. The elements of Ocampo's poster that are also common to many of the TGP's collectively made prints are its use of caricature; its unequivocal and clearly defined message; its portability; and its aim to reach a large and broad audience.

Leopoldo Méndez's print *Profesor Ildefonso Vargas* (figure 4.3) portrays the murder of a schoolteacher at the hand of a Cristero, or radical supporter of the Catholic Church, an institution engaged in a power struggle with the government in the two decades after the Revolution.

The years from 1926 to 1929 were the most violent, and the war that took place then was precipitated by specific measures taken by government and church officials. The government closed church schools and convents, ordered the deportation of foreign-born priests, directed the closing of churches where opposition to the 1917 Constitution had been publicly expressed, and restricted the number of priests in proportion to the lay population (L. Meyer 1190; Knight 504). In July 1926, the Catholic Church ordered the cessation of church services in protest (L. Meyer 1190). During the prolonged Cristero backlash that persisted throughout the Cárdenas presidency, rural schoolteachers, perceived as state infiltrators in small, remote, and typically very conservative

FIGURE 4.3. Leopoldo Méndez, *Profesor Ildefonso Vargas*, 1939. Lithograph. Reprinted in Hannes Meyer (ed.), *TGP México: El Taller de Gráfica Popular, doce años de obra artística colectiva*, p. 90. Photograph by Ryan Long.

towns, were often victims (Caplow, *Leopoldo Méndez* 147). Giving a sense of the grave danger teachers faced, Hannes Meyer's presentation of *En el nombre de Cristo*, the portfolio that includes *Ildefonso Vargas*, is preceded by the phrase "En memoria de los 200 maestros rurales asesinados en cumplimiento de su deber, por los cristeros: 1936–1938" (In memory of the 200 rural teachers killed in line of duty by the Cristeros: 1936–1938) (*TGP México* 90). Caplow explains that Méndez gathered information about murdered schoolteachers by reading newspaper articles and by speaking with his fellow TGP artist Alfredo Zalce, whose experience with the Cultural Missions provided him with knowledge about the murders (*Leopoldo Méndez* 149). As an example of how the TGP co-operated with the Mexican state, Caplow also points out that Méndez worked with the Secretaría de Educación Pública (Ministry of Public Education), or SEP, on the series (*Leopoldo Méndez* 149; "Asesinato" 153).

As is the case with Ocampo's Hirohito poster, Méndez's print effectively conveys movement and menace. The teacher struggles for his life, one hand grasping the murderer's left leg while he continues writing on his blackboard. The murderer, who "wears the same clothing worn by fascist thugs in other Méndez prints" (Caplow, "Asesinato" 154), attacks the blindfolded teacher from behind, either stabbing him, as Caplow argues ("Asesinato"153), or strangling him, as it appears to me. (The backward motion of the murderer suggests to me the force required for strangling.) Caplow observes that Méndez included the journalistic accounts of the murders he portrays in his lithographs and that in the case of Vargas's murder, Cristeros had written "Viva Cristo Rey" (Long Live Christ the King), their battle cry, on the blackboard ("Asesinato" 153). The writing of the incomplete sentence in the image, then, is a particularly compelling example of the print's dynamism. Clearly foregrounded and highlighted as the single object with the most white space within its contours, the teacher's hand dominates the bottom third of the print. The hand's angle, its location along the print's vertical axis, and its size in relative proportion to the murderer's right hand are elements that establish a clear visual parallel with the murderer's action, which, as I noted above, appears less clearly defined than the teacher's. Writing, the print implies, is stronger than killing. The incomplete sentence leaves open the possibility that something other than "Cristo Rey" finishes it, such as, "Mexico," "Cárdenas," or "the Revolution."[10] The hand's prominence and the open-ended nature of what it writes argue that the Revolution's goals were still unmet and suggest that teachers such as Vargas were willing to fight to the death with the pen, not the sword, in order to achieve them.

FIGURE 4.4. Ángel Bracho, *¡Victoria!*, 1945. Linocut. Poster in the collection of the Ibero-Amerikanisches Institut, Berlin. Photograph by Ryan Long.

Ángel Bracho's linocut print that appears on the 1945 poster celebrating the end of World War II (figure 4.4) is similar to Ocampo's prewar condemnation of the Japanese invasion of China in the grotesque directness of its symbolism. Signs of the defeated forces occupy the image's bottom half, among them the broken swastika, the burning fasces, and the fallen Iron Cross. The lines formed

FIGURE 4.5. Alfredo Zalce, *El río Palizada*, 1945. Lithograph. Reprinted in Hannes Meyer (ed.), *TGP México: El Taller de Gráfica Popular, doce años de obra artística colectiva*, p. 125. Photograph by Ryan Long.

by the swastika, the bayonet, the fasces, and the eagle's claw intersect at the point at which the bayonet delivers the fatal blow to a vampire-like Hitler's already damaged visage. The "destrucción total del fascismo" (total destruction of fascism) celebrated along the poster's bottom line is conveyed precisely by the brutal fragmentation that characterizes the image's lower half. The text immediately beneath the image makes clear the crucial role the TGP attributes to the Soviet Union. In the image, the red star's prominence—indicated by its size, its central foregrounded position, and the lines that emanate from it and fill the half of the image that represents victory—reinforces the text's message. Not surprisingly, the bayonet that kills Hitler supports the flying red flag.

Like Méndez's depiction of Vargas's murder, Zalce's *El río Palizada* (The Palizada River) portrays a national scene (figure 4.5).

Unlike Méndez's print, however, Zalce's is idyllic, an affirmative and idealized representation of the indigenous population of Mexico's Yucatan Peninsula and thus also an effort to promote a more inclusive conception of the Mexican nation, one that recognizes and honors cultural difference. In contrast to the TGP's more political prints, *El río* is less directly historical. There is nothing in the image that situates it in the year in which it was made, for example. Human activity is central for creating a tension with nature, but the latter almost overtakes the image. Nature's dominant but by no means menacing presence suggests that the people in the image are part of the natural world and that they move peacefully through it. The numerous tree roots that anchor the image's vertical axis to the bottom horizontally oriented portion defined by the river communicate a message of strength and depth in association with indigenous culture. Like Ocampo's, Zalce's lithographic technique was featured by Meyer in *TGP México*. The soft, round forms that characterize Zalce's print correspond with its tranquil, aesthetically pleasing content.

Elizabeth Catlett's 1947 portrayal of an ethnic and gender minority group in her image of Sojourner Truth is more defiant than Zalce's (figure 4.6).

Catlett's linocut incorporates a U.S. figure into the TGP's efforts to promote justice and equality, coinciding with the well-established global nature of the group's inclusive and resistant politics. The abolitionist and defender of women's rights gazes directly at the print's viewer while her finger points skyward, two trajectories that move beyond the frame of the image and that are represented within the frame by the juxtaposition of vertical and horizontal lines. These multidirectional dynamic elements are condensed in the figure of the cross on the book's open page. The cross supports the idea that the upraised finger is an appeal to a higher power, one that coincides with the demand to the viewer made by Truth's gaze. The viewer is thus compelled to make a religiously supported moral choice to continue Truth's struggle, perhaps, as the book implies, by learning and studying the teachings of the Bible.

The final print I analyze also uses the dynamic lines of a linocut to suggest a moral connection between earthly and transcendent forces. Méndez's *Pequeña maestra, qué grande es tu voluntad* (Little Teacher, How Great Is Your Force of Will), from 1947 (figure 4.7), was one of several prints that he made for Mexican feature films.[11]

Projected onto the big screen as backdrops for opening and closing credits, these prints achieved the grandeur of muralism while maintaining the ephemeral nature of most of the TGP's work, all the while reaching a broad audience.

525 La negra Sojourner Truth luchó por los derechos de las mujeres y los negros. Grabado, 14.5 × 22.2 cm. 1947.
Sojourner Truth fought for the rights of women as well as negroes.

FIGURE 4.6. Elizabeth Catlett, *La negra Sojourner Truth*, 1947. Linocut. Reprinted in Hannes Meyer, *TGP México: El Taller de Gráfica Popular, doce años de obra artística colectiva*, p. 66. Photograph by Ryan Long.

Hannes Meyer explains that the set of ten prints for *Río Escondido*, which includes *Pequeña maestra*, were made into a limited edition portfolio of 150 copies (*TGP México* 94). Méndez's *En nombre de Cristo* and Zalce's *Estampas de Yucatán*, among many others by several different artists, were also portfolios produced by La Estampa Mexicana. To gain a sense of the tensions that resulted from the need to balance popular art with financial stability, one might find it helpful to note, for example, that the sale price of the *Río Escondido* portfolio listed at the back of Meyer's *TGP México* is 90 pesos or US$20 (for sale abroad), significant sums well beyond the means of the populations the TGP aimed to reach and whose interests it defended.

Around the diminutive figure of a young woman, *Pequeña maestra* features the degree of precariousness, uncertainty, and vulnerability that many Mexicans of the time indeed faced. The woman's profession also places her in danger, as illustrated by Méndez's series about murdered schoolteachers from nearly a decade earlier. Her head just beneath the horizon line, the teacher at first glance appears overpowered by the bleak landscape that surrounds her. She is protected, however, by the force of history, here manifested in the tangible forms of the Mexican flag, an enormous eagle, and a man holding a spear in one hand (which, like the bayonet in Bracho's linocut, sustains a flag) and pointing toward the teacher's destination with the other. Their figures do not cast a shadow but instead illuminate a path whose predominant lightness will converge outside of the image's frame with the other lines made by white spaces in the print,

FIGURE 4.7. Leopoldo Méndez, *Pequeña maestra, ¡qué inmensa es tu voluntad!*, 1947. Linocut. Poster in the collection of the Ibero-Amerikanisches Institut, Berlin. Photograph by Ryan Long.

especially the lines that designate the horizon and those that form the cutting edge comprising the eagle's beak, the spear's point, and the man's finger. Mexico's revolutionary destiny, as in the print condemning Vargas's murder, is unrealized; but it is guaranteed by the combined efforts of individual persistence and a transcendent national project.

The collective and individual struggles, including defeats and victories, evident in Méndez's prints depicting schoolteachers help to develop a visual narrative whose hoped-for progressive movement is clearly illustrated in the contrast apparent between the first and last prints I analyze, *Deportación* and *Pequeña maestra*, respectively. The train in the former heads toward the left side of the image, whereas the teacher in the latter moves to the right, following the direction of letters on a Spanish-language page and providing a corrective to the world gone mad of the murdered schoolteacher whose hand moves toward the left. The lantern uncovers Nazi atrocities; the teacher's hand in the Vargas print is bright and strong; the path in *Pequeña maestra* cuts through the darkness. In these and other prints, denunciation coincides with a critical vision for change that defines the artist's role as essential.

In hindsight, it may seem easy to classify the TGP's politically critical art as naïve, excessively associated with Mexican state ideology, or both. On the other hand, and as this brief introduction to the TGP has aimed to show, the lasting vitality of the group's work continues in the intersections of its national and international thematics, the complexities of its individual and institutional relationships, the variety of its forms of artistic expression, and the contemporary relevance of the problems its artists addressed more than half a century ago, the urgency and severity of which the TGP's works continue to expose.[12]

NOTES

1. See Prignitz for discussions of perennial contentious issues, including the distribution of the revenue generated from sales of prints (74–78); governance (74–77); external politics, such as the TGP's political allegiances or oppositions (176); and the overall quality of the TGP's work (177, 180–81). Important to the demise of the TGP's most active period was the dispute over whether to participate in the Segunda Bienal Interamericana de Pintura, Grabado y Escultura de la Ciudad de México (Second Interamerican Biennial of Painting, Printmaking, and Sculpture of Mexico City), which some members wanted

to boycott in protest of David Alfaro Siqueiros's imprisonment in 1960. Those who opposed the boycott included Méndez and others with whom he had long aligned himself, including Mariana Yampolsky, Alberto Beltrán, and Pablo O'Higgins (179–81). See also Caplow for detailed histories of disputes about pricing, in 1940 (*Leopoldo Méndez* 157–58), and governance, in 1950 (*Leopoldo Méndez* 221–22).

2. See Caplow for a summary of Siqueiros's critique of the TGP (*Leopoldo Méndez* 156–57).
3. See Reyes Palma for a useful summary of the tensions between artists and the government in the decades following the Revolution.
4. For histories of the LEAR and the political issues that shaped its trajectory, see also Prignitz-Poda ("Liga"); Reyes Palma (31–32); Wechsler ("*Propaganda Gráfica*" 64–68); and Caplow (*Leopoldo Méndez* 121–22). As is the case with the quotation from Prignitz-Poda, all translations from the Spanish are mine unless otherwise noted.
5. Richards places the end of the TGP's political vitality a decade earlier, in 1950, arguing that the postrevolutionary government's shift to the right in the 1940s and the TGP's increasing emphasis on marketability and fine art prints worked together to dilute the political edge that had characterized the TGP's work (1–4, 210–17). In her biographical study of Leopoldo Méndez, Deborah Caplow provides a detailed account of the personal and political factors that led to Méndez's gradual withdrawal from the TGP in the 1950s and the subsequent dissolution of the group as it had previously existed (221–30). Prignitz provides valuable insight into the TGP's entire trajectory, including the decades following Méndez's departure. Particularly interesting is her discussion of how the TGP failed to maintain a politically critical position in the 1960s and 1970s (198–211). Wechsler's terse conclusion, from 2007, is notable, and in line with Richards's assessment: "Although it continues to operate to this day, the TGP's first ten years remain its most vital" ("*Propaganda Gráfica*" 76).
6. This is Kay B. Adams's translation, which appears side by side with the Spanish in Meyer's book. In this essay all translations into English from Meyer's 1949 book are Adams's.
7. To the best of my knowledge, Prignitz's book remains the most comprehensive account of the TGP. Its list of members also includes brief bibliographies and catalogs of individual artists' prints (279–304).
8. During his time with the TGP, from 1945 to 1947 (Prignitz 303), White produced a lithograph titled *Black Sorrow* (1946), evidence of his work with

African American themes. Catlett's *Sharecropper* (1952) is a linocut portrayal of African American life as well. I discuss a different print by Catlett in greater detail elsewhere in this chapter.

9. See Merfish for a discussion of the TGP's satirical work.
10. A blogger whose screen name is "acrisort" makes this observation in an interesting analysis of the print. See http://acrisort.blogspot.com/2012/09/una-mirada-cercana-en-nombre-de-cristo.html.
11. See Caplow for an overview of Méndez's work for filmmakers (*Leopoldo Méndez* 203–4).
12. For a thorough and detailed history of the TGP, Helga Prignitz's book *El Taller de Gráfica Popular en México, 1937–1977* (1992) is especially useful. Deborah Caplow's book *Leopoldo Méndez: Revolutionary Art and the Mexican Print* (2007) is outstanding for its presentation of Méndez and the context that shaped him as well as for its beautiful reproductions of significant prints. Hannes Meyer's album is important for its author's first-hand knowledge of the TGP's members and their work, as well as for its emphasis on theme, format, and design. It is titled *TGP México: El Taller de Gráfica Popular, doce años de obra artística colectiva/TGP México: The Workshop for Popular Graphic Art, a Record of Twelve Years of Collective Work* (1949). The webpage of the Los Angeles County Museum of Art has a good collection of TGP prints at https://collections.lacma.org/node/580931. The site accompanies its fine reproductions with specific information about each print, including artist, medium, date, and dimensions.

WORKS CITED

Adès, Dawn. "The Mexican Printmaking Tradition c. 1900–1930." *Revolution on Paper: Mexican Prints, 1910–1960*, edited by Mark McDonald, University of Texas Press, 2009, pp. 11–25.

Caplow, Deborah. *Leopoldo Méndez: Revolutionary Art and the Mexican Print*. University of Texas Press, 2007.

———. "Un asesinato/A Murder." Translated by Pilar Villela. *Gritos desde el archivo: Grabado político del Taller de Gráfica Popular, Colección Academia de Artes/Shouts from the Archive: Political Prints from the Taller de Gráfica Popular, the Academia de Artes Collection*, edited by Pilar García de Germenos and James Oles, UNAM, 2008, pp. 153–54.

Castro Leal, Antonio, et al., editors. *El libro negro del terror nazi en Europa*. Editorial "El libro libre," 1943.

Knight, Alan. *The Mexican Revolution*, vol. 2, *Counter-revolution and Reconstruction*. University of Nebraska Press, 1986.

McClean, Alison. "Committed to Print: Printmaking and Politics in Mexico and Beyond, 1934–1960." *Revolution on Paper: Mexican Prints, 1910–1960*, edited by Mark McDonald, University of Texas Press, 2009, pp. 27–42.

Merfish, Beth. "Caricatura/Caricature." Translated by Pilar Villela. In Pilar García de Germenos and James Oles, eds. *Gritos desde el archivo: Grabado político del Taller de Gráfica Popular, Colección Academia de Artes/Shouts from the Archive: Political Prints from the Taller de Gráfica Popular, the Academia de Artes Collection*, edited by Pilar García de Germenos and James Oles, UNAM, 2008, pp. 71–81.

Meyer, Hannes, editor. *TGP México: El Taller de Gráfica Popular, doce años de obra artística colectiva/TGP México: The Workshop for Popular Graphic Art, a Record of Twelve Years of Collective Work*. Translated by Kay B. Adams and M. D. de Berdecio, La Estampa Mexicana, 1949.

———. "El Taller de Gráfica Popular/Workshop for Popular Art in Mexico/Die Werkstatt für graphische Volkskunst in Mexico/L'atelier d'art graphique populaire de Mexico." *Graphis*, vol. 6, no. 30, 1950, pp. 156–63.

Meyer, Lorenzo. "El primer tramo del camino." *Historia general de México*, edited by El Colegio de México, vol. 2. El Colegio de México, 1976, pp. 1183–271.

Prignitz, Helga. *El Taller de Gráfica Popular en México, 1937–1977*. Translated by Elizabeth Siefer, Instituto Nacional de Bellas Artes, 1992.

Prignitz-Poda, Helga. "Liga de Escritores y Artistas Revolucionarios (LEAR)." *México ilustrado: Libros, revistas y carteles, 1920–1950*, edited by Salvador Albiñana, Editorial RM, 2010, pp. 252–53.

———. "Taller de Gráfica Popular (TGP)." *México ilustrado: Libros, revistas y carteles, 1920–1950*, edited by Salvador Albiñana, Editorial RM, 2010, p. 260.

Reyes Palma, Francisco. "Utopías del desencanto/Utopias of Disenchantment." Translated by James Oles and Pilar Villela. *Gritos desde el archivo: Grabado político del Taller de Gráfica Popular, Colección Academia de Artes/Shouts from the Archive: Political Prints from the Taller de Gráfica Popular, the Academia de Artes Collection*, edited by Pilar García de Germenos and James Oles, UNAM, 2008, pp. 27–37.

Richards, Susan Valerie. *Imaging the Political: El Taller de Gráfica Popular in Mexico, 1937–1949*. Dissertation, University of New Mexico, 2001. UMI, 2001.

Taller de Gráfica Popular. "Estatutos/Introduction." Translated by James Oles and Pilar Villela. *Gritos desde el archivo: Grabado político del Taller de Gráfica Popular,*

Colección Academia de Artes/ Shouts from the Archive: Political Prints from the Taller de Gráfica Popular, the Academia de Artes Collection, edited by Pilar García de Germenos and James Oles, UNAM, 2008, pp. 22–25.

Wechsler, James M. "*Propaganda Gráfica*: Printmaking and the Radical Left in Mexico, 1920–1950." *Mexico and Modern Printmaking: A Revolution in Graphic Arts, 1920 to 1950*, edited by John Ittman, Yale University Press, 2006, pp. 55–77.

———. "Taller de Gráfica Popular: The Life and Drama of Mexico." *Mexico and Modern Printmaking: A Revolution in Graphic Arts, 1920 to 1950*, edited by John Ittman, Yale University Press, 2006, pp. 208–23.

5

TEACHERS

Educating Cohesion: The Teacher as an Agent of the Postrevolutionary State

DAVID S. DALTON

PRIMARY MATERIALS:

- *La raza cósmica* (The Cosmic Race) by José Vasconcelos (essay, 1925)
- *Alfabetización: Aprendiendo a leer* (Literacy: Learning to Read) by Diego Rivera (mural, 1928)
- *La maestra rural* (The Rural Teacher) by Diego Rivera (mural, 1932)
- *Río Escondido* (Hidden River), directed by Emilio Fernández (film, 1947)
- *Maclovia*, directed by Emilio Fernández (film, 1948)
- *Salón México*, directed by Emilio Fernández (film, 1949)
- *Los olvidados* (The Young and the Damned), directed by Luis Buñuel (film, 1950)
- "Final alterno de *Los olvidados*" (Alternate Ending to *The Young and the Damned*) (video, available on YouTube)
- "Luvina," in *El llano en llamas* (The Burning Plain) by Juan Rulfo (short story, 1953)

IN 1921, JOSÉ VASCONCELOS ACCEPTED THE POSITION of *secretario de educación pública* (secretary of public education). One of the leader's first actions in this capacity was to fund ways—both in the classroom and through state-sponsored art—to inculcate *mexicanidad* in the masses.[1] The politician had long believed that the state needed to educate its Amerindian population in the ways of European society and aesthetics. Indeed, his seminal essay *La raza cósmica* (The Cosmic Race, 1925) asserts that because Mexico's pervasive "fealdad" (ugliness) results from indigenous ignorance, the country can beautify itself only through a robust education program (26–27). This belief colored how he executed the Misiones Culturales (Cultural Missions)—one of the most long-lasting legacies of his tenure—which sent "apostles of culture" to rural areas in hopes that they would civilize the country (Lewis 180–82; Palou 16–22). The most celebrated actors of the Cultural Missions were rural teachers, whom the state charged with redeeming Amerindians, women, and children by incorporating them into the mestizo state (Benjamin 479).[2] Art funded by the Secretaría de Educación Pública (Secretariat of Public Education), or SEP, celebrated Vasconcelos's Cultural Missions by deifying teachers. But as the twentieth century progressed and social problems persisted, artists began to take a more critical approach to the Cultural Missions and particularly to teachers and education. As I show in this chapter, throughout the last century—and even to the present—artistic representations of teachers served as excellent barometers for gauging popular sentiments toward the governing regime.

The connection between educators and the state was no mistake; teachers sat at the core of government-funded modernizing missions, particularly as they "assimilated" indigenous children in rural and urban settings. Given their desire to transform Mexican society, teachers often found themselves at odds with entrenched structures of power, especially local *caciquismo* (Kapelusz-Poppi 35–38).[3] The teachers' (mythic) steadfastness in the face of great personal danger cemented their position as national heroes within the popular imaginary until at least the 1940s. This rings clear in two murals that Diego Rivera painted in the SEP offices at the request of Vasconcelos: *La maestra rural* (The Rural Teacher) and *Alfabetización: Aprendiendo a leer* (Literacy: Learning to Read). *La maestra rural* shows a woman surrounded by children in the desert while a revolutionary soldier on horseback keeps watch in the distance. She may not participate militarily in the Revolution, but as she sits unarmed next to the nation's children, she risks her life as much as any soldier. Rivera furthers the ties between teachers and soldiers in *Alfabetización*, in which a teacher gives books to both children and soldiers. The message of these murals rings clear: armed peasants may have overthrown Porfirio Díaz and Victoriano Huerta, but schoolteachers will ultimately rebuild the nation by educating the people into a cohesive national identity and assimilating even the nation's military heroes.[4]

Similar ideas appeared in state-sponsored cultural production during the subsequent decades, but no artist promulgated official discourses more effectively than Emilio "El Indio" Fernández, a film director who used the silver screen as a "celluloid school" (Tuñón 466–68). Numerous critics have written about how the director—along with his cinematographer, Gabriel Figueroa—employed filmic techniques to inculcate nationalistic discourses in their audience (Ramírez Berg 15–17; Mraz 107–8),[5] but El Indio's support of the Cultural Missions has received markedly less attention. Fernández revered rural teachers and medics, but he ultimately exalted educators as the greatest actors of the state. In *Río Escondido* (Hidden River, 1947), for example, a medical doctor admits his unworthiness to teach and states that "para ser maestro hay que tener manera de santo" (in order to be a teacher you have to be like a saint).

For Fernández, teachers are secular saints who intercede in the lives of their (indigenous) students (Dalton, "Embodying Modernity" 109–33; Hershfield, *Mexican Cinema* 70). His films were often paternalistic; as Joanne Hershfield notes, El Indio's cinema viewed Amerindians as children whom the state must coerce toward modernity and redemption ("Screening" 268–69). Within the discursive framework of his films, teachers have to show their indigenous pupils the shortcomings of their "primitive" cultures and help them to attain modernity. This is especially clear in *Maclovia* (1948), which tells the story of José María, an illiterate indigenous fisherman, who deeply loves Maclovia, the daughter of Tata Macario, mayor of Janitzio. Because of José María's poverty and ignorance, Tata Macario refuses to approve of their romance, threatening instead to kill his daughter if the two so much as look at each other. José María decides to attend school with the local children so that he can learn to write love letters and correspond with Maclovia without being seen. The teacher, don Justo, is strict at first, but as his name implies, he is ultimately fair. He takes a liking to José María and helps him write a letter to Maclovia. When she receives it, the young woman begs don Justo to teach her to read. While the focus of this film is the romance between the protagonists, the teacher sits in the background as the catalyzing force that brings them together.

Beyond facilitating the lovers' communication, don Justo also molds them into worthy partners for each other; reading and writing become a means by which they can circumvent "backward" traditions and participate in modern Mexico. Throughout the film, Janitzio represents indigenous communities that supposedly resist statist understandings of modern society. The film reinforces this reading by showing that José María becomes a suitable mate only after learning to read and thus assimilating to the mestizo state. Unlike a traditional foundational fiction, where two lovers from different social strata consummate their love and thus allegorically reconcile different segments of the population (Sommer 30–51), José María and Maclovia are both indigenous. They become ideal suitors as they transcend their indigeneity and internalize the values of the state. This fact underscores don Justo's central role in transforming them into compatible spouses.

The teacher serves as a liaison not only between the lovelorn but between the local community and state actors. Early in the film, a group of soldiers comes to the island and requests to speak with the local priest, Tata Macario, and don Justo. Ironically, it is not the religious leader but the teacher who facilitates communication between the mayor and the military leaders. For example, he tells the commanding officer of Janitzio's strange custom that forbids locals from leaving the island or marrying "fuereños" (outsiders). As the teacher helps two segments of Mexican culture to better understand each other, he becomes a conciliatory, uniting agent between them. Not all state actors are as benevolent as the teacher; one of the soldiers, Sergeant Genovevo de la Garza, takes a liking to Maclovia and attempts to take her for himself, despite local traditions that forbid such actions. The sergeant justifies his disrespect for indigenous peoples and cultures by asserting the privilege that his clear eyes—which signal him as mestizo—give him. Noting de la Garza's intentions, don Justo approaches Tata Macario and requests Maclovia's hand for José María. This scene is essential to asserting the teacher, rather than the military, as the soul of the postrevolutionary state. Certainly, Fernández advocates the assimilation of the Amerindian to the mestizo state, but he also decries the superiority complex of many soldiers of European descent. When the circumstances arise, don Justo must defend indigenous people from corrupt officials who disregard the values of the postrevolutionary state that they supposedly represent.

While one component of don Justo's work is to temper the prejudice of state officials like de la Garza, his primary concern is to counteract indigenous "primitivity." One of the best ways for him to do this is by convincing local residents to leave Janitzio and interact with the rest of the country. He achieves this goal with his prized students at the end of the movie, when José María and Maclovia are forced to leave town after an altercation with de la Garza. The sergeant continues to accost Maclovia even after she marries José María; her newlywed husband hits the sergeant and is sentenced to death. Maclovia agrees to be the sergeant's mistress if he will spare José María's life. Luckily, José María escapes before his execution, and he flees the island with Maclovia, killing de la Garza in the process. They cannot return home because the locals will stone Maclovia to death for consenting to a marriage with a *fuereño*, so the couple must leave Janitzio behind.

The lovers' education plays a key role in their resistance to local customs. Maclovia's decision to give herself to de la Garza in exchange for José María's life certainly reflects her love, but it also demonstrates that she no longer views Janitzio's marriage laws as legitimate. José María demonstrates similar growth when he accepts Maclovia's decision to live with de la Garza (a decision that would have saved his life) where the rest of the town would not. Of course, beyond overcoming their supposedly essentialistic "primitivity," they have also stood against mestizo/criollo racism and affirmed the potential of indigenous Mexico. Don Justo does not figure prominently in this section of the film, but his influence lingers in the background. His lessons have helped the characters to see through the injustices of local customs and to give them the confidence to confront discrimination against their people. As the film comes to an end, the two characters have embarked on a journey that will presumably take them to a more modern—and perhaps urban—part of the country, where they will contribute economically, culturally, and spiritually to their nation.

Maclovia optimistically proclaims the feasibility of assimilating indigenous Mexico to the state, but national art began appraising education efforts more harshly by 1950. Whereas Fernández's film celebrates the incorporation of indigenous actors to the state, the cultural production of the following decade charged local and national leaders with ignoring those people who migrated to urban areas. Luis Buñuel, an exiled Spanish film director, was especially dissatisfied with the official narratives propagated in state-sponsored film (Acevedo-Muñoz 58). As such, it is of no surprise that his masterpiece *Los olvidados* (The Young and the Damned, 1950) is one of the most canonical works to question officialist discourses surrounding postrevolutionary schools. The director certainly does not view education as negative per se, but he draws attention to state failures to educate Mexican youth. At its core *Los olvidados* is about urban violence and crime, but a key subtext is that delinquency is the result of rampant hopelessness among the poor.

Unlike its state-sponsored artistic forebears, which generally held modernity to be a positive ideal toward which Mexico should aspire, the film begins with several shots panning across major metropolitan areas throughout the world before ending in Mexico City's Zócalo. During these shots, a dubbed voice states:

> Las grandes ciudades modernas, Nueva York, París, Londres, esconden tras sus magníficos edificios hogares de miseria que albergan niños malnutridos sin higiene; sin escuela; semillero de futuros delincuentes. [. . .] Sólo en un futuro próximo podrán ser reivindicados los derechos del niño y del adolescente para que sean útiles a la sociedad. México, la gran ciudad moderna, no es excepción a esta regla universal. Por eso esta película, basada en hechos de la vida real, no es optimista, y deja la solución del problema a las fuerzas progresivas de la sociedad.
>
> Behind the magnificent buildings of modern major cities like New York, Paris, and London hide poverty-stricken homes that harbor malnourished, unhygienic children; uneducated; a breeding ground of future criminals. . . . Only in the near future the rights of children and adolescents will be respected, so they can be useful to society. Mexico City, the large modern city, is not an exception to this universal rule. That is why this film, based on real events, is not optimistic, and it leaves the solution of the problem to society's progressive forces.

According to this statement, Mexico has perhaps been too successful in its emulation of the great modern cities of Europe and North America.[6] The imposition of modernity has produced delinquency and inequality in Mexico City and other urban centers, both at home and abroad.

Even as he distances himself from the modernizing discourses that have produced disastrous social consequences, Buñuel returns to the same language as his ideological opponents. The problem—at least as framed in this preamble—is not social injustice or the marginalization of the urban poor; instead it is the delinquency that these situations create. Rather than couch his critique in terms of a more equitable future with greater upward mobility—which would emphasize the living conditions of urban youth—the narrator invokes a possible future in which the "forgotten" young people of the world can be "useful" to society. Far from invoking a moral imperative to provide greater opportunities for the poor, Buñuel employs a pragmatic argument, saying that the state needs to help the poor out of self-interest. Because education is the most effective way for the state to intervene in the behavior and attitudes of its youth, it stands to reason that "progressive forces" must ultimately reshape society in the classroom. Yet one of the underlying themes of the film is the incompetence of educators' attempts to reform and educate at-risk children and adolescents.

The movie begins as El Jaibo—a criminal in his late teens—escapes from the *escuela correccional* (reformatory school) and reunites with members of his street gang. One of these is Pedro, a young boy of between eleven and thirteen years, who has recently adopted a life on the streets. The duo engages in all kinds of criminal mischief, and at one point Pedro witnesses El Jaibo murder Julián, the person who allegedly turned him in to the police a year earlier. After this, Pedro decides to reform and finds work at a blacksmith shop; however, El Jaibo stops by, steals a knife, and frames Pedro, who is later sent to an agrarian correctional school. Access to education plays a key role within the film's positive and negative spaces. It is ironic that neither Pedro nor El Jaibo attend school until after they are arrested, a fact that leads them to equate the classroom with prison. The ideal of an education proves so elusive that even when he decides to live within the law, Pedro must do so by finding work in a low-skill position. This makes him more vulnerable than he would be if he were in school; had Pedro been in class, he never would have been in a situation where El Jaibo could frame him. Buñuel, then, holds the state accountable for the violence plaguing mid-twentieth-century urban centers because it fails to provide poor youth with the necessary tools and opportunities for creating a better future for themselves. Instead, it forces them to negotiate life in the urban jungle on their own. Of course, *Los olvidados* did not achieve its canonical status by parroting an official line that prescribed more schools to resolve the problems facing Mexico. Beyond decrying the lack of educational options for children in postrevolutionary society, Buñuel also asserts that the schools that do exist are ill equipped to help young people overcome the struggles they face on a daily basis.

Pedro's inability to attend school creates the conditions necessary for his unjust arrest; afterward, his experience at an incompetent correctional education facility culminates in his murder. When he arrives, two male teachers say that they can teach him how to read, write, and contribute to the economy. Pedro never speaks except to deny that he stole the knife; nevertheless, the teachers soon decide to teach him how to raise animals. It would be imprecise to interpret these men as "bad"; however, their paternalistic attitude toward Pedro blinds them to the very real threats that he faces every day. In one scene, for example, Pedro steals eggs from the school and hurls one toward the camera; it explodes on the lens. According to Pedro Poyato, Buñuel uses this scene to transform his viewers into objects—rather than mere witnesses—of violence (177–78). I would further extend his argument and suggest that this sequence creates a type of (filmic) Brechtian distancing as it draws attention to the movie's performed nature, which in turn opens up both the film and the society it represents to greater scrutiny. As he accentuates the constructed nature of his movie, Buñuel draws attention to an equally artificial performance within some schools. This filmic means of critiquing state institutions becomes especially noteworthy because this scene catalyzes the events that lead to Pedro's climactic murder.

When the director of the school learns of Pedro's thievery, he decides not to punish him but to give him fifty pesos with the charge to buy cigars at a nearby store. Pedro leaves, and at this moment El Jaibo finds him and steals the money. Pedro later tracks El Jaibo to his home and attempts to kill him; however, El Jaibo beats Pedro to death. What is perhaps most tragic about the film is that the school fails its charge to provide Pedro a safe education. By ignoring the dangers lurking just outside of his school's doors, the principal effectively sends Pedro to his death. The film's greatest commentary on education is not that the government fails to provide schools for its students but that the school system as currently constituted is incapable of dealing with the realities of urban life. Viewed in this light, simply hiring more teachers and building more schools will not suffice; the state will have to do a better job of training those people with whom it entrusts its youth.

Buñuel and his collaborators certainly recognized the extent to which their work challenged state doctrines. As Víctor Fuentes notes, "Aquí no se restablece ningún orden, divino o humano" (Here no order is reestablished, divine or human) (104–6). Indeed, the movie's lack of (happy) resolution makes its bleak outlook so powerful and subversive that Buñuel and his financiers, particularly Oscar Dancigers (Acevedo-Muñoz 74), feared the film would never make it past the censors. In an effort to avoid losing all of their production costs if the movie was banned, the director filmed an alternate ending in which Pedro kills El Jaibo before returning to school. This version concludes with a low-angle shot that captures the boy as he enters the arched doorway of the school while triumphant nondiegetic music plays in the background. The alternative ending consists of only two minutes of footage, but it completely alters the film's discourse. Rather than critiquing state actors who fail to understand the realities of life in the ghetto, it trumpets state schools and correctional facilities as the only places capable of redeeming lost urban youth. In this way, it echoes the sentiment of films—such as those of Emilio Fernández—in which the state overcomes serious problems through quality teachers. The alternate ending was filmed so that

Buñuel would be able to show the movie even if the censors refused to permit the original version. In order to ensure this version's approval, the scene would have to counteract the overriding discourse that pervaded the rest of the film. As such, this apocryphal ending provides great insights into Buñuel's own mind, not because it reflects his ideals, but because it shows just the opposite. In signaling the school as the savior of Mexican youth in the closing frame of his alternate ending, Buñuel reminds the viewers that as currently constituted, the opposite is actually the case. Incompetent teachers have disseminated official doctrines in a top-down fashion for decades, but they will not be able to reach urban (or rural) youth until they take into account the feedback of their pupils.

Midcentury critiques of education at times discussed urban schools,[7] but most artists focused on rural schools.[8] Of all of the texts discussing rural teachers, perhaps none is more masterfully crafted than Juan Rulfo's 1953 short story "Luvina."[9] One of the most canonical stories to be published during the twentieth century in Mexico,[10] the plot centers on a conversation in a bar between a disillusioned *maestro rural* (rural teacher) and his recent replacement, Camilo. Throughout the story, the former teacher tells Camilo of the difficulties inherent to life in San Juan Luvina, which is the epitome of rural "primitivity." Front and center in the story is the notion that, despite their initial (admittedly paternalistic) excitement and commitment to improving the lives of their rural and indigenous countrypeople,[11] rural teachers lose heart when conditions are not as they imagined. Luvina is a dry, dead space where the lack of water and shelter makes life almost unbearable for the locals. Ultimately, Rulfo paints a picture of two entities—the civilizing forces from the urban center and those from the rural periphery—who are incapable of communicating with or even understanding each other. Much of the town's struggles stem from its institutionalized relegation to the national periphery. This fact suggests that despite national rhetoric to the contrary, it would go against the interests of those in power to incorporate Luvina into the mestizo state.

Incomplete state attempts to export modernity have torn Luvina apart. Men leave the town for years at a time to find work, and they return just frequently enough to bring food and supplies and impregnate their wives before once again leaving. Although it is never mentioned in the text, this economic system—which the residents refer to as "la ley" (the law) (107)—is a direct result of modernization and urbanization. Unlike *Maclovia*, which celebrates indigenous emigration from their "backward" communities, "Luvina" shows the devastating effects of mass migration on rural communities both socially and economically. The promise of modernity, which rural teachers preached in their classrooms, played an integral role in further isolating towns like Luvina. As millions of rural peasants migrated to urban centers like Mexico City (Dion 76), they bought into a narrative positing that Mexican citizens like themselves would enjoy the spoils of modernity if they assimilated to the modern economy. However, while cities grew exponentially, small towns like the fictional Luvina remained on the periphery, unable to participate in the macroeconomic achievements of the state.

Beyond being cut off from the national economy, Luvina also loses all of its male workforce. The town is cut off from both the past (the men no longer carry out the functions of their forefathers) and the future (a town whose children grow up only so that they can leave has nothing to look forward to). One of the retired teacher's harshest critiques occurs at the beginning of the story when he states that Luvina "está plagado de esta piedra gris con la que hacen la cal, pero en Luvina no hacen cal con ella ni le sacan ningún provecho" (Luvina is infested with that gray stone they make lime from, but in Luvina they don't make lime from it nor do they make any good out of it) (99). Camilo's critique reflects the capitalistic view that the environment is a natural resource for the people to exploit. In failing to mine the lime near their homes—a process that could be hazardous to people's health—the town has not upheld the postrevolutionary state's capitalistic values. Rather than live the traditional (read: backward) lifestyle that they have inherited from their forebears, the state would prefer that they mine and export their resources. Of course, because all young men leave town upon reaching the age of fifteen, Luvina lacks the workforce necessary for extracting the rock.

Cal, or lime, carries a paradoxical allegorical weight within Mexico. On the one hand, it is an agent of death; people use it to kill germs and insects, and if handled improperly, it can kill people as well. On the other hand, people use it to grind corn and make tortillas, the basis of most diets. These ties to both life and death make *cal* into a perfect metaphor for the fictitious Luvina and the numerous real communities on which it is based. As a faraway town in a rapidly industrializing nation, Luvina has become a site of contradictions, a city that is neither fully alive nor completely dead. It is perhaps this fact that leads the former teacher to classify the town as a purgatory existing between redemption and perdition. Of course, his previous function as an educator has made him (perhaps unwittingly) part of the machinery that has produced miserable conditions in Luvina. In one of the more comical segments of the story,

Rulfo offers a biting criticism of government failures to provide necessary infrastructure for the town to progress. The former teacher tells of a time when, exasperated with Luvina's perpetual poverty, he stood before the inhabitants and begged them to move somewhere better, promising them that the government would help them in their endeavors. But the people simply responded that "el gobierno no [tiene] madre" (the government is a son of a bitch) (108). This vulgar banter underscores the failures of the state to gain the confidence of the rural indigenous masses. As Lanin A. Gyurko notes, in this town, "social institutions have all but vanished" (462). The conditions in Luvina, then, ultimately reflect the government's lack of investment in rural communities. As such, it is not surprising that the people of Luvina view any action by the postrevolutionary state with contempt. Their suspicion of authority leads them to view the *maestro rural* not as a well-intentioned champion of the masses but as an out-of-touch bureaucrat who has no true interest in their community. This lack of trust ultimately results in even the school ceasing to function as a social institution, which facilitates Luvina's further relegation to the periphery.

Despite Rulfo's recognition that failed government policies have contributed heavily to the conditions in the community, he also criticizes certain mentalities within Luvina—and, by extension, other rural sectors in the country—that further isolate peripheral Mexican communities. Beyond questioning the state's ability to help them leave their town, the residents ask, "Si nosotros nos vamos, ¿quién se llevará a nuestros muertos? Ellos viven aquí, y no podemos dejarlos solos" (If we leave, who will take our dead? They live here, and we cannot leave them alone) (108). This question draws attention to the fact that, beyond the government's failures to help the rural population, there are also numerous structural factors that keep people tethered to where they live despite poor living conditions. As the case of Luvina shows, these traditions are especially limiting to women and the elderly; men leave town in search of work at a young age, but tradition dictates that their wives and parents stay behind to remember the dead. This focus on the past is irreconcilable with the postrevolutionary values of progress, yet it shapes the agency of rural Mexicans in very real ways. Viewed in this light, state-sponsored education has spawned two contradictory tendencies that, if fully observed, will necessarily tear the town apart. On the one hand, the rapidly modernizing state entices young males into leaving town in search of gainful employment. On the other hand, the need to hold on to the town's roots has made it so that nobody, especially women, children, and the elderly, can leave town. The resulting fractures within families, communities, and the town are the leading cause of Luvina's purgatorial condition.

From an officialist perspective, rural teachers should facilitate their students' assimilation to the modern economy by encouraging them to migrate to urban centers. Amit Thakkar, for example, views the teacher as a "colonizing" actor who somewhat paradoxically attempts to share the "Divine Light" of the secular state with rural Mexico (75–76). Yet an overriding theme throughout the story is the teacher's inability to fully colonize the town. Rather than convert the people to the state's future-oriented notions of progress, he ultimately retreats to a bar several miles outside of town. As he does so, the residents lose their only (admittedly tenuous) tie to the state; more importantly, they can no longer enjoy the benefits of an education or contribute economically to the nation. Beyond simply failing in his endeavors, the retired teacher now stays at the bar, where he demoralizes new teachers before they set foot in the town. If, as he suggests, Luvina is purgatory, then it is at least partially the teacher's doing. His failure to reach the town's inhabitants—and his eventual decision to give up—has done nothing to curb the town's fragmentation. His conversation with Camilo in the bar embodies the incompetence of the government as his own words serve to prejudice the replacement's attitudes regarding the town before he arrives. Clearly, the teacher, rather than serving as a redemptive agent of the state, is a tired, beaten figure whose minimal contributions to postrevolutionary society are at best inconsequential and at worst counterproductive.

The teacher remains a central figure within Rulfo's story, yet his representation differs greatly from that of the more propagandistic works of the decades immediately following the Revolution. What began as a proclamation of the state's goodwill has gradually become a discussion of state failures in providing its youth with the quality education they deserve.[12] A focus on the artistic representation of education—and particularly of teachers—in Mexico is especially useful in creating courses, because it is a theme that connects a wide array of literary and cultural production. Furthermore, the subject matter is approachable for young students in the United States because it allows them to build on their own experiences in the classroom. As we view the representations and critiques of education within Mexico, we are able to identify the overriding sentiments toward the state that abounded during a specific time and place. This in turn can help Mexico enthusiasts—be they students, teachers, or scholars—to gain a deeper understanding of the political attitudes in the nation during particular moments in its history.[13]

NOTES

1. At its core, *mexicanidad* refers to an ideology that fetishizes modernity while celebrating Mexican cultural heritage. See Gilbert M. Joseph and Timothy J. Henderson (9).
2. Beyond its overt allusions to race, the mestizo state was ultimately a state-sponsored construction that conflated racial hybridity with economic and technical modernity. See Joshua Lund (x–xi).
3. See Rodolfo Usigli's *El gesticulador* (The Impostor) for a theatrical take on the dangers facing idealistic teachers.
4. Ruben Flores' 2014 book *Backroad Pragmatists: Mexico's Melting Pot and Civil Rights in the United States* asserts that Mexican educators were highly successful in assimilating diverse segments of the population. Their success was so great that U.S. civil rights leaders used them as a model for their own work.
5. Dolores Tierney observes that the academy has been uncritical of the relationship between Fernández and the state, thus ignoring many of the breeches between his own thought and that of postrevolutionary leaders (2–3). This is not to say that Fernández did not engage concepts of *mexicanidad*; instead, it means that Fernández's views were not always synonymous with those of the state.
6. Ernesto Acevedo-Muñoz notes that the film was originally received as an affront to Mexico, and it gained prestige only after enjoying a great deal of success in Europe (57–58).
7. See, for example, José Emilio Pacheco's 1981 novel *Las batallas en el desierto* (Battles in the Desert). Another great text is Gustavo Sáinz's *Gazapo* (1968), a countercultural novel about young school-age children in 1960s Mexico.
8. The academy has already recognized that Elena Garro's play *La dama boba* (A Lady of Little Sense, 1968) uses metatheater to criticize the paternalistic nature of the Misiones Culturales (Cultural Missions); see Lisenby (15). In a previous article, I have noted that Rosario Castellanos's *Balún Canán* shows a Comitán in which the quality of a person's education depends on the combination of race, gender, and heritage; see Dalton ("Educating").
9. Nahum Megged lauds the story's "profundidad y perfección" (depth and perfection) (103).
10. Many critics have asserted clear ties between "Luvina" and Rulfo's masterpiece, *Pedro Páramo* (Jiménez de Baez 946; Kulin 351–57; Gyurko 461–62). The

similarities between the works makes "Luvina" an especially appropriate text for undergraduate students.

11. While there is no explicit reference to the indigeneity of the town, critics like Megged have painstakingly signaled numerous elements of indigenous culture woven throughout the work (103–5).
12. As evidenced by Juan Carlos Rulfo's documentary *De panzazo* (Scraping By) (2012)—which offers strong criticisms of the state of education in the early twenty-first century—the role of education continues to be a central theme in Mexican art.
13. For further reading I strongly advise instructors to assign Thomas Benjamin's "Rebuilding the Nation" alongside an abridged reading of *La raza cósmica*. The aforementioned book chapter frames education as a means for incorporating women, children, and Amerindians into the nation-state. This framework will allow students to see how constructs of race and gender interfaced one with another in postrevolutionary projects of education.

WORKS CITED

Acevedo-Muñoz, Ernesto R. *Buñuel and Mexico: The Crisis of National Cinema*. University of California Press, 2003.

Benjamin, Thomas. "Rebuilding the Nation." *The Oxford History of Mexico*, edited by Michael C. Meyer and William H. Beezley, Oxford University Press, 2000, pp. 467–502.

Buñuel, Luis, director. *Los olvidados*. Performances by Alfonso Mejía, Roberto Cobo, and Estela Inda. Ultramar Films, 1950.

Castellanos, Rosario. *Balún Canán*. 1957. FCE, 2007.

Coffey, Mary K. *How a Revolutionary Art Became Official Culture: Murals, Museums, and the Mexican State*. Duke University Press, 2012.

Dalton, David S. "Educating Social Hierarchies in Rosario Castellanos's *Balún Canán*." *Chasqui: Revista de Literatura Latinoamericana*, vol. 43, no. 2, 2014, 150–60.

———. *Embodying Modernity in Mexico: Race, Technology, and the Body in the* Mestizo *State*. Dissertation, University of Kansas, 2015.

Dion, Michelle. *Workers and Welfare: Comparative Institutional Change in Twentieth-Century Mexico*. University of Pittsburgh Press, 2010.

Flores, Ruben. *Backroad Pragmatists: Mexico's Melting Pot and Civil Rights in the United States*. University of Pennsylvania Press, 2014.

Fuentes, Víctor. *Buñuel en México: Iluminaciones sobre una pantalla pobre*. Instituto de Estudios Turolenses, 1994.

Garro, Elena. *La dama boba*. 1968. *Un hogar sólido, y otras piezas* by Elena Garro, Press de la University Veracruzana, 1983, pp. 175–246.

Gyurko, Lanin A. "Rulfo's Aesthetic Nihilism: Narrative Antecedents of *Pedro Páramo*." *Hispanic Review*, vol. 40, no. 4, 1972, 451–66.

Hershfield, Joanne. *Mexican Cinema/Mexican Woman, 1940–1950*. University of Arizona Press, 1996.

———. "Screening the Nation." *The Eagle and the Virgin: Nation and Cultural Revolution in Mexico, 1920–1940*, edited by Mary Kay Vaughan and Stephen E. Lewis, Duke University Press, 2006, pp. 259–78.

Jiménez de Baez, Yvette. "Juan Rulfo: De la escritura al sentido." *Revista Iberoamericana*, vol. 55, 1989, 937–52.

Joseph, Gilbert M., and Timothy J. Henderson. "The Search for 'Lo mexicano.'" *The Mexico Reader: History, Culture, Politics*, edited by Gilbert M. Joseph and Timothy J. Henderson, Duke University Press, 2002, pp. 9–10.

Kapelusz-Poppi, Ana María. "Physician Activists and Development of Rural Health in Postrevolutionary Mexico." *Radical History Review*, vol. 80, 2001, pp. 35–50.

Kulin, Katalin. "Luvina y Comala: Dos caras de la misma realidad." *Acta Litteraria Academiae Scientiarum Hungaricae*, vol. 23, nos. 3–4, 1981, 351–57.

Lewis, Stephen E. "The Nation, Education, and the 'Indian Problem' in Mexico, 1920–1940." *The Eagle and the Virgin: Nation and Cultural Revolution in Mexico, 1920–1940*, edited by Mary Kay Vaughan and Stephen E. Lewis, Duke University Press, 2006, pp. 176–95.

Lisenby, David. "Decolonizing Tepan: Adaptive Resistance and Alternative Nationhood in Elena Garro's *La dama boba*." *Chasqui: Revista de Literatura Latinoamericana*, vol. 42, no. 1, 2013, 109–18.

Lund, Joshua. *The Mestizo State*. University of Minnesota Press, 2012.

Megged, Nahum. "Fondo indígena, antisímbolo y problemática moderna en 'Luvina' de Juan Rulfo." *Nueva Revista de Filología Hispánica*, vol. 27, no. 1 (1978), 103–12.

Mraz, John. *Looking For Mexico: Modern Visual Culture and National Identity*. Duke University Press, 2009.

Pacheco, José Emilio. *Las batallas en el desierto*. 1981. Tusquetts, 2010.

Palou, Pedro Ángel. *El fracaso del mestizo*. Paidós, 2014.

Poyato, Pedro. "Circuito enunciativo de agresión y mundo originario en *Los olvidados* de Buñuel." *Pandora: Revue d'etudes hispaniques*, vol. 6, 2006, pp. 171–85.

Ramírez-Berg, Charles. "The Cinematic Invention of Mexico: The Poetics and Politics of the Fernández-Figueroa Style." *The Mexican Cinema Project*, edited by Chon A. Noriega and Steven Ricci, UCLA Film and Television Archive, 1994, pp. 13–24.

Rulfo, Juan. "Luvina." *El llano en llamas*. Editorial RM y Fundación Juan Rulfo, 2005, pp. 99–109.

———. *Pedro Páramo*. Cátedra, 2007.

Rulfo, Juan Carlos, director. *De panzazo*. La Media Luna Producciones, 2012.

Sáinz, Gustavo. *Gazapo*. Ace Press, 1968.

Sommer, Doris. *Foundational Fictions: The National Romances of Latin America*. University of California Press, 1991.

Thakkar, Amit. *The Fiction of Juan Rulfo: Irony, Revolution and Postcolonialism*. Tamesis, 2012.

Tierney, Dolores. *Emilio Fernández: Pictures in the Margins*. Manchester University Press, 2007.

Tuñón, Gloria. "Una escuela en celuloide: El cine de Emilio 'Indio' Fernández o la obsesión por la educación." *Historia Mexicana*, vol. 48. no. 2, Oct.–Dec. 1998, pp. 437–70.

Usigli, Rodolfo. *El gesticulador*. 1938, cdigital.dgb.uanl.mx/la/1020082047/1020082047_010.pdf. Accessed 3 Apr. 2015.

Vasconcelos, José. *La raza cósmica*. Porrúa, 2010.

6

MURDER

M for *Murder*: Mexico and Its *Democratic* State

FERNANDO FABIO SÁNCHEZ

PRIMARY MATERIALS

- *Del porfirismo a la Revolución* (From the Dictatorship of Porfirio Díaz to the Revolution) by David Alfaro Siqueiros (mural, 1957–66)
- *Ensayo de un crimen* (Rehearsal of a Crime) by Rodolfo Usigli (novel, 1944)
- *El hombre sin rostro* (The Man Without a Face), directed by Juan Bustillo Oro (film, 1950)
- *El complot mongol* (The Mongolian Conspiracy) by Rafael Bernal (novel, 1969)
- *El infierno* (Hell), directed by Luis Estrada (film, 2010)
- *La muerte en El muro de la verdad* (Death on "The Wall of Truth") by Fernando Fabio Sánchez (photograph, 2012)

"MURDER" AND "ASSASSINATION" are expressed through the same word in Spanish: *asesinato*.[1] *Asesinato* does not reveal, however, whether the victim is an important individual nor what the attacker's reasons are (generally either faith or politics). The term *magnicidio* might be a more accurate translation of "assassination." *Asesinato* vis-à-vis *homicidio* describes the material and temporal advantage of the killer over his or her victim and encapsulates the hideousness of murder. When the word *asesinato* is uttered, a crime against humanity is denounced. It demands restitution and punishment by human or divine laws. In Mexico, one of the primary elements of political power and the metanarrative called "Modern Mexico" has been the act of murdering (and assassinating), both in historical fact and in artistic representation. This chapter is a study of murder (*asesinato*) in crime fiction, film, and history in modern and contemporary Mexico. It analyzes, on one hand, how the *democratic* Mexican state has ensured its continuation in power and promoted the imposition of the capitalist model since the 1920s; on the other hand, it examines how the aesthetic representation of murder and assassination questions the meaning and causes of the state's murderous behavior, deconstructing the narrative of a modern and democratic Mexico.

INTRODUCTION: THE *ROOTS* OF MEXICO

David Alfaro Siqueiros reflects on the notion of death in the series of mural panels titled *Del porfirismo a la Revolución* (From the Dictatorship of Porfirio Díaz to the Revolution, 1957–66), as previously portrayed in the murals in the Secretaría de Educación Pública and the Colegio de San Ildefonso, among others, by Diego Rivera and José Clemente Orozco in the 1920s. In one of the panels of Siquieros's series, the revolutionary family that guided the movement and gave birth to the nation is shown: Francisco I. Madero, Aquiles Serdán, Venustiano Carranza, Eufemio and Emiliano Zapata, Álvaro Obregón, Plutarco Elías Calles, Francisco "Pancho" Villa, and Felipe Ángeles. Most of the members of this revolutionary family were executed, assassinated, or murdered. Madero was killed along with José María Pino Suárez during the coup finally led by Victoriano Huerta in 1913. Ángeles was betrayed and captured in 1919; he was executed after undergoing an unjust court-martial trial process in the city of Chihuahua. Emiliano Zapata was murdered in Chinameca in 1919 by order of Venustiano Carranza, and in 1920 Carranza himself was shot in Tlaxcalantongo during an uprising nationally led by Obregón. It is widely believed that in 1923 Obregón ordered the execution of Pancho Villa in Parral, and in 1928, Obregón fell prey to gunshots fired by the supposed lone assassin and religious extremist José de León Toral. Also shown in the mural is Plutarco Elías Calles, the last major *caudillo* of the Revolution, who was exiled by Lázaro Cárdenas in 1936, an act that could be interpreted as a sort of "parricide light" (Krauze 378–85).

In Siqueiros's mural, a homogenized narrative is proposed, in which the caudillo occupies the position of martyr and becomes a member of a national family along with his sibling executioner. The fact that they died in power struggles or over attempts to carry out their agendas is displaced. Benedict Anderson has called similar processes "reassuring fratricide" (199–203). The deaths of the "heroes" of the revolutionary era played a key role in the creation of "Modern Mexico." This role would be not only at the level of symbolic interpretation and representation but also, and most importantly, at the level of political necessity. In other words, the death of the opposing caudillo embodying an ideology and economic and social program needed to occur in order for a unitary regime to emerge. This prolonged "war of winners" was a phase that mainly involved what Alan Knight labels "macro-political violence" (33). This type of violence "is collective, organized and directed towards macro-political goals (the capture of state power, the transformation of the state or national 'project')" (33). The Carrancistas and, later on, the Sonorans executed macropolitical violence through different modalities that included, among many others, military and mercenary violence. Besides the pacification of the Mexican territory, the "winners" of the fratricidal revolutionary battle were "premised on a broadly capitalist economy" (25) and relegated the popular demands of the "losers" (that is, land reform) to the struggle of micropolitical violence. This type of violence is also collective but "geared to some (limited, often local) socio-political purpose" (38). One must say that the relative peace of the 1920s was achieved when the surviving parties created strategic alliances but also through death. We could add the names of lesser-known caudillos to the list of killed leaders, such as Lucio Blanco, Arnulfo Gómez, and General Francisco Serrano. Serrano and Gómez opposed Obregón during his second presidential campaign. Serrano died in 1927 on his way to Cuernavaca, near the town of Huitzilac, at the hands of General Claudio Fox. Gómez died later in Veracruz.

Obregón's murder was (tragically, but also very conveniently) key in the formation of the official party later to be known as the PRI (Partido Revolucionario Institucional). Obregón's death generated a polarization in the various political and military factions of the country. During his final report to Congress, Obregón's successor, Calles, made public his plan, which comprised three parts: (1) "to do away with the hegemony of caudillo, or dictatorial personalities within the government," (Nava Nava 17); (2) "to remind the political and military actors who viewed the problem of presidential succession in conspiratorial terms that there existed constitutional means of resolving the issue of the absence of the head of state" (17); and (3) "to exhort the political and ideological factions that operated within the political system—those that embodied the 'revolutionary vision'—to join forces in a true 'organic party' that would oversee, discipline, and reconcile the political interests of the different groups" (17–18). The Partido Nacional Revolucionario (PNR) was born, which in 1938 would become the Partido Revolucionario Mexicano (PRM), and, in 1946, the Partido Revolucionario Institucional. With the creation of this "organic party," power was highly centralized. This centralization was also achieved through a presidential institution. As Claudio Lomnitz proposes, the centralization of power had been an obsession in Mexico since the nineteenth century (109). This obsession was consummated in 1928 with Obregón's assassination, an act that in the national imagination gave birth to the PRI, or the so-called perfect dictatorship that governed the country continuously for seventy-two years.

Let us return to Siqueiros's *From the Dictatorship of Porfirio Díaz to the Revolution.* In another panel in the series, a row of cadavers representing the nation denotes the war's death toll. The corpses laying on the ground, side by side, seem to represent a river or a vanishing stairway, which leads the viewer to an ashy, crimson sky. The yellow sun dyes the swirling clouds. Whether the sun is setting or rising depends on the spectator's interpretation. We could explore two interpretations. According to the representation of revolutionary violence in José Clemente Orozco's *La trinchera* (The Trench, 1926) and *La destrucción del viejo orden* (The Destruction of the Old Order, 1926) in San Ildefonso and in Diego Rivera's *La sangre de los mártires revolucionarios fertilizando la tierra* (The Blood of the Revolutionary Martyrs Fertilizing the Earth, 1926) in the Universidad Autónoma Chapingo, death is not only the result of the armed conflict but also an objective and productive force. Death is an instrument that establishes order, unity, and ultimately, the fulfillment of revolutionary ideals. In these murals, the contradictions of history are displaced. The content of the past is resignified and becomes an aspiration for the future. The Revolution, as seen since the presidency of General Calles (1924–1928), has been reshaped into an everyday struggle. A new Mexico is on the horizon, but it would require a continuous effort by the nation and the state for modern Mexico to materialize. In this context, the sun is rising in Siqueiros's mural. The Revolution is the path that leads the nation to the future. Death becomes, then (and again), a synonym for progress.

Starting in the 1920s, political and economic stability became indicators of the achievements of the Revolution. However, it was not until the 1940s that a policy of capital accumulation and large-scale industrialization was fully (and finally) adopted. This policy change likewise led to the greater importance of urban centers, mass media, consumer markets, and foreign investment. Ironically, precisely in the 1940s, Mexico underwent its first and most significant break with the revolutionary-agrarian past, including its most notable manifestations of President Cárdenas's socialist policies. The decades of developmentalism, or the *milagro mexicano* (the so-called Mexican Miracle), began. The state has inclined toward capitalist policies until the present day. One can argue that one interruption occurred during the 1970s, when President Luis Echeverría Álvarez (1970–76) saw himself as the new Lázaro Cárdenas (Agustín 2) and redistributed land, turned the country inward, and cooled Mexico's relationship with the United States. Nonetheless, capitalist policies continued until they superseded the social legacy of the Mexican Revolution of 1910. In the 1990s, neoliberal policies were fully adopted. Postrevolutionary institutions, such as the ejido, disappeared or were weakened, which set things in motion for the difficult present that almost all Mexicans face.

Let us now contemplate Siqueiros's mural from the perspective of a setting sun. We can imagine that the muralist's critical genius encoded in this panel the cost of progress until the second decade of Mexican developmentalism. Let us visualize then that the row of the dead also represents progress's toll of death until the present. In order to envision this extraordinary amount of mortality we would have to add new categories of death. We would have to speak not only of the people affected negatively by urbanization and industrialization, those marginalized individuals who are impacted by poverty and sickness, but also of those people who are directly attacked by criminal groups and the institutions of the state, such as the Policía Estatal and the army. These are deaths of the people who are attacked inside and outside of their homes; people whose bodies have not been found and are declared missing; people who are murdered individually or en masse; hundreds of children, women, and migrants who are enslaved or butchered for organs. The growing number of deaths as a consequence of the capitalist imposition of development and neoliberalism has become the narrative for "Modern Mexico." These deaths would be a derivation of what Slavoj Žižek calls "systemic violence" (2), which is ideological, economical, and/or institutional, or, according to Rudolph Rummel, democide or "death by government" (32). "All homicide in post-revolutionary Mexico is political," Pablo Piccato states (104), in accordance with Jorge Aguilar Mora and Carlos Monsiváis. And this is the same story that murder fiction (both literature and film) and all its subgenres tell us about modern and contemporary Mexico.

In the works analyzed in the following pages, assassination and murder are acts that simultaneously delineate, transcend, and dismantle the symbolic boundaries of the narrative called "modern Mexico." These works echo the process by which the leading organic intellectuals during the 1920s laid down the basis of this narrative. In both the muralist movement and the novels of the Revolution, the work of the postrevolutionary intellectual is conceived of as a foundational act. In this way, the collective imagination attempts to fuse the interior world of the work of art to the exterior world (Anderson 30). Writing and painting serve to define the boundaries of the nation. Furthermore, in this decade and the following, as we have seen in Siqueiros's murals in the 1950s and the 1960s, the deaths of the assassinated and murdered caudillos serve as cornerstones upon which is erected a narrative corpus that the postrevolutionary state uses to legitimize itself and its economic model to the masses. With the passing of time, this narrative is simultaneously consolidated and renegotiated, progress and modernity being among its key elements. In the crime genre, however, the act of killing is restaged, and its meaning is shifted. The act of murder or assassination is a critical reading of the relationship between "Mexico" and the governing regime, between "Mexico" and modernity, illustrating the coherence of the country's symbolic universe and, in a gradual way, revealing its disintegration, as we will see below.

ENSAYO DE UN CRIMEN BY RODOLFO USIGLI: CRIMES FOR THE MEXICAN MIRACLE

Classic mystery fiction is a modern artifact that talks about modernity by employing modern means. This genre creates a narrative that intends to show the restitution of a disrupted social order by exercising intelligence and relying on the apparatuses of the modern nation-state. Edgar Allan Poe suggests, in his prologue to "The Murders in the Rue Morgue" (1841), the need to create a new type of reader for a new type of "hero," one whose heroism resides in his use of intellect rather than physical prowess. This search for truth by means of logic is the central characteristic of modern thought, an epistemological system that displaced the theological underpinnings of the premodern era in favor of scientific reasoning, whose end is utilitarian rather than dogmatic.

Classic mystery fiction is also a genre of completion. Roland Barthes states that the hermeneutics of this genre function through a paradoxical dynamic that is static yet changing. From the beginning, an enigma is maintained through the lack of an answer, and this empty vacuum is filled through the process of assigning a guilty identity. The murderer is declared responsible for a crime and then is punished by civil society. This void is also filled with a narrative. As Tzvetan Todorov proposes, the structure of the murder mystery is based on two stories (A and B) that are in search of each other. Story A is the story of the crime, while story B is the story of the investigation (42–45). Story A ends before story B begins, and most of the time, even before the work of fiction does. The former is a story of action, with the latter being a story based on the production of knowledge. Therefore, it is very significant that the first important work of murder fiction in Mexico is a novel that produces knowledge in an urban setting and in relation to modernity. *Ensayo de un crimen* (Rehearsal of a Crime, 1944) by Rodolfo Usigli scrutinizes the act of murder as an exercise of political and aesthetic principles in Mexico City.[2]

Usigli is best known for his plays *El gesticulador: Pieza para demagogos en tres actos* (The Impostor: A Play for Demagogues in Three Acts, 1937), *Corona de sombra* (Crown of Shadows, 1943), *Corona de fuego* (Crown of Fire, 1960), and *Corona de luz* (Crown of Light, 1963). The author also wrote poetry and two novels, *Ensayo de un crimen* and *Obliteración* (Obliteration, 1973), the former being by far the more important of the two. Luis Buñuel directed an eponymous film adaptation in 1955. However, the film does not correspond faithfully to the contents of the novel. Buñuel conceived his version as more than a mere adaptation of the book. He mentions in his memoirs that he was more interested in the character's obsession than in the roman à clef aspect of Usigli's work (112). Outside of Mexico, the film was given the title *La vida criminal de Archibaldo de la Cruz* (The Criminal Life of Archibaldo de la Cruz), further underscoring the free adaptation of Buñuel.

In the novel *Ensayo de un crimen*, Roberto de la Cruz, the protagonist, strives to carry out an *acte gratuit*, a murder without a motive. His desire to do this is awakened in an antique shop where he discovers a beautiful silk-lined music box (16). The box plays Waldteufel's "The Red Prince," which causes the protagonist to recall his teenage ambitions: to become either a saint or a great criminal. Opting for the latter, he undertakes to plan a murder by leaving clues that the police agencies find indecipherable and by erasing any possible connection between the perpetrator and the victim, between the *deed* of the former and the *reality* of the latter. The protagonist selects Patricia Terrazas and Count Schwartzemberg as victims and decides to kill them, yet he fails in both attempts; nonetheless, secret killers who are identified at the end murder both victims. In the end, Roberto de la Cruz manages to kill only Nena Cervantes, his wife, whom he mistakes for Lavinia, his former friend and protégée.

The "unmotivated intention" that guides Roberto de la Cruz is undermined by a deliberate process of selecting his victims in accordance with political strategies related to the modern Mexican state. Near the end of the novel, de la Cruz confesses at the police station that "he always longed to commit the most gratuitous and the most *Mexican* of crimes" (294; my emphasis). This revelation exposes the desire to paradoxically encode "Mexican-ness" by way of murder. The basic outlines of the national character are set forth from the beginning of the novel through the murderer's process of selecting his victims, and in the denouement it becomes clear that the sociopolitical aspect of the murders is also part of the novel's interpretative mission.

The character Patricia Terrazas represents the undesirable bourgeoisie that the Revolution has supposedly purged from the national landscape. Following the victim's death (not at the hands of de la Cruz, of course), it is revealed that Terrazas "was originally from Chihuahua and was a member of one of the most important families in the country. . . . Although the Revolution took a great toll on the Terrazas' family fortune, Miss Patricia, an only child who remained unmarried until her tragic death, inherited a sum that allowed her to live very comfortably" (89). Terrazas's murder can be interpreted as a settling of scores, the victory of the forces of social change that wipe out an iniquitous fortune accumulated during the corrupt and oppressive Porfirio Díaz dictatorship.

Count Schwartzemberg, the second victim, represents, just like Terrazas, a subject who appears unfit to join the project of forming the postrevolutionary nation. The main difference is that his life revolved around the capital's nightlife in bars, red-light districts, and other centers of decadent popular culture. He is also homosexual. Count Schwartzemberg, according to the protagonist of Usigli's novel, does not possess an identity listed in the country's desirable groups. Killing the count thus becomes an attempt to define the discourses of power (based mainly on machismo and elitism) that define the undesirable subjects who can be eliminated. A few years later, in 1950, a cinematic killer would also eliminate marginal urban subjects who otherwise might deform the project of an urbanized, modern nation. In *El hombre sin rostro* (The Man Without a Face), directed by Juan Bustillo Oro, Juan Carlos Lozano kills women (mainly prostitutes) during moments of schizophrenia. In the film, it is revealed that Juan Carlos commits these acts of violence against women because of an unresolved sin from his past. Bustillo Oro's serial killer can also be seen as an allegorical exposition of the debates over "Mexican-ness" during the *desarrollista* phase of Mexico's mid-twentieth-century project of modernization.

The desire to kill Patricia Terrazas and Count Schwartzemberg in *Ensayo de un crimen* reactivates the destructive/regenerative impulse of the Revolution. The difference is that this reactivation is carried out with ironic nuances in an urban and industrial context. The Revolution, symbolized by the music box, inspires the murderous designs of Roberto de la Cruz. His violent impulses stem from the manifestation of a trauma experienced during the decade-long period of armed struggle. When de la Cruz was a boy of eight or nine, a solider friend of his father's took him to the town square as a group of revolutionaries were coming into town. The child witnessed the moment when the solider (in boots and moustache, à la Kaiser Wilhelm) shot a passerby just to flaunt his power. As the mortally wounded man fell to the ground, an organ grinder played "The Red Prince."

The soldier's actions can be interpreted as a sort of Mexican recontextualization of Andre Breton's claim that the simplest surrealist act would be to run down the street with a pistol in hand randomly shooting at passersby, an inexplicable action that not only violates the law but also gives way to the sublime by subverting ethics in favor of aesthetics. In Mexico City, as Roberto de la Cruz relives this moment from his past, he replicates the soldier's desire to kill and also revives the concept of the motiveless crime, an act that mirrors the desire for an autonomous work of art. In a similar vein, the chaotic violence of the Revolution is transformed into a discourse that attempts to objectify itself (to eliminate its contradictions) in order to produce a coherent narrative of national foundation (O'Malley 5). According to de la Cruz's explanation of his crimes at the end of the novel, the murderer in *Ensayo de un crimen* mocks the postrevolutionary state for using death as a nation-building method. He also imitates the muralist movement, the novels of the Revolution, and the historic monuments and ceremonies related to the foundation of the modern Mexican nation. As mentioned before, these are cultural events and artifacts through which the postrevolutionary regimes first contemplated the Revolution's chaotic violence as the origin of a new narrative that displaced the contradictions of history, erased the past, and legitimated political power.

The knowledge that emerges from *Ensayo de un crimen* problematizes the discourses of power that articulate "Mexico" as an idea. Although Roberto de la Cruz does not reach his objectives, the novel elaborates on a solid critique of the postrevolutionary state. At the end of the novel, Roberto de la Cruz's poetic intention is lost, and he is ultimately left with his unintended parodical intent. The protagonist's *crimes* are then rehearsals (*ensayos*) because they are not executed as they were conceived. Also, the crimes are considered texts (that is, "essays," another translation of the word *ensayo*), which reflect upon the past, present, and future of the Mexican nation in relation to politics, aesthetics, and murder.

EL COMPLOT MONGOL BY RAFAEL BERNAL: THE DARK SIDE OF THE MEXICAN MIRACLE

In the writings of Juan Rulfo, we encounter violent subjects who seek to destroy paternal figures that are incarnations of power. Such scenes can be connected to a similar desire to assault the institution that has managed to centralize power in postrevolutionary Mexico. The postrevolutionary state became the neurotic and threatening father, the mythical ogre whose children seek to destroy him. It is not illogical to propose the use of Octavio Paz's oxymoron of the "philanthropic ogre" as a metaphor for the state during the 1950s and '60s. In *El complot mongol* (The Mongolian Conspiracy, 1969) by Rafael Bernal, this latent desire of destruction is present; murder in this text talks about a possible termination of the state a year after the student massacre in Tlatelolco in 1968. *El complot mongol* is structured around the conventions of the spy novel, one of the subgenres of crime fiction. It would exemplify Jon Thompson's idea of this type of novels: "it is no longer just the fates of individuals that are at risk, but . . . the fate of a . . . nation; indeed, in many cases, what is at stake is the course of history itself" (85). However, *El complot mongol* is more; it is a dynamic and hybrid text, a spy novel (Stavans 95) that also contains elements of the hard-boiled and thriller traditions (92). It has also been called "a foundational novel of Mexican *noir* literature that is also one of the best Mexican novels of this [the twentieth] century because of its creative joy, its depth of thought and its admirable knowledge of the Mexican psyche" (Giardinelli 253). Critics and readers would agree that *El complot mongol* is the first novel of the so-called *neopolicíaco latinoamericano*. This genre has been defined as a type of murder mystery that has its roots in the American noir novel and that deals with topics of national import (Belibrea-Enríquez 39). As stated by Paco Ignacio Taibo II, among the main characteristics of the *neopolicíaco* are "the obsession with cities; a recurring thematic trend of the problems of the state being the catalysts of crime, corruption, and police misconduct" (qtd. in Argüelles 14).[3] In the following section I will present derivative classifications of the *neopolicíaco* and of crime fiction in general.

Back to Bernal, who also penned more typical examples of the classic murder mystery, such as *Un muerto en la tumba* (A Dead Man in the Grave) and *Tres novelas policíacas* (Three Detective Novels), both published in 1946. In *El complot mongol*, the *pistolero*, Filiberto García, who as a young man was an executioner of one of Villa's leading generals, is commissioned by a Mexican police official identified as "El Coronel" (The Colonel) and by another mysterious character (whom we later discover to be Rosendo del Valle) to take three days to investigate the veracity of certain rumors circulating through Mexico City's Chinatown. Rumor has it that a plot has been hatched in Communist China to assassinate the U.S. president during his upcoming trip to Mexico. García carries out his investigation with two foreign agents: an American by the name of Richard P. Graves and the Russian Ivan Laski. The three move throughout the city in search of information related to the possible assassination plot or other issues that could affect "international peace." In addition, Laski (according to García's speculations) is trying to confirm whether Communist China is organizing a counterrevolution in Cuba to subvert Russian hegemony on the island.

Near the end of the novel, García discovers that the inhabitants of Mexico's Chinatown are not plotting to assassinate the president of the United States but are actually involved in drug trafficking. García learns that the supposed international conspiracy is in fact a local plot constructed by General Miraflores and Rosendo del Valle to assassinate the Mexican president and impose a military junta. As the novel explores the validity of Mexico's postrevolutionary national institutions, the intrigue of international espionage presented at the beginning of the book (along with the references to Mexico's participation in the Cold War) recedes to the background. These national institutions were supposed to result in a state founded in the rule of law rather than a regime legitimized by armed forces.

In the end, García manages to save the country and the president, but he perceives no transcendence in his actions. García is an individual who has completely detached himself from notions of patriotism or duty to country, despite enjoying a privileged position within the inner circles of the government. He follows the conspiracy through to its final consequences only to avenge the death of Martita, the Chinese woman with whom he is in love. The sentence "There has been one death too many" (a reference to Martita) is repeated several times in the novel. Bernal's protagonist acts without Mexico being his ulterior motive, for his role is clearly that of a critic of the established order. At the same time, García's position is similar to the role of those politicians who supposedly have the good of the nation as their ultimate objective, but nevertheless pursue personal interests and financial profits. García's irreverence throughout the novel is not an attempt to reactivate the symbolic structure of the nation. Rather, García reflects upon the weakness and emptiness of this symbolic field. His declarations are analogous to the event that threatens the very structure of the nation: the possible assassination of the Mexican president.

Assassination appears connected not only to the notion of the survival of the nation but also to the national historical past. When García informs the Colonel about the local conspiracy, the memory of an important political assassination from the past emerges: that of "General Obregón, president-elect" (188). As mentioned in the introduction to this essay, Obregón's death at the hands of José de León Toral in 1928 did not call into question the strength of the government but, rather, served as the basis for the creation of the official party. The events that took place in the restaurant La Bombilla were immediately transformed into a sacrifice for the country. Four decades later, in the realm of literary imagination, an assassination is thought to be on the verge of provoking a national catastrophe. According to the Colonel, the country might be traversing "one of the worst moments of our history" (189). As he explains, a plot against the president "is very grave for Mexico. We have created a legal order out of the Revolution, a legal order that cannot be broken. Do you understand what that is, García? A government under the rule of law. That's worth more than the lives of a few crazy people" (188). He then insists, "A government of laws. That is what we must safeguard at all cost" (189).

With the mention of Obregón's death, *El complot mongol* also alludes to the idea that the assassination of the leading caudillos of the Revolution served to found the national order. The assassination of a political figure is a privileged scene in postrevolutionary Mexican art, which represents and reflects the foundation of the modern Mexican nation. From Martín Luis Guzmán's novel *La sombra del caudillo* (The Shadow of the Leader, 1929) and Usigli's play *El gesticulador* (1938), to Julio Bracho's 1960 film *La sombra del caudillo*, Jorge Ibargüengoitia's novel *Relámpagos de agosto* (Lightning of August, 1965), and *El complot mongol*, the act of murder or assassination has consistently been linked to state-sponsored violence in postrevolutionary Mexican literature.

The assassination of the Mexican leader in Bernal's novel deals with circumstances diametrically opposed to those of 1928, when Obregón was killed. In this way, Bernal's novel represents the symbolic erosion and death of postrevolutionary Mexico. It speaks of the deterioration and the delegitimization of the national symbols as well as of the belligerent emergence of an era ruled by "progress" and politicians who are "building Mexico" from "the bars and cocktail lounges" (11). This apparently secondary discussion that the novel leads into is a sort of denouement that circularly questions one of the main themes Filiberto García's character raises from the beginning of the novel: the relationship between Mexico and the United States. The assassination of the U.S. president could unleash conflicts between the two superpowers of the Cold War. But not only that, it could harm the most important state-sponsored project of the postrevolutionary era: Mexico's entrance into the international arena as a modern nation. This is the "white-glove Revolution" (92), the "revolution" that belonged to the group of technocrats who, starting in the 1940s, fully applied the capitalist model to bring about a Mexican Miracle and that Filiberto García saved with all the sorrow of this heart.

A LONG GONE MIRACLE: THE *SUPRA POLICÍACO* AND *EL INFIERNO* BY LUIS ESTRADA

Many years have passed since the end of the Mexican Miracle. Starting in the 1990s (and even before) neoliberal policies were implemented as an attempt to bring Mexico once again to the group of developed nations. However, many events changed Mexico's promised destiny. During that decade, Mexico went through one of its greatest crises in the twentieth century. The Ejército Zapatista de Liberación Nacional (Zapatista National Liberation Army), or EZLN, uprising in Chiapas was the beginning of the 1994 crisis, which was deepened by the collapse of the peso, the assassination of PRI presidential candidate Luis Donaldo Colosio in Tijuana, and the implementation of the North American Free Trade Agreement (NAFTA). Colosio's assassination has been the subject of numerous noteworthy novels, such as *Un asesino solitario* (1999) by Elmer Mendoza, and films, such as *Colosio: El asesinato* (2012) by Carlos Bolado.

The Zapatista revolt exposed the fact that the social structures of postrevolutionary Mexico were in a dire state of decay, almost on the verge of death. Lorenzo Meyer called the 1990s "the second death of the Mexican Revolution." The first "death" occurred in 1947, when Cosío Villegas wrote his essay "La crisis de México," announcing, paradoxically, the fact that developmentalism was not included in the Revolution's objectives. This second "death" came about when the "Mexican elite was finally able to bury its Cid and stop pretending that its actions and objectives were still inspired by that formidable, but distant massive uprising that took place at the beginning of the century" (Meyer 11–12). Roger Bartra states that starting in 1994, one can speak of a "post-national" Mexican condition. It can be described as a scenario in which the government's ideological networks of legitimization with respect to the idea of nation have lost their cohesiveness (19). Murder and other crime fiction have reflected major events that have occurred during this age of national disintegration. For instance, in the closing scene of the film *Amores perros* (Love's a Bitch, 2000) by Alejandro González Iñárritu, the protagonist and assassin of the third story of the film, the Chivo, walks along what could be described as a contemporary Rulfian wasteland, the now eroded symbolic space of the nation. The land that was once seen as fertile fields (for example, the nation in Rivera's murals) and the intellect's dream of urban order and progress during the first half of the twentieth century has now transformed into the ruins of both agrarian and industrial Mexico. The utopias of early- and mid-twentieth-century Mexico collapsed. The convulsive decade of the 1990s came to an end in July 2000 with the presidential election of Vicente Fox of the Partido Acción Nacional (National Action Party), or PAN, marking the end of the PRI's seventy-year reign as Mexico's official political party.

Glen S. Close coined the term "post-*neopolicíaco*" in *Contemporary Hispanic Crime Fiction: A Transatlantic Discourse on Urban Violence* (2008). This term refers to novels written at the turn of the century that view "urban violence as depoliticized, intimately subjectified, and decisively removed from reductive schemes of moral containment" (53). These are novels that abandon the conventions of mystery and detective fiction. In these works, the activity of the murderer, or the criminal, is no longer connected to issues of national concern. Such novels would include Olivier Debroise's *Lo peor sucede al atardecer* (The Worst Happens at Dusk, 1990), Hernández Luna's *Yodo* (Iodine, 1998), and Guillermo Fadanelli's *La otra cara de Rock Hudson* (Rock Hudson's Other Face, 1997) and *Lodo* (Mud, 2002).

Along these lines, during the first decade of the twenty-first century we observe the abundant emergence of a type of novel and film that abandons the postrevolutionary, nationalistic rhetoric. As the *neopolicíaco* does, they present topics of political concerns and deal with violence and one or various murder crimes. The main difference is that these works go beyond the conventions of murder fiction and all its subgenres, creating a lack of certainty, with no possibility to clearly define the notions of good and bad. In these works there is no investigation per se or emphasis on detecting, nor is there realistic access to justice and delivery of punishment to culprits. The civil society is exposed as vulnerable before the judicial and political orders, and the state appears to be infiltrated by the crime or is seen as a direct crime agency. These novels and films speak of corruption, drug mafias, human trafficking, migration, urban poverty, and all forms of killing: murder, assassination, disappearances, hunting, systematic death, feminicides, and mass murder. Death is seen as an economic phenomenon or related to globalized systems of production, specifically illegal systems, such as drug trafficking, kidnapping, extortion, or simply the creation of political power. These works are quite dynamic and often intersect with diverse genres, such as suspense, drama, farce, comedy, and adventure. Yet the constant is the violation of human rights and the representation of impunity. It is the civil society's nightmare under the rule of corrupt politicians and criminals.[4]

If the *neopolicíaco* is the most immediate observable crime genre in Mexico, one can argue that the exploration and reformulation of the poetics of such a genre in new political, social, and aesthetic contexts has created a new category. The films and novels in this group fit within what we can call "supra-*policíaco*." As I have pointed out, these types of works represent murder, assassination, and other crimes without privileging the detection or the presence of police forces, and if the police appear, the works conclude with indeterminacy about what occurred. There is no possible access to legal justice or even to a poetic one. However, there is an implied demand for justice in these works. The failed access to justice in the story creates a necessity for action in the social realm, because justice can still be attained if civil society acquires critical awareness and exercises its democratic rights. The public will be the ultimate authority regarding justice and change; it will be a suprapolice.

Alongside this diverse literary corpus, another genre that emerged during the late twentieth and early twenty-first century is the *narcocorrido*, one of the most recent versions of the Mexican ballad, performed by a *banda sinaloense* or a *conjunto norteño*. This musical manifestation is rooted in traditional *corridos* from the Revolution and postrevolutionary Mexico and even from before (see Edberg). The *narcocorrido* presents a parallel version of history and nationalism to an audience who has become familiar with and even supportive of what Helen Redmond in her article "The Political Economy of Mexico's Drug War" identifies as "narcocapitalism." These ballads narrate stories of trafficking, some successful, some tragic, some even fantastic. They glorify drug lords (both male and female), the thrill of the criminal life, and power. Los Tigres del Norte, Los Tucanes de Tijuana, El Komander, Los Huracanes del Norte, Chalino Sánchez, and Grupo Exterminador are among the most famous performers of this genre. This was the time governed by the PAN president Felipe Calderón. It was a society at war against drug lords. It was a period of celebratory nationalism, devoid of legitimacy but enchanted by the magical numbers two hundred and one hundred: the two-hundred-year anniversary of Mexico as a free nation and the one-hundred-year anniversary of the Mexican Revolution.

The film *El infierno* (2010) by Luis Estrada takes place in this context and debates whether Mexico has pursued progress through justice or crime. This film, as do *Ensayo de un crimen* and *El complot mongol*, deviates from the values proposed by the governing regime and presents the state as a criminal, a violent entity. It also, by presenting the act of assassination and murder, speaks of both the symbolic and, most importantly, the material destruction of the criminal state and its associates—in other words, of postrevolutionary Mexico itself. We also can say that *El infierno* narrates the rise and fall of a low-life rural criminal, whose story can be found in a *narcocorrido*.

El infierno is the third film in Luis Estrada's tetralogy about Mexico's relationship with political power. *La ley de Herodes* (Herod's Law, 1999) is a critique of the formation of modern Mexico during the developmentalism of President Miguel Alemán Valdés (1946–52). The film itself is understood as a critique of the neoliberal regime of the 1990s since it showed symbols of political power, such as the national flag, the Mexican Constitution, and the emblems of the two historic parties, the PRI and the PAN. When it was made, the film was censored and its exhibition prohibited. Finally, it was released in 1999 after pressure from the media. In the second installment from his tetralogy, *Un mundo maravilloso* (A Wonderful World, 2006), Estrada creates a rhetorical parody of the *foxiato*, the period of Vicente Fox's presidency (2000–2006), taking as a central motif the government's promise of granting houses to the majority of the country's populace. In *El infierno*, the central themes are drug trafficking, the war between the drug lords and the government of President Felipe Calderón, and bicentennial celebrations. The fourth film, *La dictadura perfecta* (The Perfect Dictatorship, 2014), is an analysis of the role of the media in Mexican democracy. With high doses of farce like the previous films, *La dictadura perfecta* conceives the government of Enrique Peña Nieto as a fraud of political power in which the president is the marionette of the economic and criminal groups that support him.

In *El Infierno*, Benny García (Damián Alcázar), the main character, sets off for the United States in the 1980s and comes back to Mexico twenty years later. His return to the town of San Miguel is a narrative device through which a contrast is created between the past and the present. Benny, as well as the viewer, discovers the situation into which the region has descended, a synecdoche or metaphor for the entire country. Gradually, Benny recognizes the levels and workings of the regional mafia. He finds out that his brother, known as El Diablito, died as a member of the mafia's group of hit men, leaving a wife and son. Benny attempts to look after them. However, not having the legal means to earn enough money, he asks for help from one of his oldest friends. El Cochiloco (Joaquín Cosío) gets him an interview with don José Reyes (Ernesto Gómez Cruz), the local mafia boss. And so Benny becomes a member of the cartel. With Benny, the viewer enters the world of the mafia and gets to know its logic. Don José Reyes is not only a drug trafficker but also a respected rancher, businessman, and distinguished individual in national political and social circles. The photos hung on the great wall in the office where Benny's interview takes place show don José with recognizable public personalities, such as Pope John Paul II and President Vicente Fox. Don José even speaks of the progress of the nation and blames the problems of Mexico on the United States and the Mexican political elite. Don José is a benevolent despot, a paternalistic criminal, a philanthropic ogre whose only problem is confrontation with the cartel boss who intends to take control of the region: Don Francisco Reyes, his own brother (also played by Gómez Cruz).

The film is explicit. Mercenary violence has taken the place of microviolence, as describe by Knight; that is to say, the mercenary groups are the ones who control the economic and social changes in the region. Similarly, the mercenaries have influence over the local government and control the municipal and state police. In addition, the mafia bosses are the principal benefactors of education and appear celebrating national ceremonies with primary-school children and teachers. Nevertheless, the intention of the film is not only to denounce the fact that mercenary groups control the regions of Mexico. Rather, the film suggests that the mercenaries, governmental institutions, and commercial groups have been one and the same for a long time and have created the current hell. Corruption occurs at regional and federal levels. When Benny decides to accuse don José of his crimes, he is betrayed by Captain Ramírez (Daniel Giménez Cacho). Captain Ramírez is in charge of a federal witness-protection program; however, he also serves the mafia lords. Benny is turned over to don José for his immediate death.

But Benny manages to escape. Realizing that mercenary violence has escalated the levels of macroviolence, he decides to carry out his final act of subjective violence. During the nighttime ceremony of September 15 celebrating the bicentennial, led by don José (who now is the mayor of San Miguel), Benny hides in the festival crowd carrying a machine gun. When don José mistakenly pronounces the hero's name of the traditional Grito de Dolores, Benny shoots with deadly aim at all of the powerful individuals who can be found on the podium. He takes the lives of bodyguards, police, don José and his wife, and even the bishop. The scene, similar to Diego Rivera's mural *La quema de los Judas* (The Burning of the Judases, 1923), is bloody and does not cease showing gestures of farce. However, the visual composition is conclusive. Don José falls dead over the central pulpit from which, seconds before, he had given the Cry of Dolores for independence, and blood flows over the image of the Mexican national eagle. The image is a double metaphor: on one side is the allegory of Mexico bloodied by the so-called war on drugs, being a representation of the more than 50,000 souls lost among the deaths and disappearances of the just six-year term of President Calderón; and on the other side, it is a direct attack on the representations of that grand narrative called "modern Mexico" that politicians and criminal organizations have utilized in order to impose systems of control, development, exploitation, and, above all, death. In this scene from *El infierno* we find ourselves before the execution of that desire that was shown in a latent state in *El complot mongol* in the 1960s. We witness, in brief, the complete destruction of the system that over the course of a century had used murder/assassination to construct political and economic power.

El infierno represents this concept of symbolic death from the start. The film proposes a series of intertextual connections in which the horizontal time of the narration interacts with spatial structures of action; throughout the film the characters move through places marked with significance, and this contact produces meanings that are also part of the message of the film. In this case, the film constructs a series of references to classic Mexican cinematography, specifically to films such as Fernando de Fuentes's *Allá en el Rancho Grande* (Out on the Big Ranch, both the original version of 1936 and the remake of 1949), Emilio Fernández's *Salón México* (Salon Mexico, 1949), and Ismael Rodríguez's *Los tres García* (The Three Garcias, 1947), among others. The film, in this way, aims for the genre of *campirano* (an idealized representation of the countryside) and the nationalist cinema of the so-called Golden Age. It dismantles the idealization of the countryside, the rancher, the loving mother (the source of moral and spiritual harmony), and traditional poetics—both urban and rural—that served as articulations of the culture, which in this time were cornerstones of political power. Moreover, there are references to the low-budget action and trafficking film genre that appeared in the 1970s. Mario Almada (1922–2016) makes a cameo, a stellar appearance; Almada was a very popular actor, especially for his roles in urban westerns and action films during the 1980s. On the one hand, *El infierno* pays an homage to the actor; on the other hand, it suggests the actor is a temporal point of reference: that world he represents, relegated culturally to the margins, is now a central part of national survival.

Thus, Estrada's fourth film talks about the symbolic disintegration of a language that, in the first part of his tetralogy, belonged only to the PRI and that now, freed from this historical connection, has been appropriated as well by the PAN, the ruling regime in the first decade of the twenty-first Mexican century. Hell is that Rulfian wasteland that civil society inhabits, not only the ruin of rural and industrial Mexico, but also the space where there take place dismemberments, beheadings, and above all confrontations between brothers, all being scenes that physically and symbolically refer to decomposition. The fratricide, a motif that had already been introduced in *Amores perros* in 2000, now turns apocalyptic. In *El infierno*, the brothers Cucaracha and the bosses José and Francisco Reyes all kill one another, dismantling the union that in the 1920s served as a founding force, as it is expressed in Mexican muralism. Along the same line, in the scene of the mass murder, the image of the national eagle spurting blood is not only an allegory of the bullet-riddled country and the realization of a destructive desire but an expression of the lack of power in the symbol itself. This vacuum stands out above all in moments of national celebrations during the bicentennial. However, as we have seen, this empty space has been created over the course of the twentieth century as the governing regime imposed death before justice, crime before legitimacy. That is what murder fiction and its subgenres tell us about Mexico.

CONTEMPORARY MEXICO

Wikipedia has an article titled "List of Massacres in Mexico." One can argue that Wikipedia exchanges democratic mediation for content precision—although it could be one of the few websites that could resist censorship. The article lists twenty-seven scenes of mass murder since the Tlatelolco massacre in 1968. The

FIGURE 6.1. Artist unknown, *La muerte en El muro de la verdad*, 2012. Graffiti on plastic. Photograph by Fernando Fabio Sánchez.

consensus, according to the article, is that the state and mercenaries are responsible for such acts against humanity. The perception of the state is openly negative. For instance, during the renovation of the Alameda Central in Mexico City in the summer of 2012, the majority of messages written on the plastic greenish wall surrounding the park identified both historical parties, the PAN and the PRI, President Calderón, and future president Enrique Peña Nieto as agents of violence, acting far apart from the interests of the people. The character of Death with the mask falling off Peña Nieto stands out among all the graffiti and collective statements. The toll of death is very heavy in civil society, and the populace has stated its cry for justice on *El muro de la verdad* (The Wall of Truth), as the anonymous canvas was called (figure 6.1).

In the media and in forums of social activism, the massacres in Acteal, Chiapas (1997), and Atenco, Estado de México (2006), and the mass kidnapping in Ayotzinapa, Guerrero (2014), among others, are mentioned compulsively. However, the lesser-known massacres in San Fernando, Tamaulipas (2011), and Allende, Coahuila (2011), still await the social winds of discontent and claims of justice in federal and international courts. It is undisputable that we should add to that list the bloody attack on women in the state of Mexico: 1,767 women died violently from 2005 to 2013, and between 2011 and 2015 more than 1,500 disappeared (Reuters).

It is difficult to speak the truth in Mexico. Journalists and social activists have also died. Silence appears to be the imperative. Fiction, as well as social media and democratic websites such as Wikipedia, are among the few receptacles of truthful reality, as Héctor Domínguez-Ruvalcaba states in his book *Nación criminal: Narrativas del crimen organizado y el Estado mexicano* (Criminal Nation: Narratives of Organized Crime and the Mexican State, 2015). Fiction reveals what journalism is obligated to shut out, just as crime fiction does and has done in postrevolutionary Mexico. The pages and images of these works are full of blood and death by government.[5]

NOTES

1. The following essay is an extension of the ideas on the subject exposed in my book *Artful Assassins: Murder as Art in Modern Mexico* (2010). All variations of the original translation from the book have been made with the authorization of Professor Stephen Clark. I thank Karen Popp, Max Shue, Ashley Heath, Gerardo García, and Amanda Petersen for their comments and suggestions.
2. Throughout nineteenth-century Mexican literature, texts appear in which a police agency plays a leading role, such as Luis G. Inclán's *Astucia, el jefe de los Hermanos de la Hoja; o, Los charros contrabandistas de la Rama* (Astucia, the Chief of the Brotherhood of the Leaf; or, The Charro Smugglers of La Rama, 1865), or Manuel Payno's *Los bandidos de Río Frío* (The Bandits of Río Frío, 1891). However, these crime novels do not follow the structure of the classic detective story: they do not open with the typical mysterious homicide in need of resolution, nor do they display a process of reestablishment of social order through a detective's "reading" of a criminal story. In *Los bandidos de Río Frío*, Judge Bedolla appears utterly unconcerned with justice as he evolves from pursuer of criminals to perpetrator of a crime, thus in some ways foreshadowing the poetics of hard-boiled American detective fiction. In *Los bandidos de Río Frío*, we see that Mexico is still a long way from achieving centralized and effective oversight of its population by its police agencies. The bandidos and the Relumbrón syndicate work under multiple identities in a territory that has yet to become a modern nation-state. Thus, the world of this novel is similar to that of the picaresque, in which appearance and reality have no correspondence.
3. Some later works that can be related to the *El complot mongol*'s poetics are Jorge Ibargüengoitia's *Las muertas* (The Dead Ones, 1977) and *Dos crímenes* (Two Crimes, 1979), Carlos Fuentes's *La cabeza de la hidra* (The Hydra Head, 1978), Rafael Ramírez Heredia's *Trampa de metal* (The Metal Trap, 1979), Federico

Campbell's *Pretexta* (1979), and Taibo II's *Días de combate* (Days of Combat, 1976) and *Cosa fácil* (Easy Thing, 1977). Taibo II explored almost exclusively the conventions of the *neopolicíaco*. Writers then followed his model extensively. The novels that have been linked to Taibo II include Ramírez Heredia's *Muerte en la carretera* (Death on the Road, 1986), Hugo Valdés Manríquez's *El crimen de la calle Aramberri* (The Crime of Aramberri Street, 1994), Enrique Serna's *El miedo a los animales* (The Fear of Animals, 1995), Juan Hernández Luna's *Tabaco para el puma* (Tobacco for the Puma, 1996), Orlando Ortiz's *Una muerte muy saludable* (A Very Healthy Death, 1996), Élmer Mendoza's *Un asesino solitario* (A Lone Assassin, 1999), Rolo Diez's *Papel picado* (Confetti, 2003), and Eduardo Antonio Parra's *Nostalgia de la sombra* (Nostalgia for the Shadow, 2003).

4. A few works in this heterogeneous group are the novels *Conducir un tráiler* (Driving a Trailer, 2008) by Rogelio Guedea; Víctor Ronquillo's *Sicario: Diario del Diablo* (Hit Man: The Devil's Diary, 2009); Alejandro Almazán's *Entre perros* (Among Dogs, 2009) and *El más buscado* (The Most Wanted Man, 2012); Bernando Fernández's *Hielo negro* (Black Ice, 2011); Iris García Cuevas's *36 toneladas* (36 Tons, 2011); Luis E. González O'Donnell's *El olor del dinero* (The Smell of Money, 2011); Hilario Peña's *Chinola Kid* (2012); and César López Cuadras's *Cuatro muertos por capítulo* (Four Dead Bodies per Chapter, 2013); and the films *Batalla en el cielo* (Battle in Heaven, 2005), directed by Carlos Reygadas; Carlos Carrera's *El traspatio* (Backyard, 2009); Gerardo Naranjo's *Miss Bala* (2011); *El infierno* (Hell, 2010) by Luis Estrada; Carlos Bolado's *Colosio: El asesinato* (Colosio: The Assassination, 2012); Luis Mandoki's *La vida precoz y breve de Sabina Rivas* (The Early and Brief Life of Sabina Rivas, 2012); Diego Quemada-Diez's *La jaula de oro* (The Golden Cage, 2013); and Amat Escalante's *Heli* (2013), among others.
5. In addition to the works analyzed in this chapter, see the following abridged list of Mexican murder and crime short stories, novels, and feature films: "Un crimen provisional" (A Provisional Crime, 1926) by Arqueles Vela; *Vida y milagros de Pancho Reyes, detective mexicano* (Life and Miracles of Pancho Reyes, Mexican Detective, n.d.) by San Alfonso Quiroga; *La obligación de asesinar* (The Obligation to Kill, 1946) by Antonio Helú; *El crimen de Insurgentes: Comedia policíaca en tres actos* (The Crime of Insurgentes Avenue: Police Comedy in Three Acts, 1949) by Antonio Helú and Adolfo Fernández Bustamante; *Un muerto en la tumba* (A Dead Man in the Grave, 1946) and *Tres novelas policíacas* (Three Detective Novels, 1946) by Rafael Bernal; *Los*

mejores cuentos policiales mexicanos (The Best Mexican Detective Short Stories, 1955), edited by María Elvira Bermúdez; *Los albañiles* (The Builders, 1964) by Vicente Leñero; *Morirás lejos* (You Will Die Far Away, 1967) by José Emilio Pacheco; *Días de combate* (Days of Combat, 1976), *Cosa fácil* (Easy Thing, 1977), *Algunas nubes* (Some Clouds, 1985), *No habrá final feliz* (There Won't Be a Happy Ending, 1989), *Regreso a la misma ciudad y bajo la lluvia* (Return to the Same City and Under the Same Rain, 1989), *Amorosos fantasmas* (Loving Ghosts, 1990), *Sueños de frontera* (Dreams of the Border, 1990), *Desvanecidos difuntos* (Vanished Deaths, 1991), and *Adiós Madrid* (Good-Bye Madrid, 1993) by Paco Ignacio Taibo II; *Las muertas* (The Dead Ones, 1977) and *Dos crímenes* (Two Crimes, 1979) by Jorge Ibargüengoitia; *La cabeza de la hidra* (The Hydra Head, 1978) by Carlos Fuentes; *Trampa de metal* (The Metal Trap, 1979) and *Muerte en la carretera* (Death on the Road, 1986) by Rafael Ramírez Heredia; *Pretexta* (1979) by Federico Campbell; *Lo peor sucede al atardecer* (The Worst Happens at Dusk, 1990) by Olivier Debroise; *El crimen de la calle Aramberri* (The Crime of Aramberri Street, 1994) by Hugo Valdés; *El miedo a los animales* (The Fear of Animals, 1995) by Enrique Serna; *Tabaco para el puma* (Tobacco for the Puma, 1996) and *Yodo* (Iodine, 1998) by Juan Hernández Luna; *Una muerte muy saludable* (A Very Healthy Death, 1996) by Orlando Ortiz; *La otra cara de Rock Hudson* (Rock Hudson's Other Face, 1997) and *Lodo* (Mud, 2002) by Guillermo Fadanelli; *Un asesino solitario* (A Lone Assassin, 1999), *El efecto tequila* (The Tequila Effect, 2004), and *Balas de plata* (Silver Bullets, 2008) by Élmer Mendoza; *Amores perros* (Love's a Bitch, 2000) by Alejandro González Iñárritu; *Papel picado* (Confetti, 2003) by Rolo Diez; *Nostalgia de la sombra* (Nostalgia for the Shadow, 2003) by Eduardo Antonio Parra; *Batalla en el cielo* (Battle in Heaven, 2005) by Carlos Reygadas; *Conducir un tráiler* (Driving a Trailer, 2008) by Rogelio Guedea; *El traspatio* (Backyard, 2009) by Carlos Carrera; *Sicario: Diario del Diablo* (Hit Man: The Devil's Diary, 2009) by Víctor Ronquillo; *Entre perros* (Among Dogs, 2009) and *El más buscado* (The Most Wanted Man, 2012) by Alejandro Almazán; *Hielo negro* (Black Ice, 2011) by Bernando Fernández; *36 toneladas* (36 Tons, 2011) by Iris García Cuevas; *El olor del dinero* (The Smell of Money, 2011) by Luis E. González O'Donnell; *Miss Bala* (2011) by Gerardo Naranjo; *Chinola Kid* (2012) by Hilario Peña; *Colosio: El asesinato* (The Assassination, 2012) by Carlos Bolado; *La vida precoz y breve de Sabina Rivas* (The Early and Brief Life of Sabina Rivas, 2012) by Luis Mandoki; *Cuatro muertos por capítulo* (Four Dead Bodies per Chapter, 2013) by César López Cuadras; *La jaula de oro* (The Golden Cage, 2013) by Diego

Quemada-Diez; *Heli* (2013) by Amat Escalante; and *La dictadura perfecta* (The Perfect Dictatorship, 2014) by Luis Estrada.

WORKS CITED

Agustín, José. *Tragicomedia mexicana*. 3 vols. Planeta, 1990.

Anderson, Benedict. *Imagined Communities: Reflections on the Origin and Spread of Nationalism*. 1983. Verso, 1991.

Argüelles, Juan Domingo. "Entrevista con Paco Ignacio Taibo II: El policíaco mexicano, un género hecho con un autor y terquedad." *Tierra Adentro*, vol. 49, 1990, pp. 13–15.

Barthes, Roland. "Delay and Hermeneutic Sentence." *The Poetics of Murder: Detective Fiction and Literary Theory*, edited by Glenn W. Most and William W. Stowe, Harcourt Brace Jovanovich, 1983, pp. 118–21.

Bartra, Roger. *La sangre y la tinta: Ensayos sobre la condición postmexicana*. Océano, 1999.

Belibrea-Enríquez, Mari Paz. "Paco Ignacio Taibo II y la reconstrucción del espacio cultural nacional." *Confluencia*, vol. 2, no. 1, 1996, pp. 38–56.

Bernal, Rafael. *El complot mongol*. 1969. Joaquín Mortiz, 1997.

Buñuel, Luis, director. *Ensayo de un crimen/The Criminal Life of Archibaldo de la Cruz*. 1955. Water Bearer Films, 1993.

———. *Mi último suspiro*. Plaza y Janes, 1982.

Bustillo Oro, Juan, director. *El hombre sin rostro*. 1950. Mexinema Video de México, 1995.

Close, Glen S. *Contemporary Hispanic Crime Fiction: A Transatlantic Discourse on Urban Violence*. Palgrave Macmillan, 2008.

Domínguez-Ruvalcaba, Héctor. *Nación criminal: Narrativas del crimen organizado y el Estado mexicano*. Ariel, 2015.

Edberg, Mark C. *El Narcotraficante: Narcocorridos and the Construction of a Cultural Persona on the U.S.-Mexico Border*. University of Texas Press, 2004.

Estrada, Luis, director. *El infierno*. 2010. Gussi, 2013.

Giardinelli, Mempo. *El género negro*. 1984. Universidad Autónoma Metropolitana, 1996.

Iñárritu, Alejandro González, director. *Amores perros*. 2000. Studio, 2001.

Knight, Alan. "War, Violence, and Homicide in Modern Mexico." *Bulletin of Latin American Research*, vol. 32, 2013, pp. 12–48.

Krauze, Enrique. *Biografía del poder: Caudillos de la Revolución Mexicana, 1910–1940*. Tusquets Editores, 1997.

"List of Massacres in Mexico." *Wikipedia*, en.wikipedia.org/wiki/List_of_massacres_in_Mexico. Accessed 6 Oct. 2015.

Lomnitz, Claudio. *Deep Mexico, Silent Mexico: An Anthropology of Nationalism*. University of Minnesota Press, 2001.

Meyer, Lorenzo. *La segunda muerte de la Revolución Mexicana*. Cal y Arena, 1992.

Nava Nava, Carmen, et al. *Ideología del Partido de la Revolución Mexicana*. Centro de Estudios de la Revolución Mexicana Lázaro Cárdenas, 1984.

O'Malley, Ilene V. *The Myth of the Revolution: Hero Cults and the Institutionalization of the Mexican State, 1920–1940*. Greenwood, 1986.

Picatto, Pablo. "Homicide as Politics in Modern Mexico." *Bulletin of Latin American Research*, vol. 32, 2013, pp. 104–25.

Poe, Edgar Allan. *Murders in the Rue Morgue, and Other Stories*. Kessinger, 2004.

Redmond, Helen. "The Political Economy of Mexico's Drug War." *International Socialist Review*, http://isreview.org/issue/90/political-economy-mexicos-drug-war. Accessed 5 Feb. 2017.

Reuters. "Decretan alerta de género por feminicidios en Edomex." *El economista*, 28 July 2015, eleconomista.com.mx/sociedad/2015/07/28/decretan-alerta-genero-feminicidios-edomex. Accessed 6 Oct. 2015.

Rummel, Rudolph. *Death by Government*. Transaction Publishers, 1994.

Sánchez, Fernando Fabio. *Artful Assassins: Murder as Art in Modern Mexico*. Translated by Stephen Clark, Vanderbilt University Press, 2010.

———. *La muerte en El muro de la verdad*. 2012, photograph, Mexico City.

Siqueiros, David Alfaro. *Del porfirismo a la Revolución*, 1957–66, mural, Castillo de Chapultepec, Mexico City. *Mexican Muralists: Orozco, Rivera, Siqueiros* by Desmond Rochfort, Chronicle Books, 1998, p. 200.

Stavans, Ilan. *Antihéroes: México y su novela policial*. Joaquín Mortiz, 1993.

Thompson, Jon. *Fiction, Crime, and Empire: Clues to Modernity and Postmodernism*. University of Illinois Press, 1993.

Todorov, Tzvetan. "The Typology of Detective Fiction." *The Poetics of Prose*. Blackwell, 1977, pp. 42–45.

Usigli, Rodolfo. *Ensayo de un crimen*. 1944. Secretaría de Educación Pública, 1986.

Žižek, Slavoj. *Violence*. Picador, 2008.

7

SOLITUDE

ROBERT MCKEE IRWIN

PRIMARY MATERIALS

- “Canción mixteca” (Mixteca Song) by José López Alavés (music, 1915)
- *Nostalgia de la muerte* (Nostalgia for Death) by Xavier Villaurrutia (poetry, 1938)
- *Cuando los hijos se van* (When Children Leave Home), directed by Juan Bustillo Oro (film, 1941)
- *Soledad*, directed by Miguel Zacarías (film, 1947)
- *Angelitos negros* (Little Black Angels), directed by Joselito Rodríguez (film, 1948)
- *Un día de vida* (One Day of Life), directed by Emilio Fernández (film, 1950)
- *Víctimas del pecado* (Victims of Sin), directed by Emilio Fernández (film, 1951)
- *El diario de José Toledo* (The Diary of José Toledo) by Miguel Barbachano Ponce (novel, 1964)
- *Después de todo* (After Everything) by José Ceballos Maldonado (novel, 1969)
- *La pasión según Berenice* (The Passion of Berenice), directed by Jaime Humberto Hermosillo (film, 1976)
- *El lugar sin límites* (The Place Without Limits), directed by Arturo Ripstein (film, 1978)
- *Soledad*, directed by Rafael Banquells (telenovela, 1980)
- *Las púberes canéforas* (The Adolescent Canephores) by José Joaquín Blanco (novel, 1983)

- *Mil nubes de paz cercan el cielo, amor, jamás acabarás de ser amor* (A Thousand Peace Clouds Encircle the Sky), directed by Julián Hernández (film, 2004)
- *Babel*, directed by Alejandro González Iñárritu (film, 2006)
- *Me decían mexicano frijolero* (They Called Me Mexican Beaner), Roberto Rangel's testimony as written by Ana Luisa Calvillo (testimonial narrative, 2015)
- "Soledad" by Enrique Fabregat Jodar, performed by Chavela Vargas (music, 1963)
- "Acá entre nos" (Just Between Us) by Martín Urieta, performed by Vicente Fernández (music, 1992)
- "El favor de la soledad" (Solitude's Favor), written and performed by Gloria Trevi (music, 2008)
- "Huelo a soledad" (I Smell Like Solitude), written and performed by Ana Gabriel (music, 2001)
- "La jaula de oro" (The Golden Cage) by Enrique Franco, performed by Los Tigres del Norte (music, 1984)
- "La retirada" (The Retreat) by José Alfredo Jiménez, performed by Javier Solís (music, 1965)
- "Querida" (Dear Love) and "Debo hacerlo" (I Must Do It), written and performed by Juan Gabriel (music, 1984, 1988)
- "Amor eterno" (Eternal Love) by Juan Gabriel, performed by Rocío Dúrcal (music, 1978)

"THE SENTIMENT OF SOLITUDE," writes Octavio Paz, "is not an illusion . . . but rather the expression of a real fact: . . . truly we are alone" (22).[1] Solitude, for Paz, is a key concept—if not *the* key concept—underlying Mexican national culture, a thesis laid out methodically in his 1950 book-length essay *El laberinto de la soledad* (The Labyrinth of Solitude). Paz's essay is grounded in Mexican history, with ample references to Mexican and world letters: poetry, philosophy, political discourse. It refers as well to groups of people, including mestizos, workers, pachucos, homosexuals, and women, whom Paz contemplates but whom he has not studied up close in a rigorous way, as would, say, an ethnographer. His notions of Mexican solitude are based on consideration of a corpus of erudite writings and on speculation regarding a host of more marginal groups whose own ideas of Mexican culture he neglects to explore. He therefore seems to overlook the importance of the theme of solitude in Mexican culture beyond the confines of the lettered city.

This essay on Mexican solitude follows up on Paz's provocations, seeking out some of the best-known deployments of notions of solitude in Mexican cultural production, where its significations often end up at odds with those put forth by Paz. Solitude, it would seem, is indeed a concept that runs deep in Mexican culture. However, the sentiments and meanings it evokes differ significantly from those described by Paz. If Mexico is a labyrinth of solitude, it is a solitude that is much more emotive, more histrionic, more communal, more cathartic, more colorful, and more fun than the dreary labyrinth proposed by Paz.

THE SOLITUDE OF LOS HIJOS DE LA CHINGADA

Paz's landmark essay was not universally well received upon its original publication (323); however, its critical analysis of Mexican history, extrapolated to posit tangible manifestations of a distinctly Mexican national subjectivity, was provocative and in many ways credible. Over the years the essay came to serve as a point of reference on Mexican national idiosyncrasy; for many students, the essay has indeed functioned as an introduction to national culture. Over time, as Paz's prestige as a poet and thinker grew, the essay took on more and more weight. When he became Mexico's first Nobel laureate in literature in 1990, its significance intensified even further, perhaps excessively so, becoming what one critic (taken somewhat out of context) refers to as "omnipotent solitude" (García Canclini 90). As Paz himself states, the essay "was an attempt to describe and comprehend certain myths; at the same time . . . it has itself become another myth" (328). Its influence cannot be underestimated; Enrico Mario Santí lays out its echoes in major literary works such as Juan Rulfo's *Pedro Páramo* and Carlos Fuentes's *La muerte de Artemio Cruz* (The Death of Artemio Cruz) (127). It has generated a whole school of discourse on the Mexican national character (Uranga, Ramírez, Díaz Guerrero, Aramoni, González Pineda) and is an unavoidable reference for just about any study of Mexican national culture from the 1920s through the 1950s and beyond. It is even cited as a justification for a scientific study on "loneliness as a psychological phenomenon" in Mexico (Montero y López Leña and Sánchez-Sosa).

However, critiques have been incessant. On the one hand, more recent generations have deconstructed Paz's arguments, along with the broader range of nationalist symbols the archetypes that became its protagonists (*el gran chingón*, the long-suffering mother, the pachuco, Don Nobody, among others) embody.

Roger Bartra's *The Cage of Melancholy*, for example, mocked Mexican nationalism—with Paz as a major target—with the idea of hastening the country to move beyond it and enter what he would later call "the post-Mexican condition" (*Blood*). Claudio Lomnitz-Adler targeted the hegemony of Paz's vision in a book provocatively titled *Exits from the Labyrinth*.

Others have argued that Paz's solitude was an invention. As Enrique Krauze puts it in an essay called "La soledad del laberinto" (The Solitude of the Labyrinth), "No one in Mexico, except for Octavio Paz, had seen in the word 'solitude' a trait constitutive, or we might even say essential, of the country and its men, its culture and its history" (20); indeed, Mexicans are actually "particularly gregarious, a 'we' before an 'I,' not an atom but a constellation: a people, a community, a neighborhood, a brotherhood, a friendship and, above all, unwashed but solid as the mountainous masses, a family" (20). Krauze's thesis is that the "solitude" of the essay was principally Paz's own, the product of his feelings of not fitting in, his cool relationship with his father, his early economic struggles: "'The Labyrinth of Solitude' can be read as the Rosetta Stone of his biography" (24).

Paz's notion of Mexican solitude, existentialist in nature, is grounded in Mexican history. Mexicans, according to Paz, are untrusting because of the nation's history of colonial subjugation. He defines "Mexican-ness" in distinctly masculine terms (Mexican femininity is a separate subject, addressed below), noting that the Mexican macho "is a hermetic being, enclosed in himself" (34), exhibiting a veneer of invulnerability, of stoicism in the face of adversity. The key manifestations of this masculine Mexican-ness are those of simulation—"claiming to be what one is not" (44)—and dissimulation—"making oneself invisible," aspiring to "pass unnoticed" (46). The only way for the oppressed to show their fortitude and maintain a sense of pride would be to never allow any weakness to show through, to "no rajarse nunca" (never back down), to not "open" themselves up to reveal fears or fragilities (33).

Whether or not Paz was on target in his attempt to define psychological traits that might arise from nationally identified cultural patterns or constructions of history is the subject of debates too numerous to evaluate here. Instead, our focus will be on how the theme of solitude seems to resonate in Mexican cultural production in ways that go beyond the concepts offered by Paz—that is, how other notions of solitude that have little to do with bucking up and trying to appear strong in the face of danger are cultural commonplaces that Paz never seriously considered but are fundamental to contemporary notions, fragmented though they may be, of Mexican (post)national culture.

MATERNAL ABJECTION

Whether because she is a popular actress or because she is foreign, Libertad Lamarque does not enter into Paz's analysis, despite the fact that the Argentine chanteuse became, upon her exile from Argentina in the mid-1940s, one of the biggest box office draws and beloved stars of the golden age of Mexican cinema. She was already a major international celebrity when she arrived in Mexico in 1946, known both as arguably the most popular tango singer of her generation and as a major film actress and referred to by her fans as "la novia de América" (America's girlfriend). The superior international distribution of Mexican cinema and its studios' acumen in figuring out how to best make use of her talents made her into an even bigger superstar. Already in her late thirties by this time and no longer marketable as a "girlfriend" (although this moniker was still used early on, as indicated below), Mexican cinema cast her as a more mature woman, frequently as a mother.

While the Mexican mother, selfless and long-suffering, is itself an archetype analyzed by Paz (83, 93), it is not one associated in any clear way with solitude. Her maternal devotion to her children and faithfulness to her husband would seem to make her an inherently social being. Women, moreover, are described by Paz as inherently open; therefore, unlike the stoic macho, the mother is emotional, passive but demonstrative. She does not dissimulate her vulnerability; instead, it defines her and her relationships with her family. Thus, the archetypical Mexican mother of Mexican cinema, following this vision, is the character represented by the actress Sara García in *Cuando los hijos se van* (When Children Leave Home, directed by Juan Bustillo Oro, 1941) and other films, a woman deeply embedded in her extended family and the personal struggles of each of its members. The film portrays conflicts of modernization and urbanization as the new generation adopts values at odds with those of their parents; while disputes with their father seem insurmountable, their mother, even when she disagrees with their actions and motivations, remains devoted to them. Thus, even when her children leave home, she remains deeply connected to them, and even when she diverges from her husband's severity, she remains faithfully at his side. It is hard to fit the Mexican mother archetype into any scheme of solitude.

However, Libertad Lamarque's cinematic maternity is something completely different. Lamarque entered into voluntary exile in Mexico after her feuding with a minor actress named Eva Duarte came to a head when Duarte's protector, Juan Perón, became president of Argentina, and Eva, whom he had married a few months earlier, became a powerful first lady. Lamarque was blacklisted across the Argentine film industry, which forced her to eventually accept an offer from the Mexican studios. While her first film, a romantic comedy in which she was paired with the Mexican superstar Jorge Negrete, was a box office failure, her second film, a musical tearjerker more in line with the style of films in which she was used to acting, was a big hit. The film was titled *Soledad* (directed by Miguel Zacarías, 1947).

In this film, Libertad Lamarque is Soledad, brought as an orphan from Argentina to Mexico by a wealthy Mexican family who raised her to be their maid. As a young woman, she is seduced by their son, but he soon abandons her to marry a girl from an affluent family whom his mother deems appropriate. The mother then coerces Soledad into giving up her newborn baby daughter to her son and his new, infertile wife. Soledad, who is working in a low-class cabaret act, sacrifices her personal happiness so that her daughter might be raised in a comfortable home. The pain of this forced separation marks Soledad's life, even as she takes on a new stage name, Cristina Palermo, and pursues a singing career (later becoming a superstar billed as "la novia de América," the very epithet that had been used to promote Lamarque in her Argentine films). The bulk of the plot plays out in this later period, with Palermo forging a highly successful career but remaining always and forever alone (orphaned beginnings, abandoned by the father of her daughter, separated in absolute terms from her only daughter) in ways never experienced by archetypical Mexican mothers, such as the Sara García character mentioned above, who are always surrounded by family.

When Soledad's daughter, Evangelina, a spoiled brat who has no idea that the woman who raised her (now deceased) was not her biological mother, meets Palermo, she treats her with great disdain. Soledad, meanwhile, learns that Evangelina's well-being is at risk, as her family fortune is being gambled away by Evangelina's father. Soledad makes an anonymous intervention to keep the family afloat, yet another selfless sacrifice that her daughter, who continues to loathe her, fails to comprehend. It is perhaps significant that Soledad is explicitly Argentine in this film (as Lamarque's characters are in many others), as she is made to undergo, in utter solitude, a degree of maternal suffering never experienced by any Mexican film heroine. Yet the film is Mexican, and this maternal solitude, a fixture in Lamarque melodramas such as *La loca* (The Madwoman, 1952) and *La marquesa del barrio* (The Marchioness of the Neighborhood, 1951), comes from a distinctly Mexican perspective (this painful sacrifice of the abnegating mother is a major trope only in Mexican cinema). Lamarque's Soledad is not so much an Argentine mother imported to Mexico but, rather, an extreme extrapolation of the self-sacrificing Mexican mother projected onto an Argentine character.

And while the Mexican industry used the already internationally successful Lamarque to fortify its position in foreign markets (Szurmuk and Castro Ricalde), these Mexican genre films took the histrionics of earlier successes like *Cuando los hijos se van* to new levels. Melodrama, well established as a key genre of the Mexican culture industry, appealed broadly to Mexicans across social classes, as its stylistic conventions were applied not only to films marketed to the masses (as was the case with Lamarque's works) but also to more aesthetically ambitious projects, including many of the internationally acclaimed works of Emilio Fernández (discussed below). Solitude, performed through the heightened emotional charge of melodrama, became, during the golden age period (roughly 1936 through 1955), an effective means of nation building by fomenting the idea of an imagined community of shared "tears and desire" (López).

Indeed, in this era of Mexican cinema, it is not only Lamarque who represents the extreme vision of Mexican motherhood that implies sacrifice, alienation, and solitude. Mexican taste for melodrama brings similar figures to the screen in films such as *Angelitos negros* (Little Black Angels, directed by Joselito Rodríguez, 1948), in which an Afro-Cuban mother allows her white-looking illegitimate daughter to be raised as white in the family for whom she works as a servant. Her daughter, who grows up racist, knows her only as her nanny and treats her with disdain. In *Víctimas del pecado* (Victims of Sin, directed by Emilio Fernández, 1951), a prostitute played by Ninón Sevilla rescues an illegitimate baby tossed in the trash by a colleague who fears losing the affections of her pimp. The Sevilla character loves the child like her own but must defend him from abuse by the pimp, whom she ends up killing. The self-sacrificing stepmother is sent to jail (although she is pardoned and released at the end of the film). Much of the plot of *Un día de vida* (One Day of Life, directed by Emilio Fernández, 1950) takes place at the home of a character named Mamá Juanita, who has already lost two sons in the Mexican Revolution. The third is on death row for treason, for supporting Emiliano Zapata, an affront to the leadership of Venustiano Carranza. Everyone hides this fact from Mamá Juanita when her son is released for a day so that he can return to her village and celebrate her saint's day. The main tension of the film is in the desperate love of the mother for her only remaining son, whom she is about to lose. When he ends up before the firing squad, Mamá Juanita confesses that she knew about his fate all along. The great tragedy of the film is the death of a patriot and the abject suffering of his devoted mother, who is now left in utter solitude.

Mexico's golden age of cinema declined in the late 1950s, but Mexicans' taste for tearjerkers and anguished mothers did not cease, as the genre of the Mexican soap opera gradually entered its own golden age. Lamarque took on the name Soledad once again in a 1980 Mexican telenovela titled *Soledad* (directed by Rafael Banquells), which also became a huge hit. This Soledad again makes drastic sacrifices, giving up an illegitimate child so that he might be raised in a comfortable and upstanding household, maintaining her secret from her son even as he treats her with bitter contempt, confessing to a murder she didn't commit and going to jail to protect an unappreciative stepdaughter, later facing her son's rejection due to her poverty, and so on. Lamarque once again took the Mexican motherhood trope to a campy extreme.

UNREQUITED LOVE

The Mexican taste for cultural representations of extreme emotional suffering is not limited to mother figures in popular films and soap operas. Mexican popular music has a long tradition of deeply felt tears and anguish, with solitude as a popular theme. Chavela Vargas, the Costa Rica–born singer of Mexican romantic ballads, famously declared that solitude is the price of liberty ("Chavela"). One of her best-known songs is "Soledad" (written by Enrique Fabregat Jodar), in which she sings in her trademark pained voice of being abandoned by her lover, leaving her alone amid a "convent-like silence."

The theme of abject sacrifice in romantic love, accompanied by abandonment and solitude, is commonplace in Mexican popular music, from José Alfredo Jiménez's "La retirada" (The Retreat) ("Leave me something as a souvenir / a tear and a kiss / and a strand of your hair / Don't take anything of mine / because you already have it all / I am yours and only yours") to Vicente Fernández's "Acá entre nos" (Just Between Us) ("I want you to know the truth / I have never stopped adoring you / there in my woeful solitude"). Singer-composer Juan Gabriel took the genre of desolately tragic ballads to a new level with songs like "Querida" (Dear Love), in which the phrases "Look at my solitude" and "Come to me because I'm suffering in this solitude" are repeated again and again, and "Debo hacerlo" (I Must Do It), in which "Oh what solitude, oh what solitude" is a catchy refrain. One of his all-time most popular compositions,

"Amor eterno" (Eternal Love), offers a new twist—it is a love ballad sung to a corpse: "Dark solitude I am living / the same solitude as your tomb." More recent variations on the theme include Ana Gabriel's "Huelo a soledad" (I Smell Like Solitude) and Gloria Trevi's "El favor de la soledad" (Solitude's Favor).

Paz's discussions of human relations stand in stark opposition to those seen in these deeply engrained conventions of Mexican popular culture. For Paz, Mexican men are "masked," emotionally closed, unwilling to surrender or even reveal their affections, much less confess to feeling the deep pain of unrequited love. And while women, especially mothers, are abject by nature, sexual relations are described only in terms of the verb *chingar* (82–90), a vulgar term that translates roughly as "to fuck over." It implies a violent penetration, a rape that leaves the woman violated and the man detached, invulnerable, and confirmed in his position of power. While a woman's abnegation might be expected (in "Huelo a soledad," Ana Gabriel wallows in self-pity: "My hope dies, it no longer can be saved / and no one can awaken my dreams / and speak to me with tenderness of love / Oh! How alone I am / Oh! I am dying"), its depths are not considered by Paz, for whom woman remains "an enigma" (73). Thus, Gloria Trevi's desperate plea, "Solitude, solitude, solitude / do me a favor I beg you / make him feel what I feel," is not strictly in contradiction to Paz, but neither is this desperate masochism something that Paz explores. Indeed, the abject confessions of suffering and solitude in the Mexican romantic ballads, when performed by men like Jiménez or Fernández or Gabriel, run utterly against the Mexican national character described in *The Labyrinth of Solitude.*

Interestingly, Juan Gabriel, perhaps the most successful Mexican songwriter of all time, has been viewed as having helped to redefine Mexican masculinity, not by opposing the *machista* notions of Mexican national culture described by Paz, but rather by transforming them. Hernán Bravo Varela sees Juan Gabriel's melodramatic flamboyance as a symbol of triumph in "the battle against a parochial and machista nationalism. In his 'dark solitude,' Juan Gabriel offered the same victory to popular music and culture."

NEW GENERATION SOLITUDE

The Mexican national character of the mid-twentieth century is often associated with that particular moment in which Mexican nationalism was well consolidated, whether through state-sponsored muralism, the novel of the Mexican

Revolution, the "Mexican school of cinema" exemplified by the work of Emilio "El Indio" Fernández and his production team (including, notably, cinematographer Gabriel Figueroa), the various cultural projects associated with *indigenismo*, and *ballet folklórico*, or more generally through the establishment of Mexico's bureaucracy of cultural administration (Instituto Nacional de Bellas Artes, Instituto Nacional de Antropología e Historia, Fondo de Cultura Económica, and similar institutions). However, by the 1960s, Mexico's myths began to splinter. Youth culture and social protests, along with radical arts production, called into question national myths. Most devastating to nationalist myth building was the decline and fall of Mexico's once-booming film industry, whose foreign audiences, as well as many Mexican viewers, lost interest, and revenues plummeted beginning in the late 1950s. Much of Mexico's film production in the 1960s consisted of cheaply produced B movies, formulaic genre pictures with little, if any, pretension of aesthetic or social value. At the same time, a new generation of auteur-style directors arose. Shut out of the old studios, they were forced to produce their films independently, with unpredictable access to state support and starkly limited access to national and international distribution channels; the work they created under these conditions offered new production values.

In his generation-defining study of Mexican cinema from the late 1960s to the early 1980s, Charles Ramírez Berg ironically asserts that it is not the nationalist cinema of the 1940s and '50s but, rather, Mexico's bleaker post–golden age film production that may be most unambiguously characterized as a "cinema of solitude." He attributes the rise of the theme of alienation as a defining trait of Mexico's cinema to the various social upheavals of the 1960s and '70s: "Women are estranged because of their ascendance; men because of their powerlessness; gays, the poor and Mexican Indians because of their marginalized status" (2). For Ramírez Berg, then, Mexico's solitude is not a consequence of colonial history that leads Mexican men to close themselves off emotionally, masking their vulnerabilities behind façades of machismo. Instead, it is a much more generalized state of alienation that enacts the breakdown of national myths. Mexican national culture can no longer be understood through the "sexist, elitist, and class based" vision of Paz (4); nonetheless, Ramírez Berg argues that solitude, this time applied to a much broader Mexican demographic, becomes a defining trope of Mexican cinema in this later period.

Thus, Berenice, the widowed heroine of Jaime Humberto Hermosillo's *La pasión según Berenice* (1976), lives in utter alienation from the world, in the house of her incapacitated elderly godmother, because of rumors that circulate in her provincial city of Aguascalientes about her possible responsibility for the death of her husband in a fire. The characters of *El lugar sin límites*, Arturo Ripstein's acclaimed film of 1978, are likewise radically alienated beings. An aging transvestite performer and his prostitute daughter, both living in isolation in a small-town bordello, along with Pancho, a young married man who is severely indebted to his domineering father-in-law and struggles to resist his repressed desires for sexual relations with the transvestite, are characters who could not have been incorporated within the national mythology because of their sexual transgressions but who were fast becoming a visible part of the Mexican national landscape by the 1970s.

SEXUAL TRAGEDY

Paz references sexuality indirectly on several occasions in *The Labyrinth of Solitude*. At one point Paz implies that an open male homosexual (assumed to be one playing a passive "female" role: "Mexican homosexuality is tolerated, on the condition that it is a question of the violation of a passive agent" [43]) has more in common with the abject Mexican woman than with the solitary and closed Mexican macho; at another, Paz also suggests that Mexican machismo itself has something inherently homosexual about it ("It would not be difficult to also perceive certain homosexual inclinations [in the Mexican macho], such as the use and abuse of the pistol, a phallic symbol . . . , the penchant for closed masculine fraternities, etc." [90]). From these conflicting references, it is difficult to know whether Paz considered Mexican homosexual men to fit into his scheme as inherently Mexican (and therefore as solitary as the machos) or as un-Mexican others, better thought of outside the realm of the national.

However, the question of male homosexuality arises implicitly at another moment in Paz's essay, one in which gender roles are not the primary focus. During his discussion of the Day of the Dead, he cites a Mexican poet whose work expresses, he argues, fundamentally Mexican views toward death. Xavier Villaurrutia's poetry, at least with regard to his most acclaimed works, is all about death, his definitive collection of poems titled *Nostalgia for Death*. Paz cites a single Villaurrutia poem, "Décima muerte" (Death in *Décimas*), from this collection, although given his essay's thesis about Mexican solitude, he might have quoted another, "Nocturno solo" (Nocturne: Alone), a brief ten-line verse that opens with the line "Solitude, boredom" and portrays an image of an abject solitude, characterized by emptiness and an implicit longing for companionship.

Villaurrutia's poems in general are set in dark, lonely places, where the poetic voice, which often seems to be longing for human contact, finds only echoes or shadows. However, some other poems do include references to other beings. "Nocturno eterno" (Nocturne: The Eternal) refers to "men" who "shrug their shoulders and pass by," and other poems ("Nocturno de los ángeles" (L.A. Nocturne: The Angels) are much more explicit in describing nocturnal scenes of male homosexual street cruising. Indeed, *Nostalgia de la muerte* has been taken as a foundational text of gay male Mexican literature (Quiroga, Irwin, Balderston). Thus it might be said that Mexican homosexuality is also deeply linked to solitude. This idea, not explored by Paz, later plays out repeatedly in Mexican cultural production.

The solitude of the male homosexual in a national culture grounded in machismo is more intuitively logical than the solitude of the macho, who would seem to occupy a place of much greater power and security. *Machista* culture is often inherently homophobic—perhaps a product of those "homosexual inclinations" signaled by Paz, above—making it very difficult for avowed homosexuals to express or fulfill their sexual desires openly.

Miguel Barbachano Ponce's *El diario de José Toledo* (The Diary of José Toledo, 1964), sometimes cited as Mexico's first gay novel, portrays the deep isolation felt by a young homosexual man when he is abandoned by his male lover, who appears to be fleeing the inevitable tragedy that their relationship would bring into both of their lives. José Toledo's profound and painful solitude becomes unbearable, and the novel ends with his suicide. This anguished, lonely yearning is repeated in later Mexican novels, such as Luis Zapata's *En jirones* (In Shreds, 1985), and as recently as 2003 in Julián Hernández's film *Mil nubes de paz cercan el cielo, amor, jamás acabarás de ser amor* (A Thousand Peace Clouds Encircle the Sky), in which the lovelorn introspective protagonist wanders the city streets alone, haunted by images of his former lover. Male homosexual solitude takes on slightly different forms in novels such as José Ceballos Maldonado's *Después de todo* (In the End, 1969) or José Joaquín Blanco's *Las púberes canéforas* (The Adolescent Canefores, 1983), which present the trope of an older solitary homosexual man in pursuit of much younger lovers, more ambiguous and less committed in their sexualities. In the latter, the protagonist asserts that the life of a homosexual is characterized by "long walks and long episodes of solitude" (21). Jorge Arturo Ojeda's *Octavio* (1982) and Luis Zapata's *El vampiro de la colonia Roma* (Adonis García, 1979) offer more optimistic visions of Mexican homosexuality, though these are no less rooted in an inevitable solitude. Indeed, ostracism and loneliness are essential traits of the life of the male homosexual in Mexican gay literature, at least through the mid-1980s (Marquet 114); as León Guillermo Gutiérrez affirms, "the protagonists [of this literature] are young men immersed in anguished solitude" (284).

It seems, then, that Paz's more elitist approach to the Mexican cultural mainstream occludes the most striking and emotionally charged understandings of solitude for Mexican culture, which I am suggesting are more prominently associated with more marginal categories of subjectivity (mothers, homosexuals, unrequited lovers) and more palpably visible in popular rather than lettered culture (popular music and cinema, minor literary genres, television soap operas).

EMIGRANT SOLITUDE

A final, amply disseminated representation of Mexican solitude involves another archetype that figures prominently in Mexican popular culture: the emigrant. Paz does not pay significant attention to emigrants in *The Labyrinth*, which he wrote soon after studying at the University of California, Berkeley, in the mid-1940s. He elected to dedicate the first chapter of his study of the Mexican national character to a Californian figure who is neither a Mexican citizen nor identifies as Mexican: the pachuco, the Mexican American zoot-suiter. Passing quickly over a handful of observations concerning Mexican emigrants, he focuses his attention on a generation of youth that was born in the United States and that "does not belong anywhere" (19). Referencing the Los Angeles Zoot Suit Riots of 1943, Paz claims that "the pachuco is the prey that adorns himself to call attention to the hunters. Persecution redeems him and ruptures his solitude" (20). The zoot-suiter, further popularized in Mexico through the films of the comedian Tin Tan, is not developed as an emblem of Mexican solitude elsewhere in Mexican cultural production, where if anything this figure implies substantial camaraderie. But the Mexican emigrant is another story.

The lyrics of "Canción mixteca" (Mixteca Song), originally composed in 1915 by José López Alavés, do not reflect, as its title would imply, any essential characteristics of the Mixtec people of the Oaxaca region, aside from their historical patterns of migration. "Canción mixteca," often sung amid sobs and other cries of anguish, is something of a Mexican emigrant's lament, opening with the line "How far I am from the land where I was born!" Its refrain is a cry of pain: "Oh, Land of the Sun! I long to see you / now that I live far away without light, without love." It is often performed with the dramatic lineup of a mariachi band, intensifying its emotional impact. Its lyrics are few, simple, and easy to memorize, inviting audiences to sing along, to shout and howl in the background, to weep in expression of their own nostalgia for their homeland, of their own solitude: "Upon seeing me so alone and sad, any leaf in the wind / would be brought to tears, would wish to die of emotion." The title notwithstanding, the lack of specific geographical or cultural references (the Land of the Sun could be just about anywhere in Mexico) permits identification on the part of Mexican migrants in general (whether those who move from country to city or those who leave for abroad), while the melodramatic tone of the lyrics summons a highly emotional participation, making this song of abject solitude something of a de facto national anthem for emigrants.

"Canción mixteca" inaugurates a tradition of expressions of sorrow and solitude on the part of emigrants. Another immensely popular musical expression of this lament can be seen in the Tigres del Norte classic "La jaula de oro," which recounts very explicitly the experience of an undocumented emigrant, who is fully "established" in the United States and has a family, but sings woefully of his inability to return to his beloved Mexico because of his compromised legal status. He complains, "What good is money / if I am like a prisoner?" He has achieved the success, but not the happiness, of which he dreamed. His kids answer him in English and feel no connection to their ancestral land. He is separated in absolute terms from Mexico and alienated from his own family; the song concludes, "And even though the cage is golden / it is still a prison."

While "La jaula de oro" describes the case of alienation within a family that lives under the same roof, many other emigration stories recount separation from the family. Most definitely based in reality, this archetype of the lone emigrant who crosses the border, with or without documents, seeking fortune on his or her own, often thousands of miles from home, is well known.

The story of Martín Ramírez, who emigrated from Los Altos de Jalisco to California in the 1920s, is typical. Ramírez left behind a wife and four children (a fifth on the way), with communication back home limited to a crude exchange of letters among semiliterates. Apparently this generated major misunderstandings, and after a few years away, he decided never to return. Ramírez ended up alone and penniless and was picked up, indigent and incoherent, on the streets of Stockton, California, in the early 1930s. Despite the nationwide movement to repatriate Mexicans throughout the years of the Depression, Ramírez was sent to a California mental hospital and spent the rest of his life a ward of the state (he died in 1963). From his confinement, he began producing art with found materials, obsessively repetitive images characterized by systems of concentric lines. The most emblematic of these is the figure of a lone rider. While Ramírez rarely spoke and never explained his art, critics have assumed his riders to be self-portraits, expressing nostalgia for his Jalisco ranch, the power he felt as a young man on horseback, but also his absolute solitude in the United States. Once confined, he was rarely visited by anyone aside from a professor of art therapy, who spent significant time studying him for a few years. Of his Mexican family, only a nephew came to see him on a single occasion (Espinosa and Espinosa; Anderson).

A more recent example of the solitude of the emigrant appears in the Hollywood film *Babel*, directed by Mexican filmmaker Alejandro González Iñárritu, presents several stories, one focused on the experiences of a Mexican emigrant, Amelia. As a nanny, she lives as if she were a family member of a well-off Anglo-American couple. But she is not family; she is an employee. When her employers are off on vacation, she finds herself in a position of being expected by her own family in Mexico to attend a wedding there but can't leave her employers' children alone. She decides to attend the wedding, taking the children with her across the border. Without a letter from the parents authorizing this movement, she is unable to bring them back into the United States. After a series of horrific twists, including their crossing the border illegally and getting lost in the desert, Amelia, who had largely given up her personal life for the family that employed her, ends up losing everything she had worked and sacrificed for when she is deported back to Mexico. The family, who had elected not to press charges despite the grave danger into which their children had been placed, were powerless to impede her deportation, making clear that whatever bonds she had established in the United States were ephemeral and insubstantial. Amelia had come to the country alone and was ejected from it starkly alone.

Stories of emigrants are often bleak, particularly when their lives clash with immigration or police authorities in the United States. Such is the case of Roberto Rangel, an emigrant from Michoacán whose autobiographical story won the Premio Bellas Artes de Testimonio Carlos Montemayor, a national testimonial narrative prize, in 2013 and was published two years later, through the mediation of journalist Ana Luisa Calvillo, as *Me decían mexicano frijolero*. This fast-moving story recounts the protagonist's original undocumented crossing into the United States, his subsequent deportation, and his eventual return, in which he ends up an informant for the narcotics division of the Fresno Police Department. He is not protected by the police detectives for whom he works; instead, they abuse him and eventually, as he tells it, frame him for murder. Illiterate and unable to defend himself in English, ignorant of the legal system in which he has become entwined, and without any network of friends or community to aid him, he is ultimately convicted of murder and sentenced to fifty-seven years in prison. His story is extreme in many ways; he is subject to violence, including rape; separation from loved ones, including his children; and the constant fear that he will be unmasked to drug gangs as an informant or turned over to immigration authorities as an illegal alien. Once incarcerated, his solitude is absolute. It is perhaps ironic that his story is told from a maximum security prison in Soledad, California.[2]

NOTES

1. Note that this and all subsequent translations to English are my own, unless otherwise indicated.
2. For further reading, see Bartra, *The Cage of Melancholy*; Irwin, *Mexican Masculinities*; Lomnitz-Adler, *Exits from the Labyrinth*; Monsiváis, *La cultura mexicana en el siglo XX*; Moreno Rivas, *Historia de la música popular mexicana*; Palou, *El fracaso del mestizo*; Paranaguá, *Mexican Cinema*; Ramírez Berg, *Cinema of Solitude*; and Yépez, *La increíble hazaña de ser mexicano*.

WORKS CITED

Anderson, Brooke Davis. "Silence and Memory: Fifty Years of Literature About Martín Ramírez." *Martín Ramírez*, edited by Brooke Davis Anderson, Marquand Books, American Folk Art Museum, 2007, pp. 41–51.

Aramoni, Aniceto. *Psicoanálisis de la dinámica de un pueblo*. Universidad Nacional Autónoma de México, 1961.

Balderston, Daniel. *El deseo, enorme cicatriz luminosa: Ensayos sobre homosexualidades latinoamericanas*. Beatriz Viterbo, 2004.

Banquells, Rafael, director. *Soledad*. Televisa, 1980.

Barbachano Ponce, Miguel. *El diario de José Toledo*. 1964. Prèmia, 1988.

Bartra, Roger. *Blood, Ink, and Culture: Miseries and Splendors of the Post-Mexican Condition*. Translated by Mark Alan Healey, Duke University Press, 2002.

———. *The Cage of Melancholy: Identity and Metamorphosis in the Mexican Character*. Translated by Christopher Hall, Rutgers University Press, 1992.

Blanco, José Joaquín. *Las púberes canéforas*. Océano, 1983.

Bravo Varela, Hernán. "Oscura soledad." *Milenio*, 3 Sept. 2016, www.milenio.com/cultura/laberinto/juan_gabriel-oscura_soledad-amor_eterno_e_inolvidable_0_803919719.html. Accessed 22 Apr. 2017.

Bustillo Oro, Juan, director. *Cuando los hijos se van*. Grovas-Oro Films, 1941.

Calvillo, Ana Luisa. *Me decían mexicano frijolero*. Ficticia, Instituto Chihuahuense de la Cultura, Instituto Nacional de Bellas Artes, 2015.

"Chavela, la 'dama del poncho rojo,' en frases." *Vanguardia*, 17 Apr. 2012, www.vanguardia.com.mx/chavelaladamadelponchorojoenfrases-1266869.html. Accessed 5 Aug. 2015.

Díaz Guerrero, Rogelio. *Estudios de psicología del mexicano*. Antigua Librería Robledo, 1961.

Espinosa, Víctor, and Kristin Espinosa. "The Life of Martín Ramírez." *Martín Ramírez*, edited by Brooke Davis Anderson, Marquand Books, American Folk Art Museum, 2007, pp. 19–39.

Fernández, Emilio, director. *Un día de vida*. Cabrera Films, 1950.

———, director. *Víctimas del pecado*. Cinematográfica Calderón, 1951.

García Canclini, Néstor. "La poesía de Octavio Paz: De la palabra a la escritura." *Cahiers du monde hispanique et luso-brésilien*, vol. 21, 1973, pp. 89–103.

González Iñárritu, Alejandro, director. *Babel*. Paramount Pictures, 2006.

González Pineda, Francisco. *El mexicano, su dinámico psicosocial*. Editorial Pax-México, 1959.

Gutiérrez, León Guillermo. "La ciudad y el cuerpo en la novela mexicana de temática homosexual." *Anales de Literatura Hispanoamericana*, vol. 38, 2009, pp. 279–86.

Hermosillo, Jaime Humberto, director. *La pasión según Berenice*. Corporación Nacional Cinematográfica, 1976.

Hernández, Julián, director. *A Thousand Peace Clouds Encircle the Sky* (*Mil nubes de paz cercan el cielo, amor, jamás acabarás de ser amor*). Nubes Cine, 2004.

Irwin, Robert McKee. *Mexican Masculinities*. University of Minnesota Press, 2003.

Krauze, Enrique. "La soledad del laberinto." *Letras Libres*, vol. 22, Oct. 2000, pp. 20–27.

Lomnitz-Adler, Claudio. *Exits from the Labyrinth: Culture and Ideology in the Mexican National Space*. University of California Press, 1992.

López, Ana. "Tears and Desire: Women and Melodrama in 'Old' Mexican Cinema." *Mediating Two Worlds: Cinematic Encounters in the Americas*, edited by John King, Ana López, and Manuel Alvarado, British Film Institute, 1993, pp. 147–63.

Marquet, Antonio. "Ofensivas discursivas en la narrativa gay (para sobrevivir en heterolandia)." *Literatura Mexicana*, vol. 16, no. 2, 2005, pp. 89–115.

Monsiváis, Carlos. *La cultura mexicana en el siglo XX*. El Colegio de México, 2010.

Montero y López Leña, María, and Juan José Sánchez-Sosa. "La soledad como fenómeno psicológico: Un análisis conceptual." *Salud Mental*, vol. 24, no. 1, Feb. 2001, pp. 19–27.

Moreno Rivas, Yolanda. *Historia de la música popular mexicana*. Océano, 1979.

Palou, Pedro Ángel. *El fracaso del mestizo*. Ariel, 2014.

Paranaguá, Paulo Antonio, editor. *Mexican Cinema*. Translated by Ana López, British Film Institute, 1996.

Paz, Octavio. *El laberinto de la soledad/Posdata/Vuelta a El laberinto de la soledad* 1950/1970/1978. Fondo de Cultura Económica, 1999.

Quiroga, José. *Tropics of Desire: Interventions from Queer Latino America*. New York University Press, 2000.

Ramírez, Santiago. *El mexicano: Psicología de sus motivaciones*. 1953. Grijalbo, 1977.

Ramírez Berg, Charles. *Cinema of Solitude: A Critical Study of Mexican Film, 1967–1983*. University of Texas Press, 1992.

Ripstein, Arturo, director. *El lugar sin límites*. Conacite Dos, 1978.

Rodríguez, Joselito, director. *Angelitos negros*. Producciones Rodríguez Hermanos, 1948.

Santí, Enrico Mario. "Introducción." Octavio Paz, *El laberinto de la soledad: Edición crítica de Enrico Mario Santí*, Cátedra, 1993, pp. 11–132.

Szurmuk, Mónica, and Maricruz Castro Ricalde. "Latin American Rivalry: Libertad Lamarque in Mexican Golden Age Cinema." *Global Mexican Cinema: Its Golden Age*, edited by Robert McKee Irwin and Maricruz Castro Ricalde, Palgrave Macmillan, British Film Institute, 2013, pp. 107–31.

Uranga, Emilio. *Análisis del ser mexicano*. Porrúa y Obregón, 1952.

Villaurrutia, Xavier. *Nostalgia de la muerte*. Sur, 1938.

Yépez, Heriberto. *La increíble hazaña de ser mexicano*. Planeta, 2010.

Zacarías, Miguel, director. *Soledad*. Águila Films, 1947.

Zapata, Luis. *El vampiro de la colonia Roma*. 1979. Grijalbo, 1990.

8

DEMOCRACY

The Idea of Democratic Transition

IGNACIO M. SÁNCHEZ PRADO

PRIMARY MATERIALS

- *Vuelta* (monthly print magazine, 1976–98)
- *Entrada libre* (Free Entrance) by Carlos Monsiváis (chronicles, 1987)
- *La jaula de la melancolía* (The Cage of Melancholy) by Roger Bartra (essay, 1987).
- *Re* by Café Tacuba (music, 1994)
- *Todo el poder* (Gimme the Power) by Fernando Sariñana (film, 1999)
- *Crack: Instrucciones de uso* (Crack: Instructions for Use) by Ricardo Chávez Castañeda et al. (manifestos, 2004)
- *La era de la discrepancia/The Age of Discrepancies*, edited by Olivier Debroise and Cuauhtémoc Medina (exhibition catalog, 2007).

THE IDEA OF "DEMOCRATIC TRANSITION" in Mexico is the predominant narrative that structures various events ranging from the beginning, in the 1970s, of the slow decline of the one-party system constructed by the Mexican Revolution to the return of the twentieth-century ruling party, the Partido Revolucionario Institucional (PRI), to the presidency in 2012. This is a soft chronology, and scholars and analysts generally differ on the timeline, depending on the elements considered to establish it. The initial point usually hovers between the Tlatelolco massacre of 1968 and the earthquake of 1985, and the discussion is generally concerned with the moment in which the monopoly of power exercised by the PRI begins to decline. Similarly, the final point of the period is considered to be either 2000, when Vicente Fox beat the PRI candidate to become president, thereby starting a new era in Mexico, or 2012, when the PRI returned to power, effectively reversing an important part of the transition. Some scholars consider that the transition is still an ongoing process.

Regardless of the chronological definition of the period, it is clear that at the core of the idea of democratic transition in Mexico lies the emergence and evolution of a competitive electoral system that would replace the absolute monopoly of the PRI in government positions. This narrative is the center of José Woldenberg's *Historia mínima de la transición democrática en México* (Minimal History of the Democratic Transition in Mexico, 2012). Woldenberg, a former chair of Mexico's electoral authority and an architect of Mexico's current voting system, periodizes the transition on the basis of legal electoral reforms and their outcomes in the production of both independent voting institutions and the gradual achievements of opposition parties in conquering offices, from state governorships and congressional seats to the presidency. Woldenberg's account is a prime example of the core notion of democratization and democratic transition in Mexico. Its kernel has always been the opposition to the PRI and the strategies through which citizens erode the party's dominance. Thus, the electoral process is always at the center of discussions because it is generally believed that the ballot box would empower Mexican citizens to dislodge power from the PRI. The complexity of the notion of democratic transition is that the mere electoral component, while crucial, fails to fully account for the process of democratization in Mexico.

When one takes a more comprehensive look at the past few decades of Mexican history, it becomes clear that a series of parallel processes took place and that their analysis is indispensable in order for one to make sense of what the Mexican democratic transition is, or was supposed to be, and how much of it actually took place. One should at least highlight three processes that accompanied the erosion of the PRI. First, the Mexican democratic transition is closely tied to the emergence of economic neoliberalism. Indeed, one of the conditions that made possible the opening of the Mexican political system was the economic crisis cycles experienceed by the country, most notably the ones resulting from the collapse of oil prices and the banking nationalization in the early 1980s.

As scholars like Sarah Babb have observed, this allowed the Mexican economy to be placed in the hands of U.S.-trained technocrats who would begin the process of slowly dislodging the protectionist, clientelist economy constructed by the PRI. It is patently clear that electoral reforms ran parallel to phenomena more directly related to economic liberalization. For instance, some elements of media diversification (such as the rise of cable television and the emergence of Televisión Azteca and other alternatives to the Televisa media monopoly) were directly tied to the privatization of state assets. But perhaps more importantly, economic neoliberalization introduced an important paradox in the democratic transition process, since electoral progress has been unable to compensate for the rise in economic inequality resulting from economic reforms. As Alexander Dawson compellingly argues in his history of the post-1989 period, "Democracy in and of itself is a poor antidote to increasing inequality within global capitalism" (165). Dawson contends that political liberalization in Mexico did not necessarily mean an increase in political participation by the country's poorest (many of their organizations, like urban popular associations and unions, are frequently chastised by the middle and upper classes because of their disruption of economic centers) or in palpable outcomes regarding their quality of life. Consequently, one has to read the democratic transition as a paradoxical set of political gains that occurred against the backdrop of economic reforms (privatization, reduction of welfare structures, free trade) supported by the business classes but that have generally had results ranging from the neutral to the outright disastrous for the lower classes.

A second phenomenon is the rise and strengthening of Mexico's civil society, or at least of the idea (or myth) of an active civil society. An early representative text in this matter is Carlos Monsiváis's *Entrada libre* (Free Entrance, 1987). Subtitled *Chronicles of a Society Organizing Itself*, this book gathered stories of citizenship organization during two moments when the government failed to respond to crisis (the 1985 earthquake in Mexico City most prominently, but also the 1984 gas explosions in San Juanico) and unexpected political uprisings (such as the turmoil surrounding the electoral victory of opposition leader Leopoldo de Gyves in Juchitán). Along with fellow chronicler Elena Poniatowska, whose *La noche de Tlatelolco* (Massacre in Mexico, 1971) was an early expression of civil society narratives around the 1968 massacre, Monsiváis was deeply influential in developing a narrative of a civil society that would organize outside of state institutions in order to democratize society from below. This notion of a civil society that would stand up in resistance to the overwhelming role of the state under the PRI developed in different parts of the political and intellectual spectrum. A very important venue for this was the magazine *Vuelta*, founded by Octavio Paz and other important writers after government-supported groups ousted Julio Scherer García and his team from the directorship of the newspaper *Excélsior*, one of the few critical voices in the 1970s. Scherer would move on to create the magazine *Proceso*, which remains a controversially contrarian publication. Paz, who was ousted at the same time from *Excélsior*'s cultural supplement *Plural*, proactively used *Vuelta* to publish the work of major intellectuals self-identified as liberal or even libertarian (like Enrique Krauze or Gabriel Zaid), articulating important ideas regarding civil society and the transition. Paz published in 1978 the seminal essay *El ogro filantrópico* (The Philanthropic Ogre), a thorough and influential critique of the Mexican state and of the opposition parties on both the left and the right. This was followed, in subsequent months and years, by a constant flow of critiques of the monopoly of the PRI and advocacy for electoral democracy. Two notable essays are Krauze's "Por una democracia sin adjetivos" (For a Democracy Without Adjectives, 1982), which used the election of President Miguel de la Madrid as a springboard to argue for the need of a more representative government, and Zaid's "Escenarios sobre el fin del PRI" (Scenes on the End of the PRI, 1985), which sought to imagine the end of the system (Flores). A final magazine of note is *Nexos*, a long-running publication directed by Héctor Aguilar Camín. *Nexos* began as a left-leaning journal, featuring major figures of the democratic left (notably Carlos Pereyra). During the Salinas de Gortari presidency, it aligned itself with technocratic neoliberal policies and became a very important medium of dialogue between neoliberalism and civil society. In recent years, it has refashioned itself—particularly in the political dialogue between Aguilar Camín and Jorge Castañeda—as a magazine that seeks political alternatives to contemporary Mexican issues. While *Vuelta* was firmly rooted in the authority of literary intellectuals, *Nexos* has historically featured political scientists, pundits, and social scientists, notably José Woldenberg, Claudio Lomnitz, Ciro Murayama, and others (Sánchez Prado, "Democratic Dogma").

The third process is the visibilization of a considerable number of social agents and actors who spent the bulk of the twentieth century hidden under (or repressed by) ideologies of political and cultural nationalism fostered by the PRI. Since the 1970s, for instance, indigenous peoples and movements have gained a new visibility, mostly pushed by the uprising of the Ejército Zapatista de Liberación Nacional (EZLN), which placed indigenous rights at the center of Mexico's political agenda. In addition to the Chiapas-based Zapatistas, indigenous activism includes various movements from specific groups, such as the Purépechas and the Otomís, related to the protection of their land and resources from neoliberal development and the drug trade, as well as an array of social organizations that address distinct causes important to the many dozens of indigenous communities in the country. Indigenous peoples' activism stands in direct contradiction to historical PRI rule in many ways, not only because their claims to cultural specificity are a rejection of nationalism homogenization, but also because their fight for autonomy is a result of the erosion of the PRI's hegemony in local areas. Indigenous peoples are not the only social group that organized into a distinct political actor (in this case the EZLN). Feminist and LGBTQ social causes are central to the development of modern Mexico. From trenches such as the journal *Debate Feminista*, the democratic transition empowered women and people of nonbinary sexual identities to fight for causes such as abortion rights, same-sex marriage and adoption rights, labor rights, and other antidiscrimination policies. Finally, among many other causes that undoubtedly deserve mention, one should also point to the emergence of a diversity of local movements, from urban popular organizations to dissident labor unions, who constantly challenge forms of social order and political power engendered in the long dominion of the PRI, which is still very much part of the structures of power and domination ruling the country today.

Precisely because the democratic transition has rendered visible an important contradiction between formal and informal politics, it should not be surprising that historical accounts of the period frequently produce counterinterpretations claiming that no democratic transition actually took place or that said transition was by and large a failed process. Political scientist Arturo Anguiano, for instance, calls the period "endless dawn" rather than "democratic transition" and suggests that the decline of the political and social order of the twentieth century did not beget democracy but, rather, a succession of "broken changes" in which social actors are unable to find alternatives when facing a crisis that is not, in Anguiano's estimation, national but global (16). Anguiano's reading suggests that the democratic transition was in fact a collapse of the structures of revolutionary nationalism that came about as part of a larger set of globalizing trends, which, under the rubric of neoliberalism, rendered Mexico's struggles against authoritarianism insufficient, given that larger structural factors related to global economic and political flows escape the ideological purview of these models. A similar point is posed by Jo Tuckman, who speaks of a "democracy interrupted." Tuckman, the Mexico correspondent of the British newspaper the *Guardian*, registers in various dispatches a series of phenomena resulting from policies tied to the democratic transition: the rise of drug-cartel violence, the gradual collapse of the rule of law, and the increase in economic inequality, among others.

The key to understanding the larger counternarratives to the idea of democratic transition lies in the particular interpretation of the consequences resulting from the gradual collapse of twentieth-century PRI hegemony. Most actors tend to agree that the monopoly of power held by the PRI was a generally negative thing and that its breakup was a desirable goal. Yet when piecing together all the different interpretations, one can see that the fall of the PRI resulted primarily from two contradictory factors. One was undoubtedly internal: the large-scale mobilization of different sectors of civil society was essential to the breakup. This was achieved because resistance to the PRI grew from the 1960s to the 1990s across the ideological spectrum. Certainly the left played an important role, begetting the student movement of 1968 and the radical guerrillas of the 1980s, to later participate in the democratization process thanks to the formal incorporation of the Communist Party into electoral politics, under the leadership of Arnoldo Martínez Verdugo, and the formation of a large-scale front to favor the candidacy of Cuauhtémoc Cárdenas in 1988 (Carr 225–330). Liberal sectors grouped under the aforementioned publications *Vuelta* and *Nexos* were most certainly central in defining democracy as a key narrative for a post-PRI society, and both magazines were important spaces of encounter between left-wing and right-wing thinkers. Authors of the historical left, even those in the Communist Party, such as Roger Bartra, Jorge Castañeda, and Martínez Verdugo, dialogued with intellectuals who fashioned themselves as critics of Communism of the Soviet kind, such as Octavio Paz and Gabriel Zaid. Moreover, as various actors in the process recently assessed, the long-standing tradition of liberalism in Mexico (which can be traced back to the nineteenth century) went through a process of reinvention that resulted in a plural and contradictory ideological spectrum that ranges from the left to the right and that includes diverse opinions regarding different tenets of liberalism, most notably the role of the free market in a contemporary society (Aguilar Rivera). And, of course, the right wing also played a main role. Mostly under the Partido Acción Nacional (National Action Party), or PAN, the Mexican right historically organized in resistance to postrevolutionary reforms, such as the separation of church and state, the privatization of the oil industry in the 1930s, and the statist model of economics and politics. In the 1980s, particularly under the leadership of figures like Manuel Clouthier, Francisco Barrio, and Carlos Castillo Peraza, the PAN emerged as a peculiar form of a democratic right-wing party that placed some of its most radical elements (fascist components, orthodox Catholic doctrinaires) in the background, allowing for the leadership of an intellectual class (which included Castillo Peraza and Santiago Creel) and of politicians inclined toward probusiness postures and economic modernization policies. Vicente Fox, the first president of Mexico not spawned by the PRI, came from this movement (Loaeza).

Yet the undeniably democratic reorganization of society at the level of political parties and civil-society mobilization was accompanied by the willful participation of Mexico in neoliberalism, including the PRI and large sectors of the opposition. As a response to the economic crises of the 1980s and the PRI's growing inability to sustain the state-centered governance model, President Carlos Salinas de Gortari enacted a wide agenda of economic reform, which included large-scale privatization of industries such as banking and telecommunication, the undoing of the land reforms of the 1930s, the unraveling of the alliances between labor unions and the PRI, and even the Jacobin approach to church-state relationships. Following the model of post-Soviet transitions and encouraged by institutions such as the International Monetary Fund and the World Bank, the 1990s PRI (with considerable support from PAN legislators) put into place an economic consensus that very much remains the norm today. In fact, when the PRI returned to power in 2012, it enacted a series of political reforms (including an educational reform that radically changed the labor rights of teachers, a labor reform that encouraged flexibilization, and an energy reform that opened the doors to partial privatization of oil and electricity) that were supported not only by the right wing but even by a significant sector of the left grouped under the Partido Revolucionario Democrático (Party of the Democratic Revolution), or PRD. This doubling down on neoliberal economic policy explains a lot about the contradictory views that many Mexicans hold regarding the democratic transition. Although Mexicans today enjoy important liberal freedoms unavailable in the 1970s (including higher levels of freedom of speech and of the press), the increase in the possibilities of political participation has not stopped the implementation of reforms that are, by and large, quite unpopular among large sectors of the population. In 2016, the time of this writing, Mexico is attesting to the consequences of this division: a significant number of the actors involved in the democratic transition are very much on board with neoliberal reforms, which they defend as part of the necessary modernization of countries, while other social sectors (students, teachers, peasants, and the like) have used the possibility of mobilization to protest those reforms. As Irmgard Emmelhainz extensively discusses in the 2016 book *La tiranía del sentido común: La reconversión liberal de México* (The Tyranny of Common Sense: The Neoliberal Reconversion in Mexico), neoliberalism functions as a sort of "tyranny of common sense," in which economic political doctrines that have, at times, devastating effects on the everyday life of Mexicans are sustained as necessary to modernization and as practical approaches to governance. The divide in Mexico, one could say, is a matter of focus. If one places emphasis on political freedoms, the diversification of the political landscape, and the existence of a more or less functional electoral order, one would definitely embrace the idea of a democratic transition. However, if one has felt the brunt of the economic effects of neoliberalism, one would be more likely to question whether a democracy exists in Mexico at all.

This divide is key to understanding the culture that has emerged three decades since the election of Carlos Salinas de Gortari. Precisely because the general signifier used to describe the process ("democratic transition") is widely contested, culture has become a central site of struggle to construct the meanings of recent history and the present. Literature, critical theory, cinema, theater, popular music, and the visual arts are all spaces of challenge and redefinition of Mexico's present situation. Insofar as cultural devices were central to the construction of postrevolutionary nationalism and the political hegemony upon which it rested, it is not surprising that a central element of the democratic transition is a wide reconstitution of the cultural sphere. Early thinking in the democratic transition was aimed at the gradual questioning of the tradition of *mexicanidad*, or "Mexican-ness." In *La jaula de la melancolía* (The Cage of Melancholy, 1987), Bartra argued that the long tradition of writings by anthropologists, philosophers, writers, and other intellectuals in search of positive and essential traits to define Mexico and Mexican identity constituted the symbolic backbone of what he called the "imaginary networks of political power." In Bartra's analysis, ideas such as Octavio Paz's "solitude" or the Hyperion philosophers' search for a "Mexican Being," along with attempts at defining the collective psychology of "the Mexican" and anthropological studies that connected fieldwork to received notions of "the indigenous" or "the mestizo," were all naturalizations of incorrect stereotypes that validated the hegemonic ideologies of the state at the expense of an understanding of cultural and historical specificities of diverse Mexican constituencies. This line of thinking was further explored by another cultural critic, Claudio Lomnitz, who, in books such as *Deep Mexico, Silent Mexico* (2001) and *Death and the Idea of Mexico* (2005), sought to highlight the idea that most notions of Mexico and the Mexican used today are nothing but constructed ideas with traceable historical and intellectual genealogies, which in turn illuminate specific forms of cultural and political power. This tradition of critique of the nation remains a very important practice of Mexico's transitional culture. In a more recent example, *El fracaso del mestizo* (The Failure of the Mestizo, 2014), writer Pedro Ángel Palou revisits the history of twentieth-century Mexican literature and cinema to demonstrate the ways in which cultural productions generally considered to be part of the nationalist canon already had inscribed in them the very failure of the project they were meant to embody.

The critique of the tie between nationalism and hegemony provided a language in which culture became a central pursuit and the public intellectual a central figure from the 1980s onward. This is not surprising if one considers that the liberal strain of Mexican culture already had produced two centuries of public intellectuals, mostly from the world of letters. *Vuelta* and *Nexos* were born of this impulse. But the fact is that both the democratic transition and neoliberal intellectual trends have had a profound impact on the very notion of the public intellectual in Mexico. In *El intelectual mexicano: Una especie en extinción* (The Mexican Intellectual: An Endangered Species, 2015), a book of interviews with Mexico's leading literary intellectuals (all but one of them men, most of them literary writers, essayists, or nonacademic social scientists), Luciano Concheiro and Ana Sofía Rodríguez conclude that this kind of intellectual is essentially a "species on the verge of extinction" and suggest that future intellectual pursuits will be based in collective and horizontal forms of intellectual work rather than the individualistic and vertical model fostered by historical liberalism. This may indeed be an ongoing process, but in the particular case of Mexico it takes place in contradictory ways. One can certainly point to some process of horizontal intellectualism and an expansion of the notion of public intellectual to encompass figures not in the traditional literary professions who nonetheless exercise that kind of function. This is documented, for instance, in Debra A. Castillo and Stuart A. Day's 2014 volume *Mexican Public Intellectuals*, which includes chapters on theater-based figures like Jesusa Rodríguez and Sabina Berman, social advocates like Esther Chávez Cano, and arts collectives like Fortaleza de la Mujer Maya, offering not only an expansion on the activities that constitute public intellectual figures but also a much needed gender diversification. Yet the volume also shows the presence of intellectuals in the older mold, including the Zapatistas' Subcomandante Marcos and Javier Sicilia, the poet and leader of a movement for peace and justice. Most books on intellectuals seem to overlook the emergence of a new figure: the pundit and media intellectual. Mexican magazines and electronic media are full of professional opinion makers who do not come from the lettered background of historical intellectuals, nor do they participate in the kind of horizontal practices developed by grassroots organizations. This new cohort of communicators, radio and TV hosts, narrative journalists, pollsters, and technocrats, both left and right wing, have gradually replaced traditional intellectuals and overtaken the media and public spaces historically inhabited by literary intellectuals. People like Octavio Paz and Enrique Krauze have been displaced by journalists like Carmen Aristegui, professional opinion columnists like Leo Zuckermann, and even comedians like Víctor Trujillo in the role of public intellectuals. One can certainly call these changes a democratization, insofar as a role traditionally held by a small elite has opened to new and more diverse actors. But it is also most certainly a neoliberalization, as liberal lettered knowledge becomes replaced with technocratic regimes of discourse.

Culture and the arts have also played a part in the transformations described up to this point. A landmark 2006 art exhibit, *La era de la discrepancia*, called the period between 1968 and 1997 in Mexican art "the age of discrepancies," which, as curators Olivier Debroise and Cuauhtémoc Medina explained, described both the social milieu at large and the trends in Mexican aesthetics from the period. Debroise and Medina demonstrated that this art strongly contradicted received ideas of state-sponsored notions of art and, more importantly, conveyed a significant sense of political, economic, and cultural crisis. The exhibit's catalog showed the visual embodiment of many of the ideological trends described so far. There was clearly a trend of working from below and in the margins of cultural institutions, which mirrored the ideologies of civil society and extrastate organization popular in the political opposition from 1968 onward. In the case of art, this was visible in the emergence of alternative collective nonstate galleries and the use of media and other techniques beyond traditional painting and sculpture, all decidedly questioning more institutionalized forms of Mexican art, like literature, national cinema, and muralism. Improvised Super 8 documentaries, "psychograms," fanzines, installations, and happenings all shared the same spirit: using noninstitutionalized media and spaces to produce a counterculture that challenged the heavy-handed hegemonic modes of representation built throughout the twentieth century. The retrospective provided by Debroise and Medina illuminated the ways in which the cultural languages of the Mexican transition had been long developed in marginal and alternative art circles and, just like social movements gradually challenged the PRI hegemony in the political sphere, artists like Felipe Ehrenberg, Pedro Meyer, Silvia Gruner, and Daniela Rossell were challenging symbolic and representational hegemonies of Mexican national culture.

The transformation in the cultural sphere has become evident across all symbolic productions. Literature, which occupied a central place in the construction of twentieth-century hegemonic culture, became a much different entity during the democratic transition. In the second part of the twentieth century, devices such as the "total novel" and national allegory were central to the construction both of narratives on Mexico as such and of critical representations of the PRI (Long). Authors such as Carlos Fuentes, Fernando del Paso, and Jorge Aguilar Mora all practiced different versions of this. Indeed, early transitional novels sought to adapt these techniques to the new times, as was clear in Héctor Aguilar Camín's two major novels, *Morir en el golfo* (To Die in the Gulf, 1986) and *La guerra de Galio* (Gallium War, 1991), on the oil company's union and on post-1968 journalism, respectively, and in Ángeles Mastretta's *Arráncame la vida* (Tear This Heart Out, 1985) and Laura Esquivel's *Como agua para chocolate* (Like Water for Chocolate, 1989), both notably popular novels that revised the history of the Mexican Revolution from the perspective of female protagonists. These works, however, more properly belong to twentieth-century paradigms of literary writing.

A few very important transformations took place in Mexican literature in the 1990s that set the tune for literature in the twenty-first century. The first one was the emergence of the Fondo Nacional para la Cultura y las Artes (National Foundation for Culture and the Arts), or FONCA, which radically changed the system of funding for writers and literary institutions. Based mostly on a complex system of fellowships and supported by large-scale editorial efforts, FONCA focused mainly, but not exclusively, on writers under the age of thirty-five. The peer-review system of evaluation and the creation of common spaces for writers to engage within favored the breakaway from twentieth-century literary trends (generally emphasizing Mexican-ness or political fiction), diversifying writing but also producing more self-referential spaces (Sánchez Prado, "La generación"). Related in part to this trend, a second important phenomenon was a major decentralizing of literary writing away from institutions based in Mexico City and away from traditional cultural hierarchies. Women more decisively participated in literary writing, breaking long-standing heteropatriarchal structures to produce what Nuala Finnegan and Jane Lavery call a *boom femenino*, in which leading women writers not only became central to the aesthetic development of literary fiction but also took over best-seller lists and commercial spaces. Another relevant recentering was the so-called *literatura del Norte*, a diverse cohort of writers from Northern Mexico: Élmer Mendoza, Rosina Conde, Heriberto Yépez, Eduardo Antonio Parra, Luis Humberto Crosthwaite, Cristina Rivera Garza, and Carlos Velázquez, to mention just the tip of the iceberg. Their works challenged Mexican literary *doxa* both linguistically and geographically. While it is a mistake to understand them as a single aesthetic category (they write very diverse works), it is true that they can be read as a general and diverse challenge to cultural centralism (Parra, Guzmán). Finally, a third phenomenon was the growth of transnational literary publishers in Spanish, such as Alfaguara, Planeta, and Penguin Random House, which have become crucial to the reconstitution of Mexican literature.

A good case study in this regard is the Crack group. Building on the opportunities provided by the emergent landscape, in 1996 six writers (Jorge Volpi, Eloy Urroz, Ignacio Padilla, Pedro Ángel Palou, Ricardo Chávez Castañeda, and, intermittently, Vicente F. Herrasti) launched a manifesto and a series of books. In general terms, the manifesto advocated for the right of the Mexican writer to write about subjects in addition to Mexican-ness and advocated for a Mexican novel genre that was both cosmopolitan and attuned to contemporary realities. These lofty goals gradually intersected with important changes in the Mexican and Latin American literary industry. While the early Crack novels, focused on the topic of the apocalypse, were published by a Mexican press and enjoyed circulation only in Mexico, a few years later Volpi and Padilla won major awards in Spain with World War II–themed novels about Nazism and evil, and thus they introduced the possibility of Mexican writers not writing about Mexico while still enjoying transnational recognition. Naturally, the Crack writers have many detractors, and they are often accused of selling out to commercial literary interests, or of having contradictions between their manifestos and their literary practices, or their published books not living up to their ambitions, an even more subjective charge. But it is absolutely undeniable that the Crack group changed, both in Mexico and internationally, the idea that Mexican writers should write only about Mexico, and younger (and even older) generations of authors have achieved global recognition freed from the nationalist imperative. The later success of English translations of works by authors such as Valeria Luiselli would be unthinkable without the Crack.

Another important space for assessing the democratic transition in culture is cinema. In the 1990s Mexican cinema suffered various major changes, including the decline of state-sponsored models of production, the emergence of private coproductions, the large-scale privatization of movie theaters, and the transformation of film going from a lower-class to a middle-class pursuit. Accelerated by market pressures and by the economic crisis of 1994, these changes dismantled the twentieth-century tradition of cinema as a technology for the construction of national identity as well as the use of the medium as a space of engagement for popular subjects. As scholars have noted in recent years, Mexican cinema has essentially become an apparatus that reflects democratic transition and neoliberal ideology, and it is generally concerned with critiques of the state aligned with transition ideology, economic crisis, censorship, and liberal values (MacLaird; Sánchez Prado, *Screening Neoliberalism*). The most iconic films of contemporary Mexican cinema, Alejandro González Iñárritu's *Amores perros* (2000) and Alfonso Cuarón's *Y tu mamá también* (2001), most certainly respond to this description, by staging social and economic inequality in Mexico through modern cinematic techniques aimed at audiences whose media education took place via cable television, MTV, and the U.S. sitcom. This also accounts, in my view, for the success of these films in the global sphere, insofar as media ecologies function more in transnational than in national spheres in the neoliberal era.

Perhaps more telling and to the point are the works that had great impact on domestic audiences but because of their political content lacked recognition abroad. One of them is Fernando Sariñana's slick comedy *Todo el poder* (Gimme the Power, 1999), a romp in which a documentary filmmaker and an aspiring model chase a band of robbers and ultimately unmask complicities between crime and public security authorities. The film is very iconic in its presentation of democratic transition ideologies: a distrust of long-standing state corruption, a belief in the citizen and in civil society as the sites of democracy, and the way in which members of this civil society are imperiled by crime and lack of economic opportunity. But it is also a decidedly neoliberal cultural product: it is fascinated with the power of media and creativity as instruments of public engagement; its aesthetics replicate not only the style of popular romantic comedies but also the musical sensibilities of new Mexican rock and

MTV; and the heroes, rather than belonging to the old professional bourgeoisie, exercise an aspirational form of life very much in line with neoliberal ideals. Indeed, what can be seen here is that the democratic transition produced a form of political cinema that, instead of focusing on left-wing ideology or the representation of the marginal (as was the case with the 1970s Third Cinema movement), very much echoes the concerns and anxieties of the moviegoing middle classes, who generally support the politics of the transition to democracy, and also embrace the social and economic values of neoliberalism, but experience the failures of both in delivering their idealized promises. Indeed, one could place here another one of Mexico's most important directors, Luis Estrada, who has so far produced a tetralogy of political films aimed at different aspects of the failure of the democratic transition and neoliberal economics: *La ley de Herodes* (Herod's Law, 1999), a critique of state corruption in the eve of the 2000 election; *Un mundo maravilloso* (A Wonderful World, 2006), which mocked the contrast between the optimistic renderings of the economy by neoliberal technocrats and the realities of poverty and marginalization; *El infierno* (2010), a no-holds-barred representation of the pervasiveness of drug cartels in contemporary Mexico; and *La dictadura perfecta* (The Perfect Dictatorship, 2014), a parody aimed at the alleged role that electronic media have in promoting corrupt and inept politicians. One should acknowledge here that films like these are remarkable in their ability to connect to audiences in astonishingly adverse conditions. While Mexico has a prolific industry (140 films were produced in 2015, a historical record), Mexican films have nearly no access to commercial circuits (less that 10 percent of Mexican screens show Mexican cinema, while Hollywood captures about 85 percent) and also suffer from dismal home-video and streaming distribution. This underscores how central these films are in understanding the ideologies and anxieties of the democratic transition, as their timeliness and their reflection of audience views are crucial to their success. And it is also true that cinema has had an impact in another medium. As Paul Julian Smith documents in *Mexican Screen Fiction* (2014), there is now an emerging regime of "quality TV," very much informed by cinematic aesthetics, that is transforming the hegemony of *telenovelas* in Mexican television.

A final example of democratic transition culture worth mentioning is the *rock en tu idioma* or *rock en español* movement. Mexican rock music had a peculiar history in Mexico. It flourished in the 1960s as part of the Onda movement, mostly by mimicking American music to the point that various bands emerged who sang Spanish-language covers of famous U.S. rock songs. Historian Eric

Zolov called this "refried Elvis." All of this movement came to a screeching halt in the wake of the 1971 Avándaro music festival, Mexico's response to Woodstock, when the government of President Luis Echeverría banned rock concerts, label recordings, and radio broadcasts. For nearly two decades, rock went underground, and some of its major figures, like El Tri, Rockdrigo, Javier Bátiz, and Náhuatl, developed a solid underground culture. In the 1980s this culture was documented in landmark films like *Un toke de roc* (A Hit of Rock, 1988) and *¿Cómo ves?* (What Do You Think?, 1985). As the censorship began to thaw, Mexican rock engaged in a dialogue with two other rock traditions recently liberated from dictatorial censorship, those of Argentina and Spain. This led to the "rock en tu idioma" campaign, in which the RCA record label released singles from the three countries packaged together in cassettes. The success of that venture allowed for the emergence of a full-fledged rock movement, which included venues like Rockotitlán in Mexico City, the cult radio station Rock 101, the rise of music videos and unplugged concerts on both MTV and the Telehit channel, and the rise of many important bands. As the scholar María del Carmen de la Peza Casares extensively analyzes, this movement had a lot of important angles, from aesthetic hybridity to the rise of urban popular subjectivities. Indeed, some albums from the period remain foundational and influential, as critical to one's understanding of the democratic transition as any other work. One can recall in particular *Re*, Café Tacuba's breakout album, which combined with great dexterity popular Latin American sounds with rock rhythms, and *El circo*, in which Maldita Vecindad y los Hijos del Quinto Patio turned underground cultural practices into ska-infused mainstream rock. Mexican rock of the period, which also included a revival of El Tri, as well as bands like Caifanes, Kenny y los Eléctricos, Neón, and even the pop-rock act Maná, was essential in the reconfiguration of youth cultures during the democratic transition and became the soundtrack of the generation that would live through the brunt of the impact of both democracy and neoliberalism.

In closing, I simply would suggest that one read the "democratic transition" in three dimensions: the decline of the PRI, the rise of neoliberalism, and the emergence of a thriving culture that dealt with the contradictions between the two. There is a lot of richness in the Mexican culture and politics of the late twentieth and early twenty-first centuries and also a significant amount of broken promises and failed utopias. These contradictions will certainly play out in the years to come, and all the scholarship and cultural production mentioned here, in my view, provides a departing point from which to read Mexico's present and future.[1]

NOTE

1. For people interested in the democratic transition and its pitfalls, three canonical readings are Jo Tuckman, *Democracy Interrupted* (2012); Alexander Dawson, *First World Dreams* (2006); and Arturo Anguiano, *El ocaso interminable* (The Neverending Dawn, 2006). More recently, left-leaning intellectuals have taken more critical approaches. See, most notably, John Ackerman, *El mito de la transición democrática* (The Myth of Democratic Transition, 2015); and Lorenzo Meyer, *Distopía mexicana* (Mexican Dystopia, 2016).

WORKS CITED

Ackerman, John M. *El mito de la transición mexicana*. Planeta, 2015.

Aguilar Camín, Héctor. *La guerra de Galio*. Cal y Arena, 1991.

———. *Morir en el golfo*. Océano, 1986.

Aguilar Rivera, José Antonio, editor. *La fronda liberal: La reinvención del liberalismo en México (1990–2014)*. Taurus, CIDE, 2014.

Anguiano, Arturo. *El ocaso interminable: Política y sociedad en el México de los cambios rotos*. Era, 2010.

Babb, Sarah, *Managing Mexico: Economists from Nationalism to Neoliberalism*. Princeton University Press, 2004.

Bartra, Roger. *La jaula de la melancolía*. Grijalbo, 1987.

Carr, Barry. *Marxism and Communism in 20th Century Mexico*. University of Nebraska Press, 1992.

Castillo, Debra A., and Stuart A. Day, editors. *Mexican Public Intellectuals*. Palgrave Macmillan, 2014.

Chávez Castañeda, Ricardo, et al. *Crack: Instrucciones de uso*. Mondadori, 2004.

Concheiro, Luciano, and Ana Sofía Rodríguez. *El intelectual mexicano: Una especie en extinción*. Taurus, 2015.

Dawson, Alexander S. *First World Dreams: Mexico Since 1989*. Zed Books, 2006.

Debroise, Olivier, and Cuauhtémoc Medina, editors. *La era de la discrepancia: Arte y cultura visual en México, 1968–1977/The Age of Discrepancies: Art and Visual Culture in Mexico, 1968–1977*. Turner, UNAM, 2007.

Emmelhainz, Irmgard. *La tiranía del sentido común: La reconversión liberal de México*. Paradiso, 2016.

Finnegan, Nuala, and Jane E. Lavery. *The Boom Femenino in Mexico: Reading Contemporary Women's Writing*. Cambridge Scholars, 2010.

Flores, Malva. *Viaje de Vuelta: Estampas de una revista*. Fondo de Cultura Económica, 2011.

Guzmán, Nora. *Narrativa mexicana del norte: Aproximaciones críticas*. Tec de Monterrey, University of Texas at El Paso, Eón, 2008.

Loaeza, Soledad. *Acción Nacional: El apetito y las responsabilidades del triunfo*. El Colegio de México, 2010.

Lomnitz, Claudio. *Death and the Idea of Mexico*. MIT Press, 2005.

———. *Deep Mexico, Silent Mexico: An Anthropology of Nationalism*. University of Minnesota Press, 2001.

Long, Ryan. *Fictions of Totality: The Mexican Novel, 1968, and the National-Popular State*. Purdue University Press, 2008.

MacLaird, Misha. *Aesthetics and Politics in the Mexican Film Industry*. Palgrave Macmillan, 2013.

Mastretta, Ángeles. *Arráncame la vida*. Océano, 1985.

Meyer, Lorenzo. *Distopía mexicana: Perspectivas para una nueva transición*. Debate, 2016.

Monsiváis, Carlos. *Entrada Libre: Crónicas de la sociedad que se organiza*. Era, 1987.

Palou, Pedro Ángel. *El fracaso del mestizo*. Ariel, 2014.

Parra, Eduardo Antonio. *Norte: Una antología*. Era, Universidad Autónoma de Nuevo León, Universidad Autónoma de Sinaloa, 2015.

Peza Casares, María del Carmen de la. *El rock mexicano: Un espacio en disputa*. Tintable, UAM, 2013.

Poniatowska, Elena. *La noche de Tlatelolco*. Era, 1971.

Sánchez Prado, Ignacio M. *Screening Neoliberalism: Transforming Mexican Cinema, 1988–2012*. Vanderbilt University Press, 2014.

———. "The Democratic Dogma: Héctor Aguilar Camín, Jorge G. Castañeda, and Enrique Krauze in the Neoliberal Crucible." *Mexican Public Intellectuals*, edited by Debra A. Castillo and Stuart A. Day, Palgrave Macmillan, 2014, 15–44.

———. "La generación como ideología cultural: El FONCA y la institucionalización de la narrativa joven en México." *Explicación de Textos Literarios*, vol. 36, nos. 1–2, 2007–8, pp. 8–20.

Smith, Paul Julian. *Mexican Screen Fiction*. Polity, 2014.

Tuckman, Jo. *Mexico. Democracy Interrupted*. Yale University Press, 2012.

Woldenberg, José. *Historia mínima de la transición democrática en México*. El Colegio de México, 2012.

Zolov, Eric. *Refried Elvis: The Rise of Mexican Counterculture*. University of California Press, 1999.

FILMOGRAPHY

Amores perros. Directed by Alejandro González Iñárritu, 2000.
¿Cómo ves? Directed by Renato Leduc, 1985.
El infierno. Directed by Luis Estrada, 2010.
La dictadura perfecta. Directed by Luis Estrada, 2014.
La ley de Herodes. Directed by Luis Estrada, 1999.
Todo el poder. Directed by Fernando Sariñana, 1999.
Un mundo maravilloso. Directed by Luis Estrada, 2006.
Un toke de roc. Directed by Sergio García Michel, 1988.
Y tu mamá también. Directed by Alfonso Cuarón, 2001.

DISCOGRAPHY

Café Tacuba. *Re*, Warner Music Mexico, 1994.
Maldita Vecindad y los Hijos del Quinto Patio. *El circo*, Ariola, 1991.

WEBSITES

Debate Feminista. www.debatefeminista.pueg.unam.mx. Includes the full archive of *Debate Feminista*.
Letras Libres. www.letraslibres.com. Includes the full archive of *Letras Libres* and a select archive of *Vuelta*.
Nexos. www.nexos.com. Includes the full archive of *Nexos*.

9

CLASSISM

Gente Decente and Civil Rights: From Suffrage to Divorce and Privileges in Between

EMILY HIND

PRIMARY MATERIALS

- *Y tu mamá también* (And Your Mother Too), directed by Alfonso Cuarón (film, 2001)
- *Las batallas en el desierto* (Battles in the Desert) by José Emilio Pacheco (novel, 1981)
- Letters and poems by Salvador Novo (1930–73)
- Photographs by Semo (1942–63)
- Life trajectories of María Conesa (b. 1892, d. 1978) and Virginia Fábregas (b. 1871, d. 1950)

THE NOTION OF *GENTE DECENTE* sheds light on the ongoing national failure to respect the civil rights guaranteed by law to all citizens of Mexico. In practice, the select groups that trample the civil rights of others correspond to the sectors that imagine themselves to be socially superior, the *gente decente* (decent people). The automatic deference awarded to persons of seeming "decent" status, conferred by such dubious virtues as a light skin tone, or a strong financial station, or an advantageous job and the attendant connotations of authoritative literacy skills, conditions a national debate over the abuses perpetuated by these supreme citizens. Twenty-first-century footage from Mexico City, available on YouTube, includes the video *Gentleman de Las Lomas* (Gentleman from Las Lomas), taken from a security camera in 2011, and *Las Ladies de Polanco* (The Ladies from Polanco), shot on a cell phone, also in 2011. These notorious videos, and others like them, show the despotic behavior of the *gente decente* in Mexico City as they verbally and physically abuse, respectively, a valet parking attendant and a police officer, with onlookers passively watching. The videos succinctly illustrate the despotism of the *gente decente* and can prove stressful for the viewer, thanks to the one-sided violence directed at the less economically privileged and darker-skinned workers. The colonial viewpoint that cast the indigenous peoples as inferior until they turned Catholic, and even then prohibited them from inner-circle status, grounds the contemporary workings of the *gente bien* (nice people) or the "GCU," which stands for *gente como uno* (people like oneself) (Loaeza 60). The very phrasing of these terms reveals the enduring claim not only to righteous moral standing but also to an elite collectivity. The collective identity of the *gente decente* attracts aspirants, and this resulting "we" invests the term with impressive political power.

Perhaps confusingly for outsiders, *gente decente* are not strictly defined by economic status. Julio Moreno observes that the category allowed democratically inclined mid-nineteenth-century citizens to imagine "that Mexicans could have 'class' and 'culture' without having money" (84). The opposite of *gente decente* were the "common" or "uneducated" people, which registers the cultural capital underlying this status (83). Steven Bunker's study of the Porfiriato, the dictatorship that lasted from 1876 to 1911, supports this elastic definition, and it reveals the connection between *gente decente* and the middle class, which was "as much a cultural as an economic category" (109). Bunker lists the "gente decente values" as "thrift, sobriety, hygiene, and punctuality" (109). Whether citizens professed those values in their aspiration to the middle class or as a reflection of already achieved middle-class status, the desire to belong to this group remains an overwhelming imaginative force. Jorge Castañeda reports the findings from a poll commissioned in 2011 that asked how Mexican respondents viewed themselves: "1% said 'rich,' 16% replied 'poor,' and an astonishing 82% stated that they belonged to the middle class" (60–61). Castañeda cautions that in the most optimistic of measurements, only 60 percent of Mexicans fit into the middle class in economic terms. The nebulous nature of *gente decente* means that citizens must surveil their own behavior to make sure they are following "decent" etiquette. The following analysis contemplates less discussed discriminatory prejudices based on qualities such as age, body fat, and disability.

Perhaps because of the imaginary nature of the *gente decente* in the first place, a surprising variety of qualities can threaten citizens' "decent" status and convert them into the uninfluential segment whose civil rights prove unenforceable in the corrupt legal system. Besides the YouTube videos, the analysis below suggests study of the film *Y tu mamá también* (And Your Mother Too, directed by Alfonso Cuarón, 2001), the novella *Las batallas en el desierto* (Battles in the Desert, 1981) by José Emilio Pacheco, select poems by Salvador Novo, images by the photographer Semo, and the life trajectories of the actresses María Conesa and Virginia Fábregas. All these texts and biographies share an anchoring reference in Mexico City, and yet they stretch beyond nationalism by recognizing the existence of other countries, especially the United States.

Both Polanco and Las Lomas, the neighborhoods named in the titles of the YouTube videos, mark sites of economic privilege in Mexico City. As the videos show, economically privileged Mexicans live elbow to elbow with the other social classes. Ignacio Sánchez Prado studies this interdependence in terms of *Y tu mamá también* when he observes that in the film, class segregation "is not so much a fact as an ideological perception" because "the working classes are always already there" (*Screening* 190). Cuarón's film gives repetitive earfuls of rough language and insistent eyefuls of full nudity, queer sex, and drug use, and thus may offend some audiences. These objections to the film paradoxically support the theme regarding the hypocritical sensibilities of the *gente decente*. The simple plot has Luisa Cortés, a cancer-stricken dental hygienist from Spain, abandon her adulterous husband and take a road trip to an undeveloped Mexican beach with two (also unfaithful) Mexico City youths, middling-class Julio Zapata and higher-class Tenoch Iturbide.[1] If the true upper class is best defined as the 1 percent, Tenoch's family may not necessarily rank at the very top and may fall into the category of upper middle class.[2] The film ends with Tenoch informing Julio that Luisa died a month after the trip. This chat over coffee will be the last time that Tenoch and Julio talk, because they are ashamed of the threesome they engaged in on the beach trip. The formulaic plot of the road movie finds critical energy in the film voice-over, which interrupts continuously and expands the contextual information.[3]

The voice-over takes advantage of the conclusion to set the boys' last meeting around the time of the historic PRI loss in 2000—the presidential election that led to a PAN presidency with Vicente Fox. The voice-over avoids an optimistic take on this democratic opening, which has helped the film to age well. Indeed, Mexican democracy took a turn for the worse in 2006, when PAN president

Felipe Calderón came to office and intensified a "drug war" that resulted in a six-figure death count in six years. *Y tu mamá también* silently foreshadows this civil rights disaster with the protagonists' freewheeling fondness for marijuana and other recreational drugs and with the contrasting images of the military presence on the side of the road to Oaxaca. Those forces conduct narcotics-related searches distinct from the effort to defuse the tension over the civil war in Chiapas that erupted in earnest in January 1995 and whose aftermath attracts Julio's earnest sister. The relatively ineffectual switch in power from the PRI to the PAN came to be known as the *alternancia*, and in 2012 the presidency peacefully "alternated" back to the PRI. The *alternancia* parallels the short-lived glimpse of "another way" in Julio and Tenoch's sexual tryst. Because the distanced, steady-toned voice-over seems neither optimistic nor an activist force of change, this technical device meshes nicely with a comment by the anthropologist Emily Wentzell, who writes in her study of contemporary Mexican masculinities, "In response to my questions about their own lives, the men often adopted the detached tone of a documentary voice-over and described the behaviors intrinsic to *el Mexicano* [*sic*] in the abstract" (36). Possibly, the Mexican male voice-over denotes a national rhetorical habit. It may be that Cuarón's audience felt more comfortable with alienating narrative interruptions, voiced by star actor Daniel Giménez Cacho, than might have otherwise been predicted. At any rate, the domestic popularity of national stereotypes helps to explain the survival of categories such as *gente decente*.

Rather than invent new terms, *Y tu mamá también* explores Mexican types. When Tenoch confides to his cousin Alejandro, nicknamed Jano, near the beginning of the film that he too would like to be a writer, Jano insults him by asking if he plans to write about *niños bien* (rich boys). Jano's derision regarding the possibilities for worthwhile artistic contribution by a privileged citizen predicts the academic reception of the film. For example, one critic reacted by proclaiming that "real life" happens mostly outside the protagonist's vehicle: "a lo largo del filme el director nos hace guiños para sugerir que lo interesante (o sea la verdadera vida) es lo que se halla fuera del coche" (throughout the film the director winks at us to suggest that what is interesting [that is, real life] is what is found outside the car) (Sánchez 231). This extraordinary statement indicates a hypocritical tendency toward dismissal of the "reality" of the *gente decente*, the category to which most people aspire. The insinuation surely leaves at least some critics, who are also middle class or aspire to the middle class, in an oddly self-canceling posture. Another academic analyzes, through similar reverse snobbism, a scene set in a threadbare family restaurant: "When the camera abandons the three protagonists and enters the kitchen of the modest house, . . . this detour is not to present an exotic Mexico, but to tell the young protagonists and spectators that they are missing the reality of their country" (Oropesa 93). It isn't customary for restaurant patrons to poke their heads into the kitchen, and so the expectation that the protagonists adopt the same freedoms as the camera condemns the protagonists for politely playing their roles. In other words, if Luisa, Tenoch, and Julio did not observe the hypocritical rules of *gente decente*, they might not eat in the restaurant at all.

As the interaction between Jano and Tenoch shows, the characters themselves police the manners that enforce understandings of appropriate civility. A *niño bien* cannot write well, because he isn't and *can't be* in touch with anything worthwhile, according to Jano and the nonfictional film critics. In a self-defeating move, Tenoch supports these rules when he calls Julio a *naco* (low-class jerk or yokel) for spitting at him and onto the car window: "Pinche nacote" (Fucking big-ass yokel or poser), Tenoch sneers. Julio eventually tries to take revenge by calling Tenoch a *fresa* (literally, a strawberry; figuratively, a preppy), but the lack of sting in *fresa* as compared to *pinche nacote* simply reinforces the fact that Tenoch is more securely located among the *gente decente* and therefore enjoys a superior status. It is more difficult to turn the notion of an excessively entitled citizen (*fresa*) into an effective insult, in other words, and it is relatively straightforward to use an infringement on good taste (*naco*) to strip away dignity. Novelist Xavier Velasco identifies the term *naco* as Mexico's most relished and most feared (middle-class) insult:

> Ningún mexicano sentiríase plenamente contento con la vida si no contara con al menos un semejante en quien descargar el más contundente de los insultos nacionales, mismo que como tantas palabrotas contienen solamente cuatro letras: n-a-c-o. De ahí que cada mexicano viva y se desviva para conservar o conseguir un certificado de que *no es naco*. (65; italics in original)

> No Mexican shall feel fully satisfied with life if she or he does not count on at least one similar being on whom to unload the strongest of national insults, like so many other swear words containing only four letters: n-a-c-o. Hence, each Mexican shall live and expire in order to conserve or acquire a certificate that she or he *is not naco*.

Y tu mamá también never offers alternative or more insightful categories than *fresa*, *niño bien*, and *naco*, perhaps because of this difficulty of working beyond etiquette when trying to stage a believable cross-class friendship. The discrepant manners between Tenoch and Julio—with a disgusted Tenoch using his foot to raise the toilet seat in Julio's house and a shamed Julio lighting a match after using the bathroom at Tenoch's mansion—illustrates the precarious positioning of the middle, as the lower middle and the upper middle invoke distinct realms of fear. For example, to judge from the rules implicit in Cuarón's film, the lower middle and the fallen in class (the *venidos a menos*) can believably aspire to become writers, while the upper middle can aspire to police the lower middle's writing. Thus, the *niño bien* Tenoch brings up the negative reviews of the less wealthy Jano's book, but he ultimately decides to pursue an economics major, and the lower-middle-class dental hygienist Luisa never dares to speak up among Jano's more educated "intellectual" friends when they ask her opinion, not even to recite the technical names of teeth. A frank national conversation isn't really possible under these rules, because the person and the style used to issue a message seem to take precedence over what is actually said.

Although wealth alone does not determine the boundaries of the *gente decente*, considerable financial resources can make that status seem almost unassailable. A last comment on Tenoch's more secure positioning, thanks to his wealth, emerges in his eating habits. Compared to the less wealthy Julio and Luisa, Tenoch displays the most voracious appetite. His alcohol habits match those of Julio, and both drink rum and Cokes rather than Luisa and Jano's choice of wine at a wedding, but Tenoch exceeds the rest when it comes to common-denominator snack food. He occupies the back seat of the car in low style, eating Ruffles potato chips from the bag and a Gansito snack cake. As the repeated nude scenes show, Tenoch consumes this "junk" without becoming "fat." That is, Tenoch remains immune from the usual consequences of popular taste. In his analysis of *Y tu mamá también*, Oropesa also takes an interest in Tenoch's snack habits and reminds us that the housekeeper, Leodegaria, brings him a grilled-cheese sandwich, a *platillo volador* (literally, a "flying saucer"), a seemingly throwaway line that is difficult to hear in the movie because the microphone barely catches it (99). Fans of Mexican literature will know that this dish stars as the exotic after-school snack in Pacheco's *Las batallas en el desierto*.[4]

Pacheco's novella hints at the bad taste (more or less literally) inherent in this U.S.-inspired concoction of yellow cheese, white bread, and sweetly bland condiments. The sandwich in "bad taste" in Pacheco's novella marks the bedazzled introduction of Carlitos, the protagonist, to the cook, Mariana (mother of Carlitos's schoolmate Jim), and his difference from his lower-class schoolmate Rosales, who presumably never eats such a thing. In fact, at times Rosales has trouble finding anything at all to eat. A plot summary of *Las batallas en el desierto* benefits from Hugo Verani's distinction between narrator Carlos and protagonist Carlitos. Adult Carlos remembers his boyhood crush on Mariana, which got him expelled from school, and thus Carlitos remained far from the unfolding events when, as rumor has it, Mariana fought with her politician boyfriend and committed suicide. The parallels between Cuarón's film and Pacheco's novella stretch beyond the assimilated *platillo volador*. Like the ending of *Y tu mamá también*, with Tenoch and Julio's strained final conversation, Carlitos and Rosales meet up—possibly for the last time—near the conclusion, when the boys no longer attend the same school. Rosales confesses that he has not eaten, and at Carlitos's disdainful invitation, the near-homeless youth wolfs down *tortas* (Mexican sandwiches) with such bad manners that his host watches in disgust. Because Pacheco's Rosales is much more impoverished than Cuarón's Julio, the classroom audience can see that the difference between a *niño bien* and a *naco* is defined by degree and not by a particular income bracket. If it weren't for his relatively adequate elementary-school education, Rosales might fall into the no-taste category of the flatly "poor," who cannot participate in the incompetent consumption at work in the display of *naco* bad taste. The disgust that Carlitos feels toward Rosales's bad table manners seems to reflect the idea that Rosales should know better, in other words. Narrator Carlos has previously clarified that as a boy he took a lesson in table etiquette at the Las Lomas residence of his former schoolmate Harry Atherton, where Carlitos functioned as the implicit *naco.*

If *Y tu mamá también* allows its protagonists to ignore roadside violations of civil rights, in *Las batallas en el desierto* the residents of an entire apartment building deny that the vanished Mariana and her son ever lived there.[5] Carlitos is unable to ascertain the ultimate fate of Mariana and Jim. The neighbors' silence seems understandable in view of the risks of falling out of *gente decente* status: willful obliviousness eliminates knowledge of the indecent that might threaten one's entitlement to the privileges of "decency." Because Mariana never suffers any disgrace in Carlitos's eyes, her depression-free suicide aligns with Luisa Cortés's symptom-free cancer. These women's glamorously hygienic disappearances leave the male narrators to control the story and elide the unsexy complications of disability. That is, Mariana and Luisa seem to figure as likeable *gente decente* because they aren't fully present as themselves, but rather operate as objects of desire focalized through the adult male narrators' "alienated" (but comforting) authority and the young male's star-struck but necessarily uncomprehending admiration. This gendered trope helps me to question Sánchez Prado's assessment of *Las batallas en el desierto* as a vote for democracy. Against the critics who view the novella as an exercise in nostalgia, Sánchez Prado believes that it traces the development of a social consciousness, which sets up possibilities for democracy: "Y es a partir de esta conciencia, me atrevo a sugerir, que emergerá la ideología que posibilitará la democracia" (And it is from this awareness, I venture to suggest, that the ideology will emerge that will facilitate democracy) ("Pacheco" 397). This democratic emergence seems less certain after a gender-sensitive reading. After all, the reader can never be sure where the adult narrator Carlos stands in his assessment of his own status as decent. The notion that he does not judge Mariana but only loves her probably ends up contributing to rather than combating the problem. That is, the self-constructed myth of nonparticipation that Carlos attributes to himself as a child regarding his high-minded impartiality on racial and sexual matters does not assure his decency. Contemporary scholars of bullying believe that the passive observer is as implicated as the bully.[6] The social triangles involved in bullying, among the bully, the bullied, and the bystander, suggest one way to connect the dots regarding violence in *Las batallas en el desierto*, *Y tu mamá también*, and online videos such as *Las Ladies de Polanco* and *Gentleman de Las Lomas*. Mexican literature and film hint that imperious "playground" and "dating" power dynamics may have something to do with the macropolitical scene, in other words.

It might seem a leap to travel from a film of 2001 to a novella from 1981 and then to Salvador Novo's poetry and writings from around the period 1930–50, but Mexico City allows smooth transitions because these artists and their texts, in one way or another, have intimate connections. For instance, Laura Emilia Pacheco clarifies in a picture-book biography of her father, José Emilio, that Salvador Novo used to drop by Pacheco's childhood home (18). The tightly bound social geography among the *gente decente* in Mexico City comes into play here. As mentioned, these interconnected households—though often merely middle-class enterprises—are usually staffed with domestic workers. In point of fact, Novo wrote about his housekeeper in a newspaper column. With a kind of noble amusement, he described Domitila's mistrust of his other low-ranking employees, Gonzalo and Rafael. Suspicion, rather than cooperation, seems to reign in Novo's public portrait of his household:

> Domitila ha cumplido aquí ya casi cuarenta años. Mi madre la enseñó y educó a convertirse en la ama de llaves autoritaria, cumplida y experta que me heredó y que lleva la casa, se trae de un ala al jardinero, deja largas temporadas de hablarse con Gonzalo, no suelta los manojos de llaves que sólo ella sabe de qué son; mantiene su distancia con Rafael, insiste en rendirme cuentas detalladas de sus gastos—y aún se da tiempo para atender a un sobrino suyo que se trajo (con permiso de mi madre, por supuesto) a vivir aquí desde chico; estudiar y ahora trabajar en un Banco. Raras veces tropiezo con él. ("Cartas" 25 Apr. 1973)

> Domitila has spent almost forty years here. My mother taught and trained her to become the authoritarian mistress of the household, accomplished and expert, whom I have inherited, and who manages the house; she holds by one wing the gardener, withholds for long periods speech from Gonzalo, never lets loose the bunches of keys that only she knows the purpose of; she keeps her distance from Rafael, insists on listing detailed accounts of her expenses to me—and still finds the time to attend to her nephew, whom she brought (with my mother's permission, of course) to live here as a boy; he studied and now works at a Bank. I rarely bump into him.

The passage suggests that Domitila strives to protect her family's status as second-class citizens by creating a hierarchy that disdains a third-class rung. The absence of a democratic feeling in Novo's household captures his ambivalence toward uniformly applied civil rights. On the one hand, Novo pushed the boundaries of the definition of *gente decente* by flaunting a democratic taste in male lovers and by treating his household help with relative respect.[7] On the other hand, Novo's reputation suffers from his damning late-life alignment with the corrupt presidencies of Gustavo Díaz Ordaz and Luis Echeverría and his haughty attitude toward select portions of Mexico City residents—it remains unclear if Novo thought much about the Mexicans living outside the capital. Viviane Mahieux defends the relevance of Novo's poses for the poet himself: "An intellectual stance is not about *being*, Novo suggests, it is about *performing*" (165). By fashioning a bureaucratic dandy role, Novo plays up multiples angles of decency and helps to embrace and reject, in alternating moves, the hypocrisies of that category.

Novo's autobiographical poems prove highly accessible, in various senses. A print anthology appears online and comprises poems that test the boundaries of "citizen privilege" (Monsiváis, "Material"). Novo's texts from the 1930s, such as "La historia" (History), "La escuela" (The School), and "El amigo ido" (The Absent Friend), contemplate Novo's uncomfortable positioning as a light-skinned elite child, a transplant to Mexico City as a result of the Revolution, at a time when other, less colonialist values attempted to take hold. "Escribir porque sí, por ver si acaso" (To Write Just Because, in Case) introduces the theme of fear of aging, as does the poem "Primera cana" (First Gray Hair), which explores the strategy of deciding to ignore the aging process. Poems about sexual maturity, such as "Nuevo amor" (New Love), provide a platform for the reader to think about Novo's daringly uncloseted orientation. The shift from Novo's lifetime to the twenty-first century has seen changes in civil rights for same-sex orientations. Even at the time of Julio and Tenoch's steamy sex scene in *Y tu mamá también*, same-sex couples still could not protect their relationships with a governmentally sanctioned union. Not until December 2009 did Mexico City see passage of same-sex civil union provisions. The "naturally" styled kiss between Julio and Tenoch in *Y tu mamá también* contrasts with precise instructions that Novo provides in a 1951 booklet he wrote for theater students, which concludes with a chapter titled "Hugs and Kisses" (*10 lecciones* 51–55). The tensions that reign between mid-twentieth-century Novo and twenty-first-century *Y tu mamá también*, between formality and informality, between the scripted and the spontaneous, point to stereotypical associations between youth and the "natural."[8]

Importantly, Pacheco's novella appears between Cuarón's film and Novo's performance and explores the tipping point of the rise of informality in Mexico, which was gaining ground even as Novo wrote his acting manual. While Pacheco's reader in the 1980s knows that Jim's informal ways with his mother will largely triumph over Carlos's grammatical sense of hierarchy in his family, Novo seems to operate on less "spontaneous" terrain, which may have contributed to the pressure that he felt to change and stay "young" as the manners began to shift and his age and weight evolved in the unfashionable direction. In that regard, the fat phobia that likely contributed to Novo's demise illuminates another aspect of the constellation of qualities that define *gente decente*. Novo's anxiety over his appearance reveals the democratic possibilities of glamour and the ways that appearance can either support or cancel status that is staked on performance and not just birthright. In the 1970s, Novo wrote persistently in his newspaper column about his desire to lose weight. The decision to trust a miracle-promising clinic appears in Novo's column on May 10, 1972: "Y la aventada decisión de visitar, al día siguiente, esa Clínica que se anuncia tan conveniente, convincente: tantos kilos en tantos días, sin dieta, sin molestias, sin ejercicios ni sacrificios. Garantizados" (And the bold decision to visit, the next day, that Clinic that advertises itself as so convenient, convincing: so many kilos in so many days, without a diet, without troubles, without exercises or sacrifices. Guaranteed) ("Cartas" 10 May 1972). Novo seems to have misplaced his trust, and in January 1974 he died in the gastrointestinal hospital ward from complications due to his weight-loss regimen. The hours before his death included the humiliation of being caught on a television camera without his toupee, makeup, dentures, or more than a skimpy hospital gown (Barrera 253). This episode supplies a kind of warning regarding Novo's initially successful methods to defend his *gente decente* standing. Fine manners and cultivated appearances may at first appear to secure one's "decency," but if a citizen falls ill or ages ungracefully, the grounding for that claim weakens.

On this point of the unsustainable claim to democracy by way of glamour, it proves helpful to consider Semo, the photographer mentioned in Pacheco's novella, who supposedly photographed the fictional character Mariana and who actually did photograph Salvador Novo's face and hands (for images, see García Krinsky 10, 192). Russian-born Semo, or Simón Flechine, arrived in Mexico in the early 1940s and established a photography studio in Mexico City in 1942 (Trujillo 21–22). Early advertising introduced Semo to Mexico City as "El fotógrafo de las estrellas" (The Photographer to the Stars) whose name, in self-proclaimed publicity, served as a "garantía de originalidad y buen gusto" (guarantee of originality and good taste) (Morales Carrillo 62). Artists like Semo, in other words, may have helped to define the aesthetics of *gente decente* through a possibly democratizing effect of glamour in the relatively affordable medium of the photograph.

Semo also photographed the next subject of inquiry, María Conesa, but then, who *didn't* photograph her? Conesa, the dancer, singer, and actor, dominated the Mexican stage for four decades (Monsiváis, "María" 7). Her life story provides an excellent case study of the influence of glamour on civil rights, and although her performances went largely unrecorded, images of Conesa appear on the Internet as well as in gorgeously illustrated texts, like the one by Alejandro Rosas Robles, *200 Años del espectáculo: Ciudad de México* (200 Years of Spectacle:

Mexico City, 2010). Such materials show that Conesa and most of her cohorts carried more body weight than many star dancers do today. Like Novo, Conesa did not receive much official fanfare upon her death, and like Novo, she fretted publicly about her age and fitness. By contrast, Conesa's two-decades-older colleague Virginia Fábregas does not appear to have left a record of anxiety about her elderly fitness, and, perhaps not coincidentally, she is one of the five women (among more than one hundred men) buried in the Rotunda of Illustrious Persons in Mexico City. It may be relevant to note that Fábregas remained "decent" in the traditional way until the end; she never had plastic surgery, whereas Conesa—like Novo—attempted a medical solution to the problem of aging out of the public eye. Conesa's biographer, Enrique Alonso, writes angrily about the results of Conesa's late-life decision to undergo plastic surgery:

> Un día un asesino, con título de cirujano plástico, le aseguró que le devolvería el rostro de la Conesita de principios de siglo. María aceptó con la condición de que todo se hiciera en secreto, pero el asesino, una vez consumado el crimen, lo publicó en todos los diarios. Efectivamente, la deja sin una sola arruga, pero cambió por completo sus facciones; perdió parte de la expresión de su rostro. (161)

> One day a murderer, with the title of plastic surgeon, assured her that he would return to her the face of la Conesita from the beginning of the century. María accepted under the condition that everything be done in secret, but the murderer, once he consummated the crime, published it in all the newspapers. Indeed, he left her without a single wrinkle, but completely changed her features; she lost part of the expression of her face.

Alonso explains that the surgery supported Conesa's career because Mexicans flocked to the theater to see her new face (161). For contextualizing thought, see Alexander Edmonds's *Pretty Modern* (2010), a book on plastic surgery in Brazil. Today, Brazilian doctors argue that public funds should subsidize these cosmetic procedures for women who are not wealthy. Edmonds worries about the racist ideals behind facial surgery and the sexist principles of bodily alterations that surgically "lift" women's breasts, stomachs, and buttocks to erase the signs of childbearing; these ideals seem to argue "the 'ugliness' of the maternal body" (92). Long before this Brazilian debate, an aged Virginia Fábregas displayed a heavily maternal figure onstage and in mid-twentieth-century films, and in one black-and-white publicity still she underwent a more temporary "correction": the elderly star gazes into the eyes of a younger male actor, who has strategically placed his hands so that he covers her neck up to the bottom of the sagging jawline in a gesture that seems an almost literal "face lift" (Fábregas and Reyes de la Maza 173).

Fábregas and Conesa prove a marvelously compatible pair for a biographical discussion. Fábregas is the earlier star and regarded as the more serious; Conesa, the more sexy and scandalous. Both risked losing decency through single motherhood and divorce, and they thus helped to pave the way for resetting the standard for the "decent." These women competed against each other even as they upheld common goals. Around 1907, according to the fictionalized biography by Fela Fábregas and Luis Reyes de la Maza, Virginia Fábregas recognized two threats to her theater business: the five movie theaters in Mexico City and María Conesa (77). Spanish-born Conesa ended up in Mexico to escape the child labor laws in Spain. Yet her star act in the Americas traded from the beginning on the equivocal sex appeal of her "barely legal" age. Long before turning eighteen, she earned roaring popularity as "La Gatita Blanca" (The White Kitty Cat). Monsiváis clues us in to the appeal of the song "La gatita blanca," whose double-entendre lyrics gave Conesa her lifelong nickname: the dancer's youthful innocence onstage allowed her to push the limits of decency and thus provoked delicious scandal each time she sang it ("María" 13, 15). After the kitty-cat act and before the Revolution, Conesa took a brief hiatus for unwed motherhood and then quietly married the birth father, an upper-class Mexican. Against the desires of her wealthy husband, Conesa returned to the stage in 1909, earning the almost fantastic sum of 3,000 pesos a month. A "decent" woman would not appear in stage, but this wealth—reinforced through her lavish taste in clothes—allowed Conesa to present herself as an exception. In 1910, Conesa observed the country's centennial celebrations by sewing the national eagle on her skirt—a defiance of patriotic rules that Porfirio Díaz opted to applaud. By the time of the Revolution, Conesa made use of a quick wit and a sharp knife to enter into the audience of soldiers and military brass. With merry impunity, she cut off, for instance, gentlemen's ties, a button from General Pancho Villa's clothing, and one handlebar of General Juan Andreu Almazán's prodigious moustache (Poniatowska 39). Despite her intimate knowledge of political leaders, however, Conesa did not exercise the right to vote. Women were not allowed to vote in a Mexican presidential election until 1957, and the Mexican Constitution still does not allow foreigners to participate in national politics. Nevertheless, Conesa became known as a politically inspired figure, "La Tiple de la Revolución" (The Vaudeville Dancer of the Revolution).[9] According to the composer Agustín Lara, every soldier on any side spent his first day in Mexico City visiting the shrine of the Virgin of Guadalupe in the morning and, in the evening, the theater to see María Conesa (Monsiváis, "María" 16).

Terminating her marriage proved relatively simple for Conesa. She acceded to her husband's request for a divorce around 1923 (Alonso 101).[10] Fábregas also seems to have acquired a divorce in a relatively straightforward fashion. Fábregas became pregnant by a wealthy man without being married, but unlike Conesa and her legitimizing wedding, Fábregas ultimately married someone else, because the birth father was already someone's husband. The wedding photo, from 1902, shows only one woman—Fábregas herself—among some forty-eight men in suits, which hints at the hypocrisy of the decent women who would not pose with Fábregas for the cameras (Fábregas and Reyes de la Maza 58–59). Fábregas's reputation became a matter of public defense as her husband succumbed to alcoholism. An article from September 1911, in the newspaper *El Heraldo*, covers the painful divorce under the salacious title "La vida íntima de Virginia Fábregas" (The Private Life of Virginia Fábregas) and specifies the details behind the divorce and the couple's financial ruin (Fábregas and Reyes de la Maza 107). Fábregas never recovered her once immense fortune. In sympathy and gratitude, in 1932 the Mexican government awarded the theater star a pension, although to make ends meet Fábregas continued to work until her death in 1950. Just before she died, Rosario Sansores mused in *Novedades* about Fábregas's financial fall:

> Ahora Virginia es una anciana. Toda su arrogancia, toda su hermosura ha ido desapareciendo. Virginia Fábregas no es rica, como artista al fin no guardó nada para el mañana, no pensó que su belleza tenía, como el sol, su ocaso; no meditó en la vejez terrible, la creía demasiado lejos y no la sintió llegar. Nunca dejó de trabajar, en los umbrales de la ancianidad, animosa y valiente, quería continuar luchando. Su alma, su bella alma de artista, soltará las terrenas ligaduras y se elevará a la altura donde sólo hay paz, quietud y luz. (Fábregas and Reyes de la Maza 194)

> Now Virginia is an old woman. All her arrogance, all her loveliness has been fading. Virginia Fábregas is not rich, as an artist to the end she never saved anything

> for tomorrow, she never thought that her beauty had, like the sun, its dusk; she never meditated on terrible old age, she believed it too far away and didn't feel it coming. She never stopped working, on the threshold of elderliness, she wanted to continue fighting, spirited and brave. Her soul, her beautiful artist's soul, will release the earthly bonds and will elevate to the heights where there is only peace, quiet, and light.

The moral lesson that observers extract from figures who dare to broaden the definition of *gente decente* through democratically anchored glamour shows the risks of linking the effective exercise of civil rights to perceived "decent" status.

A last case of divorce seems relevant because it contrasts with the legal successes of Conesa and Fábregas. Although in 1926, Antonieta Rivas Mercado, a wealthy Mexico City native, a writer and patron of the arts, won her request for a divorce, a reversal was upheld by a Mexican court decision of 1930; Rivas Mercado was forced to remain married to her U.S.-citizen husband (Varley 145). The legal scholar Ann Varley relates the tragic denouement: "A year after losing her appeal to the Supreme Court, Antonieta Rivas Mercado killed herself in Paris. The struggle with her husband, leading her to forge his signature on her passport and smuggle their son out of Mexico, 'certainly contributed to her suicide'" (citing Jean Franco, 113). A photo of Fábregas's passport, presumably for a trip taken in 1949, indicates her civil status as "widowed" instead of "divorced," and like all passports of the time, it leaves two blank lines for separate signatures; Fábregas signed as the "holder" of the card, and she left the lower line for the "wife" blank (Fábregas and Reyes de la Maza 192). The nineteenth-century laws of Mexico saw great amendment in the twentieth century, and as Kif Augustine-Adams reminds us, before those changes a woman's very nationality and not just her passport depended on her husband. In the nineteenth-century case of the sisters Felícitas and Enriqueta Tavares, born and raised in Mexico, marriage to Spanish citizens meant they lost their Mexican status (and their right to buy ships), according to the final decision by the Mexican Supreme Court in 1881 (65). In other words, the laws of the nineteenth century made it possible for Mexican women to become foreigners in their country of birth by dint of marriage (66). Obviously, the laws have cultivated new protections for more generally applied civil rights, and yet, as the twenty-first-century videos of the ladies of Polanco and the gentleman of Las Lomas vividly demonstrate, the full gamut of these guarantees remains out of reach for some citizens.[11]

NOTES

1. Despite analysis of these historically resonant last names in articles such as that of Acevedo-Muñoz, Sánchez Prado argues that the references act nonsensically and thus "establish a pact of distance with the viewer: there is no way one can find a situation real [*sic*] with people named like that" (*Screening* 192).
2. Oropesa's explanation of the social resonances of every setting shows how the screenplay typecasts characters by neighborhood (97–99).
3. Sánchez Prado studies the distancing effects of the narrative voice, whose use causes the sound to be muted in a given scene in order to comment on it (*Screening* 185).
4. Food and authenticity appear in Weis's review of white bread in Mexico and Novo's and Pacheco's handling of the topic.
5. Epple denounces this apparently willful lack of collective memory among Pacheco's secondary characters (41).
6. See Coloroso's analysis of the triangular patterns of playground bullying, where she argues that desensitization affects "both the bully and the bystanders" and enables them "to commit more severe acts of violence and aggression against the bullied kid" (7).
7. See Irwin's work on Novo, which summarizes his contributions to a journal aimed at taxi and bus drivers, *El chafirete*, meant as a tool to help him seduce "the most solidly built of the drivers themselves" (126).
8. Historian Cas Wouters studies Europe and the United States to argue that informalization came about in the mid-twentieth century as young people successfully spread "more outright, spontaneous, straightforward, and direct" customs, interpreted as "the (more) 'natural'" (185).
9. See Kristy Rawson for an explanation of the various categories of *tiples* (88).
10. Stephanie Jo Smith explores the complexity of divorce in the context of the Yucatán following the national liberalization of Mexico's divorce law in 1914 and the similar legal changes in the Yucatán the following year (116).
11. For further reading, aside from the texts in the Works Cited, see the following volumes. For fat studies, see Richard Klein, *Eat Fat* (Pantheon Books, 1996); and Esther Rothblum and Sondra Solovay, eds., *The Fat Studies Reader* (New York University Press, 2009). For age studies, see Margaret Morganroth Gullette, *Aged by Culture* (University of Chicago Press, 2004). For a shift in manners, see Peter N. Stearns, *American Cool: Constructing a Twentieth-Century*

Emotional Style (New York University Press, 1994). For glamour, see Carol Dyhouse, *Glamour: Women, History, Feminism* (Zed, 2010). For more images of Conesa, Fábregas, and other early Mexican stars, see Humberto Musacchio, ed., *México: 200 Años de periodismo cultural*, vol. 1 (Conaculta, 2012).

WORKS CITED

Acevedo-Muñoz, Ernesto R. "Sex, Class, and Mexico in Alfonso Cuarón's *Y tu mamá también*." *Film & History*, vol. 34, no. 1, 2004, pp. 39–48.

Alonso, Enrique. *María Conesa*. Prologue by Carlos Monsiváis. Océano, 1987.

Augustine-Adams, Kif. "El construir la nación mexicana: Matrimonio, derecho y la nacionalidad dependiente de la mujer casada en las postrimerías del siglo XIX y comienzos del siglo XX." *Orden social e identidad de género: México, siglos XIX y XX*, edited by María Teresa Fernández Aceves, Carmen Ramos Escandón, and Susie Porter, CIESAS, Universidad de Guadalajara, 2006, pp. 65–91.

Barrera, Reyna. *Salvador Novo: Navaja de la inteligencia*. Plaza y Valdés, 1999.

Bunker, Steven B. *Creating Mexican Consumer Culture in the Age of Porfirio Díaz*. University of New Mexico Press, 2012.

Castañeda, Jorge. G. *Mañana Forever? Mexico and the Mexicans*. Alfred A. Knopf, 2011.

Coloroso, Barbara. *The Bully, the Bullied, and the Bystander: From Preschool to High School, How Parents and Teachers Can Help Break the Cycle of Violence*. 2003. Updated ed., HarperCollins E-books, 2010.

Edmonds, Alexander. *Pretty Modern: Beauty, Sex, and Plastic Surgery in Brazil*. Duke University Press, 2010.

Epple, Juan Armando. "De Santa a Mariana: La Ciudad de México como utopía traicionada." *Revista chilena de literatura*, vol. 54, 1999, pp. 31–42.

Fábregas, Fela, and Luis Reyes de la Maza. *Virginia Fábregas: Actriz, pilar del teatro en México*. Fela Fábregas, 2009.

García Krinsky, Emma Cecilia, editor. *Semo Fotografía, 1894–1981*. SINAFO–Fototeca Nacional del INAH, 2001.

Irwin, Robert McKee. "*La pedo embotellado*: Sexual Roles and Play in Salvador Novo's *La estatua de sal*." *Studies in the Literary Imagination*, vol. 33, no. 1, 2000, pp. 125–32.

Loaeza, Guadalupe. *Las niñas bien*. 1985. 21st ed. Cal y arena, 1997.

Mahieux, Viviane. "The Chronicler as Streetwalker: Salvador Novo and the Performance of Gender." *Hispanic Review*, vol. 76, no. 4, 2008, pp. 155–77.

Monsiváis, Carlos. "María Conesa: Retrato antiguo para voyeur del pasado." Prologue to *María Conesa* by Enrique Alonso, Océano, 1987, pp. 6–19.

———. "Material de lectura: Salvador Novo en el centenario del autor." *Poesía Moderna* 55, UNAM, 2004, www.materialdelectura.unam.mx. Accessed 8 Aug. 2015.

Morales Carrillo, Alfonso. "El ácrata y las estrellas." *Semo Fotografía, 1894–1981*, edited by Emma Cecilia García Krinsky, SINAFO–Fototeca Nacional del INAH, 2001, pp. 60–85.

Moreno, Julio. *Yankee Don't Go Home! Mexican Nationalism, American Business Culture, and the Shaping of Modern Mexico, 1920–1950*. University of North Carolina Press, 2003.

Novo, Salvador. "Cartas a un amigo de Salvador Novo." *El Heraldo de México*, 10 May 1972. File "Novo, Salvador. No. 2 (1959–1973)," p. 71, Centro de Documentación Literaria, Mexico City.

———. "Cartas a un amigo de Salvador Novo." *El Heraldo de México*, 25 Apr. 1973. File "Novo, Salvador. No. 2 (1959–1973)," p. 112, Centro de Documentación Literaria, Mexico City.

———. *10 lecciones de técnica de actuación teatral*. Pórtico de la Ciudad de México, 1951.

Oropesa, Salvador. "Proxemics, Homogenization, and Diversity in Mexico's Road Movies." *Hispanic Issues Online*, vol. 3, no. 1, 2008, pp. 92–112.

Pacheco, Laura Emilia. *José Emilio Pacheco: A mares llueve sobre el mar*. Illustrated by Mario Rosales. Colección Así Ocurrió: Instantáneas de la historia, SM, 2014.

Poniatowska, Elena. "¡Ay, ay, ay, mi querido capitán! María Conesa." *Palabras cruzadas*. Era, 2013, pp. 27–52.

Rawson, Kristy. "Lupe Vélez Before Hollywood: Mexico's First Iconic 'Modern Girl.'" *Latin American Icons: Fame Across Borders*, edited by Dianna C. Niebylski and Patrick O'Connor, Vanderbilt University Press, 2014, pp. 85–96.

Rosas Robles, Alejandro. *200 Años del espectáculo: Ciudad de México*. Trilce Ediciones, 2010.

Sánchez, Francisco. *Luz en la oscuridad: Crónica del cine mexicano, 1896–2002*. Ediciones Casa Juan Pablos, 2002.

Sánchez Prado, Ignacio. "Pacheco o los pliegues de la historia." *Torre: Revista de la Universidad de Puerto Rico*, vol. 9, no. 33, 2004, pp. 391–99.

———. *Screening Neoliberalism: Transforming Mexican Cinema, 1988–2012*. Vanderbilt University Press, 2014.

Smith, Stephanie Jo. *Gender and the Mexican Revolution: Yucatán Women and the Realities of Patriarchy*. University of North Carolina Press, 2009.

Trujillo, Iván. "El retrato de la imaginación popular." *Semo Fotografía, 1894–1981*, edited by Emma Cecilia García Krinsky, SINAFO–Fototeca Nacional del INAH, 2001, pp. 18–23.

Varley, Ann. "Domesticating the Law." *Decoding Gender: Law and Practice in Contemporary Mexico*, edited by Helga Baitenmann, Victoria Chenaut, and Ann Varley, Rutgers University Press, 2007, pp. 145–61.

Velasco, Xavier. "La agonía del *chic* y el retorno del naco vengador." *Luna llena en las rocas: Crónicas de astronautas y licántropos*. 2005. Alfaguara, 2007, pp. 65–72.

Verani, Hugo J. "Disonancia y desmitificación en *Las batallas en el desierto* de José Emilio Pacheco." *Hispamérica*, vol. 14, no. 42, 1985, pp. 29–40.

Weis, Robert. "Por la verdad del osito Bimbo: Los intelectuales de élite, la cultura nacional y la industrialización de la comida en México." *Brújula: Revista Interdisciplinaria Sobre Estados Latinoamericanos*, vol. 1, no. 1, 2002, pp. 94–103.

Wentzell, Emily A. *Maturing Masculinities: Aging, Chronic Illness, and Viagra in Mexico*. Duke University Press, 2013.

Wouters, Cas. "The Civilization of Emotions: Formalization and Informalization." *Theorizing Emotions: Sociological Explorations and Applications*, edited by Debra Hopkins, Jochen Kleres, Helena Flam, and Helmut Kuzmics. Campus Verlag, 2009, pp. 169–219.

10

1968

Archiving Amnesia: Tlatelolco and the Artfulness of Memory

JACQUELINE E. BIXLER

El olvido está lleno de memoria.
Oblivion is full of memory.

MARIO BENEDETTI

Hay países que castigan su pasado. Hay otros que lo entierran en un ataúd.
Some countries punish their past. Others bury it in a coffin.

DENISE DRESSER

PRIMARY MATERIALS

- *La noche de Tlatelolco* (Massacre in Mexico) by Elena Poniatowska (testimonial narrative, 1971)
- *Olimpia 68* (Olympia '68) by Flavio González Mello (play, 2008)
- *Rojo amanecer* (Red Dawn), directed by Jorge Fons (film, 1990)
- Plaza de Tlatelolco and the 1968 Memorial Museum (sites of memory)
- Graphic art from 1968 and 2008 by various artists

OUTSIDE THE BORDERS OF MEXICO, few people are aware that the 1968 Summer Olympics were held in Mexico City. Even fewer know that ten days before the opening ceremony army troops and special forces slaughtered hundreds of students and innocent bystanders in the Plaza de Tlatelolco, a site of struggle and sacrifice since the days of the Aztecs. Violent death is unfortunately nothing new in Mexico, home to the Spanish

Conquest, the 1910 Revolution, the deadly earthquake of 1985, the 1994 Chiapas uprising, femicides, drug cartels, mass graves, and the presumed slaughter of forty-three disappeared students in 2014 in rural Ayotzinapa. While the demands being made by the students in '68 were not unlike those being voiced in Paris, Prague, Tokyo, California, and many other places that same year, the Mexican student movement was unique in terms of the violence with which it was squelched and the questions that were left unanswered—namely, who ordered the massacre and how many were killed?

The movement itself began on July 22 in a rather trivial way, when an excessive use of force was used to break up a skirmish between groups from two secondary schools. The brutality of the police response sparked an escalating chain of protests and repression that led to increasingly large protest marches, in which the students were joined by teachers, workers, and members of leftist political groups. As the opening of the Olympic Games approached in October, President Gustavo Díaz Ordaz decided that on the eve of its debut on the world stage, Mexico could not and would not be seen as a country that could not maintain order. His "solution" was effective; October 2 brought the death, detention, or disappearance of hundreds and the demise of the student movement. By October 3, the bodies were gone, the blood had been washed away, and the government-controlled media merely reported that a handful of students had been killed after they opened fire on the troops, while the government itself launched Operation Amnesia: "first they hide the magnitude of the tragedy, then they minimalize the numbers, propagate rumors, denigrate the protagonists, and trivialize the events and in the end there will be those who doubt that the events actually took place" (Álvarez Garín 256). Official archives remained buried until the Partido Revolucionario Institucional (Institutional Revolutionary Party), or PRI, finally lost its seventy-year stranglehold on the presidency in 2000. The challenge to the amnesia began in earnest when 1,500 unregistered rolls of film were discovered on the roof of the National Palace, scores of books and films on 1968 appeared, and the Internet provided a free and uncontrollable source of photos, videos, and testimonies. Nonetheless, the government has yet to admit blame, to punish those responsible, or to provide an accurate count of those killed that afternoon.

On October 2, 1968, twentieth-century Mexican history split into two eras: pre- and post-'68. Considered a watershed moment in Mexican history and the cornerstone of Mexico's contemporary collective consciousness, the Tlatelolco massacre marks the beginning of deep public distrust of governmental authority. Almost fifty years later, Mexicans refuse to forget October 2 and continue to demand both the truth and an end to the impunity that has protected those responsible. Mexico's writers and artists, in particular, have ensured that "el dos de octubre no se olvida" (October 2 will not be forgotten) by counteracting the politics of amnesia with a steady stream of collective memories, ranging from chronicles and commemorative books to works for the stage and the silver screen. These cultural products serve as "counter-memories," which underscore "the disparities between history as it is discursively transmitted and memory as it is publicly enacted by the bodies that bear its consequences" (Roach 26). In a process of borrowing and inventing, Mexican writers, filmmakers, and graphic artists "quote" from various types of archives (photos, film footage, newspapers, and personal testimonies) and at the same time create texts and images that recall the events of '68, reactivate memory, and prompt critical inquiry.

A number of books by Carlos Monsiváis, Paco Ignacio Taibo II, Enrique Krauze, Jorge Volpi, and others detail the student movement from beginning to end, while literary writers, cinematographers, and graphic artists recreate 1968 with pens, cameras, and other tools of the trade. This study offers just five examples of such efforts to keep alive both the memories of 1968 and the call for justice and truth: the graphic art produced during the summer of 1968 and again on the fortieth anniversary of the massacre; Elena Poniatowska's testimonial narrative *La noche de Tlatelolco* (Massacre in Mexico, 1971); the film *Rojo amanecer* (Red Dawn, 1990); Flavio González Mello's play *Olimpia 68* (Olympia '68, 2008); and the Plaza de Tlatelolco itself, a *lieu de mémoire* (site of memory) that includes a memorial to the victims as well as a permanent museum exhibit titled *Memorial del 68.*

ART AS ARCHIVE

The use of visual art as a form of expression can be traced to the earliest civilizations that inhabited the area now known as Mexico. Mayas, Zapotecs, and Aztecs, among others, carved pictographs into stone, lined their temples with murals, and performed dances and other rituals, including human sacrifice, to tell their stories and ensure their own continuity. Centuries later, their descendants likewise used visual art to ensure the continuity of the student movement, communicating among themselves and with the pueblo at large through illustrated flyers, which the students mimeographed by the thousands, stuck on walls, and distributed to motorists and pedestrians. These simple graphic productions

FIGURE 10.1. Artist unknown, untitled flyer, 1968.

announced upcoming rallies and marches, denounced the lies disseminated by the government, and conveyed the movement's commitment to the struggle.

The mass production of hand-drawn images is reminiscent of the *grabados* (prints) created by the lithographer José Guadalupe Posada (1852–1913) at the turn of the twentieth century, a time when the great majority of Mexicans were illiterate. Like Posada, the graphic artists of '68 engaged the public eye through the use of popular, easily recognizable images. This type of visual propaganda was a crucial means of communication at a time when television, radio, and newspapers were all controlled by the government. Indeed, those caught producing or posting such materials were arrested on the grounds of "social dissolution."

While many of Mexico's graphic artists were designing posters, banners, and clothing for the upcoming Olympic Games, others appropriated and parodied images such as the Olympic mascot—the peace dove—and the famous concentric rings to mock President Díaz Ordaz and the repressive measures he was taking to keep the protesters from tarnishing the shining image of a developing, democratic Mexico (figure 10.1).[1] As Luis Castañeda notes, "It was precisely the abstract simplicity of [the Olympics'] graphics and typeface that allowed for a wide range of politically charged reinterpretations" (161). The playful merging of political protest and Olympic design in these graphic highjackings reflects the incongruous combination of international showcasing and bloody repression that Mexico experienced between July and October 1968.[2]

In addition to universal symbols of peace and democracy, icons of Mexican patriotism (for instance, Benito Juárez, José María Morelos) were transgressed with chains, gags, bayonets, and army helmets. The sacrilegious deformation of such icons of nationhood was the movement's way of both underscoring and subverting the government's use of these icons to diffuse and maintain official propaganda. International images such as the *V* for victory and "Venceremos" (We will overcome), Fidel Castro, and, most importantly, revolutionary martyr Che Guevara accompanied the clamor for justice and freedom from repression.

On the fifteenth anniversary of the 1968 massacre, several of those same bold artists published *La gráfica del '68: Homenaje al movimiento estudiantil* (The Graphic Art of '68: An Homage to the Student Movement), a significant contribution to the documentation and the understanding of the role that graphic art played in the student movement. In 2004, two graphic artists at the forefront of the '68 movement published *Imágenes y símbolos del 68* (Images and Symbols of '68), a compendium of photographs, political posters, protest songs, *corridos* (ballads), poems, newspaper clippings, and testimonies from various intellectuals, writers, and student leaders (Aquino and Pérezvega). This copious multimedia collection provides one of the most thorough cultural and artistic archives of Mexico 1968.

In 2008 and in anticipation of the fortieth anniversary, another one of the original '68 artists, José Manuel Morelos, put together an exhibition of posters by forty graphic artists from various parts of Mexico.[3] While these posters are more sophisticated in format and technology than the flyers produced in 1968, they borrow heavily from the art created that summer and carry on the parodic critique of Mexico's long-standing official culture of secrecy. One of the simplest yet most powerful of these posters is one by Morelos himself (figure 10.2).

An enormous book bears the title *Mexico 68* written in the concentric-style typeface found on the official 1968 Olympics poster. Firmly bound with barbed wire, the book shows clear signs of age and neglect. The end of impunity requires the opening of all such books, an action that the government has resisted for half a century. Other posters in the series likewise convey the concept of prohibited reading or writing, with images such as newspapers and

FIGURE 10.2. José Manuel Morelos, *Mexico 68 (El genocidio no prescribe)*, 1968. Poster.

pens leaking red ink/blood. Yet others include blood stains, scars, and tattoos, all indelible images, much like the bullet-ridden walls of Tlatelolco and the memories of those who were there. As a whole, this flurry of graphic art recognizes and celebrates the creativity of the artist-activists of '68 by reworking earlier familiar images, both official and denunciatory, reminding viewers of the injustices committed, and prompting them to join in the continued demand for open records and accountability.

ARCHIVING THE ORAL: PONIATOWSKA AND *LA NOCHE DE TLATELOLCO*

The events of Mexico 1968 have inspired a number of poems, novels, essays, and chronicles. All share the objective of remembering, recreating, and denouncing the final massacre. One immediate and particularly powerful voice of dissent came from writer and journalist Elena Poniatowska, who soon arrived on the scene of the massacre to gather testimonies from survivors and other witnesses. The result of her extensive interviewing and editing is the documentary narrative *La noche de Tlatelolco*. Published independently just three years after the slaughter, it includes hundreds of testimonies that refute beyond a doubt the government's claim that the students fired first and that the casualties were limited to twenty dead, thirty-six wounded. Prefaced with graphic photographs of the young victims, the book is loosely divided into two parts—"Ganar la calle" (Take the Streets) and "La noche de Tlatelolco"—and concludes with a succinct chronology of events. *La noche* is collective memory at its finest, a mosaic of narrated images from all levels of society, including student leaders, workers, parents of slain children, residents of Tlatelolco apartments, foreign press correspondents, prisoners, soldiers, and government officials. Along with oral testimonies, Poniatowska's discursive montage includes newspaper clippings, official rhetoric, protest songs, *corridos*, graffiti, slogans, and police records. While Poniatowska does her best to let the voices speak for themselves, her presence is nonetheless felt in the organization of the fragments, the repetition of certain slogans and short party lines, the inclusion of fragments initialed "E.P.," and the insertion of passages from Miguel León-Portilla's book *The Broken Spears*, which relates the Conquest of Mexico from the point of view of the vanquished. Also, as Beth Jorgensen notes, "Poniatowska often omits the names of policemen, government officials, and prison guards, and their anonymity, in striking contrast to the careful notation of the students' names, dehumanizes the protagonists of the government's policies" (84). The object of many editions and translations, *La noche de Tlatelolco* is the most widely read account of the events that led up to and culminated on October 2. Significantly, when Luis Echeverría, Díaz Ordaz's right-hand man and presidential successor, tried to award Poniatowska the Xavier Villaurrutia literary prize, she rejected it, demanding to know who was going to give the award to the slain students. While many of Mexico's writers and artists were co-opted by President Luis Echeverría's leftist rhetoric and promise of democratic reform, Poniatowska, along with other first responders like Octavio Paz (*Posdata* [PS], 1970) and poets Rosario Castellanos and José Emilio Pacheco, refused to be swept into the fold of the man widely believed to have ordered the massacre.

REENACTING THE ACT: *OLIMPIA 68*

In 1999, playwright and former student activist Felipe Galván edited and published *Teatro del 68*, an anthology of thirteen plays that refer, either directly or indirectly, to the events of 1968. Most of these pieces consist of one act, small casts, and minimal technical requirements, which facilitate their staging by student groups. The dramatic action often oscillates between past and present, thereby highlighting the contrast between the idealistic, youthful euphoria of the 1960s and the nostalgia, disillusion, and guilt that prevailed during subsequent decades. In several cases, the characters, now politicians, find themselves forced to recognize their own betrayal of their youthful ideals. Many of these plays include popular '60s music as well as slogans often heard during the manifestations and marches, thus recapturing the spirit of joy, freedom, and empowerment that reigned prior to October 2.

While the plays written soon after the massacre—a time of censorship and official silence—normally resorted to allegory, metaphor, and absurdist techniques to make implicit references to 1968, those created later are much more explicit. One of these is Flavio González Mello's *Olimpia 68*, which was written specifically for the fortieth anniversary. Unlike other plays that deal with the events of that summer, *Olimpia 68* combines in one text the two incongruous faces of Mexico 1968: the student movement and the Olympic Games. Competitive sports and political strife converge from the title on, which refers not only to the games and their original site in ancient Greece but also to the

Olympia Battalion, the undercover paramilitary police force formed by President Díaz Ordaz to maintain order before and during the Olympics.

Olimpia 68 premiered on October 2, 2008, in the Centro Cultural Universitario Tlatelolco, a tall building that formerly housed the Ministry of Foreign Relations and from which the massacre was filmed by cameramen hired by Luis Echeverría, presumed to be the mastermind of the slaughter. Designed to resemble the University Olympic Stadium, the stage set included a small arena for track and field events. The spectators sat on stadium-style bleachers that backed up to a huge wall of glass, through which they could see the actual building from which the army snipers had opened fire on the crowd.

The scenic complexities are compounded by a cast of more than thirty actors, who play multiple roles as athletes and coaches, Olympic officials, referees, street vendors, students, army troops, and members of the special Olympia Battalion. The minimalist, microcosmic reproduction of several Olympic venues makes possible quick transitions between scenes and the impromptu creation of spaces, including a dormitory, an archaeological site, a diving pool, and a torture chamber. González Mello makes no effort to disguise his use of sports as a metaphor for the political tug-of-war waged in Mexico during the summer of 1968. Indeed, the opening scene, "Elimination Round," blatantly sets the stage for what becomes a running metaphor of violence as sport. The Olympic official initiates the usual "On your mark, get set . . . " routine, only to diverge from the final "go" by pointing the pistol at the athlete and shooting him point-blank in the back of the head. This first scene, while shocking, establishes the link between sports and political violence, athletes and student activists, corrupt Olympic officials and corrupt governmental officials.

Like the Olympic Games, the play is framed by opening and closing ceremonies, both of which begin with explosions that could be fireworks or gunfire. In the inaugural scene, the "stadium" is full of balloons, which the audience promptly equates with the massacred students, when the "athletes," wearing the white gloves that distinguished the Olympia Battalion from civilians on October 2, pop the balloons as they march around, leaving behind a trail of latex cadavers. In the last scene, a student, tortured and amnesic, sits in the empty stadium, unable to remember why he is there. A little girl sits beside him and remarks, "It's over," a simple statement that relates not only to the play but also to the Olympic Games and to the student movement (70).

While most of the dialogue and action concern the relationships that form among athletes and coaches oblivious to Mexico's ongoing political violence, the shadow of Tlatelolco is omnipresent. The cover-ups committed by athletes, coaches, and officials echo those taking place in Mexico, where "Aquí no pasa nada" (Everything's fine) was the government's stock response to external questions regarding the student protests and October 2. In a scene titled "Long Jump," the Argentine competitor is shocked to see a human hand emerge from the sand pit. The reason provided by the judge—"He buried himself"—is no more absurd than some of the reasons the government offered to parents to explain the disappearance of their sons and daughters. When the athlete expresses the desire to help free the buried victim, she is told that "it is a crime to loot archeological patrimony in this country" (11), a statement that clearly extends to the excavating of long-buried records. At the same time, the often humorous miscommunications that occur in the Olympic venues reflect the lack of communication between the student protesters and the government officials, who clearly were not speaking the same language. The Olympic judge, who rarely rouses from her siesta, is an obvious parody of the Mexican judicial system, which has taken a long nap in its reluctance to bring to justice those parties responsible for the slaughter. Likewise, the amnesia suffered by the student Julio after being severely beaten by the police is the amnesia of a generation that was forced to forget the circumstances and the illusions that led them to that fateful day. Nonetheless, González Mello's decision to write a play about a historical event that occurred while he was but an infant confirms both the survival of collective memory and the transcendence of the event itself.

FILMING THE ARCHIVE: *ROJO AMANECER*

Those who participated in the student movement of 1968 quickly recognized the power of using film to combat official history by establishing an archive of "invisible" history. The need for such an archive became clear when Mexico's media reported the events of that summer, not as they actually occurred but rather as the government saw fit. Not surprisingly, most of the film related specifically to the student movement of 1968 is documentary in nature. In fact, the majority of it was shot by university students commissioned by the Mexican Olympic Committee later.

While choppy, clandestine documentary videos appeared over the decades,[4] Mexicans had to wait twenty-two years for a full-length feature film on 1968. In 1989, director Jorge Fons was persuaded by Xavier Robles's dramatic script

Rojo amanecer to break the long taboo and make a movie that daringly recreates the events of October 2. Nearly certain that the film would be censured, if not prohibited, Fons and his actors invested their own money and used a dilapidated storage area to serve as the Tlatelolco apartment in which the family drama takes place and beyond which the national drama occurs, out of sight but ever present. The remarkably small cast, which worked clandestinely and pro bono, includes several of Mexico's most renowned actors—Héctor Bonilla, María Rojo, Eduardo Palomo, and the Bichir brothers.

Fons uses a simple yet realistic setting to portray one day in the life of a family who occupies one of the apartments overlooking the Plaza de Tlatelolco. A calendar shows the date, October 2, while a clock marks the passage of minutes and hours. One apartment and one family, consisting of three generations, serve as a microcosm of Mexican society and political life. The grandfather, a former army officer and staunch supporter of the PRI, sees the ideals of the 1910 Revolution for which he fought shattered in a hail of bullets. His son-in-law, a small cog in the bureaucratic machinery of the PRI, tries to balance his political loyalties, his patriarchal control of the family, and the fact that his two oldest sons are active members of the student movement, while his daughter struggles to mediate family conflicts at once generational and ideological.

The family domain becomes part of the national tragedy when bullets shatter the windows and the sons and wounded fellow activists seek refuge in the family's apartment. The soldiers who enter the apartment in search of student activists open fire and kill all but the youngest son, who has seen the massacre in the plaza from the apartment window as well as the slaughter of his entire family from under the bed.

Carlos Salinas de Gortari had just begun his six-year term as president when *Rojo amanecer* was ready for release. Amid widespread accusations of electoral fraud, it behooved him to permit the release of the movie as proof of the so-called *apertura* (democratic opening) and freedom of expression. There was, however, one problem: *Rojo amanecer* explicitly portrayed the role of the army in the massacre. After the movie had sat on a shelf for six months, Mexico's intellectuals launched a public campaign for its release. Negotiations between the director and the government led to the excision of two scenes that refer to the direct participation of the army. Ironically, however, the original version seems to have been pirated, with the result that most of the copies that circulate today are the uncensored version. Particularly noteworthy is the final scene, which shows the surviving child emerging from one of the large housing buildings of

Tlatelolco. Two armed soldiers march by as the boy leaves the scene. He is not just the lone survivor of that particular family, but Mexico's future, a wounded generation that has never forgotten the night of Tlatelolco.

Subsequent feature films have either failed to be completed or flopped at the box office.[5] Nonetheless, 1968 cinematography continues to perform an important ideological function: "Film makes it possible to observe historical events in images; it allows the young to appreciate the power of the student movement—which for many is very subjective—and to realize that the forms of repression have not changed" (Rodríguez Cruz 49). As time goes by and those who participated as students in the movement grow older, documentaries include more interviews with cultural historians and former student leaders. While the tone becomes more nostalgic as the years pass, the demand for truth and accountability remains as strong as ever.

SPACE AS ARCHIVE: THE PLAZA DE TLATELOLCO, PAST AND PRESENT

President Díaz Ordaz and his army could not have chosen a site more historically and symbolically laden than Tlatelolco. As Octavio Paz succinctly states, "The plaza of Tlatelolco is magnetic with history" (130). During the last phase of the Aztec empire, Tlatelolco was founded on an island adjacent to Tenochtitlán by a group of dissidents. In 1521, Tlatelolco became even more associated with resistance and sacrifice when the Aztecs, led by Cuauhtémoc, made their last stand there against Hernán Cortés and his troops. During the early years of Spanish colonial rule, a small church, La Iglesia de Santiago, was built atop the Aztec temples, a lasting symbol of the literal and metaphorical imposition of Catholicism and colonialization. Ironically, this particular church was where Bernardino de Sahagún and his fellow priests not only instructed the conquered in Spanish and Christianity, but also taught them how to preserve their own Nahua cultural history. Knowing that this kind of knowledge could lead one day to renewed resistance, the Spanish colonial government ordered the destruction of these texts, along with the codices written prior to the Conquest. This set the stage for what would become a centuries-long practice of destroying or otherwise silencing any history that does not correspond to official ideology.

Tlatelolco survived in relative obscurity until the 1960s, when a number of large, unattractive apartment buildings were erected around the existing plaza to house government employees, along with the tall, equally unattractive Ministry of Foreign Relations building. A new name, the Plaza de las Tres Culturas, was created to reflect the combination of pyramids, colonial church, and twentieth-century architecture. Still scarred with bullet holes, Tlatelolco fell even further into ruins on September 19, 1985, when a massive earthquake brought down entire apartment buildings that were later determined to have been constructed in flagrant violation of building codes. Yet Tlatelolco remains today as a *lieu de mémoire*, a memory site, whose fundamental objective is, according to Pierre Nora, "to stop time, to block the work of forgetting" in an "endless recycling of meaning" (19). Accordingly, no amount of renaming or rebuilding will obliterate the association of Tlatelolco with conquest, authoritarian rule, sacrifice, death, corruption, and deception. The Plaza of Tlatelolco will always remain a "metaphor for that past which is a buried present" (Paz 320).

In 1993, a large stone stele was finally constructed in memory of the victims: "To those who fell on October 2 in this plaza, [a list of twenty victims and their ages] and many other comrades whose names and ages are still unknown." This dedication is followed by a fragment of Rosario Castellanos's famous poem "Tlatelolco Memorial." At the same time, the Universidad Nacional Autónoma de México (the National Autonomous University of Mexico), or UNAM, was granted ownership of the building that formerly housed the foreign minister who ordered the massacre. In October 2007, the newly named Centro Cultural Universitario Tlatelolco opened a permanent exhibit titled *Memorial del 68*. In addition to a collection of Olympic memorabilia, this multimedia installation includes photos, posters, flyers, videos, news reports, interviews, and other testimonies. One otherwise empty square room is lined with a continuous photographic mural that strings together photos of the police lineups of those students arrested on October 2. Unlike Poniatowska's book of voices, however, the *Memorial del 68* exhibit "offers only a certain subset of voices and perspectives, and thus a narrow interpretation" (Ruisánchez Serra 189).

The stele and memorial exhibit were not designed to shoulder the burden of memory but, rather, to remind visitors of their duty to remember until justice is served. So ends the well-known Tlatelolco poem by Rosario Castellanos: "Recuerdo, recordemos / hasta que la justicia se siente entre nosotros" (I remember, let's remember / until justice takes its place among us). Now, as Mexico approaches the fiftieth anniversary of the massacre, hopes of retribution have inevitably begun to fade, but collective memory has not. While the former activists who have fought against silence and amnesia are aging and dying, the memories of 1968 will live on in the art, literature, and other reflections that have been created during the past fifty years.

In *Telling Ruins in Latin America*, Michael Lazzara and Vicky Unruh explain that "ruins are dynamic sites shot through with competing cultural narratives, palimpsests on which memories and histories are fashioned and refashioned. Ruins . . . do not invite backward-looking nostalgia, but a politically and ethically motivated 'reflective excavation' that can lead to historical revision and the creation of alternative futures" (3). The Plaza de Tlatelolco is a "ruin" in more than one sense. The pre-Columbian structures point to the ruins of the past, while the plaza itself, the monument, and the memorial exhibit constitute the ruins of modernity, the destruction of dreams and hope. Although Mexicans continue to wait for justice and full disclosure, the 2014 presumed massacre of forty-three students in rural Ayotzinapa and the official silence that has followed suggest that October 2, 1968, was simply one key moment in an endless historical cycle of dissent, repression, violence, and amnesia.[6]

NOTES

1. See Felipe Covarrubias, "Lance Wyman y los íconos del 68," at www.magis.iteso.mx/anteriores/028/028_ergosum_mexico_wyman.htm for examples of clever parodies based on the official Olympic images that American artist Lance Wyman designed for the XIX Olympic Games.
2. Luis Castañeda's book *Spectacular Mexico: Design, Propaganda, and the 1968 Olympics* details the convergence of architecture, design, and cultural politics from the 1940s to the 1968 Olympics. He shows that "the violence that erupted in the context of the Olympics exposed social schisms that even the carefully designed Cultural Olympiad could not hide from public view" (xv).
3. These political posters have been exhibited in various cities in Mexico, including Mexico City and Xalapa. They are available for viewing at "Exposición de carteles 40-40: A los 40 años del '68 40 diseñadores," expo40-40.blogspot.com/2008/10/jos-manuel-morelos.html.
4. See, for example, *1968 en memoria de José Revueltas* (1968), directed by Oscar Menéndez; *Años difíciles* (1977), directed by Oscar Menéndez; *Comunicados del Consejo Nacional de Huelga* (1968), directed by Paul Leduc and Alberto Isaac; *Dos de octubre, aquí México* (1968–70), directed by Oscar Menéndez; *El grito* (1968), directed by Leobardo López Aretche; *Mural efímero* (1968–71), directed

by Raúl Kamffer; *Olimpiada en México* (1968), directed by Alberto Isaac; and *Únete pueblo* (1968), directed by Oscar Menéndez.

5. A feature film, *Tlatelolco: Verano de 68*, was released in Mexico in 2013. Directed by Carlos Bolado, it was viewed more as a story of impossible young love than as a critical revisiting of the historical events of that summer.
6. As the fiftieth anniversary draws near, Mexico 1968 is sure to remain at the forefront of political discourse and cultural production. The events of that year have indeed been the subject of several recent books published in the United States: Elaine K. Carey, *Plaza of Sacrifices. Gender, Power, and Terror in 1968 Mexico* (University of New Mexico Press, 2005); Luis Castañeda, *Spectacular Mexico: Design, Propaganda, and the 1968 Olympics* (University of Minnesota Press, 2014); Ryan F. Long, *Fictions of Totality: Mexico, 1968, and the National-Popular State* (Purdue University Press, 2008); Juan Rojo, *Revisiting the Mexican Student Movement of 1968: Shifting Perspectives in Literature and Culture Since Tlatelolco* (Palgrave Macmillan, 2016); and Samuel Steinberg, *Photopoetics at Tlatelolco: Afterimages of Mexico, 1968* (University of Texas Press, 2016). In two previous publications, I cover in more detail the relationship between the visual arts and the written and unwritten history of 1968: "Mexico 1968 and the Art(s) of Memory," *The Long 1968*, edited by Daniel Sherman et al. (Indiana University Press, 2013), pp. 169–215; and "Re-membering the Past: Memory-Theatre and Tlatelolco," *Latin American Research Review*, vol. 37, no. 2, 2002, pp. 119–35.

   A short list of the numerous studies that have been published in Mexico would include Sergio Aguayo Quezada, *1968: Los archivos de la violencia* (Grijalbo, 1998); Enrique Krauze, *El sexenio de Gustavo Díaz Ordaz* (Clío, 1999); José Revueltas, *México 68: Juventud y rebelión* (Era, 1978); Jacinto Rodríguez Munguía, *1968: Todos los culpables* (Random House Mondadori, 2008); Julio Scherer García and Carlos Monsiváis (editors), *Parte de guerra: Tlatelolco 1968* (Aguilar, 1999); Paco Ignacio Taibo II, *68* (Seven Stories Press, 2003); and Jorge Volpi, *La imaginación y el poder: Una historia intelectual de 1968* (Era, 1998).

   The democratic *apertura* that occurred during the presidency of Carlos Salinas de Gortari (1988–94) provided an opening for a number of documentaries that coincided with the twenty-fifth anniversary, including *Batallón Olimpia: Documento abierto* (1998), directed by Carlos Mendoza; *A 25 años de México 1968* (1992), directed by Oscar Menéndez; *Díaz Ordaz y el 68* (1998), directed by Luis Lupone; *Luz de la memoria* (1995), directed by Julio Pliego; *Memorial del 68* (2008), directed by Nicolás Echevarría; *México 68–98* (1998), directed by Oscar Menéndez; *Operación Galeana: Historia inédita del 2 de octubre de 1968* (2000), directed by Carlos Mendoza; and *Tlatelolco: Las claves de la masacre* (2002), directed by Carmen Lira Saade and Carlos Mendoza Aupetit.

Finally, while the production of novels related to 1968 has remained steady (see Long), there has been very little production in the way of the other literary genres since the 1990s.

WORKS CITED

Álvarez Garín, Raúl. *La estela de Tlatelolco: Una reconstrucción histórica del movimiento estudiantil de 68*. Grijalbo, 1998.

Aquino, Arnulfo, and Jorge Pérezvega, editors. *Imágenes y símbolos del 68*. UNAM, 2004.

Castañeda, Luis. *Spectacular Mexico: Design, Propaganda, and the 1968 Olympics*. University of Minnesota Press, 2014.

González Mello, Flavio. *Olimpia 68*. In *El orden invisible: Arte, escena y espacio público; Memoria de los 40 años del movimiento estudiantil del 68*, edited by Juncia Avilés Cavasola. Centro Cultural Universitario Tlatelolco, UNAM, 2010.

Grupo Mira, editors. *La gráfica del '68: Homenaje al movimiento estudiantil*, 2nd ed. UNAM, 1988.

Jorgensen, Beth. *The Writing of Elena Poniatowska*. University of Texas Press, 1994.

Lazzara, Michael J., and Vicky Unruh, editors. *Telling Ruins in Latin America*. Palgrave Macmillan, 2009.

Long, Ryan F. *Fictions of Totality: Mexico, 1968, and the Popular State*. Purdue University Press, 2008.

Nora, Pierre. "Between Memory and History: *Les Lieux de Mémoire*." *Representation*, vol. 26, 1989, pp. 7–25.

Paz, Octavio. *The Labyrinth of Solitude, and Other Writings*. Translated by Lysander Kemp, Grove Press, 1985.

Poniatowska, Elena. *La noche de Tlatelolco*. Ediciones Era, 1971.

Roach, Joseph. *Cities of the Dead: Circum-Atlantic Performance*. Columbia University Press, 1996.

Rodríguez Cruz, Olga. *El 68 en el cine mexicano*. Universidad Iberoamericana, 2000.

Rojo amanecer. Directed by Jorge Fons. Cinematográfica Sol, 1990.

Ruisánchez Serra, José Ramón. "Reading 68." *Accounting for Violence: Marketing Memory in Latin America*, edited by Ksenija Bilbija and Leigh A. Payne, Duke University Press, 2011, pp. 179–206.

11

WAR

Medusa's Head: The Drug War Commandeers the People

RAFAEL ACOSTA MORALES

PRIMARY MATERIALS

- *Perseus with the Head of Medusa* by Benvenuto Cellini (sculpture, 1545)
- *Perseus with the Head of Medusa* by Rigoberto A. González (painting, 2013)
- *Los infortunios de Alonso Ramírez* (The Misfortunes of Alonso Ramírez) by Carlos de Sigüenza y Góngora (novel, 1690)
- *El periquillo sarniento* (The Mangy Parrot) by José Joaquín Fernández de Lizardi (novel, 1816)
- *Astucia* by Luis Gonzaga Inclán (novel, 1865)
- *Los bandidos de río Frío* (The Bandits of Rio Frio) by Manuel Payno (novel, 1891)
- *El Zarco* by Ignacio Altamirano (novel, 1901)

IMAGES OF THE DRUG WAR IN MEXICO have reflected ever more striking violence as the war between branches of the government and cartels continues to claim a monstrous number of lives in the country. As of this writing, approximately 120,000 murders have been linked to the war on drugs in Mexico between 2006 and 2012 (20,000 per year, approximately 6 per 1,000 people), though it is hard to provide exact numbers, as it is difficult to attribute cause for murder clearly (Robles de la Rosa). During President Enrique

Peña Nieto's term, the number of murders attributed to the drug war has been put at 65,209 for the period between January 2012 and January 2016 (21,736 per year, approximately 6 per 1,000 people) (*Blog del Narco*). These numbers include only verified murders in the country, without counting the unknown number of disappearances.

Narco News estimates that in the period 2006–2016, 11,000 deaths were attributable to the drug war in the United States, taking its data from the FBI Uniform Crime Reporting program (Conroy), though the news outlet states that for fewer than half of the yearly murders was enough information reported to be able to determine whether their causes might have involved drugs. Moreover, "currently, no comprehensive, publicly available data exist that can definitively answer the question of whether there has been a significant spillover of drug trafficking–related violence into the United States" (Conroy). From 2000 to 2012, somewhere between 14,661 and 17,309 murders and nonnegligent manslaughter cases were registered every year in the United States (Federal Bureau of Investigation).

While it is very difficult to calculate properly just how many of these murders were related to drug violence, it is clear that drug violence figures greatly into the causes of murder in both countries. According to the United States' National Institute on Drug Abuse, illicit drug overdose cases averaged 8,388 per year during the same period reported in *Narco News*, 2006–2016 (NIH National Institute on Drug Abuse 2015). As a matter of comparison, prescription drug overdose cases average 16,682 per year (NIH National Institute on Drug Abuse 2015). Illicit drug overdoses are on the rise, in spite of all the efforts to suppress these drugs (NIH National Institute on Drug Abuse 2016). Low estimates claim that the U.S. government, across its different levels, spends upward of $41.3 billion yearly on enforcement of drug prohibition laws (Miron and Waldock 1), while others assert that these expenses are up to $51 billion (Drug Policy Alliance). And yet, "while international efforts to step up drug seizures may affect availability, price and consequences associated with a particular drug (i.e., cocaine or heroin), CASA [National Center on Addiction and Substance Abuse] was unable to find evidence that such strategies have an overall impact on reducing substance abuse and addiction or its costs to government" (National Center on Addiction and Substance Abuse 58). Results have not followed actions in the drug war that is being waged in Mexico and the United States, and it has been waged for far too long not to be evaluated or reconceived in the light of its multiple failures.

If policies relating to the drug war were aimed at reducing drug consumption or drug availability, any reasonable person ought to consider by now that either the war is irretrievably lost or that the strategy by which it is being fought is entirely mistaken and should be drastically altered. What a growing number of voices tell us is that the drug war is about everything but drugs and that, in terms of its true targets, it has actually been very successful. An examination of imagery related to this struggle, such as Rigoberto A. González's painting *Perseus with the Head of Medusa*, reveals some truths about this effort. The painting shows a masked man wearing paramilitary attire, armed with grenades, an assault rifle, and a machete, standing over a naked, beheaded female body, whose head he holds up by the hair. The female body appears to have its hands tied behind its back and is sprawled at his feet. The man stares into the distance, in a defiant attitude, displaying both the actual weapon, the machete, and the figurative one, the cut-off head. This painting references Benvenuto Cellini's homonymous statue in Florence's Piazza della Signoria. Medusa, whose body lies on a pedestal with blood pouring from the neck, has just been vanquished by Perseus, who represents all that the Greeks held dear. In his hand he holds Medusa's head. Perseus was the greatest Greek hero before Heracles and was the mythological founder of Mycenae, one of the most important cities in ancient Greece. Perseus did not kill the Gorgon Medusa because she represented a threat to his land but because his king asked Perseus to bring him her head as a trophy. During my analysis I will focus on (1) the disconnect between stated goals and results in the drug war, (2) the use of drug prohibitions as a justification for the repression of dissidence in politics, (3) the history of social banditry in Mexico, and (4) the mytho-historical background of the Perseus motif in Cellini's and González's works.

For the purposes of this argument, I'm focusing on González's representation, but a whole alternative mythology has been developed surrounding *narcocorridos* (folk ballads about drug trafficking), with manifold political implications, wherein drug lords become mythological figures in order to pursue political goals, subject to many interpretations. In the line of inquiry I take, the drug war does not seem to be an answer for the problem of drug use but, rather, seems to worsen it; paths with better records of reducing the problems related to drug consumption are disregarded in favor of a war that is costly and useless. This war has other effects, too, and González's painting is very telling of the way the drug war is perceived by the people who are closest to it. It is not a war between police and criminals, but a war of the government against its people.

DRUG WAR DISCONNECT

In Mexico, the 2006 presidential election was decided by 243,934 votes, or less than 1 percent of total votes (Instituto Federal Electoral). This election was hotly contested, and after being confirmed by a tribunal, Felipe Calderón took office as president of the United Mexican States on December 1, 2006. Merely ten days afterward, the war on drugs began, leading Jorge Castañeda, a former presidential candidate and foreign relations secretary, to speculate that "what Calderón tried to do was to legitimize himself. Facing the accusations of electoral fraud that surrounded his election, he decided he needed a foundational act of his government. . . . We imagine that when he tried to legitimate himself that way, he thought it'd be easy to get in and out" (Ordaz). The president ordered Secretary of the Interior Francisco Javier Ramírez Acuña to start the Joint Operation Michoacán, sending 4,260 army troops, 1,054 Marines, and 1,400 officers of the federal Ministry of Public Safety into Michoacán as part of the official beginning of the war on drugs in Mexico. In the official communiqué, Secretary Acuña claimed that "one of the priorities of Felipe Calderón's administration as President of the Republic is to fortify safety for Mexicans and their families in every region of the country. This shall immediately bring the recovery of the public spaces that organized crime has taken away, a recovery that shall bring an end to the impunity of the criminals who put our children's health at risk as well as the tranquility of our communities" (Presidencia de la República).[1]

What became the defining cause of Calderón's presidency, the drug war, seemed to come out of nowhere. It was never mentioned during his campaign, and the country did not have a problem with high usage of narcotics according to Castañeda: "In 2008, the government carried out a survey that indicated that 0.4% of the population is comprised of addicts, that is, only 450,000 Mexicans" (Ordaz). In comparison, in 2013 in the United States, 24.6 million people, or 8.2 percent of the population, participated in past-month illegal drug use, a statistic used in order to point to possible addiction (NIH National Institute on Drug Abuse 2015). The 120,000 drug-linked murders that occurred during Calderón's presidency would represent an exorbitant cost to prevent so few Mexicans from consuming drugs, considering that illegal drugs produced just 395 deaths in 2005 and 630 in 2010 (Observatorio de Seguridad Ciudadana de la OEA).

Before Calderón's twenty-first-century drug war, President Lázaro Cárdenas, in 1940, had seemingly figured out a way to dismantle the drug trade and control the damage addicts brought to society: give the drugs away (Enciso loc. 1007). Realizing that as long as addicts were able to get their doses of opiates they would be able to lead normal lives, the Cárdenas administration set up dispensaries and stopped prosecuting addicts (Enciso loc. 1110). The overall success of Cárdenas's experiment came to an end because of American intervention led by Federal Bureau of Narcotics Commissioner Harry J. Anslinger, who, "upon learning that Mexico would create a national narcotic monopoly and that addicts could acquire drugs from official dispensaries, . . . imposed an embargo on the shipment of all medicinal drugs to Mexico as punishment" (Redmond).

Besides the controlled distribution of narcotics, holistic approaches to the treatment of addiction suggest there are better alternatives for reducing addiction than the prohibition of drugs. Most of the addiction studies related to heroin's effects are carried out using rats held in isolation in unsatisfying and inhospitable cages. In a study by Bruce Alexander in which caged rats were provided with satisfying activities, food, and society, it was found that "happy" rats decreased their consumption of morphine on their own, even if they entered the more satisfying cages after becoming addicted (Alexander 176). Following the conclusions of Alexander's study, responsibility for addiction may lie much less in the hands of those who sell the drugs and much more in those of the ones who design the "cages." Studies carried out on monkeys have shown that rigid social orders have an effect on subordinate monkeys' cocaine self-administration, as "oppressed" apes consume significantly more psychoactive substances than dominant ones (Morgan et al.). This has also been verified in humans: a massive study carried out by the U.S. Armed Forces found that even though 43 percent of soldiers in Vietnam admitted to using opiates during the Vietnam War, less than 14 percent of those previously addicted continued using opiates after being back home for more than a year (Robins, Helzer, and Davis). This last study was verified by medical tests and should lead us to question the nature of addiction even to one of the most addictive of drugs: heroin. It is a well-known fact that, other than dependence and constipation, unadulterated heroin does not cause many long-term physical complications (Merck Manual Editors 2097). The many deaths produced by the drug war ostensibly result from an effort to prevent the use of substances that could, in fact, be used safely under proper circumstances. It is impossible not to believe that there is an ulterior motive to all these deaths and war, that there are weapons that have a purpose other than preventing the use of psychotropic substances.

In terms of illicit drug use, cartels, and public safety, Calderón aimed to configure the army as the one true defender of society against organized crime, but as Castañeda states, "The main people in this government's [Calderón's] public safety bureaus are the same as in the previous government. Then, it is hard to understand how in the previous regime, those same individuals were inept or accomplices, and now they are Superman, or national heroes" (Ordaz). The war has been highly unpopular throughout the country, as it has increased the evils it was supposed to fix. Just in Ciudad Juárez, as soon as the Mexican army arrived, the killing escalated from 252 yearly murders (1993–2007) to 3,622 murders in 2010; between 2007 and 2012, 11,862 people were murdered, more than 5 people every day (*Frontera List*). This violence also produced 4,500 complaints of human rights violations between 2007 and 2010 in Juárez alone (Silva). The war didn't manage to reclaim public space or to provide safety to Mexicans.

The results of the war have been to repress and oppress some of the most vulnerable segments of the populace. More than half of Mexico's youths live under the poverty line, and youths also represent considerably more than half the deaths produced by the war (Domínguez Ruvalcaba). These killings by public security forces seem to indicate that there is an excess of Mexican youths, who are perceived as expendable and, often, as scapegoats for social problems (Domínguez Ruvalcaba). These youths have been denominated *ninis* (from *ni estudian, ni trabajan*), a neologism that mocks the fact that many youths don't work and don't study. Those who find themselves in this situation now number more than 25 percent of youths (René). As these impoverished youths find no jobs or education available to them, they end up living "in an intense presentism, for the future is an opaque referent that clouds the absence of options" (Valenzuela Arce 20). They are considered at fault because they cannot find a way to contribute economically to society, but they have no means of production, no job opportunities, no education, no capital, nor any other way to participate in the legal economy. Those who have accumulated an extraordinary amount of capital in the upper echelons of the economy blame those who are at the bottom for not working, despite a lack of jobs—a perverse situation that ends up producing the idea that the unemployed are disposable beings not entitled to their lives. The influence of the United States can be seen here, as the neoliberal model that was applied by the PRI was imported as part of the social model of supply-side economics proposed by President Ronald Reagan.

In truth, Reaganomics was more and less than supply-side economics, but like the latter it focused on the accumulation of capital, which allowed for more goods to be produced, while it supplied less money to purchase them. This was an effort to control the inflation and stagnation that characterized the economic output of the 1970s in the United States. Reagan's policies controlled inflation but also led to the creation of an underclass that could neither produce, as it had no jobs or capital to acquire means of production, nor consume, as it had no money to spend.

When the American poor, who were overwhelmingly non-Caucasian, began to turn to violence so that they could acquire a means of consumption, they became vilified. To turn to violent behavior in order to be able to uphold the maxim of consumption "is the reaction of people who are totally caught into the predominant ideology but have no ways to realize what this ideology demands of them so it's kind of a wild acting out within this ideological space of consumerism" (Žižek 30). If the culture requires of its subjects an ever-increasing consumption but gives the ability to legally carry out this dictum to a very small percentage of the population, the stage is set for organized crime as a reaction to capitalization. These two imperatives, capitalization and consumption, work hand in hand in the projects of economic liberalization that Mexico imported from the United States, intensifying the economic inequality it inherited from colonial times.

PROHIBITION'S PRODUCTS

Political scientist Charles Tilly called statecraft and banditry protection rackets, the former legitimate and the latter illegitimate (169). However, defining banditry as a protection racket is perhaps too broad to be useful, even if the link between statecraft and banditry is illuminating. In this case, the impulses for redistribution may be key, whether it is progressive distribution (tending to increase equality) or regressive distribution (tending to increase inequality).

Smuggling and expropriation have been some of the strongest sources of funds for social (progressive) redistribution: Pancho Villa smuggled cattle and guns throughout the Mexican Revolution; President Lázaro Cárdenas reappropriated oil and funded the postrevolutionary state with the proceeds; and these days, an intermingling of government forces and bandits is using the proceeds of drug running and organized crime to pay for the drug war, by means of which several factions are vying for control of the billions of dollars that the trade produces. The scale of this trade can be estimated from what the financial system launders, as "the capitalist financial system plays a decisive role in the maintenance of the global illicit drug trade. The banks are happy to manage and invest $350 to $500 billion a year in illegal drug profits for criminal organizations" (Redmond).

The most curious thing about the approach the United States has taken in the war on drugs is that very clearly not only does it not work, but it makes the problem worse, enforcing regressive policies and encouraging the drug trade by driving up prices. As Helen Redmond argues, "The development of narcocapitalism in Mexico *depended* on the enforcement of prohibition on both sides of the border. Drug production and smuggling under the dangerous conditions of illegality creates massively inflated prices for drugs." And the same is true in the United States, where these conditions create a situation in which a kilo of cocaine is worth around US$138,000 on the street (Ríos), while a kilo of gold is worth, at February 2016 prices, US$39,288 (*New York Times*). Because of prohibition, a cocaine trader can produce something three times more expensive than gold.

Drug prohibition has also manufactured a situation in which poverty's petty violence is fed with the crumbs of a globalized trade, producing ever more violent murders. In a study of causes of drug-related murders in New York in 1988, only about 14 percent were psychopharmacological (that is, they involved a substance altering the behavior of the perpetrator), while 74 percent of them were systemic (that is, they involved somebody fighting for power because the drug trade is illegal) (Goldstein, Brownstein, and Ryan 466). Such data are unavailable for Mexico, but the increase in violence when prohibition was stepped up during the Calderón administration suggests that it would not be a bad hypothesis for further study.

In spite of what authorities claim, heightened violence comes with harsher enforcement of prohibition, a practice that increases the profit of the drug trade and perhaps of those who fight the drug war as well. This disease is active on both sides of the border, as

> it's an ironic and symbiotic relationship: enforcing drug prohibition drives the corruption tax. It's estimated that $1 billion in bribes is paid to the municipal police alone every year. Cocaine traffickers spend an estimated $500 million per year in bribes. And bribery, like drugs, crosses the border. American border-patrol agents are on the payroll. In the last seven years, 144 officers and agents with U.S. Customs and Border Protection (CBP) have been arrested or indicted on corruption charges. Margarita Crispin, a former customs officer, collected $5 million

> over three years for allowing shipments of marijuana to pass through her checkpoint. With such gargantuan sums of money on offer, everyone has their price. The endemic corruption is not an aberration, but a necessary cost of doing business. (Redmond)

The enforcement of drug prohibition increases police corruption instead of restricting drug usage. This strategy is, however, an effective tool for pursuing other purposes, as comments made by Jan Brewer, ex-governor of Arizona, indicate: "I believe today, under the circumstances that we're facing, that the majority of the illegal trespassers that are coming into the state of Arizona are under the direction and control of organized drug cartels and they are bringing drugs in" (Davenport). The drug cartels are thus used as multipurpose straw men, absorbing the blame for anything the U.S. government's agent in question opposes, whether it is a neighboring country, an underperforming economy, the tax structure, or any other proposed foe.[2] The problem with trying to end prohibition is that regardless of its ineffectiveness, it is tightly interwoven with so many practices, from for-profit prisons to political scapegoating.[3] This policy is probably here to stay.

Drug prohibition doesn't contribute to public safety: "as the strategy of the Calderón administration has shown, organized crime responds to violent attacks with increasingly defensive and intimidatory measures in order to defend its assets and control of territory" (Watt and Zepeda 233). It does, however, contribute to the undemocratic control of a country's population, which, considering the timelines in which it became a primary issue in both the United States and Mexico, may be its main purpose. According to Peter Watt and Roberto Zepeda, Calderón launched his war as a reaction to his contested election in order to counteract the influence of his opponent, Andrés Manuel López Obrador (205), and in connection with the Mérida Initiative (a security cooperation agreement between the United States, the government of Mexico, and several Central American countries, with the stated aim of fighting drug trafficking, transnational organized crime, and money laundering), soldiers harassed peasant, indigenous, and antimining leaders, using the drug war as a pretext (206).

This transnational use of violence within the Mérida Initiative is a strategy that is designed beyond Mexico's plans, incorporating collaboration between the U.S. Armed Forces and Mexican security forces. General John Craddock, commander of U.S. Southern Command, articulated preoccupations about a democratic opening in Latin America in 2006, noting that "an election can present an opportunity for those with extremist views to exploit themes of nationalism, patriotism and anti-elite or anti-establishment rhetoric to win popular support," leading to a "distrust and loss of faith in failed institutions [that] have also fuelled the emergence of anti-globalisation and anti–free trade elements that incite violence against their own governments and their own people" (120). In short, the concern of U.S. planners seems as much—if not more—about threats from economic nationalism and a rejection of the neoliberal order in Mexico and Latin America than about organized crime (205).

This has led to a different conception of what the police should be in a country and, more specifically, in Mexico. In 2014 National Security Commissioner Monte Alejandro Rubido claimed that he was building a new police force inspired by the Carabineros de Chile (Beauregard). Chile's *carabineros* force participated in the country's infamous 1973 coup, which elevated General Augusto Pinochet to dictatorial power. This does not bode well for Mexico's budding democratic political organization. In fact, the police have become heavily militarized throughout the country, as is exemplified by Mexico City's massive C4I4 surveillance center (Centro de Comando, Control, Comunicaciones, Cómputo, Inteligencia, Integración, Información e Investigación). It is a panopticon installation that "originated in 2001 as a pilot effort to gentrify the historic center of Mexico City under Mayor Andrés Manuel López Obrador. He was determined to relocate informal economic activities away from the center, despite the fact that sixty percent of the population is engaged in the informal economy" (Mushkin). In it, more than two hundred people monitor cameras and data points from all over the city, specifically targeting places "where large groups frequently gather: in the city's historic center, near the Antigua Basílica de Guadalupe, and near the Universidad Autónoma de la Ciudad de México" (Mushkin). This sort of surveillance is hardly related to organized crime's patterns, whose most important functions rarely ever occur in Mexico City or in highly frequented spots, raising the suspicion that it is oriented to surveillance of activities other than drug trafficking.

SOCIAL BANDITRY AND INEQUALITY IN MEXICO

Considering the prominence of organized crime in modern-day Mexico, it's clear that the masked man in González's painting does not come out of left field. The painting does not just draw on current events, however, as Mexico has a long history of banditry. The underclasses have often taken to violent conflict as a last resort in order to defend their subsistence from large capital holders, and the presence of social banditry as a reaction to capital accumulation could actually be called a tradition in Mexico's history. As represented in literature from the outset of Mexican letters, in Carlos de Sigüenza y Góngora's *Los infortunios de Alonso Ramírez* (The Misfortunes of Alonso Ramírez, 1690), piracy was rampant on New Spain's shores as desperate people of all races found it impossible to acquire wealth, an opportunity that was all but unavailable to those who were not already among society's richest. In 1734, New Spain had the highest calculated Gini index on record (meant to analyze economic inequality, with higher being worse) and resided beyond the Inequality Possibility Frontier (representing the minimum economic distribution needed for the poor to live above biological subsistence levels) (Milanovic 80). José Joaquín Fernández de Lizardi's *El periquillo sarniento* (The Mangy Parrot, 1816), often considered Mexico's first national novel, also explores social banditry, as the protagonist, Pedro Sarmiento, participates in every sort of outlawed trade because he lacks economic opportunities, eventually becoming part of a group of bandits. The novel is told through the deathbed voice of Pedro, nicknamed "Periquillo," who laments the wasted life his society imposed on him and attempts to show others how not to follow in his footsteps. Manuel Payno's *Los bandidos de Río Frío* (The Bandits of Rio Frio, 1891) is yet another literary example of how banditry becomes a resource for those who can find few options because of economic inequality, as both the hero and the villain of the story end up in banditry because the abyss between the rich and the poor breaks up their families and careers.

Luis Gonzaga Inclán's novel *Astucia* (1865) is the story of a tobacco smuggler who rebels against a state monopoly. At the time, the tobacco trade provided a big portion of the government's income and was riddled with corruption. Lorenzo "Astucia" Cabello, the protagonist, takes up smuggling because generalized corruption prevents him from profiting from other trades and because the majority of land belongs to a few landowners, mostly the Catholic Church. When he realizes that liquor commerce already requires businessmen to defend their wares by strength, he joins with the Brotherhood of the Leaf and starts a tobacco cartel. This cartel eventually functions as a parastate, as a warrantor of the peace. Lorenzo tells a thief, "I warn you that if you set foot three leagues from here, we'll hang you from the first available tree, for we don't hold commerce nor deal with thieves; get away from here, before I instantly dispatch you to hell" (Inclán 161). Even after the cartel is taken down, the sort of expedient justice Lorenzo learned to dispense as its leader accompanies him as he takes control of a town and becomes its paramilitary leader under a simple plan "composed of only two articles: banishing revolutionaries and hanging bandits" (442). He configures himself as the good bandit: an administrator who takes possession of executive power by force for the good of the people whom he represents.

This turn toward the use of executive power coincides with a later development in the nineteenth century, when bandits became part of the police force of Porfirio Díaz. The famed rurales were Díaz's personal army, used to repress political dissent. The formation of this force followed almost to the letter the recipe put forward by Ignacio Manuel Altamirano in his novel *El Zarco* (1901), which portrayed the monopoly of violence as desirable for the government. In the novel, Nicolás Ramírez, a mestizo police officer, joins Benito Juárez's government to fight bandits and is handed powers of exception so that he may carry out his fight.

Though this section focuses on fiction as a way to gauge the verisimilitude of the bandit figure in Gonzalez's painting, more on the historic construction of the bandit can be found in several nonfiction sources. Paul Vanderwood's *Disorder and Progress* (1981) analyzes the ways in which bandits were incorporated into the same system that produced them, providing catharsis for the frustrations of the poor but ultimately reinforcing the real and ferrous gap between rich and poor (90). In *Bandidos: The Varieties of Latin American Banditry* (1987), editor Richard Slatta gathers the writings of several scholars who dismiss the idea that banditry could have been a force to be reckoned with during the independent period (the nineteenth century throughout most of Latin America). Other scholars have argued that banditry is a form of premodern political revolution imbued with the power of the will of the people when political structures deny them expression (Hobsbawm). The real effects of banditry have been copiously studied. One such paradigmatic case examines the interrelationship of government policy and banditry in the state of Mexico in 1849–1852, under Governor Mariano Riva Palacio's administration (Solares Robles). Other scholars argue that representations of bandits complicate the discourse about the relationship between rich and poor. Chucho el Roto, a notorious bandit during the Porfiriato (1876–1910), is depicted "as a capable, working-class individual who fell victim to dominant-class abuses after indulging in a relatively inoffensive life of crime" (Robinson). In Mexico's North and the U.S. Southwest, *corridos* were songs that celebrated the deeds of outlaws who were forced into a life outside the law by a single event, such as the story of Gregorio Cortez (Paredes). The proliferation of banditry in Mexico's history as what has often been the only option the poor have for exercising power has led to studies such as Chris Frazer's *Bandit Nation*, which argues that it has been the one true and definitive element of Mexican history, much as the West has been the defining element of American history in its political mythology (*Modern History Sourcebook*). The bandit, not only in Mexico but also in the Americas in general, arose in opposition to the modern project of capital appropriation that accompanied the creation of the independent republics, a rural nightmare for the elites of urban centers (Dabove 1–43).

WEAPONS OF THIS WAR

Besides modernizing his bandit subject, the choice by González to place both a machete and an assault rifle by the masked man's side seems not to be arbitrary. It harkens to the factual history of the Kaibiles, a special operations arm of the Guatemalan military who were recruited as both trainers and soldiers by Mexico's Gulf Cartel. The Kaibiles used machetes among tactics in which "they were not only trained to kill, but to do so in a bloodthirsty way. We received victims' testimony in which they tell of rituals in which they drank blood from the victims. It was part of the exemplary terror policy that the army used in that country [Guatemala]" (Redacción Proceso). As in Cellini's statue, terror features prominently in González's painting. The man is not only supposed to be an efficient killer, as the assault rifle would suggest, but also someone willing to use the terror reflected in the faces of his victims as a weapon, as a way to figuratively turn to stone those who would gaze upon the woman's head, much like Perseus wielded the Medusa's head to literally transform his enemies into statues.

From its beginning in Greek mythology, the Perseus myth has had an undertone of tyranny. The demonstration of Perseus's power was probably in Cosimo I de' Medici's mind when he commissioned Cellini's statue. During the sixteenth century, Florence became a duchy after having been a republic. This change started with Cosimo's predecessor, Alessandro, but was finished when Cosimo became grand duke of Tuscany with the support of the papal army and against the will of the Florentine people. Cosimo was intent on sending a clear message that the republic was done. When he took possession of the grand duchy, he commissioned the statue. According to Michael Cole:

> Knowing about the harsh rule of the statue's patron, Duke Cosimo I, and remembering the violent history of its site, Florence's Piazza della Signoria, many have found Cellini's "impetuous pour" to be simply gruesome. The submission of Medusa

> to Perseus's blade can remind us of real bodies that met similar or worse fates in Cellini's Florence, and the hero's triumphant act may accordingly seem the very identity of political tyranny. Both Cosimo and his predecessor, Alessandro, used the head of the Medusa as a symbol of the end of the Florentine Republic, with its horrors—Savonarola—and its highlights—Soderini and Machiavelli. It signaled the return to power of the Medici and the end of the *signoria*, which was the organ of popular representation during the republic. The statue was placed in front of the Palazzo della Signoria, which was rechristened as the Palazzo Ducale. While the statue carried other artistic meaning separated from its political content, the message sent by the Medici was more than clear: The head of Medusa wielded by Perseus represented the power of the *polis* wielded by the elites who subdued it. (215)

The situation represented by Rigoberto González in his painting is not dissimilar. It is possible to interpret the failure of the war on drugs as utter incompetence, or it can be argued that the war has been fought in a manner coherent with the symbolism of Perseus with Medusa's head. The strategies the war employs are poorly suited for its stated purposes, but they seem wonderfully suited for imprisoning, harassing, and depleting the wealth of the poorest of the poor. Even more, this war manages to do most of its work indirectly, creating the circumstances by which the bulk of the violence is not perpetrated by the state but only nudged toward its proper objectives. It is not only the machete or the assault rifle that is used against the body politic but the head of the Medusa, its own strength redirected against itself. Much as Perseus was ordered by his king to slay the Medusa, an authoritarian figure beheaded the Mexican people and appropriated their power when the war on drugs was launched and the power and wealth of the drug trade was usurped by the government.[4]

NOTES

1. This English translation, as are all others from texts in Spanish, is mine.
2. Regarding the tax structure, it has often been proposed that taxes on cash transactions will diminish the chances of money laundering, such regressive income being used to reduce progressive taxes, like income taxes.
3. In California it costs around $47,000 per year to incarcerate every inmate, for example, and a good chunk of those funds end up in for-profit prison operations (Legislative Analyst's Office).

4. Resources for further study: A branch of criticism has been devoted to these ideas, as can be found in Astorga and in Zavala, who analyze the political meaning of the mythologization of the drug runner; Valenzuela Arce, who has several sociological approaches to *narcocorridos*; and my own work, studying the allegories of banditry, among others. Juan Carlos Ramírez Pimienta has tracked the history of *narcocorridos* from their origins to today, giving context to the violence in the ballads. Some of the scholarship done on the aesthetics of the drug trade can be traced to Colombian studies of its violence and its context. Alonso Sánchez Baute and Héctor Abad Faciolince have published on the subject as well.

WORKS CITED

Acosta Morales, Rafael. "The State and the Caudillo: Legitimacy in Yuri Herrera's *Trabajos del reino*." *Latin American Perspectives*, vol. 41, no. 2, 2014, pp. 177–88.

Alexander, Bruce. "The Effect of Housing and Gender on Morphine Self-Administration in Rats." *Psychopharmacology*, vol. 58, no. 2, 1978, pp. 175–79.

Astorga, Luis. *Mitología del "narcotraficante" en México*. Plaza y Valdés, 1995.

Beauregard, Luis Pablo. "Los gendarmes de Peña Nieto." *El País*, 22 Aug. 2014.

Blog del Narco. "65 mil 209 ejecutados en lo que va de gobierno de Peña Nieto, y el cambio?" 27 Jan. 2016, www.elblogdelnarco.com/2016/01/65-mil-209-eje cutados -en-lo-que-va-de-gobierno-de-pe%C3%B1a-nieto-y-el-cambio-.html#ixzz40kj IJdrZ. Accessed 5 Feb. 2016.

Cole, Michael. "Cellini's Blood." *Art Bulletin*, vol. 81, no. 2, 1999, pp. 215–35.

Conroy, Bill. "Drug War–Related Homicides in the U.S. Average at Least 1,100 a Year." *Narco News*, 10 Mar. 2012, narcosphere.narconews.com/notebook/bill -conroy/2012/03/drug-war-related-homicides-us-average-least-1100-year. Accessed 1 Feb. 2016.

Dabove, Juan Pablo. *Nightmares of the Lettered City*. University of Pittsburgh Press, 2007.

Davenport, Paul. "Jan Brewer: Most Illegal Immigrants Are Smuggling Drugs." *Huffington Post*, 25 June 2010, www.huffingtonpost.com/2010/06/25/jan-brewer -drug-smuggling_n_626258.html. Accessed 2 Feb. 2016.

Domínguez Ruvalcaba, Héctor. "Ciudad Juárez: La vida breve." *Nexos*, 1 June 2010. www.nexos.com.mx/?p=13689. Accessed 1 May 2017.

Drug Policy Alliance. "Drug War Statistics." Dec. 2015, www.drugpolicy.org/drug -war-statistics. Accessed 10 Feb. 2016.

Enciso, Froylán. *Nuestra historia narcótica: Pasajes para (re)legalizar las drogas en México*. Kindle ed., Penguin Random House, 2015.

Faciolince, Héctor. "Estética y narcotráfico." *Revista de Estudios Hispanicos*, vol. 42, no. 3, 2008, pp. 513–18.

Federal Bureau of Investigation. "Crime in the United States by Volume and Rate per 100,000 Inhabitants, 1993–2012." www.fbi.gov/about-us/cjis/ucr/crime-in-the-u.s/2012/crime-in-the-u.s.-2012/tables/1tabledatadecoverviewpdf/table_1_crime_in_the_united_states_by_volume_and_rate_per_100000_inhabitants_1993-2012.xls. Accessed 1 Feb. 2016.

Frazer, Chris. *Bandit Nation: A History of Outlaws and Cultural Struggle in Mexico, 1810–1920*. University of Nebraska Press, 2006.

Frontera List. "Yearly Death Tolls in Ciudad Juarez." 23 Dec. 2015, fronteralist.org. Accessed 22 Feb. 2016.

Goldstein, Paul J., Henry H. Brownstein, and Patrick J. Ryan. "Drug-Related Homicide in New York: 1984 and 1988." *Crime and Delinquency*, vol. 38, no. 4, 1992, pp. 459–76.

Hobsbawm, E. J. *Social Bandits and Primitive Rebels*. Free Press, 1959.

Inclán, Luis G. *Astucia, el jefe de los Hermanos de la Hoja; o, Los charros contrabandistas de la Rama: Novela histórica de costumbres mexicanas con episodios originales*. 1865. Porrúa, 2011.

Instituto Federal Electoral. "Elección presidencial 2006." www.ife.org.mx/documentos/Estadisticas2006/presidente/nac.html. Accessed 15 Jan. 2016.

Legislative Analyst's Office. "Inmate Cost." 2010, www.lao.ca.gov/PolicyAreas/CJ/6_cj_inmatecost. Accessed 27 Feb. 2016.

Merck Manual Editors. *The Merck Manual Home Health Handbook*. John Wiley and Sons, 2011.

Milanovic, Branko. "The Inequality Possibility Frontier." Policy Research Working Paper Series, IDEAS, 2013.

Miron, Jeffrey A., and Katherine Waldock. *The Budgetary Impact of Ending Drug Prohibition*. CATO Institute, 2010, object.cato.org/sites/cato.org/files/pubs/pdf/DrugProhibitionWP.pdf. Accessed 7 Feb. 2016.

Modern History Sourcebook. "Frederick Jackson Turner: The Significance of the Frontier in American History, 1893." Fordham University, n.d., www.fordham.edu/halsall/mod/1893turner.html. Accessed 8 Nov. 2010.

Morgan, Drake, et al. "Social Dominance in Monkeys: Dopamine D2 Receptors and Cocaine Self-Administration." *Nature Neuroscience*, vol. 5, 2002, pp. 169–74.

Mushkin, Hillary. "Reconnaissance: Inside the Panopticon." *Places Journal*, Feb. 2016, placesjournal.org/article/inside-mexico-citys-c4i4-surveillance-center/?utm _source=mailchimp&utm_medium=email&utm_campaign=Newsletter+03–02–2016. Accessed 1 Mar. 2016.

National Center on Addiction and Substance Abuse. "Shoveling Up II: The Impact of Substance Abuse on Federal, State, and Local Budgets." May 2009, www.centeronaddiction.org/addiction-research/reports/shoveling-ii-impact-substance-abuse-federal-state-and-local-budgets. Accessed 2 May 2017.

New York Times. "Markets." 27 Feb. 2016.

NIH National Institute on Drug Abuse. "DrugFacts: Nationwide Trends." June 2015. *National Institute on Drug Abuse*. www.drugabuse.gov/publications/drugfacts/nationwide-trends. Accessed 30 Nov. 2015.

———. "Overdose Death Rates." www.drugabuse.gov/related-topics/trends-statistics/overdose-death-rates. Accessed 3 Feb. 2016.

Observatorio de Seguridad Ciudadana de la OEA. "Muerte por sobredosis de drogas ilícitas." 2010, www.oas.org/dsp/observatorio/database/indicatorsdetails.aspx?lang=es&indicator=361. Accessed 15 Jan. 2016.

Ordaz, Pablo. "Reportaje: Diálogo sobre la situación de seguridad en México." *El País*, 28 Nov. 2009.

Oropeza Abúndez, Carlos. *Encuesta nacional de adicciones 2008*. Consejo Nacional contra las Adicciones, 2008, www.conadic.salud.gob.mx/pdfs/ena08/ENA08_NACIONAL.pdf. Accessed 20 Nov. 2015.

Paredes, Américo. *"With His Pistol in His Hand": A Border Ballad and Its Hero*. University of Texas Press, 1988.

Presidencia de la República. "Anuncio sobre la Operación Conjunta Michoacán." 11 Dec. 2006, calderon.presidencia.gob.mx/2006/12/anuncio-sobre-la-operacion-conjunta-michoacan/#b1. Accessed 17 Feb. 2016.

Ramírez Pimienta, Juan Carlos. "De torturaciones, balas y explosiones: Narcocultura, Movimiento Alterado e hiperrealismo en el sexenio de Felipe Calderón." *A Contracorriente*, vol. 10, no. 3, Spring 2013, pp. 302–34.

Redacción Proceso. "Kaibiles: Leyenda negra." *Proceso*, 24 Sept. 2006, www.proceso.com.mx/94875/kaibiles-leyenda-negra. Accessed 2 May 2017.

Redmond, Helen. "The Political Economy of Mexico's Drug War." *International Socialist Review*, vol. 90, 2013, isreview.org/issue/90/political-economy-mexicos-drug-war. Accessed 2 May 2017.

René, Pierre-Marc. "Al país le falta una reforma de seguridad." *El Universal*, 24 Nov. 2015.

Ríos, Viridiana. "Evaluating the Economic Impact of Mexico's Drug Trafficking Industry." *Scholars at Harvard*, Spring 2008, scholar.harvard.edu/files/vrios/files/rios2008_mexicandrugmarket.pdf?m=1450932765. Accessed 29 Jan. 2016.

Robins, Lee N., John E. Helzer, and Darlene H. Davis. "Narcotic Use in Southeast Asia and Afterward." *General Psychiatry*, vol. 32, 1975, pp. 955–61.

Robinson, Amy. "Mexican Banditry and Discourses of Class: The Case of Chucho el Roto." *Latin American Research Review*, vol. 44, no. 1, 2009, pp. 5–31.

Robles de la Rosa, Leticia. "En el sexenio de Calderón hubo 121 mil muertes." *Excélsior*, 12 Mar. 2014, www.excelsior.com.mx/nacional/2014/03/12/948239. Accessed 3 Feb. 2016.

Sánchez Baute, Alonso. *Líbranos del bien*. Kindle ed., Santillana Colombia, 2011.

Silva, Mario Héctor. "CNDH reporta 4500 denuncias en Juárez." *El Universal*, 3 Sept. 2010, archivo.eluniversal.com.mx/notas/706293.html. Accessed 10 Feb. 2016.

Slatta, Richard. "Introduction to Banditry in Latin America." *Bandidos: The Varieties of Latin American Banditry*, edited by Richard Slatta, Greenwood Press, 1987, pp. 1–9.

Solares Robles, Laura. "El bandidaje en el estado de México durante el primer gobierno de Mariano Riva Palacio (1849–1852)." *Secuencia* 45, 1999, pp. 27–61.

Tilly, Charles. "War Making and State Making as Organized Crime." *Bringing the State Back In*, edited by Peter B. Evans, Dietrich Rueschemeyer, and Theda Skocpol, Cambridge University Press, 1985, pp. 169–90.

Valenzuela Arce, José Manuel. *El futuro ya fue: Socioantropología de l@s jóvenes en la modernidad*. COLEF, 2009.

———. *Jefe de Jefes: Corridos y narcocultura en México*. COLEF, 2003.

Vanderwood, Paul J. *Disorder and Progress*. University of Nebraska Press, 1981.

Watt, Peter, and Roberto Zepeda. *Drug War Mexico: Politics, Neoliberalism, and Violence in the New Narcoeconomy*. Zed, 2012.

Zavala, Oswaldo. "Imagining the U.S.-Mexico Drug War: The Critical Limits of Narconarratives." *Comparative Literature*, vol. 66, no. 3, 2014, pp. 340–60.

———. "Las razones de Estado del narco: Soberanía y biopolítica en la narrativa mexicana contemporánea." *Heridas abiertas: Biopolítica y representación en América Latina*, edited by Mabel Moraña and Ignacio Sánchez Prado, Iberoamericana/Vervuert, 2014, pp. 183–202.

Žižek, Slavoj. *Violence*. Picador, 2008.

12

FEMINICIDE

Expanding Outrage: Representations of Gendered Violence and Feminicide in Mexico

DANA A. MEREDITH AND
LUIS ALBERTO RODRÍGUEZ CORTÉS

PRIMARY MATERIALS

- *Antígona: Las voces que incendian el desierto* (*Antigone: The Voices That Ignite the Desert*) by Perla de la Rosa (play, 2004)
- *Lomas de Poleo* by Edeberto Galindo (play, 2002)
- *Backyard: El traspatio*, directed by Carlos Carrera, written by Sabina Berman (film, 2009)
- *Zapatos rojos* (Red Shoes) by Elina Chauvet (art installation, 2009–13)
- *Ánima sola* (Lonely Soul) by Alejandro Román (play, 2010)
- *Mi cabello por tu nombre* (My Hair for Your Name) by Elina Chauvet (performance art, 2014)
- *Memorial* by Lorena Wolffer (archival performance art, 2015)
- *21,000 princesas* (21,000 Princesses) by Ave Barrera and Lola Horner (mixed-media book, 2015)

FOR MORE THAN TWO DECADES, scores of women have met violent deaths in Ciudad Juárez, Mexico, which lies just across the border from El Paso, Texas. The most sensational cases involve victims who disappear and are murdered, mutilated, and abandoned in the desert. Journalist and academic Alice Driver writes that it is impossible to pinpoint when these murders, often called "femicides" or "feminicides," began and how many women and girls have been killed.[1] Noting local officials' failure to systematize death counts, she cites statistics kept by private citizen and scholar Julia Estela Monárrez Fragoso, who recorded 1,481 feminicides in Juárez between January 1, 1993, and November 15, 2012. Of these deaths, Monárrez Fragoso considers 217 the result of familial violence, 233 the result of sex crimes, and 706 the result of organized crime (Driver 5). Like many others who have attempted to locate the cause of this gendered violence, Stephen Eisenhammer suggests a strong connection between the murders and Juárez's long embrace of neoliberalism.[2] From the Border Industrialization Program of 1965, which aimed to make the region into a zone of manufacturing for export, to the boom in foreign-owned factories, known as *maquiladoras*, that accompanied the implementation of the North American Free Trade Agreement (NAFTA) in 1994, Juárez has long attracted poor, young, often female internal migrants looking for work (Eisenhammer 103–4). Living in a city powered by trade laws that favor corporations over individuals, these women find that many other laws are not enforced, especially in the geographically isolated, undeveloped parts of the city where they live.

Melissa Wright has studied how such women fall victim to what she calls the "myth of the third world disposable woman." According to Wright, a young woman of Third World origin over time comes to "personify the meaning of human disposability" and, having become "a form of industrial waste" as her body's capacity to perform manual labor is depleted, she is free to be dumped ("Introduction" 2). Wright examines this process at work in a Juárez maquiladora, where managers and engineers monitor the various body parts of women—their wrists, fingers, backs—as they work in order to "extract valuable labor from them while determining that these women are worth little value in and of themselves" (17). As their bodies become less able to perform demanding factory work, and thus devalued by the very jobs that have drawn them to Juárez, these women become easy prey in a city where police often fail to investigate crimes and courts rarely prosecute criminals (Driver 12). The use of misogynistic, patriarchal discourse by police and other officials to discredit these victims has also been well documented.[3] Such rhetoric includes the ever-popular tactic of conflating all women acting independently in public with the most well-known representative of the "public woman," the prostitute, by accusing murdered and disappeared women of having led "double lives" that contributed to their deaths (Weiner 292). It is clear, then, that Juárez's feminicides are the result of economic forces working not in isolation from but rather in concert with a complex web of social, political, and cultural factors.

The high rate of domestic-based feminicides also attests to the confluence of elements behind this violence. In her analysis of 494 Juárez feminicide victims recorded between 1993 and 2007 in the Feminicide Database at the Colegio de la Frontera Norte, Monárrez Fragoso classifies 115 of the cases as systemic sexual feminicides (those involving kidnapping, sexual violence, torture, murder, and the abandonment of bodies) and 150 of the cases as intimate feminicides (those taking place between sexual partners) (80). As more Mexican women have been driven to the workforce in the face of rising poverty, increased living costs, and the loss of government subsidies and other support systems, Mexican men have been confronted with a shift in the traditional gender-based division of the so-called public and private spheres. Mercedes Olivera theorizes that many of these men have found that "the stereotypical self-image of the *macho* makes it difficult to accept roles that are inferior either objectively or symbolically to those of their mates" (54), leading to what Deborah Weissman sees as the replication in households of the stress and disorder of the market via "increased rates of divorce, separation, household volatility, and gender violence" (233). Although such gender violence in the form of feminicide in Mexico has long been linked to Juárez, it can no longer be said to be a geographically isolated phenomenon.[4] Olivera views feminicide as "a pathology that has spread throughout Mexico," citing Monárrez Fragoso's national tally of 5,000 cases in 2002 (49). Although perhaps embraced first and most vigorously in Juárez in the early 1990s, many of the neoliberal economic policies tied directly and indirectly—via their interaction with social and cultural factors—to feminicides have been implemented nationwide in Mexico, making the diffusion of this violence unsurprising.

As feminicides have spread across Mexico, the focus of cultural production about the phenomenon has expanded. Driver notes that films, documentaries, and television miniseries, as well as "innumerable novels, works of nonfiction, poetry, short stories, and articles," have been released on the Juárez feminicides (21). Some of the earliest works featured explicit denunciations of the Mexican government, testimonies, and analyses of the forces behind the wave of gender-based violence. These investigative pieces almost always took the side of the victims and those seeking justice in the face of institutional shortcomings. Although not necessarily made in order to pursue justice in the courts, these works sought to influence the court of public opinion by exposing wrongdoings and the circumstances that allowed for the feminicides. Two of these pieces in particular have influenced later cultural production on feminicides, including the works analyzed in this chapter. In 2001, filmmaker Lourdes Portillo released *Señorita extraviada* (*Missing Young Woman*), the first of a series of documentaries related to the Juárez feminicides. The film starts with a voice-over, the director's words echoing Juan Rulfo's classic novel, *Pedro Páramo*: "I came to Juárez to track down ghosts and to listen to the mysteries that surround them." Through testimonies of the victims' relatives and the exploration of diverse hypotheses for the crimes, Portillo transcends her labor as a journalist and artist, positioning herself to denounce the injustices that have occurred in Juárez as she expresses her frustration over the systematic murder of Juárez's women. The documentary received attention from scholars, journalists, and nongovernmental organizations that fight for the rights of women, achieving a success that surpassed the borders of Mexico.

Around the same time as the debut of the landmark *Señorita extraviada*, another influential journalistic work on Juárez's feminicides was released. Sergio González Rodríguez's 2002 book *Huesos en el desierto* (*Bones in the Desert*) has become a fundamental source on the topic, both in Mexico and abroad. Utilizing his reporting background, González Rodríguez draws a wide picture of the context of the tragedies, offering documented investigations and exploring the many mysteries surrounding the feminicides. The book reveals not only the impunity enjoyed by murderers but also the complicity of police and public officials with organized crime. González Rodríguez also highlights the bravery of NGOs and feminist groups that demand justice during dire times. *Huesos* became a foundational source for Roberto Bolaño's novel *2666*, published posthumously in 2004. With ruthless realism and cruelty, the text explores the murder of women in the fictional city of Santa Teresa, a stand-in for Juárez. Bolaño's early death and *2666*'s forceful prose have made the work one of the best-known and most studied literary representations of the feminicides of Juárez.

The more recent incorporation of literary and generic intertexts represents another side to the cultural output on Mexico's feminicides. While the works examined in this chapter certainly have documentary and testimonial elements, they are also clearly marked by parodic inversions of other "texts," in both the narrow and the broad sense of the term.[5] These include classic Greek texts in the case of Perla de la Rosa's 2004 play *Antígona: Las voces que incendian el desierto* (Antigone: The Voices That Ignite the Desert) and classic Mexican texts in the case of Edeberto "Pilo" Galindo's 2002 play, *Lomas de Poleo*. Beyond specific texts, works on feminicide also dialogue with genres and various types of media, including thrillers in the case of the 2009 film written by Sabina Berman, *Backyard:*

El traspatio; social media in the case of Alejandro Román's 2010 play, *Ánima sola* (Lonely Soul); and fairy and folktales in the case of Ave Barrera and Lola Horner's 2015 mixed-media book, *21,000 princesas* (21,000 Princesses). Other works included in this chapter transcend the page by using different means of representation, as in the case of the artists Elina Chauvet and Lorena Wolffer, who have used their bodies, public spaces, and the Internet to create performances and art installations that reflect on gendered violence and feminicide. Additionally, some of the works analyzed here have expanded their geographic scope beyond the confines of Ciudad Juárez to include other Mexican cities and, in the case of *Backyard*, even other parts of the world. Through the expansion of intertextuality, representation, and geography, these artists offer audiences new ways to reflect on gendered violence in Mexico and to involve themselves in the search for justice.

RECOVERING PERSONHOOD: ANTIGONE IN JUÁREZ

Perla de la Rosa's 2004 play *Antígona: Las voces que incendian el desierto* follows the efforts of the protagonist, Antígona, to recover the body of her missing sister, Polinice. Antígona is ultimately foiled by Ciudad Tebas's Mayor Creón, who attempts to have her murdered in a drive-by shooting that instead kills her boyfriend, Hemón. Perhaps similar at first glance, the treatment of Polinice's body is markedly different than that of Polynices's in Sophocles's *Antigone*, one of the central intertexts of de la Rosa's play. Like the bodies of the victims tossed in Juárez's deserts, Thebes's King Creon leaves Polynices exposed to the elements after his nephew attacks the city-state. Adriana Cavarero has noted that Creon behaves contrary to Platonic thought as expressed in the *Republic*—which holds that the psyche is the principle of action and the body is a mere instrument—by considering Polynices's dead body to possess "a nontranscendable corporeal individuality to which the definition of enemy clings utterly" (58). It can be argued that he seeks to punish not only Polynices's soul, which cannot rest without burial rites, but also his still-individualized body. He seems to have left Polynices's corpse to be picked at by vultures, not because he views it as without value but because he views it as being highly valuable, possessing a dangerous power that must be stripped away in a very public arena.

Unlike Polynices's body, the mutilated corpses of Juárez women are initially dumped and left to decompose because the victims were commoditized, dehumanized, and devalued while alive, in line with Wright's concept of the Third World disposable woman. Ironically, this degradation imbues the dead, and not Mayor Creón, with a certain power: their corpses, if found and made known to the public, would serve as silent witnesses to the government's failure to protect its citizens. The women, invisible in life, are thus made invisible again in death in *Antígona*, as Creón has them hidden in the city's morgue to prop up the illusion that the rule of law is alive and well in Tebas. They are denied public burial, an act that presumably would humanize and reindividualize them. Creón does permit a state-sponsored burial of eight feminicide victims, whose mutilated bodies are found in a cotton field (208).[6] However, the comments made at the scene by Creón's wife, Eurídice, make it clear that the burial of these women does not represent the state beginning to recognize and rectify a problem, nor is it meant to honor the victims' memories. Rather, it is an attempt to bury growing public unrest about Tebas's vanished women, much as Juárez officials have sought to pin the feminicides on various scapegoats over the years.[7] Eurídice responds to a reporter's question about the existence of other bodies by saying that "la morgue está vacía" (the morgue is empty) and referring to the women from the cotton field as "las pocas que efectivamente se han encontrado" (the few who have actually been found) (203). By burying these women, the state has turned them into faceless symbols and propaganda tools, forced to embody all of the murdered and missing women whom Creón's government refuses to recognize.

Antígona, rightly, does not trust the government to acknowledge her sister's death, much less find and hand over her corpse. She remarks of Polinice that "aı negar su muerte también se niega su vida" (by denying her death her life is also denied) (200). A public funeral, it seems, is key to the restoration of Polinice's memory as a woman with a name, a history, and a family, and the state's many failures and indifference prompt Antígona to personally seek her sister's body. In the first scene in which she descends to the city's morgue in search of her sister, Antígona does not come across Polinice but rather another young victim, unknown. She later returns to the morgue to carry off the unknown girl for burial, indicating a commitment to the larger battle of burying and recognizing all of the feminicide victims in Tebas. It is an effort that brings to mind the tireless work of the women who have formed victims' advocate groups in the state of Chihuahua, such as Nuestras Hijas de Regreso a Casa (May Our Daughters Return Home) and Justicia para Nuestras Hijas (Justice for Our

Daughters), after growing exasperated with government officials. Just as by setting her play in a mythical city de la Rosa broadens the space and resonance of her work—Ciudad Tebas could, after all, just as easily represent the neoliberal border town Tijuana instead of Juárez—the inclusion of a protagonist with ties to a mythical figure allows de la Rosa to represent any and all Mexican women fighting for the rights of feminicide victims rather than limiting her focus to specific struggles, as is the case in documentary works.

In another expansion of the play's scope, neither Antígona nor Creón appear in nearly one-third of *Antígona*'s scenes. Instead, the work gives space to various anonymous townswomen to voice their histories of marginalization and violence (Weiner 283). In the opening scene of de la Rosa's play, a young woman, Clara, is found dead and bound in front of the home she shares with her sisters. Clara's identity as a maquiladora worker is evident from the comments her sisters make before discovering her body, as they discuss her job at the *fábrica* (factory) and her "bata de uniforme de trabajo" (work smock) (de la Rosa 190), left hanging on the wall of their home. Just moments before discovering her body, the sisters speculate that Clara's bosses at the factory "la liquidaron" (fired her) (190). Recalling Wright's theory, it seems that Clara's body was apparently marked as no longer useful at work and thus as disposable for the company. Clara is, indeed, disposed of, dumped in a heap at her doorstep. It is an opening with clear ties to both real-life events and previous adaptations of *Antigone*: In her introduction to the play, Guadalupe de la Mora notes that this scene parallels the opening of Bertolt Brecht's 1948 *Antigone* (176), which she identifies as one of *Antígona*'s three main intertexts, along with Sophocles's play and Jean Anouilh's 1944 *Antigone* (169). De la Rosa's play is thus full of overt intertexts, borrowing from mythic and theatrical frameworks and increasing the likelihood that audience members will be able to tap into familiar reference points in order to make connections with the production.

THE DEAD SPEAK: SHOUTING FROM THE LOMAS

In 2002, shortly before de la Rosa, Chihuahua playwright Edeberto "Pilo" Galindo released a play on Juárez's feminicides: *Lomas de Poleo*. Its thirteen short scenes jump between four women (Nancy, Érika, Maty, and Angélica) who abide in a mysterious, isolated shack and who eventually realize they are dead, and two male actors who portray various characters, including gang members, doctors, and government officials. As in de la Rosa's play, the female protagonists of *Lomas de Poleo* are not fictionalized versions of real-life Juárez citizens but representative characters—a *maquila* worker, a prepubescent girl, a woman who dies at the hands of acquaintances, and another killed by strangers. Overall, however, Galindo's work includes more overt references to current events. The title of the play is from the name of the isolated area of Juárez where many feminicide victims have been found; family members seek help from the police, who give them the bureaucratic runaround; and an official partly blames feminicides on bad parenting. In the introduction to the play, Galindo identifies the production's focus as Juárez's most-shocking and well-known feminicide victims: young women with dark skin and long hair, many of whom have been found with ravaged bodily markers of "femaleness"—"el seno derecho mutilado y el pezón izquierdo cercenado a mordidas" (the right breast mutilated and the left nipple bitten off) (175). Galindo's *teatro documental* (documentary theater) approach is not surprising: a self-described writer of social theater (Salazar Mendoza 48), he notes that with *Lomas de Poleo* he wanted to tackle "el problema de lleno y de frente, machín, o si no para qué hablamos, esa es mi opinión" (the problem fully and head-on, man, or if not then why do we talk, that's my opinion) (Galicia 138). In *Lomas de Poleo*, Galindo denounces the local government's attempt to hold individuals accountable for a systemic, cultural problem. The four female protagonists seemingly find peace with the arrest of their killers, but the play closes with a scene that suggests the cycle of murder and mutilation has begun again.

Although *Lomas de Poleo* has clear ties to the contemporary violence in Juárez, it restores feminicide victims' voices by establishing a dialogue with a canonical Mexican text: Juan Rulfo's *Pedro Páramo*. Like the 1955 novel, Galindo's play also features the murmurings of the dead. The playwright uses theater to allow murdered women to "speak" for themselves rather than relying on the testimonies of family members and friends to tell their stories. Feminicide victims, invisible in life and death, are made visible on stage, but they are not, much like Rulfo's Juan Preciado, immediately aware that they have entered a literal ghost town. There are, however, numerous clues in both works that point to the truth. Like Rulfo's town of Comala, the ghost Juárez in which Galindo's victims linger is an eerie, stormy, abandoned landscape where "están cerradas todas las tiendas" (all of the stores are closed) (184). The women's shack in the *lomas* (hills) is clearly a liminal space, a spirit way station between this life and the next. This liminality is reflected by Nancy and Érika's debate over whether it is dusk or dawn outside (183). Both are ambiguous, transitory portions of the day between one certainty (day) and another (night). The women are also unable to determine if time is passing slowly, passing quickly, or standing still (182), nor which direction the shack's door faces (185). Similarly, while staying with an incestuous brother-sister couple, Juan Preciado remarks that it appears "como si hubiera retrocedido el tiempo" (as if time had gone backward) (Rulfo 58). By jumping back and forth from the shack to scenes in the "real" Juárez, Galindo forces his audience to share in the victims' spatiotemporal confusion, although *Lomas de Poleo* is arguably much easier to follow than the notoriously disorienting *Pedro Páramo*. Rulfo's Juan Preciado also realizes his fate much more quickly than the murdered women, who don't know that they have died until scene 12, the second-to-the-last scene and the play's emotional climax. The audience witnesses a hysterical Érika confront Nancy in a crescendo of emotional accusations about her having hidden the truth of their violent fates, although Érika ultimately seems to resign herself to her death and leads the women away from the *lomas* in the play's final scene.

The sisterhood formed by Galindo's feminicide victims and their departure for a new realm stands in contrast to the experience of the dead in Rulfo's novel, although parallels can be found in the authors' messages to the Mexican public. Juan Preciado, who is overwhelmed to the point of death by the murmurs and voices that surround him in Comala (62), continues to hear the voices of the dead while in his shared grave with village native Dorotea (82). There is no sign that the two will ever "move on," and they pass the time by listening to Susana San Juan's memories. *Pedro Páramo*'s dead never tire "of rehearsing their complaint for the suffering brought upon them during their life by love, pride, and power" (Pope 232), and Rulfo gives free rein to flashbacks to expose the Mexican Revolution's ruthless caudillos (strongmen) who, like his titular character, have obtained heroic proportions in Mexico's national mythology. Although Galindo's Nancy, Érika, Maty, and Angélica leave their spiritual purgatory after the discovery of their bodies, three new women soon take up residence in the shack in the *lomas*. Galindo, like Rulfo, suggests Mexico will continue to rehash and repeat the past without an active attempt to change the status quo: Juárez can break free from a cycle of violence only by confronting the underlying economic, systemic, and cultural factors behind its feminicides.

MISGUIDED CATHARSIS: FEMINICIDES AND A THRILLER

De la Rosa and Galindo are far from the only playwrights to have tackled Juárez's feminicides, as dramaturges seem to have been particularly drawn to the issue.[8] Dramatist Sabina Berman wrote the script for the detective thriller film *Backyard: El traspatio*, which hit screens under the direction of Carlos Carrera in 2009. The movie follows detective Blanca Bravo (Ana de la Reguera), who fights to solve the mysteries behind the murders. As the story progresses, Blanca realizes that the killings are not the work of a serial killer, as she originally suspected. She instead uncovers a network of suspects, including criminals, politicians, and businessmen, who are involved in human and drug trafficking and exploitative labor practices. Joining Blanca's investigation are Sara (Carolina Politi), the head of a domestic violence shelter who tells Blanca more about the feminicide victims, and Peralta (Joaquín Cosío), a radio talk-show host who disseminates information about the feminicides and denounces the corruption of public officials. *Backyard* highlights the engagement of journalists and newscasters with the Juárez community, as seen in González Rodríguez's *Huesos*, as well as the help that civil organizations offer to victims of violence ignored by the state.

The women in the film are remarkably active. Despite ultimately becoming another victim of feminicide, Juana (Asur Zagada) gains greater economic and personal independence after arriving in Juárez. She enjoys her free time and takes control of her romantic life, finding a new partner once she decides to open herself to the idea of meeting new people. Her ex-boyfriend, Cutberto (Iván Cortes), struggles with Juana's newfound self-assurance. Driven by jealousy, he lets his friends convince him to participate in Juana's rape, which leads to her death. Blanca is another of the film's strong women. Even though her working environment is clearly male dominated, she commands a high degree of authority. Fed up with the impunity surrounding the murder of women, at the end of the movie Blanca takes justice into her own hands and kills Mickey Santos (Jimmy Smits), a businessman involved in the exploitation and killing of women. It's an ending that seems at odds with the movie's aims. Probably obeying the dictates of the thriller genre, Santos's death avenges his victims and offers audiences the possibility of catharsis. Such cathartic closure, however, dulls the sense of urgency needed to push viewers to action. The battle for women's lives will not be won without community involvement, as the last scene shows by presenting data on the violent murder of women in recent years. Beyond Juárez, similar crimes are reported for several other cities in Mexico as well as elsewhere in Latin America, Spain, and the United States. Feminicide, it seems, is quickly growing into a ubiquitous problem.

TWEETING DEFIANCE: SOCIAL MEDIA ON STAGE

Other recent Mexican cultural productions also highlight the spread of gender-based violence in the country. Alejandro Román's 2010 play *Ánima sola* takes place in three parts of Mexico. Through a choral structure, the play weaves together the voices of thirty-year-old Adriana, who talks from a landfill in Tijuana; twenty-seven-year-old Carmen, who speaks from a junkyard in Juárez; and eighteen-year-old Érika, who addresses the audience from the state of Guerrero. As the play progresses, spectators realize that the testimonies are sent from the afterlife; like the women in Galindo's *Lomas de Poleo*, these female protagonists are also already dead, and they describe their murders in detail. Adriana remembers how she was kidnapped by a group of hit men who believed she had betrayed them. Carmen, a single mother, fell prey to the gangs and criminal groups that roam Juárez. Érika became a collateral victim in a long-standing conflict between drug traffickers and caciques (fat cats). The stories of these three women represent the thousands of other women whom the forces of gendered violence have reduced to "lonely souls."

Ánima sola highlights the importance of denunciation in the fight against feminicides and its role in the organization of social justice movements. Besides first-person testimonies, social media also becomes a site of resistance in Román's work. Beyond its ties to the main characters, the play's title is also a reference to Adriana's sister's Twitter username. Through her account, María (aka Ánima Sola) denounces gendered violence and asks for help to spread the word about her sister's disappearance. Adriana begins a monologue by reflecting on her sister's Twitter use:

> Mientras pienso en María, a bordo de esta minivan blanca, / mi hermanita debe estar llena de pánico escribiendo / en su twitter algo como [. . .] / Qué día tan triste hoy / día primero de agosto del año dos mil nueve / hoy que mi hermana Adriana / había pasado con su hijo todo el día / hasta caer la noche / hasta que

> cuatro hombres / armados hasta en la sombra / la levantaron afuera de la casa / la subieron en una minivan blanca / [. . .] Si alguien vio algo / si alguien sabe algo / si alguien ha visto esa minivan / si alguien vio para dónde se fue / pasen la voz, con su lista de contactos / déjenme un mensaje aquí. (23)
>
> While I think of María, riding in this white minivan, / my little sister has to be full of panic writing / in her Twitter account something like . . . / What a sad day today / August first of the year two thousand and nine / today my sister Adriana / had been with her son the whole day / until night fell / until four men / fully armed in the shadows / kidnapped her outside our house / they took her with them in a white minivan / . . . If anyone saw something / if anyone knows something / if anyone has seen that minivan / if anyone saw where they went / spread the word, with your contact list / leave me a message here.

While Adriana rides in the minivan, she avoids reflecting on her seemingly inevitable demise by thinking of her sister typing on her laptop, looking for her and asking for help on Twitter. Adriana begs her sister to not stop writing: "Hermanita, haz un milagro [. . .] / No pares de buscarme, querida hermana [. . .] / Escribe, con toda la fe [. . .] / Rescátame [. . .] / Sigue escribiendo lo que sientes desde el fondo de tu corazón" (Little sister, work a miracle . . . / Do not quit looking for me, dear sister . . . / Write, with all your faith . . . / Rescue me . . . / Keep writing what you feel from the bottom of your heart) (48–49). Like other victims of feminicide, Adriana relies on others to write about the violence roiling Mexico, to make their suffering public and allow justice to prevail.

Institutional justice for murdered women, however, is hard to come by in Mexico. As Martha Estela Pérez García has discovered, NGOs have sprung up to fill the void left by ineffective governmental agencies. The Coordinadora en Pro de los Derechos de la Mujer (Coordination Committee for Women's Rights), founded in 1994, was the first of these groups to form (149). According to Pérez García, "El trabajo de las ONG creadas alrededor de esta problemática gira en torno a brindar una ayuda solidaria a las madres de las víctimas, acompañarlas en el proceso de búsqueda de sus hijas, en los trámites oficiales, así como en exigir justicia. Estos grupos se convierten en una de las pocas alternativas de ayuda para las madres de las víctimas" (The work of NGOs created to solve this problem focuses on providing aid to the victims' mothers, supporting them in the process of searching for their daughters, in official procedures, as well as in demanding justice. These groups have become one of the few alternative forms of support for the victims' mothers) (150). With the discovery of eight bodies in a Juárez cotton field in 2001, the murder of women in Juárez began to receive more attention, leading to the emergence of another group formed by relatives of killed and lost women, the previously mentioned Nuestras Hijas de Regreso a Casa. The organizations fighting against Mexico's feminicides have continued to proliferate.[9]

The movement against feminicides has received vital support from social media in the 2010s, as Román hints in *Ánima sola*. Civil groups and NGOs rely on these platforms to disseminate information and call for public support. Through websites, blogs, forums, Facebook pages, and Twitter hashtags, among other online resources, people can share visuals and opinions, quickly contributing evidence that can help resolve cases of disappeared women. Social media allow for immediate access and constant updates, resulting in the almost-viral proliferation of news and the rapid popularization of specific events, such as a march organized in 2016 in Mexico City. The demonstration, now known as #24A because it took place on April 24, 2016, was also promoted with the hashtag #VivasNosQueremos (#WeWantUsAlive). The parade aimed at expressing an open repudiation of *machista* violence, a widespread problem in Mexico, where, according to the Observatorio Ciudadano Nacional del Feminicidio (National Civic Observatory of Feminicide), on average seven women are murdered every day.

PERFORMING OUTRAGE: INSTALLATIONS, ACTS, AND ARCHIVES

Along with public demonstrations, some artists have created interactive pieces that invite members of society to reflect on Mexico's feminicides. Artist Elina Chauvet calls this *artivismo*, and it includes artistic installations and performances that try to keep alive the memory of women who have been killed or disappeared. Between 2009 and 2013, Chauvet coordinated the public installation *Zapatos rojos* (Red Shoes), which started in Juárez and traveled to Mexico City and then to Italy, Argentina, Chile, Ecuador, Spain, and the United Kingdom. The installation attempted to prompt reflection on gender-based violence and involved placing red shoes in public places like parks, squares, and busy sidewalks. By occupying a public space, the installation allowed passersby to metaphorically put themselves in victims' shoes. Chauvet's use of shoes was not arbitrary; they have become a symbol of feminicide, as they are usually found in the areas around crime scenes, along with other accessories typically associated with women, such as clothing, purses, and cosmetic products. Chauvet adds that, besides the obvious reference to blood, the color red can also be linked to "el corazón de la esperanza" (hope's heart). Chauvet at times placed the shoes in lines, representing the traces of bloody paths walked by feminicide victims. Other times, the shoes were displayed in a protest formation, the only visible sign of otherwise invisible demonstrators. The empty shoes often called the attention of pedestrians, who would get closer to take pictures, simultaneously opening a space for reflection on how and why the shoes came to be unoccupied.

Chauvet also paid tribute to murdered women with the performance *Mi cabello por tu nombre* (My Hair for Your Name). The artist cut off locks of her hair, to which she attached pink ribbons with the names of victims on them and which she then hung together to create an altar. After being completely shaved, Chauvet had the word *justicia* (justice) tattooed on her head. The artist describes her performance as

> un ritual que me conecta a las mujeres asesinadas en México, son mis emociones y pensamientos representados por mi pelo, es reconocerlas en él y devolverles su identidad, mencionar sus nombres es no dejarlas caer en el olvido, tatuar en mi cuero cabelludo la palabra JUSTICIA es una metáfora de la ausencia de la misma en mi país, ya que al crecer el cabello será cubierta dejándola invisible, como cubre la tierra los cuerpos asesinados impunemente. (*Mi cabello*)

> a ritual that links me with murdered women in Mexico, it's my emotions and thoughts represented in my hair, it's recognizing them in it and giving them back their identities, mentioning their names is not letting them fall into oblivion, tattooing on my scalp the word JUSTICE is a metaphor for the lack of it in my country, because when the hair will grow it will be covered again making it invisible, just as the soil covers the bodies murdered with impunity.

Like Chauvet, the artist Lorena Wolffer is known for involving her body in works with political messages. In *Territorio mexicano* (Mexican Territory, 1995–97), Wolffer appeared nude on a gurney while blood dripped onto her abdomen, her body serving as a representation of the passivity and suffering that Mexicans have long endured. In *Memorial*, Wolffer transcended the corporeal by using the Internet as an archival system to preserve the memory of feminicide victims. The project was defined as "[un] ejercicio ciudadano de reconocimiento y reparación de las violencias que nosotras hemos vivido, un manifiesto contra el olvido para [que] jamás se vuelvan a repetir" ([a] civic exercise of recognition and reparation for the violence we have lived, a manifesto against forgetting so that it never happens again). The link that allows the public's participation in the project can be found on the website of the Museo de Arte Moderno (Museum of Modern Art) in Mexico City,[10] although it unfortunately no longer seems to work. There remains only a description explaining the memorial: "Este Memorial honra a mujeres que han experimentado cualquier tipo de violencia, incluyendo la feminicida" (This Memorial honors women who have experienced any type of violence, including feminicide). The fact that the link to this memorial connects to a suspended site leads one to hypothesize that it has suffered a fate not uncommon in Mexico to this type of denunciation. It is possible the project is being boycotted by official institutions, for which such projects present a threat, or, in the worst-case scenario, it has vanished because of fear or a lack of interest in the community to which it is addressed.

UNHAPPY ENDINGS: FAIRY TALES AND GENDERED VIOLENCE

While performances, art installations, and the Internet are great ways of involving audiences, sometimes they run the risk of not reaching them because of the ephemeral nature of such works. When artists Ave Barrera and Lola Horner co-created *21,000 princesas* (21,000 Princesses) in 2015, they seemed to be aware of those problems. Consequently, although their book project started as a limited edition of three deluxe copies, it was later expanded to a free online version and reprinted into a simpler format for free distribution. The book blends literature, journalism, and visual arts, focusing more specifically on classic fairy tales, crime reports, serigraphy, and photography. The book opens with a foreword taken from *Las mil y una noches* (One Thousand and One Nights), which describes how King Schahriar ensured spousal fidelity by taking a new wife every night and having her killed the next morning. A photograph of crime-scene tape emblazons the following page, warning readers of the brutal stories found in the book's thirteen tabloid-like notes, which blend classic fairy tales and stories of violence against women, including feminicides, in the style of Mexican journalism known as *nota roja* (yellow journalism). The articles are embellished by black-and-white crime photos, which stand in contrast to the red serigraphs of the tales on facing pages. A disclaimer on the book's legal page states that "las imágenes empleadas corresponden a noticias de diversas fuentes y han sido adaptadas a estas reescrituras ficcionales con fines artísticos y literarios" (the images used correspond to pieces of news from diverse sources and have been adapted to these fictional rewritings with artistic and literary ends). Through the book's blending of classic and contemporary, traits of oppression and violence against women found in fairy tales such as "Little Red Riding Hood" and "The Little Mermaid" are brought forward, revealing the deep roots and normalization of such practices in Western cultures. Additionally, the jarring combination of the stories and the *nota roja* style prompts readers to consider how female victims are dehumanized by explicit, wildly popular Mexican tabloids.

It is clear that *21,000 princesas* tries to stay away from portraying only the violence of Juárez, and the authors have also expanded their scope by examining various types of gender-based violence, not just feminicides. Some of the crime notes follow the plot of their intertext, while others include only a small detail from their original source. For example, the last note, titled "¡Amordazada!" (Gagged!) and the most violent and graphic of them all, includes the name "Sherezada Vera," which links together *One Thousand and One Nights'* Scheherazade and Mexican activist Nadia Vera, who was killed July 31, 2015, in Mexico City along with four other victims: photojournalist Rubén Espinosa, Yesenia Quiroz Alfaro, Olivia Alejandra Negrete Avilés, and Mile Virginia Martín. This case attracted a lot of attention in national and international news because both Nadia and Rubén had previously expressed that they had received many death threats and said that Veracruz governor Javier Duarte would be responsible for whatever happened to them. A lack of security made them leave the state of Veracruz and flee to Mexico City, where they were finally assassinated. News coverage focused on the death of the man, Espinosa. However, many civil organizations fighting violence against women called the killings feminicides and demanded they be covered as such. By connecting Nadia Vera and Scheherazade, Barrera and Horner try to call attention to those who speak out to save themselves from the threats of a violent system: while Scheherazade told stories in order to survive the sultan's killing, Vera and Espinosa used journalism, public protest, and activism to denounce the dangers of the corrupt and oppressive state.

CONCLUSIONS

For all of the cultural production that denounces feminicides, Mexicans are also confronted with art that seemingly glorifies this gendered violence. In January 2016, Mexican singer-songwriter Gerardo Ortiz premiered a video clip for his song "Fuiste mía" (You Were Mine), which was met with controversy because it portrayed a man burning a woman after finding out that she had cheated on him. By using social media like the website Change.org, civil groups and feminist organizations protested and asked for the video to be banned, saying that it promoted feminicide (Reina). A few months later, a state of Jalisco prosecutor issued an arrest warrant for Ortiz on charges of inciting criminal activity. However, the singer was able to pay a fine of $2,700 in exchange for his freedom. While such representations can incite violence, federal authorities are targeting them to create the illusion that they are solving the problem of feminicides. It is a skin-deep approach to a sickness with much deeper roots.

Since the early 2000s, Mexicans have suffered an explosion of violence in their everyday lives, which has been captured by art and popular culture. Marginalized sectors of the population have been most impacted by this violence, specifically low-income women. The artistic representations of feminicides that have been analyzed in this chapter show that the problem of gendered violence is not limited to areas considered to be dangerous in Mexico, like border cities such as Ciudad Juárez, but is a cancer that has spread throughout the country. Contemporary works like the ones included here try to offer solutions and to create awareness among the Mexican population, to demand justice, and to try to change a culture where violence against women has been systemized. Drawing on real-life events as well as diverse texts, genres, and media, these dramaturges, writers, and artists have expanded their arsenal of representation beyond direct pleas and documentation in order to involve as much of the populace as possible. Rooted in complex causes involving all strata of Mexican society, feminicides cannot be stopped by the few, only the many.[11]

NOTES

1. Although the terms are often used interchangeably, there is substantial theoretical argumentation that differentiates between the two. *Femicide* was first

defined in writing in 1992 by Jill Radford and Diana Russell in *Femicide: The Politics of Woman Killing* as "the misogynist killing of women by men" (xi). In 2001, Russell redefined *femicide* as "the killing of females by males because they are females" (qtd. in Widyono 7). Theorists such as Rosa-Linda Fregoso and Cynthia Bejarano have advocated for the use of the term *feminicide* to describe the phenomenon in Latin America. The word *feminicide*, they argue, acknowledges the contributions made in the Global South to a concept originating in the Global North, including the understanding that this gender-based violence implicates the state as well as individuals, because it involves systemic violence that deprives women of human rights (5). Similarly, Mexican academic and politician Marcela Lagarde y de los Ríos points to *femicidio* (femicide), homicide of a woman, as a limited term in comparison with *feminicidio* (feminicide), genocide of women (xv–xvii).

2. See Driver; Olivera; Weissman; Gaspar de Alba and Guzmán; and Wright, "Introduction."
3. See Driver; and Wright, "Public Women."
4. Drawing data from records of "defunciones femeninas con presunción de homicidio" ("female deaths with a presumption of homicide"), data that do not take into account the motivation behind a killing, the authors of a 2010 government report note high rates of women being murdered not only in Chihuahua, the state that is home to Juárez, but in other states in the northeast of the country as well, including Durango, Nayarit, Sinaloa, and Baja California, as well as in Guerrero, a state located along the Pacific Ocean (Incháustegui Romero et al. 28). The authors also note increased rates of murdered women in municipalities in Nuevo León and Coahuila for 2010 (52).
5. Our understanding of parody in this chapter is taken from Linda Hutcheon's seminal 1985 publication *A Theory of Parody: The Teachings of Twentieth-Century Art Forms*, in which she identifies modern parody as a "form of imitation characterized by ironic inversion, not always at the expense of the parodied text," or, in other words, "repetition with critical distance, which marks difference rather than similarity" and thus goes "beyond mere allusive variation" (6).
6. As Jesse Weiner notes, this is a clear allusion to the discovery of eight feminicide victims in a Juárez cotton field in November 2001 (294). Thus, de la Rosa's play can be said to have elements of *teatro documental* (documentary theater), a type of theater that emerged at the end of the 1960s and often dramatizes "conflictos puntales como huelgas" (specific conflicts such as strikes) and "abusos políticos o jurídicos" (political or juridical abuses) (Freire 20).

7. Among those who have been blamed for the feminicides are the local gang Los Rebeldes, a group of bus drivers known as Los Toltecas, and the Egyptian-born chemist Abdel Latif Sharif Sharif (Messmer).
8. *Hotel Juárez: Dramaturgia de feminicidios* (Hotel Juárez: Dramaturgy on Feminicides) contains a small sampling of these theatrical works. Edited by Enrique Mijares, the 2008 anthology contains eleven plays that touch on the topic of Juárez's feminicides from different dramatic perspectives. The collection takes its name from one of these works, *Hotel Juárez* by Víctor Hugo Rascón Banda, one of Mexico's most prolific twentieth-century dramatists. According to reviewer Sarah M. Misemer, the anthology "is full of serious works, which delve deeply and honestly into the spectacles of horror occurring in many of the poorest neighborhoods of Ciudad Juárez" (218).
9. See Pérez García for more on the trajectory that many of these NGOs followed between their inception and 2005.
10. For more, go to www.museoartemoderno.com/lorena-wolffer#/memorial/.
11. For a general overview of the concept of femicide, see *Femicide: The Politics of Woman Killing* by Jill Radford and Diana E. H. Russell. For an examination of some of the factors behind these crimes in the Americas and Mexico, see *Terrorizing Women: Feminicide in the Américas* by Rosa-Linda Fregoso and Cynthia Bejarano; *Huesos en el desierto* by Sergio González Rodríguez; and *Disposable Women and Other Myths of Global Capitalism* by Melissa W. Wright. For an analysis of cultural production centering on Mexican feminicides, see *More or Less Dead: Feminicide, Haunting, and the Ethics of Representation in Mexico* by Alice Driver. To continue the examination of these recent cultural productions, see the plays in *Hotel Juárez: Dramaturgia de feminicidios*, edited by Enrique Mijares, and the stories in *El silencio de los cuerpos: Relatos sobre feminicidos*.

WORKS CITED

Backyard: El traspatio. Directed by Carlos Carrera, written by Sabina Berman. Argos Producciones, 2009.

Barrera, Ave, and Lola Horner. *21,000 princesas*. Pluralia Ediciones, 2016.

Bolaño, Roberto. *2666*. Anagrama, 2004.

Cavarero, Adriana. "On the Body of Antigone." *Feminist Readings of Antigone*, edited by Fanny Söderbäck, SUNY Press, 2010, pp. 45–63.

Chauvet, Elina. *Mi cabello por tu nombre*. 7 Jan. 2014, Galería Cuadrante Creativo, Culiacán. "Performance." *Elina Chauvet*, www.elinachauvet.com. Accessed 11 Jan. 2017.

———. "*Zapatos Rojos*." 2009-current. "Artivismo." *Elina Chauvet*, www.elinachauvet.com. Accessed 11 Jan. 2017.

de la Mora, Guadalupe. "Las voces de Antígona en Ciudad Juárez." *Cinco dramaturgos chihuahuenses*, edited by Guadalupe de la Mora, Municipio de Juárez, 2005, pp. 169–83.

de la Rosa, Perla. *Antígona: Las voces que incendian el desierto*. *Cinco dramaturgos chihuahuenses*, edited by Guadalupe de la Mora, Municipio de Juárez, 2005, pp. 187–228.

Driver, Alice. *More or Less Dead: Feminicide, Haunting, and the Ethics of Representation in Mexico*. University of Arizona Press, 2015.

Eisenhammer, Stephen. "Bare Life in Ciudad Juárez: Violence in a Space of Exclusion." *Latin American Perspectives*, vol. 41, no. 2, March 2014, pp. 99–109.

El silencio de los cuerpos: Relatos sobre feminicidos. Ediciones B, 2015.

Fregoso, Rosa-Linda, and Cynthia Bejarano, editors. *Terrorizing Women: Feminicide in the Américas*. Duke University Press, 2010.

Freire, Silka. *Teatro documental latinoamericano: El referente histórico y su (re)escritura dramática*. Ediciones Al Margen, 2007.

Galicia, Rocío. "Edeberto *Pilo* Galindo." *Dramaturgia en contexto I: Diálogo con veinte dramaturgos del noreste de México*, edited by Rocío Judith Galicia Velasco, Consejo Nacional para la Cultura y las Artes, Instituto Nacional de Bellas Artes, and Fondo Regional para la Cultura y las Artes del Noreste, 2007, pp. 127–47.

Galindo, Edeberto. *Lomas de Poleo*. *Dramaturgia del norte: Antología*, edited by Enrique Mijares, Fondo Regional para la Cultura y las Artes del Noreste, 2003, pp. 173–219.

Gaspar de Alba, Alicia, and Georgina Guzmán, editors. *Making a Killing: Femicide, Free Trade, and La Frontera*. University of Texas Press, 2010.

González Rodríguez, Sergio. *Huesos en el desierto*. Anagrama, 2002.

Hutcheon, Linda. *A Theory of Parody: The Teachings of Twentieth-Century Art Forms*. University of Illinois Press, 1985.

Lagarde y de los Ríos, Marcela. "Preface: Feminist Keys for Understanding Feminicide: Theoretical, Political, and Legal Construction." *Terrorizing Women: Feminicide in the Américas*, edited by Rosa-Linda Fregoso and Cynthia Bejarano, Duke University Press, 2010, pp. xi–xxviii.

Messmer, Marietta. "Transfrontera Crimes: Representations of the Juárez Femicides in Recent Fictional and Non-Fictional Accounts." *American Studies Journal*, vol. 57, 2012, DOI 10.18422/57-03. Accessed 22 Apr. 2017.

Mijares, Enrique, editor. *Hotel Juárez: Dramaturgia de feminicidios*. Editorial Espacio Vacío, 2008.

Misemer, Sarah M. Review of *Hotel Juárez: Dramaturgia de Feminicidios*, edited by Enrique Mijares. *Latin American Theatre Review*, vol. 43, no. 1, 2009, pp. 218–19.

Monárrez Fragoso, Julia E. "An Analysis of Femicide in Ciudad Juárez, 1993–2007." *Strengthening Understanding of Femicide: Using Research to Galvanize Action and Accountability*, Program for Appropriate Technology in Health, InterCambios, Medical Research Council of South Africa, and World Health Organization, 2009, pp. 78–83.

Olivera, Mercedes. "Violencia Feminicida: Violence Against Women and Mexico's Structural Crisis." *Terrorizing Women: Feminicide in the Américas*, edited by Rosa-Linda Fregoso and Cynthia Bejarano, Duke University Press, 2010, pp. 49–58.

Incháustegui Romero, Teresa, et al. *Violencia feminicida en México: Características, tendencias y nuevas expresiones en las entidades federativas, 1985–2010*. ONU Mujeres and INMUJERES, 2012.

Pérez García, Martha Estela. "Las organizaciones no gubernamentales en Ciudad Juárez y su lucha contra la violencia de género." *Género, feminismo(s) y violencia desde la frontera norte*, special issue of *Noésis*, vol. 15, no. 28, 2005, pp. 147–67.

Pope, Randolph D. "The Spanish American Novel from 1950 to 1975." *The Cambridge History of Latin American Literature*, vol. 2, edited by Roberto González Echevarría and Enrique Pupo-Walker, Cambridge University Press, 2008, pp. 226–78.

Radford, Jill, and Diana E. H. Russell, editors. *Femicide: The Politics of Woman Killing*. Twayne Publishers, 1992.

Reina, Elena. "Un videoclip de Gerardo Ortiz, acusado de promover el feminicidio." *El País Internacional*, 22 Apr. 2016, internacional.elpais.com/internacional/2016/03/29/ mexico/1459217973_116141.html. Accessed 11 Jan. 2017.

Román, Alejandro. *Ánima sola*. Consejo Nacional para la Cultura y las Artes Nuevo León, 2010.

Rulfo, Juan. *Pedro Páramo*. 1955. Fondo de Cultura Económica, 1971.

Salazar Mendoza, Margarita. "El teatro juarense, ¿reflejo social?" *Archipiélago: Revista Cultural de Nuestra América*, vol. 14, no. 51, 2006, pp. 46–48.

Señorita extraviada. Directed by Lourdes Portillo. Xochitl Productions and Women Make Movies, 2001.

Weiner, Jesse. "Antigone in Juárez: Tragedy, Politics, and Public Women on Mexico's Northern Border." *Classical Receptions Journal*, vol. 7, no. 2, 2015, pp. 276–309.

Weissman, Deborah M. "Global Economics and Their Progenies: Theorizing Femicide in Context." *Terrorizing Women: Feminicide in the Américas*, edited by Rosa-Linda Fregoso and Cynthia Bejarano, Duke University Press, 2010, pp. 225–42.

Widyono, Monique. "Conceptualizing Femicide." *Strengthening Understanding of Femicide: Using Research to Galvanize Action and Accountability*. Program for Appropriate Technology in Health, InterCambios, Medical Research Council of South Africa, and World Health Organization, 2009, pp. 7–25.

Wolffer, Lorena. *Memorial*. 2015. Museo de Arte Moderno, www.museoartemoderno.com/lorena-wolffer#/memorial/. Accessed 11 Jan. 2017.

Wright, Melissa W. "Introduction." *Disposable Women and Other Myths of Global Capitalism*. Routledge, 2006, pp. 1–19.

———. "Public Women, Profit, and Femicide in Northern Mexico." *South Atlantic Quarterly*, vol. 105, no. 4, 2006, pp. 681–98.

13

EL NORTE

The North in Contemporary Mexican Narrative, Poetry, and Film: Relocating National Imaginaries Beyond the Mythology of Violence

OSWALDO ZAVALA

PRIMARY MATERIALS

- *Tomóchic* by Heriberto Frías (novel, 1983)
- *Guerra en el paraíso* (War in Paradise) by Carlos Montemayor (novel, 1991)
- *La guerra de Galio* (Gallium War) by Héctor Aguilar Camín (novel, 1991)
- *Los detectives salvajes* (The Savage Detectives) by Roberto Bolaño (novel, 1998)
- *Un asesino solitario* (A Lone Assassin) by Élmer Mendoza (novel, 1999)
- *Amores perros* (Love's a Bitch), directed by Alejandro González Iñárritu (film, 2000)
- *Todo el poder* (All the Power), directed by Fernando Sariñana (film, 2000)
- *2666* by Roberto Bolaño (novel, 2004)
- *El infierno* (Hell), directed by Luis Estrada (film, 2010)
- "Los muertos" (The Dead) by María Rivera (poetry, 2010)
- *Miss Bala* (Miss Bullet), directed by Gerardo Naranjo (film, 2011)
- *Poemas de terror y de misterio* (Poems of Terror and Mystery) by Luis Felipe Fabre (poetry, 2013)
- *Te diría que fuéramos al río Bravo a llorar pero debes saber que ya no hay río ni llanto* (I'd Tell You to Come with Me and Cry at the Rio Grande but You Must Know That There Is No Longer a River nor Tears) by Jorge Humberto Chávez (poetry, 2013)

THE 1999 PUBLICATION of Élmer Mendoza's *Un asesino solitario* (A Lone Assassin) synthesized the raw political and economic crisis that Mexican society had experienced nationwide in the last years of the twentieth century. The confusion of one of the characters in the novel illustrates the generalized chaos of the time:

> Fito se sentía desalentado de la vida, que no entendía nada, no se explicaba qué había ocurrido: cayó el socialismo, el muro de Berlín, había guerras, racismo, hambre, enfermedades incurables, Fidel estaba valiendo madre, esos pedos, no comprendía cómo se estaba acomodando el mundo. (23)

> Fito felt discouraged about life, he felt that he did not understand anything, he could not explain to himself what had happened: socialism fell, the Berlin wall, there were wars, racism, famine, incurable diseases, Fidel was going down, all that shit, he did not understand how the world was being rearranged.[1]

The main character in the novel is Jorge Macías, known as Yorch (George), an assassin from the state of Sinaloa working for an obscure intelligence unit of the Mexican government. Macías is hired to kill the presidential candidate in the 1994 election, a direct reference to the assassination of Luis Donaldo Colosio, the candidate of the Institutional Revolutionary Party (PRI),[2] who was gunned down in the border city of Tijuana that year. The innovative use of popular language allows Mendoza to represent a "new" Mexico that first appeared in novels such as *El complot mongol* (The Mongolian Conspiracy, 1969), the great police noir by Rafael Bernal in which a Mexican detective investigates an international plot against the president of the United States during the latter's visit to Mexico. In both novels, a multiplicity of mafias, police corporations, undercover agents, and common criminals within and outside government struggle for power, although even the protagonists ignore who is behind the various levels of conspiracy. In Mendoza's story, the overwhelmed Yorch repeats the one truth of this new world order: "unas veces se pierde y otras se deja de ganar" (sometimes you lose and sometimes you stop winning) (228).

Un asesino solitario nevertheless goes beyond any previous Mexican police novel written in the 1990s. Its difference consists in rendering visible the transformations and catastrophes brought about at the end of the twentieth century. But detective fiction is only one of the changing genres in the narrative of those years. Toward the end of the 1990s, the Mexican literary field experienced a profound decentering with the emergence of many writers who gradually made dominant various themes related to the crisis. In the national imaginary, the geography of the crisis was located mainly in the northern states. However, its origin (the governing elite) and temporality (1994 was the watershed year) were of national and international scope. The convulsion began on January 1, 1994, with the uprising of the Zapatista National Liberation Army (EZLN) in the southern state of Chiapas, simultaneous with the implementation of the North America Free Trade Agreement (NAFTA). Then on March 23, the PRI presidential candidate, Colosio, was killed in Tijuana. On September 28, the assassination of José Francisco Ruiz Massieu, head of the same party, followed. Finally, on December 20, only days after the December 1 inauguration of President Ernesto Zedillo, the Mexican currency, the peso, experienced one of the worst devaluations of its history.

Political scientist José Woldenberg presided over the Federal Electoral Institute, which managed the 2000 presidential election when the PRI lost for the first time after seven consecutive decades in office. Woldenberg recalls 1994 as a decisive year in the modern history of the country:

> 1994 fue un año duro, cargado de preocupantes presagios. Pero fue también un año de promisorias innovaciones que coadyuvaron a la construcción de un escenario democrático. Lo que en ese año sucedió dejó una importante estela y vale la pena recordarlo porque modeló—en alguna medida—lo que hoy México es. (7)

> 1994 was a difficult year, loaded with worrisome omens. But it was also a year of promissory innovations that helped in the construction of a democratic stage. What happened that year left an important wake, and it is worth remembering it because it was a model—to a certain measure—of what Mexico is today.

Other events contributed to the disintegration of the PRI nationalist project and led to a democratic reform that paradoxically brought more instability, violence, and official corruption. Two key years marked irreparable fissures that would ultimately produce, among other factors, the collapse of the presidential system: 1968 and 1985. The first is the year of the student massacre in the Plaza de las Tres Culturas in Tlatelolco, Mexico City, which evidenced the criminal side of the repressive state. The second brought the earthquake that partially destroyed the capital, a tragedy that revealed a dysfunctional federal government and the rise of what the writer, critic, and activist Carlos Monsiváis saw for the first time as civil society. The same year, 1985, marked another event in Mexico's political history: the shuttering of the Federal Security Directorate (DFS), the government agency whose duties over previous decades included disciplining organized crime. With its dismantling, multiple extraofficial power players were marginalized from the political system that until then had exercised an implacable national hegemony. By the 1990s, these cracks in the system resulted in the violent confrontation of rival groups within the government as well as the guerrilla uprising in the south and the broken national economic policy. Thus, according to Woldenberg, the zeitgeist of 1994 carried a "sign of death" (101).

The political narrative published in the early 1990s reflected the still prevalent authoritarian state rule. In 1991, for example, two important novels depicted the governing system at the height of its power in the 1970s: Héctor Aguilar Camín's *La guerra de Galio* (Gallium War) and Carlos Montemayor's *Guerra en el paraíso* (War in Paradise). Both dramatize guerrilla movements, state violence, police power, vulnerable media, and a subdued civil society with limited agency. As the decade came to an end, however, the image of the repressive state and its obscure political affairs was replaced by that of an unstable government falling into chaos. It is logical that in the map of national unrest, the zone of greatest conflict was the furthest from the capital of the functional state. Tijuana emerged, opposite Mexico City, as the space of absolute negativity: the site where the system's leaders were betrayed and killed. In this sense, more than portraying a given reality, the changing political narrative mediates in the narrative structure of *Un asesino solitario*. The new paradigm made the crisis of the state synonymous with the disjointed national territory. In literary and audiovisual productions, an imaginary about the North as the exceptional region of failure gradually overtook the rest of the country: the narrative of the failed state has now become the new, accepted *real* of Mexico's cultural productions.

In what follows, I will analyze this paradigm of interpretation precisely as a discursive strategy with historical roots in the late nineteenth century that were radicalized in the following decades, to the point that the North has become the ultimate frontier of Mexican modernity. For this purpose I study not how artists born or located in the northern states conceptualize the region but rather how certain works of art allow for a productive understanding of the North as a privileged space of geopolitical signification in Mexico, in particular after 1994. Suspending for now the "intellectual colonialism" (Tabuenca Córdoba 421) that critic María Socorro Tabuenca suspects in the works of writers who do not herald from the North but who have written about it—Carlos Fuentes, Paco Ignacio Taibo II, Laura Esquivel, among others—I will comment on works by novelists, poets, and filmmakers who may not come from the North, might not reside there, or, in some cases, are not even natives of Mexico, but who nonetheless have contributed significantly to the country's most important cultural trends in the last decades of the twentieth century and the first decades of the twenty-first.

As Viviane Mahieux and I analyzed in the introduction to *Tierras de nadie*, it may be argued that the North first appeared in the national cultural imaginary with the publication of Heriberto Frías's *Tomóchic* (1893). This testimonial novel narrates the real massacre of the residents of a small town in Chihuahua's mountain range, a mass killing perpetrated by the federal army under the orders of the dictator Porfirio Díaz. The town of Tomóchic had committed the intolerable transgression of challenging federal and state power by organizing its own government body and expelling all official and ecclesiastic authorities. The massacre may have served to extend the symbolic reach of Porfirian modernity, but nothing could stop the dictatorship's collapse two decades later with the 1910 Revolution. The irony, of course, is that the North, the same geopolitical space that consolidated Díaz's nationalist project at the end of the nineteenth century, became, one hundred years later, the very site widely held to be the locus of the present-day crisis of the modern Mexican project.[3]

The first years of the twenty-first century saw a proliferation of cultural productions about the North precisely as the real and symbolic region of national decomposition due to its systemic poverty, official corruption, and the rise of organized crime in the context of the neoliberal era. The phenomenon of drug trafficking in particular has clearly become the major reference of the North, configuring a persistent national and international imaginary revolving around a permanent security crisis within the state and civil society.[4] While there certainly is a vast corpus of literature, music, and film that does not focus on the drug trade when representing the North, I seek to shed light on the complex discourse around the notion of "national security." First articulated in the United States, "national security" has become a central logic of government in Mexico; it has transformed our current understanding of that country's waves of violence as the constitutive condition for life in the northern states.

As sociologist Fernando Escalante Gonzalbo explains, the discourse on national security derived from a growing distrust of the notion of the welfare state in the 1980s that led to a general antigovernment attitude in the neoliberal era.

Without the protection of social assistance institutions and with a decaying judicial system, there emerged a *fantasy* in which the perception of crime and the crime statistics are no longer equal. In fact, as Escalante Gonzalbo explains, the national homicide index remained stable and even *decreased* throughout the 1990s and most of the 2000s. Despite this fact, the national imaginary prevailed in representing a state of chaos, with organized crime and official corruption as the endemic conditions afflicting society.

The symbolic decentering of national tradition at the turn of the twenty-first century may also be seen through the important literary works of Chilean author Roberto Bolaño. This is certainly the case of *Los detectives salvajes* (The Savage Detectives, 1998), a novel in which three marginal young poets, self-declared "enemies" of Octavio Paz, abandon Mexico City to help a prostitute escape from her ruthless pimp. The four of them drive to the northern desert of Sonora state in search of a lost avant-garde poet whose work they barely know but whom they passionately wish to follow. When the poet is accidentally killed, two of the young writers embark on a long exile through various countries and continents.

Also set in the North of Mexico, Bolaño's extraordinary novel *2666*, published posthumously in 2004, revealed the sociopolitical coordinates of the discourse on the national security crisis. This ambitious work explores two key phenomena of the new *perception* of crime—femicides and the drug trade—in the country's most notorious city: Ciudad Juárez, at the U.S.-Mexico border.[5] The novel, divided into five interconnected parts, explores centuries of Western history, linking many of its most violent atrocities: slavery, the Holocaust, sexism, drug trafficking. Most of the action takes place in the fictional border city of Santa Teresa—modeled after Ciudad Juárez—where hundreds of women have disappeared in what is referred to as the phenomenon of femicide. For one reason or another, the main characters converge in Santa Teresa, where the crimes go on with impunity. One of the characters describes the femicide in an intriguing light: "No one pays attention to these killings, but the secret of the world is hidden in them" (348).

At the end of the novel, however, the people of Santa Teresa find another form of survival in their community, staying together to celebrate the holidays despite the rampaging crime: "The Christmas holidays in Santa Teresa were celebrated in the usual fashion. There were *posadas*, piñatas were smashed, tequila and beer were drunk. Even on the poorest streets people could be heard laughing. Some of these streets were completely dark, like black holes, and the laughter that came from who knows where was the only sign, the only beacon that kept residents and strangers from getting lost" (631). It is this resilient gesture of communal survival that perhaps best describes Bolaño's novel. As the border people struggle with the most difficult acts of violence, their basic need for collective life never wanes. As the killing continues, unlikely policemen, politicians, journalists, and organizers begin to seek out solutions to the crimes, refusing to accept the role of victim and the indignation assumed by most common citizens. Philosopher Roberto Esposito studies a certain ethos inherent to the notion of community in Western modernity that is certainly at the base of Bolaño's writing: "Community is both necessary and impossible. Human history harbors this wound, which corrodes and voids it from within. Our history is only interpretable in proportion to this 'impossibility' from which it nevertheless originates, in the form of a necessary betrayal: We inhabit the margin between what we owe and what we can do. So much so that when we do attempt to construct, realize, or effect community, we inevitably end up turning it into its exact opposite—a community of death and the death of community" (15). Destroyed by the horror of hundreds of women brutally murdered, Santa Teresa's community resists in the margin of Mexican modernity that paradoxically forces it into becoming a community by virtue of being excluded from the nation.[6]

Bolaño's novel showed the political limits of the discourse on the crisis of national security by narrating the daily life of a struggling border city in all of its criminal complexity. However, what had been mainly a perception of crime gained irrefutable *materiality* with President Felipe Calderón's strategy against drug trafficking. His government (2006–12) was responsible for a "war" against the so-called drug cartels, which led to more than 121,000 killings and more than 30,000 forced disappearances.[7] This level of violence has no precedent in the history of drug trafficking in Mexico. In fact, as documented by specialists such as sociologist Luis Astorga, from the 1970s on, the federal government established effective police controls across the country to limit and manipulate the smuggling of illegal drugs.[8] With that strategy, as Astorga explains, the state conceived a discursive matrix through which it imposed a certain understanding of the drug trade. Decades of police reports, press releases, intelligence documents, diplomatic exchanges, news interviews, and the like articulated a new vocabulary and narrative sense to describe all things "narco." Eventually, a cultural *habitus* mediated most of the common "narco" knowledge in the field of cultural productions. By the end of 2012, it was widely accepted that "drug cartels," especially those based notoriously in the northern states, posed a real challenge to state power, with criminals better trained and armed, and with even more resources and intelligence capabilities, than the Mexican army and the federal police themselves. While some journalists and academics have questioned the official narrative about drug trafficking, most writers, musicians, filmmakers, and conceptual artists have reproduced uncritically the government's assessment of the national security crisis.

But the North has also become the geopolitical source for a current of cultural productions that not only challenge the mythology of violence but also reconfigure the region as a viable ethicopolitical community. The works of Daniel Sada, César López Cuadras, and Víctor Hugo Rascón Banda, among others, have articulated a counterhegemonic approach to the North of Mexico with its own historical and political specificity. The poetry of Jorge Humberto Chávez, a native of Ciudad Juárez, must be read in this context. His collection *Te diría que fuéramos al Río Bravo a llorar pero debes saber que ya no hay río ni llanto* (I'd Tell You to Come with Me and Cry at the Rio Grande but You Must Know That There Is No Longer a River nor Tears, 2013) articulates memories and affects of border subjectivity experienced in the years of Calderón's drug war. This intimate and lyrical poetry draws from news reports, personal remembrances, and the political implications of the violence destroying the North's social tissue. It is worth considering the entire poem "Otra crónica," as it sums up the relevance of the collection:

> On October 6th of this year Armando El Choco mentioned at a party that they were looking for him
> and they found him a month later that morning he was warming up his car's engine to drive his daughters to school
> in 1967 we'd go to the Rio Grande to wash the barrio cars first Chato's [Flatface] then Bogar's [Bogart] and finally Huarache Veloz [Flyin' Flip-flop]
> in 1990 policemen used to go to the Rio Grande to fish from the banks for young girls waiting to cross over to El Paso
> in the year 2010 the Grande almost no longer a river a *migra* and Sergio Adrián age 13 he fought with a stone in his hand and the agent with a revolver
> that same year in a store in Salvácar the clerk refused to pay the ransom and got shot in the head
> and 17 of his neighbors were hunted down one by one while celebrating the touch-football game they had won
> oh young sons of Cadmus I know you'd rather be anywhere else but you are here today old Ovid sang

> and you woman taken out of your house and then threatened that they'd kill your husband if you didn't go on your last car ride
> I'd tell you to come with me and cry at the Rio Grande but you must know that there is no longer a river nor tears (Chávez, "Two Poems")

Each couplet names real crimes, combined with a melancholic instant, such as the 2008 killing of journalist Armando Rodríguez or the 2010 killing of a Juárez child shot from the U.S. side of the Rio Grande by a Border Patrol agent. The memories of the murders are preserved as the poetic voice seems to address both the poet's community and the reader, who either joins in the remembrance or learns about the crimes as a newcomer among the locals. The importance of this poetry resides in the fact that it is the very community that recalls its own, writing against the mythology of violence and showing how border people have not renounced their social contract, which has instead been broken by official power dynamics. With this, Chávez joins other poets who have approached the violence in the North with literary projects defying the official narrative. Such is the case of Luis Felipe Fabre and María Rivera. In *Poemas de terror y de misterio* (Poems of Terror and Mystery, 2013), Fabre turns to the violence in commercial movie trailers in which the seeming victims of femicide, for example, return as vampires attacking the living, showing violence as consumerist spectacle. With her poem "Los muertos" (The Dead), Rivera draws from leftist Latin American poetic traditions, in particular the works of Pablo Neruda and César Vallejo, in order to enumerate the innocent victims of the violence across the country, rejecting both the notion that violence occurs only in the conflicted regions of the North and the government's claim that most of the murders occur between rival gangs of traffickers.

Film productions in Mexico have also been deeply affected by the official discourse on national security. Two significant films released in 2000 eloquently captured the effects of this perception of crime: Fernando Sariñana's *Todo el poder* (All the Power) and Alejandro González Iñárritu's *Amores perros* (Love's a Bitch). In both, Mexico City appears in a state of emergency, ridden with police corruption, complicit gangs, and moral bankruptcy. Ten years later, the movie industry relocated that crisis to the northern region, where gender violence, extreme poverty, and drug trafficking allegedly ruled over all aspects of society. Two films, among many others, mark this latter displacement: Luis Estrada's *El infierno* (Hell, 2010) and Gerardo Naranjo's *Miss Bala* (Miss Bullet, 2011). In the first, Benny, the protagonist, is deported back to his native town in northern

Mexico after spending years as an undocumented migrant worker in the United States. Upon his return, he finds that his birthplace is in the middle of a drug feud between two brothers who are responsible for a constant bloodbath permeating all institutions, leaving a wake of death and despair for those who survive it. Ignacio Sánchez Prado discusses how Luis Estrada's film "has no qualms about presenting the complete destruction of a northern Mexican town and its inevitable surrender to the cartel" (153). But more than a critique of the state's actual surrender to organized crime, in my opinion the film plays on the anxieties of Mexican society *after* the adoption of neoliberalism as the government's ideology. *Miss Bala* transfers this prevalent fear to the urban setting of Tijuana, the same city where the PRI presidential candidate was assassinated nearly twenty years earlier. The film tells the unexpected journey of a young woman who aspires to enter a beauty contest but finds herself instead working for a local drug gang. Powerless, she is forced to accept the favors of a kingpin in order to enter the beauty contest in exchange for her unconditional collaboration in various criminal activities. The audience sees the story from her point of view, and like her, it is left confused after witnessing a military assault that fakes the killing of the drug lord, who is last seen placing his signature baseball cap on the dead body that authorities will later, during an official press conference, claim is his remains. The film shows an ironic parallel between the beauty contest and that press conference, both structured to produce symbolic power plays disciplining the body politic of the young women of the North, at the mercy of a cruel aspirational society and its clandestine economy. In sum, the Mexican cinema of the early twenty-first century has consistently reimagined the North as the ground zero of the irruption of violence resulting from the corruption of the state and the cold dominance of late capitalism.[9]

More than two decades since the violence of 1994, the field of cultural productions has been profoundly influenced by the idea that Mexico's national project has failed and that this failure has transformed the entire north of the country into a sort of no-man's-land, which gives the title to Eduardo Antonio Parra's celebrated collection of short stories, *No Man's Land* (2004). As we retrace our steps back to the 1999 publication of *Un asesino solitario*, it is clear how this and the other works discussed here explored the most pressing symbolic events of the turn of the century. These novels, films, and poetry, however, did so without designating the North, and much less the border region, as the tragic zone of postnational failure. The North is rather seen as that privileged space of signification in which the violence of Mexican modernity, which affects the entire country, is experienced with more intensity. At one point in Mendoza's novel, the professional assassin Jorge "Yorch" Macías talks to a university professor who laments the historical defeat of Mexico's national project. Yorch ponders: "lo más doloroso para él era que al final la razón la tendríamos los cabrones como yo" (the most painful thing for him was that in the end, fuckers like me would be proven right) (26). This sharp mockery may be read as a caricature of the obedient hit man who chooses never to question the extent of his criminal actions within the corrupt official system. But as the novel unfolds, Yorch discovers that he himself may be sacrificed by the system as well. The conspiracy will ultimately turn against all the agents who made it possible. The survivors, like Yorch, will face the ethicopolitical demand of forming a new community, as in Bolaño's novel *2666* or Chávez's poetry. Their Mexico may not be the same nation-state conceived a century earlier, but their share of the territory may still be recognizable, beyond all political distortions, in their creative imaginations.

FURTHER READING

FICTION

Chávez Díaz de León, Miguel Ángel. *Policía de Ciudad Juárez*. Océano, 2012.

Crosthwaite, Luis Humberto. *Estrella de la calle sexta*. Tusquets, 2000.

Herrera, Yuri. *Trabajos del reino*. 2004. Periférica, 2008.

López Cuadras, César. *Cuatro muertos por capítulo*. Ediciones B, 2013.

Parra, Eduardo Antonio. "La fábula del narcotráfico." *Letras Libres*, Sept. 2005, pp. 79–80.

Rascón Banda, Víctor Hugo. *Contrabando*. 1991. Mondadori, 2008.

Rivera Garza, Cristina. *La cresta de Ilión*. Tusquets, 2002.

Sada, Daniel. *El lenguaje del juego*. Anagrama, 2012.

———. *Porque parece mentira la verdad nunca se sabe*. Tusquets, 1999.

Silva, César. *La balada de los arcos dorados*. Almadía, 2014.

SECONDARY SOURCES

Bowden, Charles. *Juárez: The Laboratory of Our Future*. Aperture, 1998.

———. *Murder City: Ciudad Juárez and the Global Economy's New Killing Fields*. Nation Books, 2010.

García Canclini, Néstor. *Culturas híbridas: Estrategias para entrar y salir de la modernidad*. Grijalbo, 1990.

Mignolo, Walter. *Local Histories/Global Designs: Coloniality, Subaltern Knowledges, and Border Thinking*. Princeton University Press, 2000.

Ramírez-Pimienta, Juan Carlos, and Salvador C. Fernández, editors. *El norte y su frontera en la narrativa policiaca mexicana*. Plaza y Valdés, 2005.

Sánchez Prado, Ignacio. "El sublime objeto de la frontera." *Tierras de nadie: El norte en la narrativa mexicana contemporánea*, edited by Viviane Mahieux and Oswaldo Zavala, Tierra Adentro, 2012, pp. 43–53.

Vulliamy, Ed. "As Juárez Falls." *The Nation*, 9 Dec. 2010, www.thenation.com/article/156996/ju%C3%A1rez-falls. Accessed 20 June 2011.

Wald, Elijah. *Narcocorrido: A Journey into the Music of Drugs, Guns, and Guerrillas*. HarperCollins, 2001.

Webb, Gary. *Dark Alliance: The CIA, the Contras, and the Crack Cocaine Explosion*. Seven Stories Press, 1998.

NOTES

1. All English translations are mine unless otherwise indicated.
2. This and most other acronyms are from the original Spanish terms.
3. A key work signaling this crisis is without doubt Luis Humberto Crosthwaite's *El gran pretender* (The Great Pretender, 1992). The novel delves into the life of marginal cholos who struggle to maintain their barrio united against the harassment of the police, rival gangs, and their own internal divisions. The plot captures what Octavio Paz foresaw in his seminal essay *The Labyrinth of Solitude* (1950), which opens with a cultural critique of the pachuco as a liminal border subject of Mexican modernity.
4. For a study on the emergence of popular "narconovels" as a result of such imaginary, see my article "Imagining the U.S.-Mexico Drug War: The Critical Limits of Narconarratives."
5. As I mentioned before, homicide rates, in fact, steadily decreased until 2008, when the so-called war against drugs was ordered by President Felipe Calderón, militarizing cities including Juárez, as I will discuss later in this essay. Additionally, as border researcher Molly Molloy has noted, the national and international perception of Juárez femicides does not coincide with statistical data on gender violence: "Female murder victims have never comprised more than 18 percent of the overall number of murder victims in Ciudad Juárez, and in the last two decades that figure averages at less than 10 percent. That's less than in

the United States, where about 20 to 25 percent of the people who are murdered in a given year are women. Ciudad Juárez is experiencing profound social distress, and the elevated violence in the city is a continuing crisis. But this idea that Juárez is a place of disproportionate violence against women is a misperception" (Hooks). See Molloy's website *Frontera List* (fronteralist.org) for more statistical analysis on organized crime in Mexico.

6. For a thorough analysis of *2666* and the rest of Bolaño's fiction, see my book *La modernidad insufrible: Roberto Bolaño en los límites de la literatura latinoamericana contemporánea* (2015).
7. The figures of the victims of violence during the Calderón government come from the National Institute of Statistics and Geography (INEGI), an autonomous and decentralized research center based in the city of Aguascalientes. See La Redacción and Turati.
8. See my article "Las razones de Estado del narco: Soberanía y biopolítica en la narrativa mexicana contemporánea" for an analysis of the historical relationship between the state, organized crime, and cultural imaginaries of drug trafficking.
9. For complete analyses of the historical transformation of Mexican cinema at the turn of the twenty-first century, see Sánchez Prado and Smith.

WORKS CITED

Astorga, Luis. *Seguridad, traficantes y militares: El poder y la sombra*. Tusquets, 2007.

Bolaño, Roberto. *2666*. 2004. Translated by Natasha Wimmer, Farrar, Straus and Giroux, 2008.

———. *The Savage Detectives*. 1998. Translated by Natasha Wimmer, Farrar, Straus and Giroux, 2007.

Chávez, Jorge Humberto. *Te diría que fuéramos al río Bravo a llorar pero debes saber que ya no hay río ni llanto*. Fondo de Cultura Económica, 2013.

———. "Two Poems." Translated José Ramón Ruisánchez and Tamara R. Williams, *Literal*, vol. 36, Spring 2014, p. 44, literalmagazine.com/two-poems-by/. Accessed 27 Apr. 2017.

Escalante Gonzalbo, Fernando. *El crimen como realidad y representación*. El Colegio de México, 2012.

Esposito, Roberto. *Terms of the Political: Community, Immunity, Biopolitics*. Translated by Rhiannon Noel Welch, Fordham University Press, 2013.

Hooks, Christopher. "Q&A with Molly Molloy: The Story of the Juarez Femicides Is a 'Myth.'" *Texas Observer*, 9 Jan. 2014, www.texasobserver.org/qa-molly-molloy-story-juarez-femicides-myth/. Accessed 28 Apr. 2017.

La Redacción. "Más de 121 mil muertos, el saldo de la narcoguerra de Calderón: Inegi." *Proceso*, 30 July 2013, www.proceso.com.mx/?p=348816. Accessed 28 Apr. 2017.

Mahieux, Viviane, and Oswaldo Zavala, editors. *Tierras de nadie: El norte en la narrativa mexicana contemporánea*. Tierra Adentro, 2012.

Mendoza, Élmer. *Un asesino solitario*. 1999. Tusquets, 2001.

Monsiváis, Carlos. *"No sin nosotros": Los días del terremoto, 1985–2005*. Ediciones Era, 2005.

Parra, Eduardo Antonio. *No Man's Land*. Translated by Christopher Winks. City Lights, 2004.

Sánchez Prado, Ignacio. *Screening Neoliberalism: Transforming Mexican Cinema, 1988–2012*. Vanderbilt University Press, 2014.

Smith, Paul Julian. *Mexican Screen Fictions: Between Cinema and Television*. Polity, 2014.

Tabuenca Córdoba, María Socorro. "Las literaturas de las fronteras." *Por las fronteras del norte: Una aproximación cultural a la frontera México–Estados Unidos*, edited by José Manuel Valenzuela Arce, Fondo de Cultura Económica, 2003, pp. 393–427.

Turati, Marcela. "Desaparecidos: Las listas caóticas." *Proceso*, 13 Mar. 2013, www.proceso.com.mx/?p=336112. Accessed 28 Apr. 2017.

Woldenberg, José. *Violencia y política*. 1995. Cal y Arena, 2014.

Zavala, Oswaldo. "Imagining the U.S.-Mexico Drug War: The Critical Limits of Narconarratives." *Comparative Literature*, vol. 66, no. 3, Summer 2014, pp. 340–60.

———. *La modernidad insufrible: Roberto Bolaño en los límites de la literatura latinoamericana contemporánea*. North Carolina Studies in the Romance Languages and Literatures, University of North Carolina Press, 2015.

———. "Las razones de Estado del narco: soberanía y biopolítica en la narrativa mexicana contemporánea." *Heridas abiertas: Biopolítica y representación en América Latina*, edited by Mabel Moraña and Ignacio Sánchez Prado, Iberoamericana/Vervuert, 2014, pp. 182–202.

14

MEDIA

Media from Above/Media from Below: An Alternative Topography of the Mexican Mediascape

MAGALÍ RABASA

PRIMARY MATERIALS

- *Retrato de la burguesía* (Portrait of the Bourgeoisie) by David Alfaro Siqueiros (mural, 1939–40)
- *Nada, nadie: Las voces del temblor* (*Nothing, Nobody: The Voices of the Mexico City Earthquake*) by Elena Poniatowska (collective chronicle, 1988)
- *La toma de los medios en Oaxaca* (The Taking of the Media in Oaxaca), produced by Jen Lawhorne and Arnaldo Peña (documentary video, 2007)
- #YoSoy132 (#IAm132) (social media, 2012)

THE IMAGES WERE STRIKING: dozens of photographers gathered in public places, holding up their cameras in one hand and white flowers in the other, while wearing simple black-and-white paper masks bearing the face of their murdered colleague, thirty-one-year-old photojournalist Rubén Espinosa. On July 31, 2015, Espinosa was tortured and killed along with four women—among them, #YoSoy132 activist Nadia Vera—in an apartment in the Narvarte neighborhood of Mexico City.[1] He had recently fled Veracruz, where he and Vera had both worked for several years, amid increasing threats directed at them and a general climate of violence toward and particular repression of journalists.[2] Immediately, the Internet was flooded with demands of #JusticiaParaLxs5 (Justice for the 5)[3] as well as the increasingly, and disturbingly, common call for greater protection for journalists. The protests online and in the streets of Mexico over the weeks that followed were at once unique and eerily familiar in a country that ranks among the most dangerous places for journalists. While much could be said about the significance and broader context of this tragedy, it is clear that the murder of Lxs5—and the popular responses that followed—illustrate the way that in Mexico today the media is a field of extreme antagonisms and, increasingly, of violence.

If we follow the conflicts over control of the media back through the history of Mexico, where do they lead us? As far back as the early sixteenth century we can see evidence of the ways that the practices of a nascent media, in what would later be named Mexico, were deeply affected by the economic interests propelling an inherently capitalist colonial enterprise.[4] The invasion and subsequent "conquest" led by Hernán Cortés in 1519 was the subject of many volumes of chronicles penned by both the invaders and the indigenous inhabitants, which represent the earliest mediatic—which is to say, printed and published—appearances of the encounter that would result in the formation of the nation now called Mexico.[5] As Ángel Rama argues in his conceptualization of the "lettered city," the Spanish Crown attempted to maintain its discursive control through regulation of reading and writing and the cultivation of a class of *letrados* (men of letters) who would serve the colonial interests. Parallel to this process was a growing and evolving tension between textual and nontextual modes of representation (29). While official control over public access to information became less overt, and the powers shifted after independence, in the late nineteenth century Porfirian Mexico stood out among its Latin American neighbors for the considerably lesser degree of freedom that journalists enjoyed there (88). The Mexican Revolution of 1910 provoked a transformation of the role of media in Mexico for several reasons. First, because representation was a significant issue being fought for, popular groups associated with the revolutionary armies developed mediatic tools to accompany the armed struggle. Second, as Zuzana Pick shows in her 2010 study of media in the Revolution, the timing was opportune, as the popularization of photography and the advent of cinema provided new tools with which to document the Revolution and disseminate information.

In the decades that followed the Revolution, as its radical ideals became increasingly diluted and the Revolution itself was paradoxically institutionalized in the Partido Revolucionario Institucional (Institutional Revolutionary Party), or PRI, the erosion of democratic principles was accompanied by a progressive centralization and concentration of the media. With the neoliberal reforms of the late twentieth century, by the beginning of the twenty-first century it was widely accepted that, like other aspects of social and political life, "los medios de comunicación y su contenido han sido devorados por las leyes del mercado, por el negocio y el afán de lucro" (the media and its content have been devoured by the laws of the market, by business, and by the pursuit of wealth) (Flores Olea). As countless news stories can prove, today in Mexico, with the nation caught in the grips of a seemingly endless war, control of the media is a profoundly financially motivated endeavor that pits independent and nonconforming media against the most powerful political and economic forces in the country. As the snapshot with which this chapter opens shows, the current state of what journalist Dawn Paley has named "drug war capitalism" places journalists not only in the crossfire but directly in the crosshairs, subject to censorship, repression, and direct acts of violence.

In this chapter, I examine the tensions at play in the Mexican mediascape through its representations in a varied selection of twentieth- and twenty-first-century cultural productions. In doing so, I adapt cultural anthropologist Arjun Appadurai's concept of the mediascape (9) to the analysis of "*the* media," in the sense of *los medios*, rather than "media" more broadly, while also building on media theorist Clemencia Rodríguez's analysis of the "fissures in the mediascape" created by alternative media producers. As the title suggests, this chapter looks at expressions of both mainstream media (which I call "commercial media," following the Centro de Medios Libres) and independent, or grassroots, media. The objective is not to reassert dichotomous categories but, rather, to examine works of art that highlight the tensions at play between "media from above" and "media from below."[6] Unlike most of the other contributions to this volume, the concept at the core of this particular chapter has a double character: the objects being analyzed (the works of art) are also examples of the subject they represent (media). In this sense, in each section I perform a multidimensional analysis, paying close attention not just to the form and content of the works but also to the contexts and processes of their production and circulation.

RETRATO DE LA BURGUESÍA BY DAVID ALFARO SIQUEIROS

"¡Trabajadores de todo el país, de vosotros depende la estabilidad de nuestra propia prensa! ¡Sería un crimen sin nombre no contraarrestar la influencia funesta de la prensa burguesa, con el empuje sano de la prensa proletaria!" (Workers of the whole country, the stability of our own press depends on you! It would be an unspeakable crime to not counteract the terrible influence of the bourgeois press with the wholesome energy of the proletariat press!) (Siqueiros, qtd. in Tibol, *Textos* 30). With these words, in 1924 Mexican artist David Alfaro Siqueiros called for support for the political newspaper he helped launch, suggestively named *El Machete*. Siqueiros, most well known for his place in the trio of Mexican muralists that also included Diego Rivera and José Clemente Orozco, was a radical figure who, despite his on-and-off ties to the postrevolutionary governments, was in constant tension with political and economic elites. A muralist first and foremost, Siqueiros used multiple platforms to develop his political agenda as an artist. In the early 1920s, he organized a union of political painters and sculptors, as well as cofounding *El Machete*, which first served as the official publication of the (short-lived) union and later as the official mouthpiece of the Mexican Communist Party, of which he was a member. In the 1924 propaganda piece for the paper quoted above, Siqueiros describes *El Machete* as a collaborative effort that connects dozens of illustrators and printmakers, "all the revolutionary writers in Mexico," and experts in social matters, while relying on the energy of the workers of Mexico to build its force as a revolutionary media outlet (30).

Siqueiros was imprisoned on numerous occasions and was a staunch critic of what he perceived to be an increasingly conservative political climate in Mexico, directing some of his critique toward other artists. He questioned the radical potential of his fellow muralists, as Mary K. Coffey describes in her 2012 study of Mexican muralism, *How a Revolutionary Art Became Official Culture*: "He asserted that Orozco's subject matter and use of dynamic symmetry led to political cynicism, while Rivera's required a 'microscopic examination' that immobilized his audience before massive painted 'lectures'" (49). With what Coffey identifies as his "cinematographic mural paradigm"—a result of his relationship with the Soviet filmmaker Sergei Eisenstein—Siqueiros sought to activate his audience by confronting the "fascist 'aesthetization of politics' with the social 'politicization of art'" (44). Following a series of projects commissioned by the administration of Álvaro Obregón and coordinated by Secretary of Public Education José Vasconcelos, Siqueiros expressed growing concern about the revolutionary potential of the official murals to reach the public and explored other venues for creating radical mass media, such as the wood-block printing that came to be featured in *El Machete*, a parallel medium that could complement muralism. In 1924, he stated of the artists who had been "tossed out" by the government, "cambiaremos los muros de los edificios públicos por las columnas de este periódico revolucionario" (we will trade the walls of the public buildings for the pages of this revolutionary newspaper) (Tibol, *Textos* 30).

Just after returning to Mexico following two years of fighting with the Republican Army in the Spanish Civil War, Siqueiros produced one of his most monumental works, *Retrato de la burguesía* (Portrait of the Bourgeoisie, 1939–40), expressing his profound indignation about the rapid rise of fascism and the spread of capitalism. While he assumed a leadership role in its design and production, he produced the mural working alongside a team of young artists he had gathered, including Mexicans and exiled Spaniards (Guadarrama Peña 73–74). As such, the mural clearly expressed Siqueiros' long-standing belief that revolutionary media must be collective in both its production and its reception (Coffey 44; Tibol, *Siqueiros* 111) and that the message of such art should be accessible to the masses through its public exhibition. These ethical-political commitments were not without conflict, however, as the realities of collaborating with a collective of artists and responding to the desires of patrons often clashed with Siqueiros's individual desires (Guadarrama Peña 75–76). Nevertheless, *Retrato de la burguesía* represents some of Siqueiros's most radical work as a muralist in Mexico, bridging his technical and aesthetic innovations with his commitment to using this craft as a powerful form of mass media.

As with any mural, the significance and permanence of its location imbues the work itself with additional meaning. *Retrato de la burguesía* was commissioned by the Sindicato Mexicano de Electricistas (Mexican Electrical Workers Union) or SME, one of the most combative unions in Mexico, founded as a rebellious force in 1914 in the context of the Revolution. The mural surrounds the main staircase of the SME's headquarters, a building designed to be multifunctional, with facilities for all facets of the workers' lives, including employment, education, health care, communication, leisure, and even housing.[7] In this sense, the new building and the mural it would house—both of which came on the heels of the historic strike of 1936—would serve as a major space of encounter and support for the multitudinous SME membership. The mural was yet another element of the education and communication strategies—which is to say, its internal media apparatus—developed by the SME to support and inspire its workers. And with its fixed position on 100 square meters of the walls of the monumental building, it was certainly less ephemeral than the *Lux* magazine published by the union and other popular print and audio media consumed by the workers.

The SME charged Siqueiros's team with the task of producing a work that would treat the themes of "imperialism, fascism, and war" (Siqueiros, qtd. in Tibol, *Siqueiros* 111). The mural itself presents an apocalyptic vision of the future of capitalism—and makes clear the role that fascism plays in maintaining it. Juxtaposed on either end of the triptych that wraps around the staircase are, on the far right, a revolutionary worker bearing a rifle and a red-and-black flag and on the far left, a human figure with the head of a parrot standing before a microphone, with three arms: one holding a miniscule violet, another bearing a fiery torch, and the third tucked in a pocket. Below the parrot are the countless diminutive soldiers being directed into a burning temple. In the center lies what Siqueiros named the "máquina infernal" (infernal machine) (Guadarrama Peña 78), "una absurda máquina-templo, que convierte la sangre de los obreros en dinero, [y] es objeto de culto de la burguesía" (an absurd machine-temple, which converts the blood of the workers into money, [and] is the object of the cult of the bourgeoisie) (Mateos-Vega). Overhead are symbols of industry: electrical towers and the chimneys of factories, with the SME flag flying above near the sun—the only bright spot in the mural—representing the solidarity and labor that power the struggle for more progressive industry and liberation.

While the mural was completed in 1940, its relevance has not faded. If anything, in the context of recent—and escalating—neoliberal attacks on labor movements (in both legislation and the media), it has been imbued with new significance. Guadarrama Peña, writing in 2010, asserts that in the context of the 2009 government attacks on the SME through the sudden closure of the Compañía Luz y Fuerza del Centro (a clear expression of the collusion between political and economic elites that Siqueiros fought against):[8] "su tema se renueva: fascismo, capitalismo e imperialismo, ya que la forma como el gobierno 'despareció' la empresa, con el objetivo real de extinguir al Sindicato, fue fascista, producto de un capitalismo dependiente a las órdenes del imperialismo" (its theme is renewed: fascism, capitalism and imperialism, since the way that the government "disappeared" the company, with the real goal of destroying the union, was fascist, a product of a capitalism that is dependent on the orders of imperialism) (82). And, like the future of the SME and its headquarters, the future of the mural is also in question. What is unquestionable is the fact that through its production, content, and location, *Retrato de la burguesía* presents a poignant and evolving statement on the power of communication in economics, politics, and war.

NADA, NADIE: LAS VOCES DEL TEMBLOR BY ELENA PONIATOWSKA

Founded on September 19, 1984, one year to the day before the massive earthquake[9] that destroyed huge swaths of Mexico City and killed more than 25,000 people,[10] the daily newspaper *La Jornada* emerged as the only major media outlet to welcome "the ones without a voice" (Poniatowska, *Nothing* 313).[11] This is how Elena Poniatowska—widely considered one of the most important and influential writers in Mexico—describes *La Jornada* in the final pages of her 1988 book *Nada, nadie: Las voces del temblor* (Nothing, Nobody: The Voices of the Mexico City Earthquake). The book, which constitutes a major act of denunciation of the ineptitude, recklessness, and violence of the government of President Miguel de la Madrid in the wake of the earthquake, is an extension of Poniatowska's daily newspaper columns following the earthquake. As she notes in the concluding pages, "Public officials have had all the electronic and print media at their service" (313). The reports and chronicles she published first in *La Jornada* and later in her book present a different view: of the voices excluded from the official stories and of the individual and collective subjects who created the force that came to be recognized as "civil society," mobilizing the most significant rescue, recovery, and reconstruction efforts in the wake of the earthquake.

When Poniatowska began chronicling the experiences of the people of Mexico City in the aftermath of the earthquake, she did so with the intention of publishing her articles in the newspaper *Novedades*, where she had been employed since 1955. As she describes in an interview with critic Cynthia Steele published in 1989, the newspaper soon refused to continue publishing her articles: "Empecé a amargar al periódico *Novedades*, hasta que me dijeron que ya no les diera los artículos, porque, yo creo, habían recibido una orden del gobierno. Me dijeron: '¡No! Eso deprime muchísimo a la gente y ya no hay que hablar de eso'" (I started to rub them the wrong way at *Novedades*, and finally they told me not to give them more articles because, I think, they had received an order from the government. They said to me: "No! It's making people really depressed and we shouldn't talk about it anymore") (Steele and Poniatowska 102). She goes on to explain how, with a new article in her hand, she walked from the *Novedades* office to the nearby office of the newly founded *La Jornada*—which would come to use the slogan "espacio para todas las voces" (space for all the voices)—where they accepted her text and went on to publish her writing about the earthquake daily for the next three months.

But the book she would publish three years later is more than a mere compilation of those articles. Over more than three hundred pages, Poniatowska writes with, compiles, and edits the "voices of the earthquake," creating a montage of heterogeneous sources that breaks with the objectivity, linearity, and brevity of conventional journalism. And as a print book, it also departs from the ephemeral nature of most journalism, which is published on disposable newsprint, immediately discarded, and replaced by the next day's edition. In both its form and its content, *Nada, nadie* transmits the sense that both the scale of the destruction and chaos of the earthquake and the spontaneous response and action of the people could not be accounted for otherwise. The event demanded a necessarily fragmented, extensive, subjective, and raw documentation of the experiences of those who lived it. The kinds of spontaneity and decentralization that characterized the responses to the earthquake are in many ways reproduced in the form of the book itself.

In this sense, with *Nada, nadie* Poniatowska reasserts her position as a groundbreaking writer of the distinctly Latin American genre of *testimonio*. This genre of nonfiction—which saw its boom beginning in the 1960s with the publication of works such as Miguel Barnet's *Biografía de un cimarrón* (Biography of a Runaway Slave, 1966)—actively, though not unproblematically, disrupts the singularity and hierarchy that shape how "history" is produced, through a politicization of memory and first-person narration. As critic Beth Jörgensen asserts in her study of Poniatowska, *testimonio* "offers an alternative view of official, hegemonic history" (68), and, we might add, of current events or "news." While Poniatowska's *testimonios* are themselves varied in form and approach, one of her earlier publications can, in many ways, be said to most intimately accompany *Nada, nadie*. *La noche de Tlatelolco: Testimonios de historia oral* (Massacre in Mexico), published in 1971, similarly denounces the actions of the government, compiling testimonies and chronicling the events leading up to and following the massacre of several hundred students in Mexico City on October 2, 1968, just days before the Olympics were to be held there (see chapter 10, "1968," by Jacqueline Bixler in this volume).[12] Rosario Alonso Martín describes both books as "textos incómodos que constituyen una denuncia de los poderes institucionales" (uncomfortable texts that constitute a denunciation of institutional powers), and they are, indeed, uncomfortable to read. Referring to *Nada, nadie*, Poniatowska reveals her own discomfort in producing it: "me cansé, me desesperé, no pude manejar ese material. . . . Era como decirle a México, 'Ya, tomen su libro, ahí está, yo ya no puedo, ya no puedo'" (I got tired, I gave up, I couldn't handle the material. . . . It was like saying to Mexico, "Here, take your book, there it is, I can't anymore, I just can't") (Steele and Poniatowska 104). As a journalist and a writer and editor of *testimonios*, Poniatowska is never outside of the experiences she relates to the reader. Despite not having been immediately affected by the destructiveness of the earthquake, like many residents across Mexico City, Poniatowska was actively involved in the recovery efforts that followed, just as she participated in the popular responses to the 1968 massacre (102). And that ongoing political engagement and commitment, or *compromiso*, to the collective subjects she seeks to give voice to in her writing continues today, as she accompanies, among other groups, the family members of the forty-three disappeared rural students from Ayotzinapa, Guerrero, in their struggle for justice. As the title of the 1988 book states, in the case of the earthquake (just as with Tlatelolco before it and other tragedies that followed), "*Nada* de todo aquello se olvida. *Nadie* podría contar solo esta historia" [*None* of all of that can be forgotten. *Nobody* can tell that story alone) (Poniatowska, *Nada* back cover).

LA TOMA DE LOS MEDIOS EN OAXACA, PRODUCED BY JEN LAWHORNE AND ARNALDO PEÑA

"¡Como un reconocimiento a todos los medios de comunicación que han sido muy honestos en esta lucha magisterial!" (In recognition of all of the media outlets that have been very honest in this teachers' struggle!) Over a *cumbia* rhythm, the voice of Oaxacan musician Che Luis opens the 2007 documentary *La toma de los medios en Oaxaca*, a low-budget, transnational collaboration between U.S. filmmaker Jen Lawhorne, Mexican activist Arnaldo Peña, and the Oaxacan collective Radio Zapote. The thirty-nine-minute video is composed primarily of interviews with participants in the 2006 popular rebellion, combined with archival footage from two independent media producers (Mal de Ojo TV and Vanguardia Proletaria) as well as still photographs from Indymedia Oaxaca. There is no voice-over narration, and the firsthand testimonies are only briefly interrupted by just a few bits of text on the screen, written by the producers to contextualize the events being recounted. The film zooms in on three different moments between June and August 2006 when commercial and government media outlets were seized and occupied by members of the popular movement. The first is the student takeover of Radio Universidad de Oaxaca on June 14, 2006, following the violent police raid on the popular occupation of the main plaza of Oaxaca's capital, which included the destruction of Radio Plantón. In the weeks that followed, Radio Universidad was transformed from an institutional media outlet dedicated to promoting the interests of the university administration to serving as a "radio de denuncia" (radio of denunciation) that functioned as the main media hub for the APPO (Popular Assembly of the Peoples of Oaxaca). The second moment came on August 1, 2006, when a group of women called for a "marcha de cacerolas" (march of pans) to bring more attention to the strength and magnitude of the movement that the commercial media, specifically the national station Televisa and the Oaxacan state TV station, Canal 9, were actively minimizing and underreporting. After the march arrived at Canal 9, the women demanded "a few minutes to put on the air the real story of Oaxaca" (Lawhorne and Peña),[13] and when they were refused, they decided to take over the station and began to operate it themselves. The final moment documented in the film came just weeks later, on August 21, 2006, when, following yet another police attack, members of the APPO took over twelve radio stations.

The film itself is an exercise in popular and independent media production that takes as its subject the struggle over media in the context of the 2006 rebellion in Oaxaca, which began with the annual teachers' strike, grew into a widespread call for the resignation of then-governor Ulises Ruíz, and ultimately culminated in the founding of the APPO. The producers are themselves participants in the reality that they document on the screen, a direct manifestation of the independent media ethos "¡Toma los medios, sé los medios, haz los medios!" (Take the media, be the media, make the media!) (Centro de Medios Libres). The focus of this short, raw documentary is not the popular movement but, rather, the role of the media in popular politics and the tensions and antagonisms at play in the struggle for communication.

La toma de los medios en Oaxaca closes with a lengthy interview with Dr. Bertha Muñoz, also known as La Doctora Escopeta (Doctor Shotgun), a Oaxacan activist and key leader of the 2006 movement. From off screen, we hear Arnaldo Peña ask her why there was so much repression and so many attacks against Radio Universidad, the most important radio station seized during the popular movement. Muñoz responds, "Oaxaca is a state of the republic where it appears modernity has not arrived . . . people live in *cacicazgos* [chiefdoms] as if we were in the time of Porfirio Díaz. Oaxaca is the state with the greatest number of indigenous people in the country. It has sixteen ethnicities . . . sixteen indigenous groups that in some way for 500 years have resisted being destroyed as a people" (Lawhorne and Peña). Another interviewee says that Oaxaca has long been an important hub of community radio stations, many of which are run by indigenous communities. The statements of these two interviewees make evident that it is precisely the long history and current reality of both indigenous resistance and indigenous media that the government perceives as a threat. And the space where control of the media takes place becomes a site where that antagonism is especially visible.

In her 2013 book *Indigenous Media in Mexico*, anthropologist Erica Cusi Wortham discusses the ways that indigenous media projects (video in particular) have shifted from an explicit identification as "indigenous" to broader affiliation and identification with what she calls "alternative media" and what I identify as independent media, or *medios libres*. As Wortham explains, this shift is, in part, a result of a process through which indigenous media producers who had previously been tied to government institutions (most notably the Instituto Nacional Indigenista, or National Indigenous Institute) "succeeded in shaking off institutional dependency and became increasingly aligned with the Zapatista movement, and, more recently, with the popular movement in Oaxaca" (13). And in this sense, it could be said that the move from "indigenous" to "independent" media is evidence of a transformative moment in the more than five-hundred-year antagonism between the Mexican state and the nation's indigenous groups, in which indigenous movements increasingly distrust the state and prioritize autonomy from its institutions as a central axis of struggle.[14] This, in turn, serves to align indigenous struggles (and media) with other groups who similarly seek to represent themselves as a means of countering repressive state policies that further marginalize them: youth, women, LGBTQ people, workers, students, and the rural and urban poor. Such marginalized groups are the ones that came together in Oaxaca in 2006 to form the APPO, connecting a diversity of struggles and experiences under the common objective of ousting then-governor Ulises Ruíz, perceived by the people to be a symbol of the corruption and violence that plagues state institutions across Mexico. As Wortham's study documents and *La toma de los medios* demonstrates, Oaxaca is a key site for tracing those processes and for understanding how the struggle for independent media in the twenty-first century is also a struggle for autonomy from the state and capital, whose interests are represented by the commercial media. As one of the voices featured in *La toma de los medios* asserts, "I hope this movement has made the media realize that it's necessary to transform mass media and that the mass media must be pluralistic" (Lawhorne and Peña). At the time that the documentary was made, a new era of digital media was fully under way, giving ordinary citizens greater possibilities of documenting their reality and of producing and distributing independent media. The video was made with basic digital technology and was distributed directly "de mano a mano" (hand to hand) in the form of inexpensive DVDs and later through online video platforms, like Vimeo, that allow for free downloading of media. Independent media, in the form of documentary video, community radio, and print and online journalism, was the immediate precursor to what we now call "social media"—and which exploded in Mexico as a tool of protest at the close of the first decade of the twenty-first century. The common threads that connect the earlier independent media with the more recent social media are distributed (or decentralized) production and consumption, open access, and, most significantly, the political objective of countering the overwhelming power of commercial media.

#YOSOY132

In mid-2012, less than two months before the highly contested presidential elections that would ultimately bring the long-ruling PRI party back into power after a twelve-year absence, a new social movement led by university students burst onto the scene, with a name like none before it: #YoSoy132 (#IAm132). The hashtag that precedes the name marks the movement as a product of the social media generation. The symbol itself is a tool used to disseminate digital information on a given topic—be it in the form of text, photographs, video, or audio—by making the key words easily searchable and compiled via online social networking platforms like Twitter and Facebook. While the use of hashtags and social media platforms by social movements was not new in 2012, it could be said that #YoSoy132 was the first movement named for a hashtag.[15] But where did this hashtag come from, and what does it mean?

On May 14, 2012, a group of students from the Universidad Iberoamericana Ciudad de México (Ibero-American University Mexico City) uploaded a hastily edited video to YouTube titled *131 Alumnos de la Ibero responden* (131 Students from the Ibero Respond). The video opens with raw footage of a large crowd gathered on the campus of the Universidad Iberoamericana—among the most elite private universities in Mexico—following an appearance by PRI presidential candidate Enrique Peña Nieto on May 11. Over the sounds of the crowd booing and chanting, we hear a muffled voice identified by a caption on the screen as Arturo Escobar, spokeperson for the Partido Verde (Green Party), a member of the PRI's coalition:

> Hay un grupo de . . . no quiero decir jóvenes. Ya están mayorcitos. Calculo de treinta o treinta y cinco años para arriba. Incitando. No pasaban de veinte personas. . . . La información que se nos da al final es que grupos cercanos a Andrés Manuel López Obrador [candidato presidencial por el Partido Revolucionario Democrático] estuvieron promoviendo y organizando este tipo de actos. (*131 Alumnos*)

> There's a group of . . . I don't want to say young people. They're older. I'd say they're upwards of thirty or thirty-five. They're inciting. No more than twenty people. . . . The information we got at the end was that groups close to Andrés Manuel López Obrador [presidential candidate for the Party of the Democratic Revolution] were promoting and organizing these kinds of acts.

But the voice-over and the images do not match. They were edited together to expose the inaccuracy of the report presented by Escobar. While he describes a small group of "older" people, the video shows a crowd of hundreds of clearly college-age students in their late teens and early twenties. Escobar's version was the one that was later reproduced and echoed by the PRI and commercial media outlets across Mexico, who claimed that the protesters were "provocateurs" trained and organized by the opposition and that they were not, in fact, Ibero students. The video then cuts to a white screen with red text that reads: "Los Estudiantes respondemos" (The students respond). Over the next ten minutes, 131 students face the camera—from their homes, their classrooms, their workplaces—and state their names and student identification numbers while holding up their Ibero ID cards, affirming, "No somos acarreados, no somos porros. Nadie nos entrenó para nada" (We aren't instigators, we aren't *porros*.[16] No one trained us for anything). In the hours and days that followed, *131 alumnos de la Ibero* quickly became a top "trending topic" on Twitter, and soon the hashtag #YoSoy132 began to circulate, as students and others across Mexico (and beyond) identified themselves as the one hundred and thirty-second student in a show of solidarity.

When the students confronted Peña Nieto at the Ibero on May 11, 2012, their message was very direct: they demanded that he discuss his role as governor of the state of Mexico in the deadly repression unleashed against protesters in the town of Atenco on May 3 and 4, 2006.[17] He evaded the questions, responding only by saying that he had acted legitimately, and quickly ducked out of the event. The students followed him as he attempted to exit the campus, yelling "¡Asesino! ¡Atenco no se olvida!" (Murderer! We will not forget Atenco!) and other chants—and this was the moment captured in the footage that opens *131 Alumnos*. The case of Atenco, which Peña Nieto and his media partners worked hard to erase from his public image, was significant not only because of the brutality and lawlessness of the state and the police but also because of the tremendous manipulation of commercial media representations of the events in the days and weeks that followed.[18] In this sense, the students at the Ibero were bringing attention not only to Peña Nieto's role in the violent repression and criminalization of protesters but also to his deep, long-standing ties to media giants, most notably Televisa, which controls nearly 70 percent of the television audience share in Mexico (Gómez García and Treré 4).[19] The attempts to delegitimize their protest by accusing them of not being students but, rather, trained and planted provocateurs from the opposition were in some ways reproduced by media reports of the mass movement that followed, which downplayed the agency of the young people at the helm of #YoSoy132 and portrayed the movement as a spontaneous, sudden political awakening of Mexican youth (Reguillo).

Over the weeks that followed, students across the country—united by the hashtag #YoSoy132—organized assemblies, rallies, and marches, calling for a democratization of the media and especially bringing attention to the direct role the superpowers Televisa and TV Azteca played in electoral politics. With the presidential election fast approaching, the movement quickly gained tremendous momentum, and it was further intensified after the *Guardian* (UK) published an exposé on June 7, 2012, accusing Televisa of having sold Peña Nieto "favourable coverage in its flagship news and entertainment shows and used the same programmes to smear" his opposition, populist leftist candidate Andrés Manuel López Obrador (Tuckman). The reports provided the documentation to prove what many already knew, revealing a paper trail showing that the alliance dated back at least several years. The calls to "democratize the media" had everything to do with a broader call for true democracy in Mexican politics. As journalist Laura Carlsen asserts, #YoSoy132 brought to the forefront "recognition of the media's enormous influence to distort democracy and the interlocking relations between economic and political elites that determine so much of how people see their world. As children of mass media like no other generation before them, they know its power and resent that it is wielded by so few" (13).

The impact of the movement and its message was the product of the critical consciousness of these "children of mass media" combined with their mastery of the new communication technologies that seem to actively resist the centralization that characterizes print and television media in Mexico: online social media. The use of YouTube, Facebook, Twitter, and customized websites and blogs to generate and disseminate their denunciations and demands demonstrated the potential of social media to create "fissures in the mediascape" (Rodríguez). The movement, embodied by a hashtag, traveled across different spaces and platforms, where individual and collective actors in turn constructed their own expressions of the common demand for democracy. As of this writing, three years later, it can be said that #YoSoy132 set in motion a continuous rejection of Peña Nieto—and the "interlocking relations between economic and political elites" (Carlsen 13) that he represents—by the young people who have long been criminalized by his party, the PRI, in collusion with the commercial media.

CONCLUSION

The Mexican mediascape is a battleground for democracy. Control of the technology, economics, and language of communication and knowledge has been a central site of conflict in the more than five hundred years of what Bolívar Echeverría calls the "conquista inconclusa" (unfinished conquest) (242). The media, in its polyvalent manifestations, is the name given to those tangles of technologies and practices of representation, information, and propaganda used by both elite and subaltern groups in their efforts to constitute themselves as collective subjects and advance their social, political, cultural, and economic desires, be they of domination and expansion or of resistance and survival. What the works of art gathered in the essay show is the way that control of the medium is control of the message and vice versa.[20] And what the case of the Mexican mediascape makes so evident is the fragile symbiotic relationship between pluralism of media and democracy.

The context, production process, and message of Siqueiros's *Retrato de la burguesía* affirm the central role of communication in not only political and economic domination but also in war. Created on the heels of the Spanish Civil War, just as the horrors of World War II were unfolding, the mural presents images and concepts that seem to foreshadow the pervasive and multifaceted violence of capitalism—and the progressive erosion of democracy—in the war being waged in twenty-first century Mexico. Poniatowska's chronicle of the 1985 earthquake activates fragmentation and decentralization as an aesthetic and political strategy for representing—and intervening in—unspeakable tragedies. The independent media represented in and by *La toma de los medios en Oaxaca* highlights the role of media as a permanent axis of struggle for indigenous communities in their assertion of self-determination and their construction of autonomy from the state and capital. The documentary also signals the new possibilities for the pluralization of media that emerge from the combination of old and new communications technologies. And the social media mobilized by the young people at the helm of #YoSoy132 demonstrates the potential of new media to intervene in and disrupt the extreme concentration of communications in the hands of a minute political and economic elite. Plurality, decentralization, and collaboration are commonalities that run through the various works of art examined in this essay, in their form and content, and it could be said that these are foundational concepts of democracy. If we take the logic of the "conquest" of Mexico to be one of appropriation, conversion, and expansion, the Mexican mediascape is a salient site for examining and understanding the antagonisms and tensions that make that process "unfinished" more than five hundred years later.[21]

NOTES

1. #YoSoy132 refers to a social movement led by university students that emerged in the time leading up to the 2012 presidential elections in Mexico. The final section of this chapter discusses the movement in greater detail.
2. The state of Veracruz is considered the most dangerous state in Mexico for journalists (Elizarrarás). Before their murders, Vera and Espinosa were both vocal opponents of then-governor and PRI member Javier Duarte, denouncing the repression, corruption, and violence that characterized his regime. Protests largely centered on Duarte's responsibility for their murders.
3. All translations mine unless otherwise noted.

4. Here I follow Walter Mignolo, Aníbal Quijano, Enrique Dussel, and others who argue that capitalism began in 1492.
5. I place the term "conquest" in scare quotes following journalist John Gibler in his 2009 book *Mexico Unconquered*, where he argues that Mexico is "a nation divided, not conquered" (5), referring to Mexican philosopher Bolívar Echeverría's assertion that "the process of the Conquest is an enterprise that has *not* finished . . . the Conquest of America is still ongoing" (qtd. in Gibler 5–6).
6. I use this spatial metaphor to represent a relational dynamic rather than fixed positions of power, privilege, et cetera. In doing so, I draw on popular uses of the concept of "los de abajo" (those from below), as in the eponymous Mariano Azuela novel, and "desde abajo" (from below), as in contemporary Zapatista communiqués. My conceptualization of these categories is also inspired by subaltern studies scholars, including Ranajit Guha, who developed the idea of "subaltern" as a relational category.
7. As described by Guadarrama Peña: "oficinas sindicales, sala de asamblea, servicio médico, cooperativa, escuela, biblioteca, área para editar la revista *Lux*, gimnasio, casino, oficina de solicitantes de empleo, imprenta, habitaciones y servicios generales" (union offices, assembly room, medical services, cooperative, school, library, area for editing the magazine *Lux*, gym, casino, employment office, press, bedrooms and general services) (73).
8. On October 11, 2009, 44,000 electricity workers from the SME were fired, after President Felipe Calderón ordered the closure of one of two nationalized electricity companies, Compañía Luz y Fuerza del Centro. The mass layoffs sparked a movement not only of electricity workers and their families but also of a broad swath of Mexican society in protest against the socioeconomic inequalities in Mexico and the corruption of Calderón.
9. As the translators of the English edition noted (Camacho de Schmidt and Schmidt xxv), while the Mexico City earthquake disaster actually consisted of two major tremors over two days, September 19 and 20, 1985, it is generally referred to as "the earthquake," in the singular. I follow this practice as well.
10. Although many estimates figure the casualties at around 10,000, I refer to the figure calculated by La CEPAL (the Economic Commission for Latin America and the Caribbean) and cited by Poniatowska in her essay on the twentieth anniversary of the earthquake (Poniatowska, "20 años después").
11. The English edition was published in 1995 as *Nothing, Nobody: The Voices of the Mexico City Earthquake*, translated by Aurora Camacho de Schmidt and Arthur Schmidt. I refer to this translation in all direct quotes.

12. The English translation of *La noche de Tlatelolco* was published in 1975 as *Massacre in Mexico*.
13. I refer to the English subtitles for all direct quotes from the video.
14. The Zapatista movement is the most evident expression of this.
15. For example, the Arab Spring, L@s Indignad@s, and the Occupy movements of 2011 made widespread use of Twitter and Facebook, as did other so-called Twitter revolutions. At the time that I am writing this, another "hashtag social movement" has emerged here in the United States: #BlackLivesMatter. This movement has sparked important conversations about collective authorship, appropriation, and decentralized organization in the era of social media.
16. The concept of *porros* is difficult to translate as it is a very particular phenomenon in educational institutions in Mexico. *Porros* are organized, violent groups of youth—often actual students—who are hired or planted by external forces, be they the police, political parties, or other administrative powers, with the objective of threatening or attacking student organizers and protesters.
17. On May 3 and 4, 2006, acting as governor of the state of Mexico, Enrique Peña Nieto sent thousands of police officers (state and federal) into city of San Salvador Atenco, where they brutally repressed a protest organized by the local community as well as members of the caravan of the Zapatista's Otra Campaña (Other Campaign). The horrific violence included the murder of two young men, rampant police brutality, arbitrary detentions, random raids of private homes, acts of torture, and the sexual assault of forty-seven women by police officers. Hundreds of people were arrested, with nearly a dozen held as political prisoners for several years.
18. The documentary *Romper el cerco* (Breaking the Siege, 2007) (Défossé and Viveros) provides excellent analysis of the role of the commercial media in the aftermath of Atenco.
19. The other 30 percent is controlled by TV Azteca. Together the two stations control 99 percent of the television audience share in Mexico (Gómez García and Treré 4). This is particularly significant given that 95 percent of households in Mexico own at least one television.
20. This is, of course, a reference to media theorist Marshall McLuhan's aphorism "The medium is the message" (McLuhan and Fiore).
21. Suggestions for further study: Though this chapter does not discuss radio, it is, without a doubt, an important arena to look at in order to understand the Mexican mediascape. Two studies that bridge important moments in the history of radio in Mexico are *Radio in Revolution: Wireless Technology and State*

Power in Mexico, 1897–1938 by J. Justin Castro (University of Nebraska Press, 2016) and *Radio Nation: Communication, Popular Culture, and Nationalism in Mexico, 1920–1950* (University of Arizona Press, 2000). For analysis of indigenous radio in the late twentieth century, José Manuel Ramos Rodríguez has published several studies that provide an important overview.

WORKS CITED

131 Alumnos de la Ibero responden. YouTube, uploaded by RECREO, 14 May 2012, www.youtube.com/watch?v=P7XbocXsFkI.

Alonso Martín, Rosario. "Poniatowska: El compromiso de consignar." *La Jornada*, 10 Aug. 2008.

Appadurai, Arjun. "Disjuncture and Difference in the Global Economy." *Theory, Culture & Society*, vol. 7, 1990, pp. 295–310.

Barnet, Miguel. *Biografía de un cimarrón*. Instituto del Libro, 1967.

Camacho de Schmidt, Aurora, and Arthur Schmidt, translators. "Foreword: The Shaking of a Nation." *Nothing, Nobody: Voices of the Mexico City Earthquake* by Elena Poniatowska, Temple University Press, 1995.

Carlsen, Laura. "Mexico's Youth Protest a Return to the Past." *Dissent*, vol. 60, no. 1, 2013, pp. 10–15.

Centro de Medios Libres. *Toma los medios, sé los medios, haz los medios*. El Rebozo, 2013.

Coffey, Mary K. *How a Revolutionary Art Became Official Culture*. Duke University Press, 2012.

Défossé, Nicolás, and Mario Viveros, directors. *Romper el cerco*. Canal 6 de Julio, Promedios de Comunicación, 2007.

Echeverría, Bolívar. *Vuelta de siglo*. Era, 2006.

Elizarrarás, Rodrigo. "Veracruz, la entidad más peligrosa para ser periodista." *Animal Político*, 4 Aug. 2015.

Flores Olea, Victor. "Nueva ley de medios." *La Jornada*, 26 Apr. 2010.

Gibler, John. *Mexico Unconquered: Chronicles of Power and Revolt*. City Lights, 2009.

Gómez García, Rodrigo, and Emiliano Treré. "The #YoSoy132 Movement and the Struggle for Media Democratization in Mexico." *Convergence*, vol. 20, no. 4, 2014, pp. 1–15.

Guadarrama Peña, Guillermina. *La ruta de Siqueiros*. Centro Nacional de Investigación, Documentación e Información de Artes Plásticas, 2010.

Guha, Ranajit. *Elementary Aspects of Peasant Insurgency in Colonial India*. Duke University Press, 1999.

Jörgensen, Beth. *The Writing of Elena Poniatowska: Engaging Dialogues*. University of Texas Press, 1994.

Lawhorne, Jen, and Arnaldo Peña, producers. *La toma de los medios en Oaxaca*. 2007.

Mateos-Vega, Mónica. "Evoca *Retrato de la burguesía* la necesidad del arte contestatario." *La Jornada*, 15 June 2009.

McLuhan, Marshall, and Quentin Fiore. *The Medium Is the Message*. Penguin Books, 1967.

Mignolo, Walter. *The Idea of Latin America*. Wiley, 2005.

Paley, Dawn. *Drug War Capitalism*. AK Press, 2014.

Pick, Zuzana. *Constructing the Image of the Mexican Revolution: Cinema and the Archive*. University of Texas Press, 2010.

Poniatowska, Elena. *Nada, nadie: Las voces del temblor*. Era, 1988.

———. "'Nada, nadie: Las voces del temblor,' 20 años después." *La Jornada*, 14 Sept. 2005.

———. *La noche de Tlatelolco: Testimonios de historia oral*. Era, 1971.

———. *Nothing, Nobody: The Voices of the Mexico City Earthquake*. Translated by Aurora Camacho de Schmidt and Arthur Schmidt, Temple University Press, 1995.

Quijano, Aníbal. "Colonialidad del poder, cultura y conocimiento en América Latina." *Dispositio/n*, vol. 24, no. 51, 1999, pp. 137–48.

Rama, Ángel. *The Lettered City*. Translated by John Chasteen, Duke University Press, 1996.

Reguillo, Rossana. "Reflexiones iniciales en torno a #YoSoy132." *Blog de la redacción*, 28 May 2012, www.magis.iteso.mx/redaccion/reflexiones-iniciales-en-torno-yosoy132. Accessed 25 Nov. 2015.

Rodríguez, Clemencia. *Fissures in the Mediascape: An International Study of Citizens' Media*. Hampton Press, 2001.

Steele, Cynthia, and Elena Poniatowska. "Entrevista: Elena Poniatowska." *Hispamérica* vol. 18, nos. 53–54, 1989, pp. 89–105.

Tibol, Raquel. *Siqueiros: Vida y obra*. Colección METROpolitana, 1974.

———. *Textos de David Alfaro Siqueiros*. Fondo de Cultura Económica, 1974.

Tuckman, Jo. "Computer Files Link TV Dirty Tricks to Favourite for Mexico Presidency." *Guardian* (UK), 7 June 2012.

Wortham, Erica Cusi. *Indigenous Media in Mexico: Culture, Community, and the State*. Duke University Press, 2013.

15

NET.ART

DEBRA A. CASTILLO

PRIMARY MATERIALS

- Mejor Vida Corp. (MVC), created by Minerva Cuevas (web-based nonprofit corporation, 1997–present)
- Transborder Immigrant Tool (TBT) by Ricardo Domínguez, Micha Cardenas, Amy Sara Carroll, and other collaborators in b.a.n.g. lab's Electronic Disturbance Theater (GPS system with experimental poetry)

NET.ART HAS been around for more than twenty years as of this writing, reaching a peak in the early 2000s and morphing more recently into what are often called "post-Internet" aesthetic projects. Originally parodying the kinds of pretensions (and the contemporary commercial snob appeal) retroactively associated with avant-garde art movements, practitioners of the loosely connected group of artists associated with net.art quickly developed their own theoretical and aesthetic core through the writings of scholar-artists like Mark Amerika, whose widely distributed Avant-Pop Manifesto is one of the signal contributions in thinking about the intersections of new media technologies, artistic practice, and the emergent self in the times of Web 2.0.[1] Unsurprisingly, for a (non)movement in which the critique of conventional/commercialized art world legitimacy has always been a primary point of entry, there has also always been a subset of net.art practitioners who quickly focused on exploring the potentiality of the networked web art medium for other kinds of critique, including for more overtly political-aesthetic purposes: tactical media art, for instance, which brings into question the highly corporatized forms of accessing media (browsers, navigation, advertisements, et cetera) through deployment of such tactics as pop-up interventions; or hacktivism, often using the mechanism of denial of service attacks or the aesthetic possibilities of manipulating the HTTP 404 (web page not found) error.

Fifteen years later, the same artists find themselves living in radically different times, as Artie Vierkant writes in 2010, in a trenchant critique of earlier net.art efforts: "New Media is here denounced as a mode too narrowly focused on the specific workings of novel technologies, rather than a sincere exploration of cultural shifts in which that technology plays only a small role. . . . In the Post-Internet climate, it is assumed that the work of art lies equally in the version of the object one would encounter at a gallery or museum, the images and other representations disseminated through the Internet and print publications, bootleg images of the object or its representations, and variations on any of these as edited and recontextualized by any other author." Michael Connor adds: "It no longer makes sense for artists to attempt to come to terms with 'internet culture,' because now 'internet culture' is increasingly just 'culture.' In other words, the term 'postinternet' suggests that the focus of a good deal of artistic and critical discourse has shifted from 'internet culture' as a discrete entity to the reconfiguration of *all* culture by the internet, or by internet-enabled neoliberal capitalism." Walter Benjamin would be cheering: finally, the work of art has lost its pretensions to aura, while retaining a cutting-edge focus on the intersection of culture and capital.

From its founding, net.art has always had a strong Hispanic participation, and many of the key early artists combined activism with their aesthetic work, a commitment that continues in post-Internet interventions. One of the most prominent early practitioners, Daniel García Andújar (Spain), remains one of the most internationally visible figures. His elaborate website, available in nearly twenty languages, speaks to his fundamental creative role among technologically influenced artists as well as to his commitment to social change, as evidenced already by his early Technologies To The People Foundation and his domain irational.org (still the host of Minerva Cuevas's Mejor Vida Corp., about which more will be said below). One of his typical early creations was the "Street Access Machine" (figure 15.1), which Iris Dressler describes as

FIGURE 15.1. Daniel García Andújar, "Street Access Machine," from Technologies To The People Foundation website, 1997.

a combination system made up of reading device, special credit card, and public online access, which allows the homeless and other fringe groups to enter the world of plastic money and E-commerce. The trademark-protected "Street Access Machine," whose design announced the i-Mac Generation in 1996, is perfectly marketed with a corporate identity and comprehensive advertising campaign—flyers, posters, and merchandising materials. Nothing is missing except the corresponding product. Andújar is not concerned with virtual capital for all, but more so with naming the structures of exclusion so gladly denied during the course of the omnipresent cyber-euphoria.

Dressler's point is a crucial one; the "Street Access Machine" is conceptual rather than mechanic, an artistic project located on a website rather than a street corner.[2]

Tania Bruguera (Cuba), the founder of the Arte Útil (Useful Art) movement, which has important central loci in Havana and New York City, also celebrates the impetus of social critique in these new artistic projects but exhorts the collaborators in Arte Útil to commit to a practice that goes beyond merely "naming the structures of exclusion" associated with early projects like "Street Access Machine." As a practitioner who bridges the generations between early net.art and the post-Internet, Bruguera does not define herself or the work of her collaborators solely within the net.art realm. Likewise, not all of the projects applauded by the Asociación de Arte Útil show the influence of technologically framed aesthetic practices. Drawing inspiration from thinkers like Paolo Freire and Augusto Boal, who blend pedagogy, performance, and attention to the structural inequalities in society, Bruguera puts more emphasis on how to conceive of art broadly as a tool that, according to the criteria listed in one of her manifestos, "must be implemented and function in real situations . . . [must] have practical, beneficial outcomes for its users . . . [must] re-establish aesthetics as a system of transformation." Thus, "the artworks in the *Arte Útil Lab* are propositions to generate and refine our thinking through public conversation" (Asociación de Arte Útil). This sounds marvelous in principle; however, I would suggest that almost every term in this list can be read ambiguously. What is "real," who are "users," what do we mean by "aesthetics" in a "system" defined by "transformation," where do we locate "the public"? Who decides? In the context of an artistic practice defined by access to, and interfacing with, contemporary media technologies, the answer is clearly a subset of literate humans, albeit a shifting and continually evolving body of thinking subjects.

Brian Rotman argues that "not only is thinking always social, culturally situated, and technologically mediated, but that only by being these things can it happen in the first place" (91). Accordingly, if we locate "the public" within the context of theorists like Rotman or Amerika, the self is postulated as the evolving posthuman entity, essentially a media effect, and they see the horizon of theoretical imagining as a technocultural artifact. For Rotman, the analog model of linearity and abstraction facilitated and/or imposed by alphabetic writing increasingly strains against other kinds of theorization (the boom in affect theory and the renewed interest in phenomenology are, for him, symptoms of this strain). Thus, Rotman sees new forms of theorization, performance, and understandings of self arising from the influence of parallel computing and pluridimensional visualization; these technologies, he says, "are inculcating modes of thought and self, and facilitating imaginings of agency, whose parallelisms are antagonistic to the intransigent monadism, linear coding, and intense seriality inseparable from alphabetic writing" (3). He builds explicitly on previous work such as that by N. Katherine Hayles, arguing, as Timothy Lenoir's summarizes, that human consciousness in its choice of "metaphors, narrative, and other interpretative linguistic modes we use for human sense making of the world around us do the work of conditioning us to behave as if we and the world were digital" (Lenoir xi). This "as if" is crucial to the projection of the emergent, leaky self at this juncture: "Perhaps the first question to ask about the psyche in a technologized milieu is not really one of identity and persona, of 'who' the emergent self is, but *what* and *how* is the self. How is it assembled and transformed by mechanic processes, ubiquitous mediation, and ever smarter, more interactive, techno-systems?" (Rotman 81).

Likewise, in his sui generis theoretical study (book and website) *remixthebook*, Mark Amerika proposes "to create a cross-disciplinary approach to the way contemporary theory is performed and to anticipate future forms of writing that challenge traditional modes of scholarly production" (xi), inviting readers to make their own mash-ups and remixes of his work, and that of others, and add them to an evolving archive.[3] In the printed book, he describes instantiations of theory that include stand-up comedy, the academic conference paper, and classroom performances—all of which have in common the central notion of self-conscious behavior performed as a routine, the kind of live action role-playing (LARPing) that for him occurs when the mind is allowed free play while immersed in network culture (xv). The body of Amerika's book takes on the challenge of this concept of remix, with attributed and unattributed quotations ("playgiarism"), mash-ups, rewritings, and reflections, all typeset in the ragged line endings that evoke poetic utterance. The website puts this theoretical intervention into practice in the digital realm with a proposal and materials for a course, a blog, and, most importantly, digital remixes in various media:

> In *remixthebook*, Mark Amerika develops a model of contemporary theoretical writing that mashes up the rhetorical styles of performance art, poetry, and the vernacular associated with 21st century social media and networking culture.
>
> Amerika, along with co-curator and artist Rick Silva, has invited over 25 contributing international artists, poets, and critical theorists, all of them interdisciplinary in their own practice-based research, to sample from *remixthebook* and

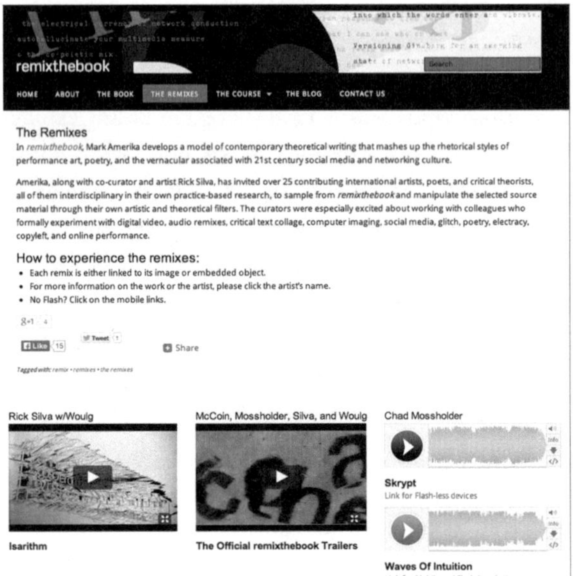

FIGURE 15.2. Mark Amerika, "The Remixes," from *remixthebook* website, 2011.

> manipulate the selected source material through their own artistic and theoretical filters. The curators were especially excited about working with colleagues who formally experiment with digital video, audio remixes, critical text collage, computer imaging, social media, glitch, poetry, electracy, copyleft, and online performance. (figure 15.2)

In this chapter, I want to bring together the three strands of net.art, Arte Útil, and post-Internet art with respect to their implications for contemporary aesthetic and critical theory through an analysis of two representative projects from the Hispanic world that engage with these questions in different ways. The case studies focus on the Mejor Vida Corp. (created by the Mexican artist Minerva Cuevas) and the Transborder Immigrant Tool (a collective project of Ricardo Domínguez, Micha Cardenas, Amy Sara Carroll, and other collaborators in b.a.n.g. lab's Electronic Disturbance Theater). While these works of art have been created at different points during the evolutionary period of net.art, one common theoretical impulse is investigating how to think about humanities/arts in a Web 2.0 environment, where the questions of property, creator, and author are always a bit blurred by collaborations, by borrowings, by hacktivist backgrounds, and by an aesthetic position that gnarls copyright conventions and disrupts understandings of the relationships between author/artist and text/art object as linear versus distributed.

These projects have in common elements related to video game architecture and aesthetics, to an engagement with the interface among technology producers and users; all share as well an awareness of those left out of the technological present/future. Both projects are fundamentally performative works, engaging the audience interactively so as to complete the artwork, and in this manner also implicitly or explicitly bringing to the fore concerns about the status of performative genres in a screen age, an age that is also marked by the rise of the posthuman alongside analysis of affect in theory circles. This user/collaborator/coperformer may be single, anonymous, located behind another screen, or, in the case of the Transborder Immigrant Tool, turned into a de facto LARPer in a deadly serious game. Both these artistic projects thus question what it means to do/create art in the twenty-first century; they grapple with the issue of the use value of art; they share a concern about their own ethical positions and the chic appeal of non-Westerners as a horizon or a threat in certain mainstream circles. Both embrace an implicit yearning toward a utopia self-engaged in a parallel rather than serial mode of apprehending our surroundings—the kind of distributed self that derives from an experience of multiple screens, picture-in-picture, the multiple layers of information in, say, Google Earth. At the same time, they also share a nostalgic element, looking back to the "real situations" of a nonscreen serial mode.

MEJOR VIDA CORP.

Mejor Vida Corp. is provocative and politically engaged. Minerva Cuevas initially began her project in 1998 as a series of live, invisible theater performances in Mexico City, eventually morphing the project into the web-based Mejor Vida Corp. (MVC).[4] Cuevas says that "Mejor Vida Corp. is not associated with one individual or author, it is publicly identified as a plural entity," albeit an entity "activated by one single person." In this way, MVC interrogates the categories of author/artist and property, especially intellectual property, including the intellectual property of the individual (i.e., copyright, which formally defines the exact monetary value of knowledge through restriction and control of

FIGURE 15.3. Minerva Cuevas, "MVC Products," from Mejor Vida Corp. website, 1998.

access), as well as trademarks and other properties of corporate identities. Says Cuevas: "MVC remains rooted in its original soil and loyal to the strategies and resources adopted in its origins. The project's impulse derives from the marginal conditions and social bitterness of Mexico City and its voice comes from there." She adds, curiously, "Abroad, MVC is not a tourist, but a traveler that asserts its true nature each time in every new context—aiming for local subversion," thus insisting on her project's translocal nature while remaining rooted in a historically particular Mexican reality ("For a Human Interface").

All of MVC's "products" and "services" are free (figure 15.3). The products include materials that the user can print and use, like Mexico City subway tickets, and barcode stickers for specific fruits and vegetables at particular stores. Other products include "magic seeds" (there is no indication of what kind of plants they would bear); "safety pills" for use on the subway (again, with no indication of the type of pill); and tear gas (available only in Mexico City). Still other products and services include letters of recommendation and student ID cards, both with prominent Mejor Vida Corp. affiliations, since Cuevas's goal is to make an artistic statement, not commit fraud.

One of the interesting features of MVC is the relation between products and services. None of the products—with the exception of the student ID card—are individualized; most of the services, on the other hand, involve individual interaction with the artist, at least at some level (the personalized recommendation letter, for example). Presumably Cuevas herself responds to requests for the "cleaning service" or "security service" (in interviews she describes doing such invisible theater actions in the past), and she or her proxy engages in the action contracted.[5] In this respect, these MVC services anticipate the current surge in online outsourcing of tasks and services that has become so familiar to us, but with the difference that these are free services, contracted by an individual customer, but at the same time it is not a service from which the individual who contracts it gains any personal benefit. Thus, Cuevas commits to a performance while not necessarily having any real knowledge of the person making the request from the other side of the screen. The audience for this performance is at least double: the inadvertent audience or curious bystander witnessing the invisible theater act, like the cleaning of Mexico City subways registered in the photograph on her website (figure 15.4), and, secondarily, the person who has

FIGURE 15.4. Minerva Cuevas, "STC Cleaning Service," from Mejor Vida Corp. website, 1998.

contracted the service and who presumably has privileged knowledge about the service but gains no privileged access.

Technically rather simple, Cuevas's MVC highlights an important element for our purposes by making the exchange of goods and services, as well as the physical body of the artist, essential aspects of the project. In the negotiation between products and services, MVC also juggles live and virtual performance, material and virtual objects. At the interface of this exchange, Cuevas asks us to think about what a better life (*mejor vida*) might be, while also provoking us as users to ask ourselves about the usefulness of artistic work.

TRANSBORDER IMMIGRANT TOOL

The Electronic Disturbance Theater continues to make use of core tactics developed at the turn of the millennium, when they began the denial of service attacks against the Mexican government, often under the auspices of Brett Stalbaum's conceptual net.art project *The Zapatista Tactical Floodnet*. Most recently, there was a similar call for participation via the thing.net blog for a spring 2014 e-graffiti solidarity action in response to the assassination of Zapatista Comandante Galeano (b.a.n.g. lab).[6] Taking their inspiration from media theorist Friedrich Kittler, who said in a memorable 1998 talk, "Only art history still knows that the famed geniuses of the Renaissance did not just create paintings and buildings, but calculated fortresses and constructed war machines," the artist-hacktivists (Ricardo Domínguez sometimes uses the term *artivists*) of the Electronic Disturbance Theater collectively contribute art pieces to nonviolent civil disobedience protests through the aesthetics of the denial-of-service attack, and they invite other collaborators to their art projects by making readily available for downloading the HTML code that will turn their computers into virtual antiwar machines. Those actions, however, are not their most notorious ones.

I began this discussion with reference to the ideological aspirations of the groundbreaking net.art practitioner Daniel García Andújar, a collaborator with and contemporary of Minerva Cuevas, and specifically to his "Street Access Machine." In some sense, the Transborder Immigrant Tool (TBT) takes up the challenge made by critics that earlier projects like these (as well as most of the Electronic Disturbance Theater actions to this day) remained in the merely theoretical-conceptual realm. The Transborder Immigrant Tool does not. An inexpensive device with a physical world application, it has been celebrated by the Arte Útil Association and harshly attacked by U.S. government agencies, for more or less the same reasons, and in both cases we easily can see why.[7] In essence, the TBT is an inexpensive cell phone with GPS capability that delivers a double product to its users/audience: bilingual poetry and the location of water drops in the border area between the United States and Mexico.

Or, at least, that is the premise and the promise. On the one hand, the code has been made open source and available for download, so that any person with access to the Internet could presumably download and use the TBT on the cheap GPS-enabled phones they have already purchased in their local Mexican Walmarts (this also assumes sufficient battery life to carry them through the desert). Likewise, the poetry and water drop instructions have been translated into indigenous languages, including Yucatec Maya, Diné, and Nahuatl, as well as Spanish, Portuguese, Russian, German, Greek, and Taiwanese, arguing for its widespread—even globalized—applicability (Reed). On the other hand, for various reasons, despite a well-publicized preliminary test of the technology, the prototype for the TBT to date remains technically glitchy in real-world scenarios, and the proposed 2011 rollout date for the app—much less the distribution of already loaded phones—was delayed indefinitely, largely because of U.S. federal government interdiction of further research. Thus, this slide between potential use and technical provisionality makes the TBT currently more of a performance piece than a functional aid to migrants, something that the Arte Útil folks for obvious reasons prefer not to highlight. In this respect, the U.S. government scrutiny and neoconservative press condemnation serve the purpose of publicizing the project's real-world application and rousing their ire (while, curiously, they also turn into literary critics and condemn the poetry on political and aesthetic grounds); at the same time, the technical incompleteness makes the TBT a utopian project in some sense not too distant from García Andujar's much earlier work (yet another example of purely aesthetic practice arguably divorced from utility). Likewise, the furor around the TBT, and the ironic validation of its usefulness by way of U.S. government interdiction, has meant that the work has garnered considerable interest in the artistic establishment. It has been featured in more than forty international performance venues, including art galleries and institutional spaces (Reed).

Domínguez and his collaborators in the San Diego–based b.a.n.g. lab[8] are academics as well as artists and activists, so it is not surprising that they have published extensively, both online and in print, on their projects and the theoretical underpinnings that support them. Domínguez's theoretical work ranges dramatically in style from more conventional academic writing to pieces like "The Ante-Chamber of Revolution: A Prelude to a Theory of Resistance and Maps," very much in the Mark Amerika vein. In general, he says the work of the Electronic Disturbance Theater is defined by a "politics of rehearsal" and an "aesthetic of minor signals and lower frequencies" (qtd. in Bird). Like other net.artists, the b.a.n.g. lab collaborators emphasize creative reuse and remix, and like Amerika and Navas, Domínguez promotes the "gesture of 'plagiarism'—a cutting and pasting of what is already an assemblage or a system that exists because immigrants are crossing multiple spaces around the world and GPS is everywhere in our cloudy global Empire" (Bird). He inserts his work within the larger history of net.art and cites as important cothinkers the novelist William Gibson, the Wachowski siblings (especially their *Matrix* film series), and European theorists Gilles Deleuze, Félix Guattari, Giorgio Agamben, and Jacques Rancière, alongside artist and remix theorist Eduardo Navas and Cameroonian philosopher Achille Mbembe. For her part, poet and collaborator Amy Sara Carroll adds the Caribbean American writer, poet, and activist Audre Lourde and the nineteenth-century U.S. thinker Henry David Thoreau, whose essay on civil disobedience is central to her work, to the group of crucial theorists serving as their dialogue partners.

GPS is fundamental to the artistic undertaking, both in its theoretical and in its practical applications. As Domínguez reminds us, GPS was originally conceived and operated as a U.S. military surveillance system, was made available to the general public in 2004, and now "has free global coverage, courtesy of the United States government" (qtd. in Bird). The TBT project has been facilitated by the ever-lower prices of disposable cell phones requiring neither a SIM card nor cell service to access GPS, and, following their general practice with other works, the creators have made the code for the project readily available for download, with the explicit hope that other groups will adopt the technology for other border circumstances: "We imagine TBT's code and gesture," says Domínguez, "as open to use on multiple borders and that it is not bound to the Mexico/ U.S. border" (qtd. in Bird). For both the U.S. government and the conservative press, the water drops have been, of course, the controversial element, and they are highlighted on the home page of the project (figures 15.5, 15.6).

Military surveillance is an important conceptual metaphor guiding the aesthetic impulse behind TBT, as well as a mechanism and a lived reality for

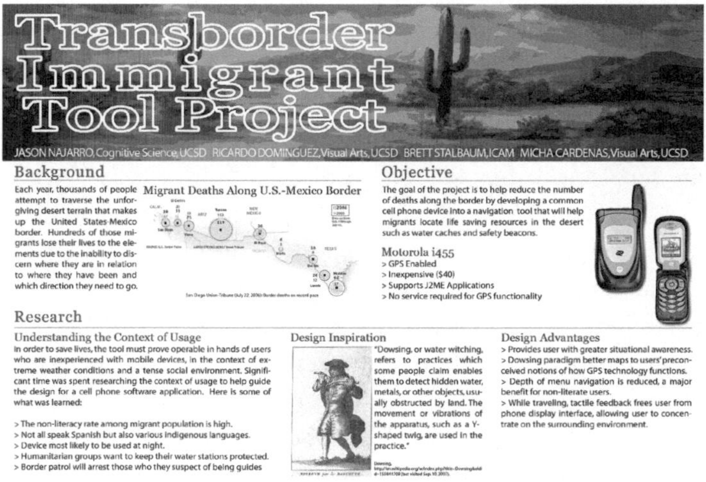

FIGURE 15.5. Electronic Disturbance Theater/b.a.n.g. lab, *Transborder Immigrant Tool Project*, n.d. Poster.

FIGURE 15.6. Electronic Disturbance Theater/b.a.n.g. lab, Transborder Immigrant Tool concept photograph, n.d. Nokia e71 cell phone, water container, and GPS system screen shot.

collaborators on the project. As Peter Andreas notes, the U.S. government and U.S.-based media frequently use metaphors of war, invasion, and natural disaster to speak about immigration from Latin America on the increasingly barricaded border, rationalizing this rhetoric by reference to the "drug war" and the "war on terror" (x).[9] Boots on the ground in the San Diego/Tijuana border region are supplemented by an ever-growing panoply of technological assistance, including a sophisticated "virtual fence" of cameras and motion sensors and a physical barrier incorporating surplus steel panels originally used to build landing strips during the Vietnam War.

Yet, as Andreas perceptively reminds us, this military metaphor has parallels in the game metaphor as well: "Border policing has some of the features of a ritualized spectator sport" (x), or a staged performance. "What makes the border a particularly challenging stage," he writes, "is that the actors are involved in a double performance, having to assure some of the audience that the border is open (to legal flows) while reassuring the rest of the audience that the border is being sufficiently closed (to illegal flows)" (10). By and large, then, for U.S. policy makers, "projecting a 'winning image' . . . has so far provided a politically viable alternative to actually winning the game" (111). In this way, he concludes, "stupid policies can be smart politics" (148). Through electronic civil disobedience acts and the Electronic Disturbance Theater, the San Diego–based artists and activists take hold of this rich substrata of demagoguery, increasing physical barriers, and heightened border surveillance to craft responses that are often more complexly theorized than their actions may at first appear on the surface.

Less discussed than the function of the GPS in the TBT is the role of the poetic texts, written by Amy Sara Carroll, a longtime collaborator in the Electronic Disturbance Theater. Nevertheless, these poems are integral to the project's conception. In this respect the TBT functions, in Carroll's words, as "dislocative media, seeking to realize the possibilities of G.P.S. as both a 'global positioning system' and what, in another context, Laura Borràs Castanyer and Juan B. Gutiérrez have termed 'a global poetic system' . . . in the mindset of Audre Lourde's pronouncement that 'poetry is not a luxury'" (qtd. in Bird). Performances of the poems are readily available in videos of Carroll's performances and talks, as well on the cell phones themselves and simulation videos of how they work; in addition, texts for many of them are published on the group's website thing.net. Written in a variety of styles, they have a practical as well as an artistic function in serving as essential references for often marginally literate immigrants. Elsewhere Carroll adds, "Los poemas ofrecen información útil para la supervivencia en el desierto; información similar a la que se puede encontrar en los manuales de supervivencia" (The poems offer useful information for survival in the desert; this information is similar to what you can find in survival manuals) ("EDT 1.0"). Here is an example of one of these poems, cited in Bird, but also widely available elsewhere. It is the specific poem from the TBT that was signaled by conservative pundit Glenn Beck for particular scorn and was transmitted, in part, on national television on September 1, 2010 (Reed):

Transition (Song of My Cells)

> Gloria Anzaldúa writes, "We have a tradition of migration, a tradition of long walks. Today we are witnessing *la migración de los pueblos mexicanos*, the return odyssey to the historical/mythological Aztlán." . . . The historical? The mythological? Aztlán? It's difficult to follow the soundings of that song. Today's borders and circuits speak at "lower frequencies," are "shot through with chips of Messianic time." Might (*O chondria!*): imagine the chips' transliteralization and you have "arrived" at the engines of a global positioning system—the transitivity of the Transborder Immigrant Tool. Too: when you outgrow that definition, look for the "trans-" of transcendental -isms, imperfect as overwound pocket watches, "off"-beat as subliminalities (alternate forms of energy which exceed Reason's predetermined star maps). Pointedly past Walden-pondering, *el otro lado* de flâneur-floundering—draw a circle, now "irse por la tangente"—neither gray nor grey (nor black-and-white). Arco-iris: flight, a fight. Of fancy. *This Bridge Called My Back*, my heart, my head, my cock, my cunt, my tunnel. Vision: You. Are. Crossing. Into. Me.

Glenn Beck found it offensive, both aesthetically and politically, and condemned it with typically apocalyptic fervor. "The poetry on this system," he said, "will destroy the border and the nation" (qtd. in Gharavi). Large stakes, indeed.[10] I leave it to the readers to ponder the survival information that a normative Mexican or Central American migrant would garner from this message.

But let us imagine that the TBT were able to work out its bugs and go into widespread distribution. If the TBT is a game—and conceivably we can view it as one, although not in the trivializing way the word is often used—then it is also important to think briefly about the players. Scholar-performers like Bertolt Brecht and Augusto Boal have long since theorized the relation among thought, performance, and audience action, whether in epic theater (Brecht) or theater of the oppressed (Boal), encouraging in each of their cases a form that sponsors critical reflection rather than catharsis. Just as Andreas conceives of border surveillance as a kind of theater, with audiences treated differentially, simulating a perfect scenario for such reflection, so too the TBT creates gamers by providing border crossers with access to these equipped cell phones, hence creating a new kind of immigrant. In a more technologically framed theoretical vein, Rotman speaks of the way the self emerges differently when patterned, not on a literate, linear, serial organization of knowledge, but rather on the fluid multiplicities of information-bearing visual images, such as maps, schematics, wire-frame renderings, scans, and the like (95). The immigrants, in unfamiliar landscapes whose clues they are unable to read, follow the poems and the GPS and the compass to trace their way through the not-yet-here of the desert and toward the scattered, life-saving water stops. This is gaming with serious material and cultural consequences; it is playing a game of life and death in the most literal sense. In this traversal of space by cell phone, the immigrants become LARPers, participating in a new kind of public culture, where the choices they have made as game players determine the future paths of their lives and where they are captive audiences to the poetic performances that take them from water stop to water stop.

I return to a quote from Rotman that I cited at the beginning of this study: "Perhaps the first question to ask about the psyche in a technologized milieu is not really one of identity and persona, of 'who' the emergent self is, but *what* and *how* is the self" (81). Toward the end of the book, he concludes with a statement of faith: "We can, I believe, embrace the para-human, to begin—haltingly, with confusion, pain, wonder, inevitable resistance, nostalgia, feelings of loss and dread, moments of intense liberating pleasure, not to say joy and surprise—become plural 'I's able to be beside ourselves in ways we're only just starting to recognize and feel the need to narrate" (104–5). One version of this narration comes to us through artistic projects like the ones that I have been describing here, and projects like these require more flexible theoretical structures than those afforded us by most traditional stories our thinkers have been telling us. Humanities 2.0, says prominent digital humanist Cathy Davidson, is premised on interactivity and openness, decentering knowledge and authority, privileging collaborative pedagogy and research. It sounds like pedagogy of the oppressed repurposed for post-Internet times. Where, then, do we look for Theory 2.0? Not in this paper, which is still in a very traditional academic style.

Perhaps we can find it elsewhere, head down, eyes on a book or a cell phone, while LARPing.[11]

NOTES

1. The term *Web 2.0* describes a modular, recombinatory, flexible platform, often relying on a bottom-up, crowdsourcing model of building information. In Michael Connor's succinct definition, "'Web 2.0' [is] a term used to describe the increasing use of centralized services rather than independent websites to share and access content online. . . . In broad strokes, these changes meant that many more people were making and sharing content online, and they were doing so through a smaller number of channels. . . . Making art 'after' the internet in 2006, then, involved being a participant-observer of an emerging internet culture." It is worth reminding ourselves that Wikipedia went online in 2001, YouTube launched in 2005, and social networking sites were growing in popularity after Facebook's 2006 expansion to anyone thirteen and older with an email address. The iPhone would be released in 2007, signaling the beginning of the smartphone era of constant connectivity.
2. García Andújar's later work moves more explicitly into creating means for access to both technology and art, as he has maintained a consistent argument that both are fundamental human rights.
3. The challenges of maintaining this project are obvious—who keeps up the website and adds new material? For instance, as of this writing, the last entries to remixthebook.com were in 2012. Eduardo Navas's *Remix Theory*, released in 2012, retains an active website.
4. The page has not changed substantially in a number of years, but as of this writing it did indicate it was last updated in March 2014.
5. A 2000 update of the website indicates a snag in the "security service" option. The service was described thusly: "The representative of the corporation will enter the Policía Judicial Federal PGR as one of its agents. You'll be able to follow the whole process here." However, since neither the Policía Judicial Federal nor the Policía Federal Preventiva had women police officers, Cuevas was unable to complete this action.
6. In summer 2014, former Subcomandante Marcos formally took on the name Galeano in recognition of and homage to his fallen comrade.

7. Since January 2010, b.a.n.g. lab has been subject to heightened surveillance from their home institution, national media, and the U.S. government (FBI's Cyber Division). Members of Congress Brian P. Bilbray, Darrell Issa, and Duncan Hunter charged the lab with violation of the Immigration and Nationality Act of 1965. Attempts were made to revoke Domínguez's tenure, and after several investigations he signed an agreement to refrain from virtual performances for four years (Reed, Bird).
8. This has always been a collective project; however, as editor of thing.net and the target of the most vitriolic attacks, Domínguez has been converted into a de facto lightning rod and is often the spokesperson for the group.
9. Of course, smuggling goes both ways: Andreas sees the United States as the world's largest smuggling target (of drugs and migrants) as well as the world's largest smuggler (of weapons, stolen cars, money, et cetera) (16).
10. It would be interesting, but beyond the scope of this article, which focuses on net.art, to think about the parallels with the more artisanal practice of the Tucson, Arizona, based NGO No Más Muertes, whose members often draw pictures (artwork) on bottles of water left in the desert, on the very practical assumption that while Minutemen and other anti-immigrant groups might poison water, they are unlikely to make art (Reed).
11. Suggestions for further reading: A broader study of the phenomenon of Mexican cultural projects that take advantage of the new media opportunities would include the thousands of websites, Facebook pages, and blogs set up by authors to promote their works, as well as interactive poetry such as that by Karen Villeda ("Poepedia," "Tesauro," "Poetuitáme"); the multiple projects of Fran Ilich (e.g., "Being Boring," Diego de la Vega, "Transcultura reciclada," "Possible Worlds"); the recent work of graphic novelist Cecilia Pego (*Exilia*); Eve Gil's "manga realism" projects, like *Sho-Shan* and the related website, *Murasaki Inku*); and Valeria Luiselli's "Swings of Harlem." For a recent overview in Spanish of figures like these, see Cleger.

WORKS CITED

Amerika, Mark. *remixthebook*. University of Minnesota Press, 2011. Companion website: www.remixthebook.com/.

Andreas, Peter. *Border Games: Policing the U.S.-Mexico Divide*. Cornell University Press, 2000.

Asociación de Arte Útil. arteutil.net/open-call/.

b.a.n.g. lab. "E-graffiti Action in Solidarity with the Zapatistas." bang.transreal.org/e-graffiti-action-in-solidarity-with-the-zapatistas/.

Bird, Lawrence. "Global Positioning: An Interview with Ricardo Domínguez." *Furtherfield*, 15 Oct. 2011, www.furtherfield.org/features/global-positioning-interview-ricardo-dominguez.

Bruguera, Tania. www.taniabruguera.com/cms/.

Carroll, Amy Sara. "EDT 1.0, EDT 2.0, EDT 3.0." *Errata*, vol. 3, 2011, issuu.com/revistaerrata/docs/errata_3_cultura_digital_creaci_n.

Cleger, Osvaldo. "La creación ciberliteraria: Definición, perfil carta de navegación para orientarse en un campo emergente." *Letras Hispanas*, vol. 11, 2015, pp. 262–80.

Connor, Michael. "What's Postinternet Got to Do with Net Art?" *Rhizome*, 1 Nov. 2013, rhizome.org/editorial/2013/nov/1/postinternet/.

Cuevas, Minerva. www.irational.org/minerva/resume.html.

———. "For a Human Interface." www.irational.org/minerva/texts.html.

Davidson, Cathy N. "Humanities 2.0: Promise, Perils, Predictions." *PMLA*, vol. 123, no. 3, 2008, pp. 707–17.

Domínguez, Ricardo. http://www.thing.net/~rdom/.

———. "The Ante-Chamber of Revolution: A Prelude to a Theory of Resistance and Maps." *Swarm*, http://www.thing.net/~rdom/Maps.html.

———. "Error 404: Democracia no encontrada." *Errata*, vol. 3, 2011, issuu.com/revistaerrata/docs/errata_3_cultura_digital_creaci_n.

———. "Sistemas geo-poéticos (GPS): Fragmentos, fractales, formas y funciones contra la invisibilidad." *Errata*, vol. 3, 2011, issuu.com/revistaerrata/docs/errata_3_cultura_digital_creaci_n.

Dressler, Iris. www.hartware-projekte.de/archiv/inhalt/andujar.htm. Link no longer accessible, but it is mirrored on other sites, including Daniel García Andújar's webpage at www.medienkunstnetz.de/works/technologies-to-the-people/.

García Andújar, Daniel. www.danielandujar.org/.

———. Technologies To The People Foundation. www.irational.org/tttp/*siteTTP/dpro.html.

Gharavi, Maryam Monalisa. "Transgressing Virtual Geographies." *Darkmatter*, 27 July 2011, www.darkmatter101.org/site/2011/07/27/transgressing-virtual-geographies/.

Hayles, N. Katherine. *My Mother Was a Computer: Digital Subjects and Literary Texts*. University of Chicago Press, 2005.

Kittler, Friedrich. "INFOWAR." Ars Electronica 98, Linz, Austria, Sept. 1998. hydra.humanities.uci.edu/kittler/infowar-tr.html.

Lenoir, Timothy. "Machinic Bodies, Ghosts, and Paraselves: Confronting the Singularity with Brian Rotman." Introduction to *Becoming Beside Ourselves: The Alphabet, Ghosts, and the Distributed Human Being* by Brian Rotman, Duke University Press, 2008, pp. ix–xxxiv.

Mejor Vida Corp. www.irational.org/mvc/english.html.

Navas, Eduardo. *Remix Theory: The Aesthetics of Sampling*. Springer-Verlag, 2012. Companion website: remixtheory.net/.

Reed, Alison. "Queer Provisionality: Mapping the Generative Failures of the *Transborder Immigrant Tool*." *Lateral*, vol. 4, 2015, csalateral.org/wp/issue/4/queer-provisionality-mapping-the-generative/.

Rotman, Brian. *Becoming Beside Ourselves: The Alphabet, Ghosts, and the Distributed Human Being*. Duke University Press, 2008.

Staulbaum, Brett. *The Zapatista Tactical Floodnet*. www.thing.net/~rdom/ecd/ZapTact.html.

Transborder Immigrant Tool. bang.transreal.org/transborder-immigrant-tool/.

Vierkant, Artie. "The Image Object Post-Internet." *Artlurker*, 2010, www.artlurker.com/wp-content/uploads/2011/03/image-object-postInternet.pdf.

CONTRIBUTORS

Rafael Acosta Morales is an assistant professor of Spanish in the Department of Spanish and Portuguese at the University of Kansas. He received his PhD from the University of Cornell in 2014. His research interests relate to political theory, Latino studies, comparative literature, and Mexican studies. His work has been published or will appear in *Revista Iberoamericana*, *Latin American Perspectives*, *Latin American Research Review*, and *Comparative Literature*, among other journals. His current book project, "Drug Lords, Cowboys, and Desperadoes: Matrixes of Violence in the Mexican American Frontier," studies how affective structures represented in stories illustrate the substrata of political behavior.

Jacqueline E. Bixler is professor of Spanish at Virginia Tech, where she teaches Latin American culture and literature and chairs the Department of Foreign Languages and Literatures. She also currently serves as the editor of the *Latin American Theatre Review*. Winner of the Alumni Excellence in Teaching Award, the Diggs Teaching Scholar Award, and the 2016 Outstanding Faculty Award from the State Council of Higher Education for Virginia, she is one of ten Alumni Distinguished Professors at Virginia Tech. A specialist on Mexican theater, she is the author or editor of six books: *Historias para ser contadas: El teatro de Alejandro Ricaño* (LATR Books, 2012); *Las mujeres y la dramaturgia mexicana del sigo XX* (with Claudia Gidi; Ediciones el Milagro, 2011); *Trans/Acting: Latin American and Latino Performance* (with Laurietz Seda; Bucknell University Press, 2009); *Voces en el umbral: El teatro* *de Rascón Banda* (with Stuart Day; Escenología, 2005); *Sediciosas seducciones: Sexo, poder y palabras en el teatro de Sabina Berman* (Escenología, 2004); and *Convention and Transgression: The Theatre of Emilio Carballido* (Bucknell University Press, 1997; translated and published in Spanish by the Universidad Veracruzana, 2000). Her articles on Mexican, Argentine, and Chilean theater have appeared in such publications as *Latin American Research Review*, *Theatre Journal*, *Gestos*, *Latin American Theatre Review*, *Conjunto*, *Tramoya*, *Revista hispánica moderna*, *Revista canadiense de estudios hispánicos*, and *Hispania*. She earned her PhD in 1980 from the University of Kansas.

Marta Caminero-Santangelo is a professor in the English Department at the University of Kansas, where she currently holds the Frances L. Stiefel Professorship and teaches classes in U.S. Latinx literatures and the literature of social justice. She is also interim director of the Center for Latin American and Caribbean Studies. Her academic research in the field of twentieth- and twenty-first-century U.S. Latinx literary studies focuses on the conjunction between literature, group identity, and the ability to promote social change. She has published numerous articles and three books: *The Madwoman Can't Speak, or Why Insanity Is Not Subversive* (Cornell University Press, 1998); *On Latinidad: U.S. Latino Literature and the Construction of Ethnicity* (University Press of Florida, 2007); and, most recently, *Documenting the Undocumented: Latina/o Narrative and Social Justice in the Era of Operation Gatekeeper* (University Press of Florida, 2016). She earned a PhD in English from the University of California, Irvine.

Debra A. Castillo is Stephen H. Weiss Presidential Fellow, Emerson Hinchliff Professor of Hispanic Studies, and professor of comparative literature at Cornell University and past president of the international Latin American Studies Association. She specializes in contemporary narrative from the Spanish-speaking world, gender studies, cultural theory, and visual studies. She is author, editor, or translator of ten books, including *Talking Back: Strategies for a Latin American Feminist Literary Criticism* (1992), *Easy Women: Sex and Gender in Modern Mexican Fiction* (1998), and (cowritten with María Socorro Tabuenca Córdoba) *Border Women: Writing from La Frontera* (2002). Her most recent books are *Re-dreaming America*, *Cartographies of Affect: Across Borders in South Asia and the Americas*, and *Mexican Public Intellectuals*.

Christopher Conway received his doctorate in 1996 from the University of California, San Diego. He is currently professor of Spanish at the University of Texas at Arlington. He is the author of *Nineteenth-Century Spanish America: A Cultural History* (Vanderbilt University Press, 2015) and *The Cult of Bolívar in Latin American Literature* (University Press of Florida, 2003). He is the editor of *The U.S.-Mexican War: A Binational Reader* (Hackett Publishing, 2010) and *Peruvian Traditions* (Oxford University Press, 2004), as well as a co-editor of *Bakhtin and the Nation* (Bucknell University Press, 2000). Conway's articles on modern Latin American literature and culture have appeared in journals such as *Latin American Research Review*, *Hispanic Review*, *Revista de crítica literaria latinoamericana*, and *Bulletin of Spanish Studies*. His current research projects focus on twentieth-century mass culture and inter-American studies.

David S. Dalton is an assistant professor of Spanish at the University of North Carolina at Charlotte. He has written seventeen published and forthcoming articles and book chapters for various journals and edited volumes. His primary research interests revolve around how science and technology inform understandings of race, gender, and nationality both in and beyond Latin America. His forthcoming book, tentatively titled *Forging the Mestizo: Technology, Modernity, and the Body in Post-Revolutionary Mexico*, is currently under contract with the University Press of Florida.

Stuart A. Day is professor of Spanish, managing editor of the *Latin American Theatre Review*, and senior vice provost for academic affairs at the University of Kansas. Before joining the faculty at KU he taught at the University of North Carolina at Chapel Hill (2000–2005), where he was a Faculty Fellow and recipient of two teaching/mentoring awards. At KU he was awarded the Kemper Fellowship for Teaching Excellence. His books include *Staging Politics in Mexico: The Road to Neoliberalism* (Bucknell University Press); *Mexican Public Intellectuals*, with Debra A. Castillo (Palgrave Macmillan); *El Teatro de Rascón Banda: Voces en el umbral*, with Jacqueline E. Bixler (Escenelogía); *Outside Theater: Alliances That Shape Mexico* (University of Arizona Press); and numerous anthologies. He received his PhD from Cornell University in 2000.

Emily Hind is an associate professor with the University of Florida, where she was voted Professor of the Year (2016–17) by the graduate students in the Hispanic literature program. She also received a University of Florida Term Professorship (2016–19) for distinguished record of research and scholarship. She has published two books of interviews with Mexican writers in Spanish, as well as a book of criticism in English,

Femmenism and the Mexican Woman Intellectual from Sor Juana to Poniatowska (Palgrave Macmillan, 2010). She was a Fulbright scholar in Mexico in 2015, and her essay on Rosario Castellanos won the Feministas Unidas essay prize. Hind has published more than twenty articles on Mexican literature and film in academic journals, and nearly as many chapters in books of collected criticism.

Robert McKee Irwin is chair of the Graduate Group in Cultural Studies and professor in the Department of Spanish and Portuguese at the University of California, Davis. He is the author of *Mexican Masculinities* and *Bandits, Captives, Heroines, and Saints: Cultural Icons of Mexico's Northwest Borderlands*, and the co-author (with Maricruz Castro Ricalde) of *El cine mexicano "se impone": Mercados internacionales y penetración cultural en le época dorada* and *Global Mexican Cinema: Its Golden Age*. Irwin is co-editor (with Mónica Szurmuk) of *Diccionario de estudios culturales latinoamericanos* (available in both Spanish and English) and (with Héctor Fernández l'Hoeste and Juan Poblete) of *Sports and Nationalism in Latin/o America*. He is editor of two "lost" literary works: Eduardo Castrejón (pseud.)'s *Los 41: Novela crítico-social* and Aurelio Pérez Peña's *Heroína*. Currently he is co–principal investigator (with Guillermo Alonso Meneses) of the Tijuana-based digital storytelling project Humanizando la Deportación (humanizandoladeportacion.ucdavis.edu/es/). He is also co–principal investigator (with Sunaina Maira) of Comparative Border Studies: Rights, Mobility, Protest, a Mellon Initiative (borderstudies.ucdavis.edu/).

Ryan Long is associate professor of Spanish at the University of Maryland. His research focuses on culture and politics in Mexico and Latin America, with an emphasis on the twentieth century. He has published articles on a range of topics, including the conflict in Chiapas, Mexican cinema, and writers such as Bruno Montané Krebs, Álvaro Mutis, Ignacio Manuel Altamirano, José Gorostiza, Juan Villoro, Laura Esquivel, and Roberto Bolaño. His first book, *Fictions of Totality: The Mexican Novel, 1968, and the National-Popular State*, was published in 2008 by Purdue University Press. He is currently working on two new book projects, one about Bolaño and another about the Swiss architect and one-time Bauhaus director Hannes Meyer, who lived and worked in Mexico from 1939 to 1949.

Dana A. Meredith is a doctoral student in Spanish literature at the University of Kansas in Lawrence. She previously obtained her Bachelor of Arts in Spanish and Bachelor of Science in journalism at the University of Kansas (2012), as well as her

Master of Arts in Spanish at the University of Kansas (2016). She is interested in studying the confluence of gender and revolutionary movements in Mexican and Brazilian culture production from the twentieth and twenty-first centuries. Although her primary focus is on narrative, she has a secondary interest in theater and serves as an editorial assistant for the *Latin American Theatre Review* at KU.

Magalí Rabasa is assistant professor of Hispanic studies in the Department of World Languages and Literatures at Lewis & Clark College in Portland, Oregon. In 2014, she received her PhD in cultural studies from the University of California, Davis, with an emphasis in feminist theory and research. Over the last decade, she has worked extensively with alternative media and popular education projects across the Americas. She is a founding member of the Colectivo Radio Autonomía (Oakland, California) and Changing Suns Press (Regina, Saskatchewan). She has published articles and commentary in the *Journal of Latin American Cultural Studies*, *Anthropology Today*, *Tabula Rasa*, *La Jornada*, Rebelión.org, and *Herramienta*, and she is a contributor to the forthcoming *Routledge History of Latin American Culture*. Her translations include the "Subalternisms" entry by Ileana Rodríguez in the *Dictionary of Latin American Cultural Studies* (University Press of Florida, 2012). Her first book project, "The Book in Movement: Autonomous Politics and the Lettered City Underground," is an exploration of print book culture in current Latin American social movements.

Luis Alberto Rodríguez Cortés is from Xalapa, Veracruz, Mexico, and has lived in the United States since 2008. He received his BA in Hispanic languages and literatures from the Universidad Veracruzana in his hometown and his MA in Spanish at Marquette University; he is now a candidate for a PhD in Spanish at the University of Kansas. His research interests are the construction and undermining of national and supranational identities during the twenty-first century, with a focus on Mexico, Cuba, and Latinx communities in the United States. More specifically, his work examines novels, films, and spaces of cultural dissemination where the idea of national identity is being put into question. Other areas of interest are the bildungsroman, the road film, and other genres related to movement and transition. Future projects deal with the spaces of cultural production in the United States where national identities are being created (especially the identities of Latin America and Mexico) and with literary products of the recent Latin American intellectual diaspora, such as the campus novel genre.

Fernando Fabio Sánchez, associate professor of Spanish at California Polytechnic State University, specializes in postcolonial Mexico. His research focuses on the concept of modernity, the representation of violence, and the role of the state in literature, painting, photography, film, and mass media. He has published *Artful Assassins: Murder as Art in Modern Mexico* (Vanderbilt University Press, 2010), in which he unveils the long record of violence in twentieth-century Mexican culture and studies the causes of the demise of postrevolutionary political cohesion that has been demonstrated in the even more violent Mexican twenty-first century. He also co-edited *La luz y la guerra: El cine de la Revolución Mexicana* (Consejo Nacional para la Cultura y las Artes, 2010). The volume is a collection of essays written by prominent scholars from Mexico, Canada, and the United States examining the cinematic corpus of the Mexican Revolution of a whole century. Professor Sánchez has also published crime fiction and is concurrently working on a novel and a study of the filmography of the Mexican film director Felipe Cazals.

Ignacio M. Sánchez Prado is professor of Spanish and international and area studies at Washington University in Saint Louis. He is the author of *El canon y sus formas: La reinvención de Harold Bloom y sus lecturas hispanoamericanas* (2002); *Naciones intelectuales: Las fundaciones de la modernidad literaria mexicana, 1917–1959* (2009), winner of the LASA Mexico 2010 Humanities Book Award; *Intermitencias americanistas: Ensayos y estudios académicos, 2004–2010* (2012); and *Screening Neoliberalism: Mexican Cinema, 1988–2012* (2014). He has edited seven scholarly collections and published more than forty scholarly articles on Mexican culture and on Latin American cultural theory.

Analisa Taylor is associate professor of Spanish in the Department of Romance Languages and Literatures at the University of Oregon. She is the author of *Indigeneity in the Mexican Cultural Imagination: Thresholds of Belonging* (University of Arizona Press, 2009) and has published essays in *Signs*, *Latin American Literary Review*, *Revista de estudios hispánicos*, and the *Journal of Latin American Cultural Studies*. Her current projects include two books: *Daughters of the Moon: True Life Stories from the Lacandon Rain Forest*, an annotated translation and scholarly edition of *Entre anhelos y recuerdos* by Marie-Odile Marion, and *Mesoamerican Stories and Strategies of Decolonization*.

Oswaldo Zavala is professor of contemporary Latin American literature at the Graduate Center and at the College of Staten Island, City University of New York

(CUNY). His most recent book is *Insufferable Modernity: Roberto Bolaño in the Limits of Contemporary Latin American Literature* (North Carolina Studies in the Romance Languages and Literatures, 2015). His article "Imagining the U.S.-Mexico Drug War: The Critical Limits of Narconarratives" won the 2015 Humanities Essay Award of the Latin American Studies Association Mexico Section. He co-edited (with Viviane Mahieux) *Tierras de nadie: El norte en la narrativa mexicana contemporánea* (2012) and (with José Ramón Ruisánchez) *Materias dispuestas: Juan Villoro ante la crítica* (2011). His current book-length investigation is "Drug Cartels Do Not Exist: A Political History of Organized Crime and State Violence in Mexico and the United States (1947–2012)."

INDEX